Avebury Reconsidered

(Photo by Ann Stringfellow)

Avebury Reconsidered

From the 1660s to the 1990s

PETER J. UCKO
Department of Archaeology, University of Southampton

MICHAEL HUNTER
Department of History, Birkbeck College, University of London

ALAN J. CLARK
The Library, The Royal Society

ANDREW DAVID
Ancient Monuments Laboratory, English Heritage

Published on behalf of
the Institute of Archaeology,
University College London

London
UNWIN HYMAN
Boston   Sydney   Wellington

Published by the Academic Division of
Unwin Hyman Ltd
15/17 Broadwick Street, London W1V 1FP, UK

Unwin Hyman Inc.
955 Massachusetts Avenue, Cambridge, MA 02139, USA

Allen & Unwin (Australia) Ltd
8 Napier Street, North Sydney, NSW 2060, Australia

Allen & Unwin (New Zealand) Ltd
in association with the Port Nicholson Press Ltd
Compusales Building, 75 Ghuznee Street, Wellington 1, New Zealand

First published in 1991

British Library Cataloguing in Publication Data

Avebury reconsidered: from the 1660s to the 1990s.
1. Wiltshire. Avebury. Neolithic monuments
I. Ucko, Peter J. (Peter John) 1938–
936.2317

ISBN 0-04-445919-X

Library of Congress Cataloging in Publication Data

Applied for

This book was edited and proofed by the authors

Typeset in 11 on 12 point Bembo by Computape (Pickering) Ltd, North Yorkshire
and printed in Great Britain by the University Press, Cambridge

Contents

List of plates

★ **Note**. In addition to the transparencies, the folder contains: duplicates of Plates 5 (Plan D), 6 (Plan C), 7 (Plan A), 8 (Plan B) and 14 (Plan E); Stukeley's panoramic view of the Kennet and Beckhampton Avenues; an analytical quadrant-by-quadrant comparison of four plans of the outer circle of the Avebury henge; and a key to the stones in Stukeley's drawings.

List of transparencies

The transparencies are included in the folder.

1   Aubrey's plan A of Avebury, from *Monumenta Britannica*.
2   Stukeley's plan E of Avebury, from the Frontispiece to *Abury*, omitting most contemporary details and the supposed second outer circle.
3   Keiller's unpublished plan of the area of the southern inner circle before excavation, with the addition of Smith's (1965) tentative scheme.
4   Aubrey's plan A of the southern inner circle.
5   Aubrey's plan A of the southern inner circle enlarged to produce a 'best fit' of the two arcs to Smith's circle.
6   Stukeley's draft frontispiece – N (Plate 32).
7   Stukeley's draft frontispiece – O (Plate 33).
8   Stukeley's draft frontispiece – P (Plate 34).
9   Stukeley's draft frontispiece – Q (Plate 35).
10   Stukeley's draft frontispiece – R (Plate 36).
11   Stukeley's draft frontispiece – S (Plate 37).
12   Stukeley's draft frontispiece – T (Plate 38).
13   Stukeley's draft frontispiece – U (Plate 39).
14   Stukeley's draft frontispiece – V (Plate 40).
15   Stukeley's draft frontispiece – W (Plate 41).
16   Stukeley's draft frontispiece – X (Plate 42).
17   Smith's (1965, fig. 70) 'tentative reconstruction', based on the excavations by Keiller.
18   Aubrey's plan B of Avebury and its environs, from *Monumenta Britannica*.
19   Reconstruction of Stukeley's 'Tour' with gaps left to fit plan E details.
20   Reconstruction of Stukeley's measured plan (Plate 15) to fit plan E.
21   Smith's (1965, fig. 70) 'tentative reconstruction' of the southern inner circle with the addition of relevant geophysical anomalies.
22   Stukeley's plan E of the southern inner circle.
23   Aubrey's plan B of the southern inner circle.
24   Smith's (1965) 'tentative reconstruction' of the northern inner circle with the addition of relevant geophysical anomalies, pasture boundaries from aerial photographs and two additional stones.
25   Aubrey's plan B of the northern inner circle.
26   Aubrey's plan A of the northern inner circle.
27   Stukeley's plan E of the northern inner circle.

Acknowledgements

An interdisciplinary project such as this one could not have been accomplished without the assistance of a great number of people, as well as those particular intimates who suffered with us but prefer to remain anonymous.

We gratefully thank the following for having taken the time to discuss aspects of our problems with regard to Avebury and/or for having read drafts of parts of the manuscripts: R. F. Alton (St Edmund Hall, Oxford), Jim Bennett (Whipple Museum of the History of Science, University of Cambridge), Timothy Champion (Department of Archaeology, University of Southampton), Thomas Coke (Royal Commission, Cambridge), Andrew Crookston (Wiltshire County Record Office, Trowbridge), Judith Field (Science Museum, London), Alison Finley (Department of English, Birkbeck College), Jane Freeman (Victoria County History of Wiltshire), Chris Gingell (National Trust, North Wiltshire), John Henry (Science Studies Unit, University of Edinburgh), David Hinton (Department of Archaeology, University of Southampton), Jim Lanagan (Royal Commission, Southampton), Susan Limbrey (Department of Archaeology, University of Birmingham), Alan Macfarlane (Department of Social Anthropology, University of Cambridge), Howard Morphy (Pitt Rivers Museum, Oxford), John Peacock (Department of English, University of Southampton), Erik Petersen (Det Kongelige Bibliotek, Copenhagen), Peter Phillips (Department of Teaching Media, University of Southampton), Sebastian Rahtz (Department of Electronics and Computing, University of Southampton), P. H. Robinson (The Museum, Devizes), Stephen Shennan (Department of Archaeology, University of Southampton), Lydia Soo (University of Illinois, Urbana-Champaign), Peter Stone (English Heritage (Education Section), South West Region) and Peter Tate (formerly, English Heritage, Avebury).

We are indebted to the Royal Society's Librarian, Mrs Sheila Edwards, and to her staff – in particular to the Society's Archivist, Keith Moore, for his alert interest in the project. We also wish to thank Bruce Barker-Benfield of the Bodleian Library and Mrs P. Colman, Librarian of the Wiltshire Archaeological and Natural History Society, for all their assistance.

We owe a particular debt to Jane Hubert (Department of Psychology, University of Southampton) for having read and commented on all of this work. Isobel Smith and Stuart Piggott have done likewise, *twice over* – we are truly grateful to both of them. Professor Piggott has requested us to record that he agrees with our re-interpretation of William Stukeley – we do this gladly, as a public recognition of Stuart's magnanimity.

We thank Mike Allen (Trust for Wessex Archaeology, Old Sarum) and Rod FitzGerald (Royal Commission, Southampton) for having undertaken field research on our behalf. The geophysical survey was undertaken by the Ancient Monuments Laboratory of English Heritage. Its outcome is the result of concerted teamwork, notably by Andy Payne was was responsible for most of the fieldwork, with Andrew David, Paul Linford, Dave Jordan and David Coombes. The 1975 survey was done by Andrew David, Alistair Bartlett and Phil Crawshaw. Subsequent data processing was the work of Dave Jordan, Andy Payne and especially Paul Linford. We would like to thank Brian Davison for his interest and encouragement, and Tony Clark (formerly, English Heritage) for helpfully discussing our geophysical results. For permission to conduct surveys over their land we are grateful to Mr R. E. Butler and Mr R. J. Hues, and also to the National Trust and their tenant farmers Mr A. A. Farthing and Mr R. Cooper.

We are grateful to Professor E. M. Jope (Oxford) for access to his unpublished manuscript on 'Avebury: Saxon and Medieval'.

Steve Shrimpton (Department of Teaching Media, University of Southampton) took the superb photographs (Plates 6, 29, 30, 50, 51 and 57) of Aubrey's plan (C), in the Royal Society. Nick Bradford (Department of Archaeology, University of Southampton) rescued us at a late stage by taking the photographs for Plates 17, 46, 47, 48, and 49.

However, our greatest debt is undoubtedly to Christopher Webster (Department of Archaeology, University of Southampton) – without him Chapter IV (particularly sections r–x) could not have been accomplished. We thank him for his many perceptive comments and for having taken the time and trouble to get to know Stukeley's records almost by heart. Above all, we acknowledge the importance of the set of analytical drawn plans which accompany this book and which are all Chris' work.

The publication of this book has been made possible by generous grants from the following bodies: Birkbeck College, University of London (Publication Fund), Council for British Archeology, English Heritage (though it should be made clear that the views expressed in this book are not necessarily those of this organization), the Publications Committee of the Institute of Archaeology, University College London, the Royal Society (Scientific Publications Grant Committee; a similar proviso applies as with English Heritage), and the University of Southampton (Research Sub-Committee of the Committee for Advanced Studies).

Illustrations are reproduced by kind permission of: Alexander Keiller Museum, Avebury (Plates 52, 55, 56, Stukeley's Panorama in folder); the Department of Western Art, Ashmolean Museum, Oxford (Plate 1); Bodleian Library, Oxford (Plates 2, 3, 7–9, 13–16, 18–27, 32–44, 60, 61, 64, 65, 70); Ancient Monuments Laboratory, English Heritage (Plates 45, 53, 54, 58, 59, 62, 63, 65, 67–9, 71); Hunterian Art Gallery, University of Glasgow (Plate 4); Ordnance Survey © Crown Copyright: Plate 45 (1975, scale 1:10 000), Plate 58 (1977, 1:2500), Plate 62 (1977, 1978, 1:2500), Plate 63 (1975, 1:2500); Plate 69 (1977, 1:2500), Plate 71 (1977, 1:2500); President and Council of the Royal Society (Plates 5, 6, 28–31, 50, 51, 57); Wiltshire Archaeological Society (Plates 11, 12); Wiltshire County Record Office (Plates 46–9).

Peter J. Ucko, Michael Hunter
Alan J. Clark, Andrew David
31 May 1990

Avebury Reconsidered

Introduction

Avebury is without question one of the outstanding prehistoric sites in Great Britain. The area enclosed within the massive bank and ditch, with its main and subsidiary circles and other features, comprises the largest henge monument with standing stones in existence. It also forms part of a unique grouping of antiquities, either still existing or whose former existence has been established by archaeological investigation, within which fresh and unexpected features are still being brought to light. This rich complex includes the avenue of standing stones leading away from the henge to West Kennet; the 'Sanctuary' on Overton Hill; and such outlying antiquities as the West Kennet Long Barrow and Silbury Hill. It is a mark of its significance that Avebury and its surroundings have (with Stonehenge) been designated by UNESCO as one of the eleven 'World Heritage Sites' in the United Kingdom, of which it is arguably the most important.

It is not surprising that Avebury should continue to engender much scholarly and public interest. In the study of British prehistory, the site as a whole is often taken as a kind of signpost for neolithic cultural complexity and endeavour (e.g. Renfrew 1973). It has also been the subject of a number of more popular expositions, including Aubrey Burl's wide-ranging and imaginatively illustrated text, *Prehistoric Avebury* (1979; reissued in 1986 in association with the National Trust), and, more recently, two publications sponsored by English Heritage, the custodians of the site: a 'Study Pack for Teachers' on *The Avebury Monuments* (Coupland 1988) and an *English Heritage Book of Avebury* (Malone 1989). Alongside these, the breadth of appeal of the mysterious is well illustrated by speculative essays with titles like *The Avebury Cycle* (Dames 1977).

Much of our current knowledge of the history of the site, as reflected in popularizing texts like those of Burl and English Heritage, derives from the work on Avebury carried out by archaeologists in the 20th century. That the monument belonged to the neolithic period was established through intermittent excavations by Harold St George Gray, on behalf of the British Association for the Advancement of Science, between 1908 and 1922 (Gray 1935). It was he who plumbed the vast depth of the henge ditch, nearly ten metres deep, and sectioned the bank, finding late neolithic flints and potsherds on the old ground surface below. Amongst his other achievements at Avebury, Gray also made an extremely thorough survey of the monument in 1912.

Following the work of Gray, we owe most of our subsequent knowledge of Avebury – as also its present state of preservation – to the determined work of investigative restoration carried out by Alexander Keiller during the 1930s. In 1934–5 (and again in 1939) Keiller and Stuart Piggott examined the northern part of the Kennet Avenue in its approach to the henge, re-erecting stones and marking the former positions of others. During 1937–9 Keiller turned his attention to excavating and restoring the western circuit of the great circle and excavated part of the south-east quadrant, finding the so-called Z stones and other stone settings. It is the

1

work of Keiller, gathered together and published by Isobel Smith (Smith 1965), which represents the starting point for much modern interpretation of the site.

Though our present knowledge of Avebury owes much to such 20th-century investigations, however, it is important to remember the extent to which the effort of men like Keiller was devoted to *reconstructing* what the site had been like before it suffered from the depredations of earlier centuries. One of the characteristics of Avebury is that – unlike Stonehenge – it does not stand isolated in the middle of open countryside. Instead, it has for many centuries been adjacent to and entangled with an English village, and the relations between the two have tended not to be good for the antiquity. As the scientist and social reformer Sir John Lubbock (later to be created Baron Avebury) put it in his *Pre-Historic Times* of 1865:

> On the whole, this appears to have been the finest megalithic ruin in Europe; but, unfortunately for us, the pretty little village of Abury, like some beautiful parasite, has grown up at the expense, and in the midst, of the ancient temple, and out of 650 great stones, not above 20 are still standing. (Lubbock 1865, 53)

This obscuring effect of the village and the lamentable despoliation of the monuments will have a large place in our discussions. Though the downthrowing and burial of stones had begun much earlier, destruction of stones for use as building materials apparently reached a peak in the decades on either side of 1700: almost the whole of the Sanctuary was destroyed in a single year, 1724, while many stones within the henge were either buried or remorselessly and thoroughly broken up by fire and water during this period.

To the damage done by such destruction of the stones for utilitarian reasons should be added the well-intentioned but crude investigations of early archae-ologists. Such disturbances have naturally focused on central locations within the site which appeared to be crucial to its function – particularly around the Cove and the Obelisk – with the result that potentially fruitful avenues for modern enquiry have been irreparably harmed. Indeed, in recognition of the lesson so learned that investigation of such a site is necessarily destructive, recent excavation has been kept to an absolute minimum and is now the subject of a more or less complete moratorium.

Against this background, special value attaches to the earliest records of the site, some of which have been extensively discussed since the 19th century. Amongst the foremost of these sources is the work of William Stukeley (1687–1765), published in his *Abury: A Temple of the British Druids* of 1743, a sequel to his *Stonehenge: A Temple Restor'd to the British Druids* of 1740. As their subtitles convey, both works were dominated by Stukeley's elaborate interpretation of these antiquities in terms of what he thought to be the beliefs and rites of the Druids and the primeval religion which, in his view, they exemplified. Although archaeologists since the 19th century have rejected Stukeley's interpretative superstructure, they have continued to admire the fieldwork that he carried out between 1719 and 1724 (Piggott 1985). Names such as the Cove, Sanctuary and Kennet Avenue, first used by Stukeley, have been employed ever since, and Stukeley's record remains indispensable for its many detailed contemporary depictions – whatever the outcome of continuing con-troversy over his postulate of a Beckhampton Avenue. In the 1920s the archaeologist

O. G. S. Crawford carried out a detailed collation of Stukeley's work with the existing state of the site, while Alexander Keiller's respect for Stukeley's record is indicated by the care he took to collect and preserve manuscript material on which Stukeley's published books were based.

In the 19th century, antiquaries investigating the history of Avebury discovered an even earlier record, that made by John Aubrey (1626–97) in his 'Templa Druidum', the first part of his *Monumenta Britannica*, begun in 1663, in which he preceded Stukeley in postulating that Avebury and other stone circles were erected by the Druids. Although Aubrey's views on this subject were publicized through the summary of them included in the revised edition of William Camden's famous *Britannia* brought out by a team of scholars in 1695, and though his own book came close to publication in the 1690s, in the event the manuscript remained unpublished until the 1980s, and still requires an adequate edition even now.[1] Aubrey actually saw and described the Sanctuary before it was demolished. In addition, he included in 'Templa Druidum' two plans of Avebury itself, one a detailed survey of the area enclosed by the bank and ditch, the other a map showing the relationship of Avebury to other antiquities in the locality, including the Kennet Avenue, the Sanctuary and Silbury Hill (these items are hereinafter referred to as plans A and B).

The first to draw more than passing attention to Aubrey's manuscript account of the site was the antiquary Sir Richard Colt Hoare (1758–1838), who transcribed lengthy sections of Aubrey's text in the second volume of his *Ancient Wiltshire*, published in 1821 (Colt Hoare 1812–21, ii. 57–64). In the 1850s and 1860s, further transcriptions of Aubrey's account of Avebury were published, together with facsimiles of his plans – at first crude (Long 1858a), then more accurate (Anon. 1862; Jackson 1862, 314–30): though Colt Hoare had referred to the plans (Colt Hoare 1812–21, ii. 66–7, 71), he had not reproduced them. As a result, Aubrey's role in discovering Avebury and making the first accurate records of it has ever since been widely acknowledged, as typically seen in general accounts of the site such as Burl's *Prehistoric Avebury* (Burl 1979).

Since the 19th century, the evidence of Aubrey and Stukeley has been constantly referred to by those trying to reconstruct the earlier state of the site. As we shall see, assessments both of the absolute and of the relative reliability of the two observers have differed markedly, and this reflects a general ambivalence about the legacy of both men, whose fieldwork was often combined with speculations which in modern eyes seem fanciful (Hunter 1975, 183ff., 230; Piggott 1985, 152–8 and passim). But what is crucial for us is a recognition that, in the light of subsequent destruction and of the inevitable incompleteness of archaeological testimony, such early records are indispensable to any attempt to understand the history of the site.

The central significance of these pioneering records makes it all the more surprising that two other 17th-century plans of Avebury have until now been almost entirely overlooked. Both of these survive in the archives of the Royal Society, having evidently been deposited there in connection with a discussion of Avebury which occurred at a meeting of the Society in July 1663: these are hereinafter referred to as plans C and D. The former is a further depiction of Avebury by John Aubrey. The latter is a plan executed by a figure whose role in the history of Avebury has hardly ever been noticed at all, Dr Walter Charleton (1620–1707). It was this savant whose presentation on the topic stimulated the discussion at the Royal Society; he also participated in the royal visit to Avebury in 1663 (see Chapter I, iv), but he is not even referred to in Burl's *Prehistoric Avebury*.

Both of these plans have been the subject of glancing footnote references – one of them, surprisingly enough, occurring in Burl's own book. Though alluding to the existence of the Aubrey plan at the Royal Society on the basis of an earlier footnote reference to it by one of the present authors, however, Burl seems to have felt no urge to investigate the matter further when researching his volume.[2] It was only in August 1988 that attention was for the first time focused on these hitherto neglected records and their implications for our understanding of Avebury.

The context – perhaps appropriately – was provided by the British Association for the Advancement of Science, which had originally taken the initiative in instigating controlled archaeological investigations at Avebury in the early years of this century. In September 1988, one of the authors of this study, Peter Ucko, Professor of Archaeology at Southampton University, organized that Association's Section H (Anthropology and Archaeology) meeting at Oxford on the subject of 'Changing Perceptions'. Avebury was chosen as the location of a case study in the archaeology of cultural landscape, and it was in the course of investigating the background for this, in the previous month, that Ucko contacted the Royal Society Library in search of fresh material, thereby learning of the existence of the two plans in the archives there.

Immediately, it became apparent that plans C and D not only doubled the extant pictorial record of the site at a crucial point in its history, but that they also differed significantly from the early documents that were already known. It is hence not surprising that in the autumn of 1988 they attracted a good deal of attention in the media, first from *The Independent*, in which a measured account of them by David Keys was published on 31 October 1988, and then both on ITN News and in BBC Radio 4's 'Science Now' programme.[3]

For one thing, Charleton's plan categorically describes features which appear to conflict with the received view of the site based on Aubrey's detailed plan in his *Monumenta Britannica* (plan A) and on the published Frontispiece to *Abury* by Stukeley (plan E), particularly in showing the Cove as comprising four, rather than three, stones, and in including a pair of stones outside each of the entrances to the site. Aubrey's Royal Society plan also differs in important respects from his plan A – in the case both of the Cove and the entrance features largely agreeing with the record of Charleton – and this therefore raised questions about the status of Aubrey's well-known record, whose extensive detail and air of authenticity have tended to give an impression of definitiveness to all its features. In fact, as we shall see, plan A is really a more problematic document than has hitherto been realized.

It soon became clear that in order fully to assess the information included in these plans and its implications, it would be necessary to investigate in detail exactly what was recorded about the site in the early modern period and the circumstances in which such records were made, and to collate the facts thus brought to light with all other relevant information about the antiquity. For this, an interdisciplinary team of investigators was assembled. In addition to Peter Ucko, bibliographical skills were provided by Alan Clark, Deputy Librarian of the Royal Society, while Michael Hunter, author of a book on John Aubrey and of other studies of late 17th-century science, was recruited as a scholar able to illuminate the background to the new documents. It was further decided to draw on the expertise of Andrew David and the Ancient Monuments Laboratory of English Heritage.

It is the collaborative work on the new documents and their significance by this team which is presented here: though originally intended to be published as an article, the study has grown into the present book. What follows is an essay in interdisciplinary collaboration which should be of considerable interest in its own right. In the course of it the authors have learnt much about each other's language of discussion, debate and writing, and arguably our insight into Avebury has benefited from this.

As the work progressed it brought to light even more new information than originally expected. In addition to a number of unexpected details about the plans themselves, much new information has come to light from other sources. From the 17th century we have new texts, including a little-known interview concerning Avebury between Charleton and a Danish visitor, Olaus Borrichius, and a hitherto unpublished account of antiquities in the Avebury area by the courtier and virtuoso Sir Robert Moray (1607/8–73), the full text of which is transcribed here as Appendix I.

Then, fresh scrutiny of the manuscript records and draft illustrations of Avebury made by William Stukeley revealed new facts about the state of the site in his time, about the manner in which he acquired his information, and about the relationship between Stukeley's own investigations and the earlier records that initially inspired this study. Indeed, it became increasingly apparent that it was artificial to deal with the 17th-century plans without devoting attention to Stukeley's record, and we have therefore included the 'ground-plot' of Avebury published as the Frontispiece to his *Abury* in our analysis (as plan E) and have also examined its background. In the course of this, we discovered a series of draft versions of this well-known document – none of them identical either with one another or with the final version – together with a lengthy written commentary on the antiquity by Stukeley which was not published in his *Abury*, an edited version of which we have printed here as Appendix II. In addition, we have reassessed Stukeley's elaborate interpretation of Avebury and the question of when and how it developed, reaching the conclusion that there is no basis for the dichotomy that has been discerned between a 'sound' early period, when he did his fieldwork, and a fanciful later one. The result is to give a new insight into the thought of this influential antiquary.

We have also utilized various 18th- and early 19th-century plans of the site which survive in Wiltshire County Record Office, a source of information about the antiquity and its surroundings which, surprisingly enough, has hitherto been ignored. In addition, we have examined the writings of 19th-century antiquaries about the site and have reconsidered the records of the 20th-century excavations: in both cases, information came to light which took on a different significance when seen in the context of the fresh data available from the 17th- and 18th-century sources. Lastly, in order to supplement our investigations into the documentary and archaeological record, an attempt was made, by the application of geophysical survey, to introduce into the debate fresh data from the ground itself. This aspect of the research coincided with a programme of survey begun in 1975 by the Ancient Monuments Laboratory of English Heritage. The results are incorporated here, and these clearly demonstrate the largely unrealized potential offered by non-destructive scientific investigation for our future understanding of Avebury and its associated antiquities.

It would, of course, have been possible simply to expound the information revealed by the early records and to leave others to assess its significance for archaeological understanding of the site. But it seemed to us important to attempt such an assessment here, not least since this in turn stimulated us to ask fresh questions of the early records. The result has been not only to add greatly to the sum of our knowledge about this crucial site, but also to suggest lines of enquiry which promise new insights into its history and context.

However, we do not wish to pretend that either our findings or their implications are straightforward: indeed, those in search of simple answers about what the site was 'really like' either in Aubrey's and Stukeley's time or in prehistory may find our work frustrating. One feature of the early records, and not least the newly discovered ones, is the extent to which the evidence that they provide shows discrepancies, and we have felt obliged to explore these in detail and to try to account for them, partly by examining the aims and preconceptions of the antiquaries who made them, and partly by collating all old and new knowledge about every feature of the antiquity, from the boundaries traversing it to the location of each of its stone emplacements.

The result is to illustrate that, if the indispensable records that survive from the period before destruction are not unproblematic, neither is the evidence that has been brought to light by archaeologists in the 20th century. Indeed, suggestive questions are posed about how perception and preconception interrelate, whether in the 17th century or the 20th: matters which deserve fuller attention than they have received hitherto.

We begin in Chapter I by giving a narrative of the antiquarian discovery of the megalithic monument at Avebury, thus setting out the context in which the plans were made. Then, Chapter II broadens the discussion by considering the aims, methods and preconceptions of the early antiquaries who studied the site, reaching a climax with Stukeley. This involves reference to various features of the early plans, but it also seemed important to our purpose to subject each of these records to the most systematic possible examination, and this follows in Chapter III. This deals with each of the early plans in turn:

> Plan A: Aubrey's 'plane-table' survey of the antiquity at Avebury itself, illustrating his 'Templa Druidum'.
> Plan B: Aubrey's map of the relationship of Avebury to other neighbouring features, also from 'Templa Druidum'.
> Plan C: Aubrey's pencil plan of Avebury, preserved at the Royal Society.
> Plan D: Charleton's plan of Avebury, also preserved at the Royal Society.
> Plan E: Stukeley's Frontispiece to his *Abury* (1743), and the drafts of this that survive.

Chapter IV continues the process of elucidation by deploying all available sources to investigate the antiquity and its surroundings, feature by feature, while Chapter V draws out the major findings from this exercise, drawing conclusions about the early documents and their effects on later interpretations of the site. Lastly, Chapter VI offers some broader reflections concerning Avebury and its future, in the light both of the new information that we have brought to light, and of the various current threats to the monument and its environs.

Notes

1   A highly unsatisfactory edition now exists in the form of Fowles and Legg 1980, 1982. For a critique of the first volume of this, see Hunter 1980; to this may be added the further criticism that, although it gives no indication of the fact, this edition completely omits Part IV of Aubrey's book, in some ways its most interesting section.

2   Burl 1979, 249 n.25, evidently derived from Hunter 1975, 158 n.8. It is perhaps worth pointing out that in the footnote cited here (and on p. 42), Burl confuses the date of the Royal Society meeting with that of the meeting with Charles II (see below, Chapter I, iii–iv). It is also odd that the same note refers to plan A without recording that this is the very plan reproduced as plate 20 of Burl's book. For a reference to Charleton's plan, see Henry 1988, 379.

3   The faulty record of these plans and the events associated with them in Malone 1989, 21–2, must be derived, without acknowledgement of her sources, from David Keys' *Independent* account and/or the presentation by one of us (PJU) at the meeting of the British Association for the Advancement of Science in Oxford in September 1988 or slightly amended repeated presentations in Southampton later in the same year or Birmingham early in 1989. On the inaccuracies of her account see further Chapter V, n.1. It is a pity that she did not establish direct contact with the authors of this book to gain accurate information on the subject rather than retailing a garbled and misleading account in this way.

I   *The antiquarian discovery of Avebury*

i. The beginnings

Although the village and parish of Avebury have a history similar to that of others elsewhere in Wiltshire, which has recently been chronicled at length (V.C.H. 1983), references to the prehistoric antiquities in the locality are rare before the period with which this book is concerned. What is apparently the first such record to survive is to be found in a charter of King Athelstan granting land at Overton to one Wulfswyth in 939, which described the boundaries of the area covered, noting how, near Kennet, these ran 'thonne north up anlang stan raethe. thonne on tha byrgelsas' (Birch 1887, 448; thorns transliterated as 'th'), 'then north up along the stone row, then on to the burying places'. This may well be a reference to the Kennet/Overton Avenue and to some of the numerous barrows in the vicinity: though in the 19th century, it was suggested that 'the burying places' referred to might be the henge at Avebury, this seems unlikely (Long 1858a, 360–1n.; Fergusson 1860, 209; 1872, 73–4). At the Wiltshire Assizes in 1289, the case arose of a murder that had taken place in 1282 at 'Waleditch', a location that was clearly in the Kennet/Avebury area, and it has been suggested that this is a reference to the bank and ditch surrounding the stone circle at Avebury, which was still called 'Wall Ditch' in various maps and estate documents of the 17th and 18th centuries (Kempson 1955; Plates 46–7). Then, in 1307, we have an isolated reference to the Avebury stones in the Cartulary of Cirencester Abbey, which was granted rights to a pathway which ran 'usque magnas petras veteres', 'as far as the great old stones'; this charter also makes reference to 'la Waldich' as a property boundary (Devine 1977, 1051).

With the onset of systematic topography in the Tudor period, Avebury received brief notices which are indicative of the dawning of curiosity about the contemporary appearance and historical associations of the countryside (Kendrick 1950, chs. 4–8; Rowse 1950, ch. 2; Moir 1964, ch. 2; Levy 1967, ch. 4; Morgan 1982). Thus in about 1540 the pioneer of such enquiry, John Leland, noted in his account of Wiltshire:

> Kenet risithe northe northe west at Selberi Hille botom, where by hathe be [sic] camps and sepultures of men of warre, as at Aibyri a myle of, and in dyvers placis of the playne. (Leland 1907–10, v. 81)

Avebury also appeared in the celebrated work of Leland's principal successor, William Camden, whose *Britannia* was first published in 1586. Camden's own recensions of the book make no reference to Avebury itself: he gave an account of Silbury Hill, professing uncertainty as to whether it was a burial-place or a kind of boundary-mark, while, of the course of the River Kennet, he noted how 'This River *Kenet* runneth at the first Eastward, thorow certain open fields, out of which there stand up aloft every where stones like rockes, and off them a litle village there is, called, *Rockley*' (Camden 1607, 185; trans. in Camden 1610, 255). In 1610, however, when Philemon Holland translated the work into English, he placed between the account of Silbury and that of the River Kennet the following note:

> Within one mile of *Selburie*, is *Aiburie*, an uplandish village built in an old Campe as it seemth, but of no large compasse, for it is environeth with a faire trench, and hath foure gappes as gates, in two of the which stand huge Stones as jambes, but so rude, that they seeme rather naturall than artificiall, of which sort, there are some other in the said village. (Camden 1610, 255)

Clearly, therefore, Holland or an informant must have visited the site (his statement that the stones were 'naturall' probably means that, in his view, they had not been placed there by human hand, though it may allude to the common tradition that megaliths, such as those at Stonehenge, had been cast artificially: Chippindale 1983, 27–8). Another possible early visitor is Sir John Harington, who, in his translation into English of Ariosto's *Orlando Furioso*, published in 1591, added to his commentary on Merlin a topographical reference which almost certainly concerns Avebury:

> that he had a castell in Wiltshire called after him *Merlins* burie, (now Marleborow) it is verie likely: the old ruines whereof are yet seene in our highway from Bath to London. Also the great stones of unmeasurable bignesse and number, that lie scattered about the place, have given occasion to some to report, and others to beleeve wondrous stratagems wrought by his great skill in Magike, as likewise the great stones at Stonage on Salisburie plaine, which the ignorant people beleeve he brought out of Ireland: and indeed the wiser sort can rather marvell at, then tell either why or how they were set there. (Harington 1591, 22)

A further reference to Avebury appeared in Inigo Jones' *Stoneheng Restored*, posthumously published in 1655, in which Jones gave a detailed description of Stonehenge, with lavish – if somewhat schematic – plans and elevations, and sought to prove that it was a Roman temple. Jones compiled this book in 1620 in response to the interest in the antiquity shown by James I and various of his courtiers (Jones 1655, 1–2), and it is just possible that they visited Avebury as well: in the early 18th century William Stukeley was to record in his fieldnotes – evidently on the basis of oral information – that 'K[ing] Ja[mes] I was at Abury in his Progress & viewd the stones very curiously' (Eng.Misc.c.533, 44bv). This, however, is otherwise unsubstantiated and it seems unlikely to be true: in the course of his book, Jones referred to '*Aibury* in North-*Wiltshire*', but only as the site of 'Quarries of the like stone' to that from which Stonehenge was constructed, noting that stones were to be found there 'of far greater dimensions then any at *Stoneheng*' (Jones 1655, 34, 36–7; see also Chapter IV, b).

Avebury was also cited in connection with Stonehenge in a further work which, though topographical, was of a somewhat different kind from Camden's, bearing witness to the enthusiasm for Baconian natural history in England in the mid-17th century: Joshua Childrey's *Britannia Baconica: Or, The Natural Rarities of England, Scotland, & Wales* (1661). Childrey noted how:

> upon the Downs between *Marleborough* and *Aubury* ... are to be found abundance of great stones, commonly called by the Country thereabout, the Gray Weathers; and at *Aubury* in an Orchard there are halfe a dozen, or halfe a score stones little inferiour to the *Stonehenge* for hugeness, some standing upright like the *Sonehenge* [sic], & others lying flat on the ground. And the Country here, like that about the *Stonehenge*, affords not a stone beside.

This confirmed him in his view of the stones at Stonehenge that, contrary to those who considered them artificial, they were 'naturall stones' which 'were *ab initio*, placed here by the God of nature' (Childrey 1661, 48–9).

ii. Aubrey and Charleton

Twelve years before Childrey published his account, in 1649, Avebury had been discovered by John Aubrey (Plate 1), as he recounted in a well-known passage of his address 'To the Reader' in his 'Templa Druidum'. Aubrey recalled how, though familiar since his childhood with Salisbury Plain and Stonehenge, he 'never saw the Countrey about *Marleborough*, till Christmas 1648', when he was invited to a house party by his aristocratic friends, the Seymours. Aubrey tells of a hunting expedition on 7 January 1649, when:

> the Chase led us (at length) thorough the Village of Aubury, into the Closes there: where I was wonderfully surprized at the sight of those vast stones: of which I had never heard before: as also at the mighty Bank & graffe about it: I observed in the Inclosures some segments of rude circles, made with those stones: whence I concluded, they had been in the old time complete. I left my Company a while, entertaining my selfe with a more delightfull indaegation: and then (steered by the cry of the Hounds) overtooke the company, and went with them to *Kynnet*, where was a good Hunting dinner provided (Aubrey 24, 23; Fowles and Legg 1980, 17f.).[1]

The text as we have it comes from a revised version made by Aubrey during the last year or two of his life, since it cites the new edition of Camden's *Britannia* published in 1695; it also uses the name 'Aubury', which is the spelling that Aubrey increasingly adopted later in life. But it is clearly adapted from an earlier version, and an overlapping draft appears among the deleted passages on the verso of Aubrey's plan A elsewhere in 'Templa Druidum', where he wrote:

> Anno 1649 January as I was hunting in the country of the Hare that game led us through the Towne, but I was so strangely surprized with the immenseness of the Antiquity that I made bold to lett my friends follow the chase, while I admired and ... these ... Ruines. This gave me the first Occasion of writing this Rhapsodie. (Aubrey 24, 39; Fowles and Legg 1980, 43)[2]

Plate 1 John Aubrey by William Faithorne, 1666: ink drawing, tinted with watercolour. Aubrey intended to have this portrait engraved for his *Monumenta Britannica* (Aubrey 24, 17). Ashmolean Museum, Oxford.

In the margin, he tried rewriting this: 'The Chase of the Hare led us to the Towne of Avebury & through the Closes there', and he also added a note about the Seymours. Though these notes cannot be precisely dated, they seem likeliest to date from the mid-1660s when Aubrey was composing the introductory material for the book. They thus juxtapose material which went into his 'To the Reader' with material deployed in the general introductory section to the work and the description of Avebury, including Aubrey's well-known remark that Avebury 'as much exceedes Stoneheng in bignesse; as a Cathedrall does, a parish church'. Their handwriting is perfectly consistent with such a dating.

As will be seen from this account, Aubrey clearly found Avebury by accident, rather than through knowledge of existing accounts, such as that in the 1610 edition of Camden. That even later on he was only vaguely aware that the antiquity had ever been referred to at all is suggested by the fact that, whereas in the draft version of the material on the back of plan A he noted 'tis strange that our Chorographers tooke no more notice of it. Mr Camden, names it only', in the reworked version of this that he included in his description of Avebury the name of the chorographer who 'only names it' was left blank (Aubrey 24, 31, 39; Fowles and Legg 1980, 33, 43). He does seem, however, to have been conscious that it was thought by some that the earthwork was defensive in purpose, taking the trouble to point out that the placing of the bank outside the ditch made this unlikely (Aubrey 24, 31; Fowles and Legg 1980, 34).

Aubrey's 'To the Reader' went on to refer to the publication of Jones' *Stoneheng Restored* in 1655, and how the discrepancies between the details of Jones' account of Stonehenge and the actual monument 'gave me an edge to make more researches'. Although this implies that the stimulus from Jones' book came in the year of its publication, in the draft on the back of plan A his critique of Jones appeared

11

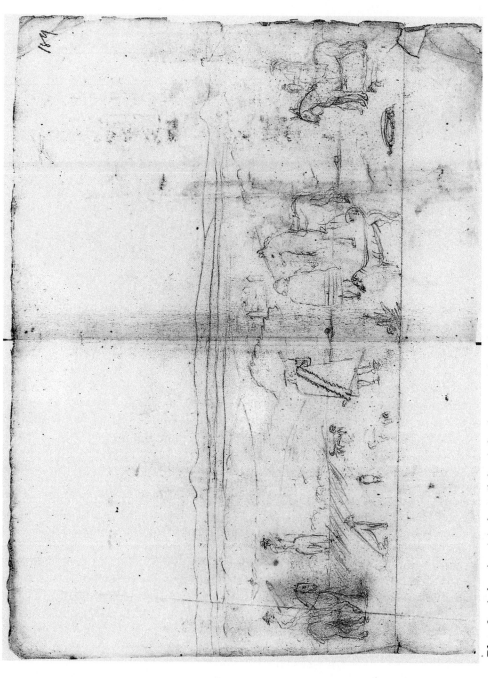

Plate 2 Aubrey's original pencil sketch for the watercolour shown in the next plate (Bodleian Library ms. Aubrey 3, 188v–9).

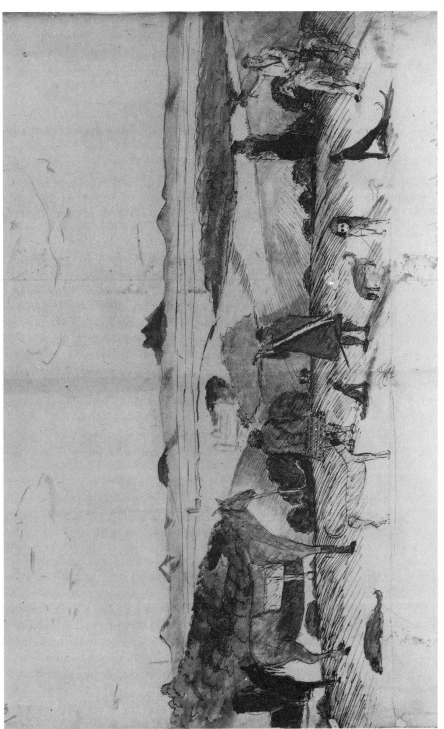

Plate 3 Aubrey's watercolour of a hawking expedition by himself, Sir James Long and others in the later 1650s (Bodleian Library ms. Aubrey 3, 186v-7).

elsewhere on the page, in immediate juxtaposition with a reference to the attack on Jones that Walter Charleton was to publish in 1663, and it is possible that his interest in Stonehenge was more a feature of the 1660s than of the decade in which Jones' book actually appeared. But Aubrey certainly made some study of Avebury before 1663, for he went on to tell 'the Reader' how 'a farther opportunity was, that my honourd & faithfull Friend Colonell *James Long* of Draycot, was wont to spend a week or two every Autumne at Aubury in Hawking, where several times I have had the happiness to accompany him' (Aubrey 24, 24; Fowles and Legg 1980, 20). James Long (1617–92) was a Wiltshire gentleman with scientific and antiquarian interests, who succeeded to a baronetcy in 1673, as Aubrey recorded in a marginal note; his house, Draycot, lay north of Chippenham. A watercolour by Aubrey showing one of these hawking expeditions on which fieldwork was also done at Avebury is reproduced on the cover of this book (and see Plates 2–3). It well illustrates Aubrey's appreciation of the 'Romantick countrey' in which Avebury was set, about which he went on in an almost lyrical vein:

> the Prospects, noble & vaste, the Downes stock't with numerous Flocks of Sheep: the Turfe rich & fragrant with Thyme & Burnet ... nor are the Nut-brown Shepherdesses without their graces. (Aubrey 24, 24; Fowles and Legg 1980, 20)

Unfortunately, though we know that Aubrey was working on both a natural history of Wiltshire and an antiquarian survey of the county in the late 1650s, none of the notes that he made at this time survive in their original form (Hunter 1975, 94–5, 149–50). On the other hand, since we know that Aubrey's plan C was completed before July 1663, it is quite possible that it was during his visits to Avebury with James Long in the autumns of the 1650s that Aubrey recorded the details entered into this pencil plan.

If Aubrey's connection with Avebury has long been well known, the role in the early history of the site of the author of plan D, Walter Charleton (Plate 4), has hitherto been strangely neglected. Charleton (1620–1707) was an active figure in scientific and medical circles in Interregnum and Restoration England. Appointed physician extraordinary to Charles I in the 1640s, he thereafter became a prolific author on scientific topics and his writings have attracted a good deal of modern scholarly attention (see Rattansi 1964; Kargon 1966, ch. 8; Webster 1967; Gelbart 1971; Sharp 1973; Frank 1980; Fleitmann 1986; Henry 1988).

Like Aubrey, Charleton found himself dissatisfied with Inigo Jones' views on Stonehenge. In Charleton's case, this was largely because collation of the antiquity with megalithic remains to be found in Scandinavia, most fully chronicled by Olaus Worm in his *Danicorum Monumentorum Libri Sex* (1643), suggested to him that the Wiltshire monument was not of Roman date, as Jones claimed, but a work of the Danes (Charleton 1663, passim). We know that Charleton corresponded with Worm about Stonehenge and its similarity to these northern antiquities, and this must have taken place before Worm's death in 1654: Charleton wrote how Worm had 'vouchsafed sometimes to honour me with his Epistles', and had 'been so liberal in his Contributions toward the maintenance of my Supposition, as to furnish me with not onely verbal Descriptions, but lively Draughts or Pictures also of sundry Antique *Danish* Monuments, as well in the Bulk and Rudeness of the Stones, as in

Plate 4 Portrait of Walter Charleton by Sir Godfrey Kneller. Hunterian Art Gallery, University of Glasgow.

the Order and Manner of their position and situation, much resembling our *Stone-heng*' (Charleton 1663, 29–30). Either, therefore, Charleton must have had access to a copy of Jones' text before it was published in 1655 – which is quite possible, since the work had been in existence for thirty-five years by that date – or he had had an independent interest in Stonehenge. This could conceivably have been stimulated by Worm, who had made efforts to establish contact with Charleton in 1650 after the publication in that year of Charleton's earliest books, and who appears to have been interested in possible analogues between English and Danish antiquities (Charleton 1663, 29; Wood 1813–20, iv. 753–4; Long 1876, 30 n. 1; Seaton 1935, 239; Worm 1968, 426, 427–8, 435; Piggott 1989, 104).

The fact that at one point in his text Charleton referred to Worm as 'not above four years past deceased' indicates that he wrote his account of Stonehenge in the late 1650s (Charleton 1663, 29). It was not, however, published until after the Restoration, when Charleton had become royal physician to Charles II and, early in 1661, a Fellow of the newly founded Royal Society, in which he was to play an active role until 1668 (Hunter 1982, 172–3). His book, the title-page of which was dated 1663, was entitled *Chorea Gigantum, or, The most Famous Antiquity of Great-Britain, Vulgarly called Stone-heng, Standing on Salisbury Plain, Restored to the Danes*. In it, he gave at length his reasons for believing that Stonehenge, like other similar antiqui-

15

ties in this country, was not of Roman but of Danish origin; he also claimed that it was not a temple, as Jones had claimed, but was 'principally, if not wholly Design'd to be a *Court Royal*, or place for the *Election* and *Inauguration* of their Kings' (Charleton 1663, sig. a1).

The latter hypothesis was obviously politically appropriate in the immediate aftermath of the Restoration, and it is not surprising to find that the work was decked out with obsequiously loyalist sentiments and dedicated to the King, as well as being prefaced by an effusive congratulatory poem by John Dryden: indeed, the copy of the work that Charleton presented to Charles II, bound in red morocco, still survives in the British Library, classmark C.76.b.20 (cf. Hunter 1989, 42–3). One author has even claimed that Charleton's hypothesis about Stonehenge's original function can be explained by his wish to ingratiate himself with the King (Chippindale 1983, 61), though this is rendered less likely by the Interregnum prehistory of the book indicated here. Charleton was also critical of Jones for the way in which he depicted Stonehenge: he reproduced the engraving of the antiquity in Camden's *Britannia*, which he considered 'to come much neerer in resemblance both to the work it self, and to the idea thereof formed in my Imagination out of its ruines, than that bequeathed to the world by *Mr. Jones*, though much more elaborate and artificial' (Charleton 1663, 13).

In the course of *Chorea Gigantum*, Charleton did refer to Avebury, but he simply echoed Jones in mentioning Avebury, along with Rockley, as a place where scattered concentrations of the stones from which Stonehenge was constructed were to be found, 'brought thither, as is vulgarly, and perhaps not untruly beleived, by the violence of the universal Deluge, and left there in vallies, as the force of the currents abated'. Charleton even noted: 'These stones I my self have often seen, in journeys to *Bath* from *London*' (Charleton 1663, 58). Clearly, therefore, when Charleton wrote his book, and still, presumably, when he prepared it for publication – the dedication to the King is dated 27 April 1662 and the imprimatur 11 September 1662 – he had not realized that Avebury was an antiquity comparable to Stonehenge.

At this point, Aubrey can re-enter our story, since it is very likely that it was he who, on reading Charleton's book, told him what he himself had known since 1649 – that Avebury was itself a remarkable ancient monument. In 1672, Aubrey was to describe Charleton as his 'old & faithfull friend' (Hunter 1975, 45 n. 3): that the two were already well acquainted in 1662 is shown by the fact that Charleton presented Aubrey with a copy of another of his books in October 1662, the month after the imprimatur of *Chorea Gigantum* (Powell 1963, 298), and that it was Charleton who proposed Aubrey for Fellowship of the Royal Society on 24 December 1662: such proposals generally indicate friendship between the persons concerned (Hunter 1982, 62, 182). Unfortunately, we do not know exactly when Aubrey first saw Charleton's book: his copy of it – if he had one – cannot now be traced. There is, among the Aubrey manuscripts in the Bodleian, a slim volume (MS Aubrey 11) comprising notes and comments on *Chorea Gigantum* which at one point Aubrey seems to have intended to incorporate in his 'Templa Druidum' (Aubrey 24, 13, 22; Fowles and Legg 1980, 5): but these are undated, and they probably date at earliest from the mid-1660s, when Aubrey was writing the work, if not later still, when he was rewriting and recopying it.

16

Nevertheless, it seems highly probable that it was Aubrey who, on first seeing Charleton's book on Stonehenge, opened its author's eyes to the true significance of Avebury, and one result was evidently that Charleton paused to study the site while travelling between London and Bath. He was a West Country man, born at Shepton Mallet, and references in the Royal Society's minutes suggest that other Fellows expected him to be knowledgeable about matters concerning Bath: at a meeting in June 1663, for instance, 'he took notice of the accretions made to the stones under the waters at Bath', while Aubrey, too, referred to views that Charleton had formed from 'his long observation' there (Birch 1756–7, i. 25, 256, 315; Aubrey 1, 161v). That Charleton spent time at Bath in the first half of 1663 may be suggested by the fact that, whereas his presence at Royal Society meetings is frequently signalled by his contribution to proceedings as recorded in the minutes, there is no reference to him at any meeting between 18 February and 20 May 1663. It is very likely to have been during this period that he made plan D, or at least the observations, measurements and notes from which it was compiled.

iii. The Royal Society meeting and its aftermath

This brings us to the meeting of the Royal Society in July 1663 when Avebury was the subject of the 'first antiquarian contribution to the Royal Society', which has been described as illustrating the Society's 'scientific spirit at work in the archaeological field' (Evans 1956, 28). The original draft minutes for the meeting on 8 July 1663 record that:

> Dr Charlton presented the Compayny with the Plan of the Stone-Antiquity at Avebury neer Marlborough in Wiltshire: suggesting, it were worth the while to dig there under a certain Triangular Stone, where he conceived would be found a Monument of some Danish King. Col. Long and Mr Awbrey were desired to make further inquiry into the same.[3]

Charleton's presentation was also referred to by Robert Hooke, the Society's Curator of Experiments, in a letter to the scientist Robert Boyle, then living in Oxford. Hooke wrote:

> Dr *Charlton* gave a description of *Aubery* in *Wiltshire*, which seems indeed by his relation a very strange piece of antiquity, and more admirable than *Stoneheng*, which he hopes to make an argument to confirm his hypothesis about that *Chorea Gigantum*. (Boyle 1744, v. 532)

Hooke's letter is undated: his account of Charleton's presentation is juxtaposed with details of the business that appears in the minutes as being dealt with at the meeting on 15 July,[4] whereas he had described the bulk of the business at the 8 July meeting in a different, also undated but presumably earlier, letter (Boyle 1744, v. 531–2). It is possible, therefore, that Charleton's presentation in fact took place on 15 July and was misplaced in the minutes: but it is likelier that Hooke had accidentally forgotten to tell Boyle about the presentation immediately after it occurred, and that he

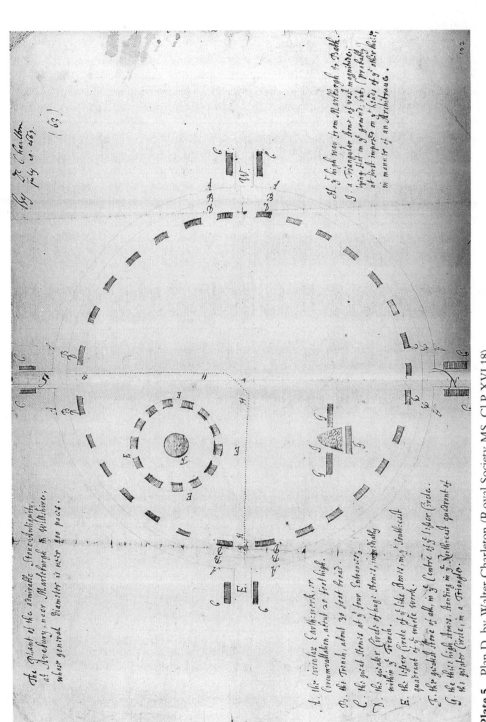

Plate 5 Plan D, by Walter Charleton (Royal Society MS. Cl.P.XVI.18).

inserted it into the subsequent letter because he deemed the matter of sufficient interest not to let it pass (though, if so, it is curious that he did not explain to Boyle that this was the case).

Plan D (Plate 5 and also in folder), which now survives in the Society's Classified Papers, is undoubtedly that presented by Charleton, though it has been overlooked by almost all previous commentators. This may in part be because the plan was until recently misdated to 1667 in the Royal Society's catalogues of its archives. Carefully drawn in ink, plan D must have been prepared in advance with a view to stimulating discussion. Indeed, it is even possible that its format is explained by the needs of the occasion, since the writing is 'upside down' in relation to a north–south alignment, perhaps for reading out by Charleton while displaying the plan to the kind of audience – of twenty or thirty – who would have been present at a Royal Society meeting at this time (see Hunter 1982, 16–17). Charleton's plan depicts the earthwork as having four entrances, outside each of which is a pair of stones. Within the main circle of stones he clearly marks the stone now known as the Obelisk with a subsidiary circle around it, while, to the north, the Cove – which is shown as comprising four stones – is depicted as standing on its own with no surrounding circle. Each feature is described in a caption, and these are reproduced in full in Chapter III.

In one caption Charleton described the Cove as comprising 'the three high stones, standing in the North-east quadrant of the greater Circle, in a Triangle', with 'a Triangular stone, of vast magnitude, lying flat on the ground; but, (probably) at first imposed on the heads of the other three, in manner of an Architrave': the reference in the minutes to Charleton's mention of 'a certain Triangular Stone' appears to echo this. It was presumably under this stone that he was claiming that 'a Monument of some Danish King' would be found, a point noted in the minutes but not in any of the captions. Background to this is to be found in his *Chorea Gigantum*, where he discussed Danish analogues to Stonehenge: possibly this was what lay behind Hooke's remark about Charleton's belief that the new site would 'confirm his hypothesis' about the better-known monument. For, though Charleton argued that the principal function of Stonehenge was as a place where kings were elected, elsewhere he followed his mentor, Worm, in postulating that megalithic antiquities might be 'Sepulchres', additionally suggesting that in certain circumstances the two functions could be combined, particularly when a king was killed in battle: this was introduced as a subsidiary hypothesis concerning Stonehenge (Charleton 1663, 48, 54). In the case of Avebury, he may either have been postulating a comparable joint function, or he may have meant that the funerary purpose was more central here than at Stonehenge: further evidence on this topic will be adduced in Chapter II.

Although it was thus Charleton who drew the attention of the Royal Society to Avebury, it was not he who was asked by the Society to investigate the matter further. Instead, this task was deputed to Aubrey and his friend, James Long, who may have been mentioned first because of his greater seniority in the Society. Not only was Long quite an active member of the Society at this stage (Birch 1756–7, i. passim; Hunter 1982, 176–7); he also lived in Wiltshire and it was in his company, as we have seen, that Aubrey had visited Avebury in the 1650s. The Royal Society's minutes often contain such instructions at this time: they do not necessarily prove that the Fellows in question were present, but they do show that they were thought likely to have an interest in the matter in hand, and in this case Charleton and/or the other Fellows present evidently saw Aubrey as an appropriate person to make further investigations, presumably because of his known interest in Wiltshire antiquities in general and Avebury in particular; his friend, Long, was probably seen as a useful assistant.

No record was kept of Fellows' attendance at meetings unless they are recorded in the minutes as speaking or making a presentation: on 8 July 1663, those who fall into this category are Charleton; Hooke; Long; Edmund Waller, the poet; and Sir Robert Moray, courtier, Scottish Privy Councillor and one of the most active Fellows of the Society at this time (it is also mentioned that a discourse by Sir Paul Neile 'was read', implying that this was done in his absence). On 15 July, those named as present were Charleton, Hooke, Long, Moray, the President, William, Viscount Brouncker, and the following other Fellows: the mathematician and divine John Pell; the doctors Timothy Clarke and William Croone; and the courtier Sir Anthony Morgan. In addition, a visitor from France, Victor Beaufort Vabres de Fresars, was present, while Dr Jonathan Goddard, who was asked to undertake a task, may or may not have been (Birch 1756–7, i. 272–80).

Though his name was not among those recorded in this way on either occasion, we know that Aubrey was present at the meeting at which Avebury was discussed, because this is confirmed in some near-contemporary notes by Sir Robert Moray which survive in the Society's archives. These notes, which may have been the subject of an oral presentation in October 1664, deal with antiquities and other phenomena 'in the country to Bathe': they are printed in Appendix I, and we will consider their content in more detail shortly. What is important here is that, describing Avebury as 'the noblest monument that I ever saw of the kinde', Moray noted how it had been 'already observed & spoken of at a meeting of the Society sc. by Mr Aubry & Dr Charleton'. He therefore forebore to describe it, in the expectation of Aubrey's measuring it exactly and bringing 'a perfect account thereof to the Society'.

The fact that Moray mentioned Aubrey's name before Charleton's makes it virtually certain that Aubrey as well as Charleton gave a disquisition about Avebury at the July meeting, when he may well have supplemented Charleton's presentation by bringing in plan C (Plate 6 and also in folder). Although neither his presentation nor his plan are noted in the minutes, there is good reason to believe that these provide a far from complete record of everything that took place at the Society's meetings (Hunter 1982, 83). Indeed, the fact that the original draft minutes for the meeting on 8 July contain a further instruction to Aubrey and Long to investigate 'a certain Tombe upon Salisbury plaine' as well as Avebury, which was subsequently deleted, suggests that this may have been a further topic which came up during the discussion and which the Secretary included in the draft instructions through a misunderstanding.

Certainly, the secretary, Henry Oldenburg's endorsement to plan C, 'By Mr Awbrey. july 8. 1663', suggests that Aubrey *did* produce this item at that meeting; the only – less likely – alternative would be that it was submitted at a later date and endorsed by Oldenburg with this date because it related to business transacted on that occasion. Whether or not the plan was specially prepared for presentation to the Society is unclear. Though the fact that it is in pencil might suggest that it was

Plate 6 Plan C, the plan by Aubrey now in the Royal Society archives (Royal Society MS. 131, 67).

produced in a hurry, it displays no signs of hasty composition, while a considerable amount of care has clearly been taken over its details and its 'well-lettered' title.

Although by the same author, this plan is strikingly different from the better-known plan A by Aubrey that appears in *Monumenta Britannica*. For one thing, in contrast both to that and to Charleton's plan, it depicts houses standing along both of the cross streets within the henge; it also appears to delineate a different and more complex set of field boundaries from those shown in plan A. It agrees with both plans in including what is clearly the Cove, which is also shown enlarged in the margin, together with a picture of Avebury church, separated from the antiquity by a river running north–south. But it accords with Charleton's plan rather than plan A in that the Cove as shown in the margin clearly comprises four stones, while the bank and ditch are shown as having four entrances, outside at least three of which – and possibly all four – stand pairs of stones. In other respects, however, Charleton's plan and Aubrey's plan C vary: indeed, this shows that they were composed independently, which strengthens their testimony on the points where they corroborate one another. In particular, within the main circle, Aubrey does not show a ring in one segment, as Charleton does, but a series of three further concentric circles of stones, with the Cove appearing as a kind of anomaly to this arrangement. Hence, though prepared by Charleton and Aubrey in the belief that they were adequate representations of the antiquity, there were some striking differences between the two plans. If both were produced at the same meeting, one can only presume that puzzled discussion must have ensued, which may have illustrated to Aubrey the inadequacies of plan C as a record of the site and made him resolve to return to look at it more fully.

Though Moray noted Aubrey's intention to 'bring a perfect account' of the antiquity to the Royal Society, in fact the subject never came up again in the Society's minutes. Antiquarian topics are relatively rare in the Society's proceedings in these early years, and the July 1663 minute dealing with Avebury is rather isolated in a record of discussions mainly devoted to scientific and technological phenomena (Hunter 1971, 188). There is, however, a kind of postscript in the form of the survival in the Society's archives of a note, or a copy of a note, addressed to Aubrey which, among other things, quoted the minutes of 8 July 1663 in instructing him 'To make further inquiry into the Stone Antiquity of Avebury, and particularly of the Monument, suspected to be under the triangular stone; which was also desired of Col: Long'. This forms part of a group of thirty-two such memoranda, including comparable notes addressed to Charleton and Long (though neither of these refers to Avebury).[5] Clearly, these memoranda belong to one of the recurrent attempts to reinvigorate the Society's business that occurred in its early years, though their exact date is uncertain. Since another of Aubrey's tasks listed in his memorandum was one that he was first asked to undertake only in November 1666, it is likely that the note dates from late 1666 or 1667, when the Society was recuperating from the disruption to its activities caused by the Great Plague and the Fire of London.[6] In any case, it failed to stimulate any further presentation of material relating to Avebury at a meeting of the Society.

In August 1663, however, there had been two further developments. The first occurred on 9 August, when a Danish scholar, Olaus Borrichius, paid a visit on Charleton, at which antiquarian topics were discussed and Charleton showed his

Danish guest various of his medical writings. Previously, Borrichius had spent several weeks in England, part of the time in London and part travelling to Oxford, Bath and other places; he described his experiences both in a journal and in a letter of 10 August to his compatriot, the medical writer Thomas Bartholinus (Borrichius 1983, iii. 16–75; Bartholinus 1663–7, iv. 516–40; Seaton 1935, 164–8). In the course of his tour, he had visited Stonehenge, about which he wrote at length in his letter, noting with satisfaction Charleton's recently published book attributing the antiquity to 'our race', and filling out the rather briefer account that he vouchsafed to his journal (this did, however, give some information omitted from the letter, including the name of the antiquity and the number of stones that it comprised) (Borrichius 1983, iii. 59; Bartholinus 1663–7, iv. 534–5; Seaton 1935, 238).

The fuller detail – and the information about Charleton's book – may have been based on Borrichius' interview with Charleton on his return to London, an interview which had taken place the very day before the letter to Bartholinus was written: we know from the journal that the two men discussed Jones' theories about Stonehenge on this occasion, with Charleton showing Borrichius Jones' plan of the antiquity and criticizing the architect's theory about its Vitruvian character. In the journal, this was presented as an appendage to the first topic of conversation which came up, an antiquity which can only be Avebury, which Borrichius described in his letter to Bartholinus in the following terms:

> Doctor Walter Charleton has made observations upon another and more magnificent monument of Danish Antiquity in the County of Wiltshire, almost the counterpart of the other at Salisbury, but a far greater labour, for here the upright stones attain the height of thirty-six, and one even of forty feet, which is called Kong-Stool, almost after the fashion of our language. He showed me a plan [Topographiam] of it. The rocks stand arranged in a circle (you would say they were Cyclops [Aetnaeos fratres diceres]), but on a regular system [certa lege], a smaller circle enclosed by a bigger; and in this circle this ingenious Doctor suspects that one of our Kings lies buried. (Bartholinus 1663–7, iv. 536; translation adapted from Seaton 1935, 238)

Borrichius' account in his journal overlaps with this fuller account in his letter to Bartholinus, but it is briefer and the description is slightly differently worded (Borrichius 1983, iii. 70). In it, the information about the size of the stones and the shape of the monument is conflated, which means that he makes it clear that the highest stone is in the middle of the inner circle, something which Borrichius did not actually tell Bartholinus, but which is precisely what one would have expected him to have been told by Charleton, since the relevant caption on plan D clearly speaks of 'the greatest stone of all, in the Centre of the lesser Circle'.[7] Indeed, it was presumably a copy of plan D – if not the original of which this was a copy – that Charleton must have shown him. Borrichius' rather arcane allusion to 'Cyclops' was clearly addressed specifically to Bartholinus and does not appear in the journal, while, more surprisingly, he also failed to record in his journal Charleton's hypothesis that Avebury was the burial site of a Danish King. Two details are slightly different in the two accounts, one that the height of all but the tallest stone is given as 34 foot in the journal, as against 36 in the letter, and the other that the tallest stone (in other words, presumably the Obelisk) was said in the journal to be called 'King-Stool', not 'Kong-Stool'. On both, the journal is probably to be preferred, the printed text of the letter having been corrupted by the typesetters through whose hands it passed, who may simply have set 36 instead of 34 by accident, and who presumably Germanicized 'King' into 'Kong'.

On the other hand, even allowing for typographical error, the dimensions that Borrichius gave for the stones are clearly exaggerated, while other parts of his record appear to represent a misconstrual on his part of what Charleton told him. Thus, though it is interesting that Borrichius' letter confirms the Royal Society minutes in reporting Charleton's hypothesis that Avebury was a royal mausoleum, he appears to have confused matters in his implication that it was in the middle of the inner circle – i.e. the south circle, the only one shown in plan D – that a Danish king was buried: as we have seen, collation of the Royal Society minutes with the captions to plan D suggests that it was in fact the Cove that Charleton meant in this connection, his reference to the stone in question as 'Triangular' almost certainly excluding the Obelisk, which is shown on his plan as circular, a shape confirmed both by Stukeley's account of it and by modern excavation (Stukeley 1743, 24; Smith 1965, 198).

As for the 'King-Stool', this is more problematic still: it may represent a further misunderstanding, or it could record a new and hitherto unknown piece of information about the antiquity. Background is provided by Charleton's description of Danish analogues to Stonehenge in *Chorea Gigantum*, where he cited Olaus Worm concerning a place of regal inauguration 'called *Kongstolon*, or Kings throne' as part of his conjecture that Stonehenge had been erected for such purposes, and, evidently referring to the stone usually called the altar, he noted:

> one Stone, in the inmost circle (now lying along and broken, but at first set upright, and then probably placed at the very centre of the whole work) whose remaining fragments put together make, according to *Mr. Jones* his accompt, sixteen feet in length; Which is as likely to have been a *Kongstolon* (as the *Danes* call theirs) or Kings throne, as an Altar. (Charleton 1663, 49, 52; cf. Worm 1643, 88)

Since we know that at Borrichius' meeting with Charleton Stonehenge as well as Avebury was discussed, the similarity of terminology could suggest that Borrichius had accidentally transferred what Charleton told him about Stonehenge to Avebury.

On the other hand, since Charleton seems to have seen such features as typical of megalithic antiquities generally, it is equally possible that he told Borrichius that there was a 'King-Stool' at Avebury too – indeed, perhaps even that his hypothesis concerning Stonehenge had been confirmed by oral tradition at the other site.[8] If so, this would imply that Charleton *did* see Avebury as combining electoral and funerary functions, and in this connection it is interesting to compare the wording of the caption to the Obelisk on his plan – 'the greatest stone of all, in the Centre of the lesser Circle' – with yet another passage of *Chorea Gigantum* dealing with 'Places designed for the Election and Inauguration of their Kings'. These were supposed to comprise rings of large stones 'for the most part twelve in number, and one stone exceeding all the rest in eminency, set in the middle' (Charleton 1663, 48–9; Worm 1643, 87): in his plan of Avebury, the circle surrounding the Obelisk is shown as having thirteen stones.

iv. The royal visit and its context

Later in August, a further, better-known series of events occurred concerning Avebury, which Aubrey records in his address 'To the Reader' in 'Templa Druidum', beside a marginal note '1663'. This is from the same version, dating from the end of Aubrey's life but presumably adapted from an earlier recension, as his account of his discovery of the site in 1649 which has already been quoted.

> King Charles IId discoursing one morning with my Lord *Brounker, & Dr Charleton* concerning Stoneheng, they told his Majestie, what they had heard me say, concerning Aubury, sc. that it did as much excell *Stoneheng*, as a Cathedral does a Parish church. His Majestie admired that none of our Chorographers had taken notice of it: and commanded Dr Charlton to bring me to him the next morning. I brought with me a draught of it donne by memorid [sic] only: but well enough resembling it, with which his Majestie was pleased: gave me his hand to kisse and commanded me to waite on him at Marleborough when he went to *Bath* with the Queen (which was about a fortnight after) which I did: and the next day, when the Court were on their Journey, his Majestie left the Queen and diverted to Aubury, where I shewed him that stupendious Antiquity, with the view whereof, He and his Royal Highnesse the Duke of *Yorke*, were very well pleased. His Majestie then commanded me to write a Description of it, and present it to him: and the Duke of Yorke commanded me to give an account of the old Camps, and Barrows on the Plaines.
>
> As his Majestie departed from Aubury to overtake the Queen: he cast his eie on Silbury-hill about a mile off: which He had the curiosity to see, and walkt up to the top of it, with the Duke of Yorke, Dr Charlton and I attending them: They went to Lacock to dinner: and that evening to *Bathe*; all the Gentry and Commonaltie of those parts waiting on them, with great acclamations of Joy, &c. (Aubrey 24, 24–5; Fowles and Legg 1980, 21–2)[9]

The 'One morning' may be dated to about 12 August 1663, if it really was 'about a fortnight' before the King's departure for Bath, which occurred on 26 August that year (Pepys 1972–83, iv. 288; Evelyn 1955, iii. 361 and n. 3). It is interesting that Aubrey states that Brouncker as well as Charleton informed the King of 'what they had heard' to be Aubrey's view of the antiquity, since this probably refers to the discussion which had taken place at the Royal Society the previous month, which Brouncker, as President of the Royal Society, almost certainly attended (although his presence was not actually noted on 8 as against 15 July). According to Aubrey's account, Charleton was again presenting him as the real expert on the site. But it has to be remembered that our knowledge of what transpired at the meeting with the King derives entirely from Aubrey's later account, and he may have implied that Charleton deferred to him more than was in fact the case. Charleton was by then equipped to vouch for the importance of Avebury for himself, and it would surely have been odd if, having shown both the Royal Society and Borrichius his own plan of the site and mentioned to them his hypothesis concerning its nature, he had not also drawn the King's attention to his own views. The conflict in testimony concerning the site may have also been mentioned, though the royal mandate to further enquiry which ensued presumably received its stimulus not least from Charles' surprise at the lack of attention paid to the site hitherto (cf. below, p. 27).

It is possible that Aubrey, in writing his account of the episode many years later, may deliberately have understated Charleton's own acquaintance with the antiquity. But, if so, this should perhaps be attributed to retrospective simplification on Aubrey's part rather than to any sense of rivalry between the two men. It is true that Aubrey was to criticize Charleton's interpretation of Stonehenge as a 'gross mistake' (Aubrey 24, 92v; Fowles and Legg 1980, 85). But even this note is otherwise respectful, and such references in Aubrey's letters as survive suggest that Charleton and he were always on good terms (Williams 1969, esp. 77, 89, 103, 263, 330, 402, 533, 620; see also Aubrey 12, 66). Moreover, though Aubrey failed to reinstate the rather flattering reference to Charleton as 'That learned Gentleman, Walt[er] Charleton M.D. (whom I name for honor-sake)' which appears in deleted form in the draft on the back of plan A,[10] this was probably because the gist of the passage was encapsulated in the note just cited and in another place in his manuscript where Aubrey referred to Charleton's views on Stonehenge (Aubrey 25, 77v; Fowles and Legg 1982, 863).

As for the 'draught . . . donne by memorid only: but well enough resembling it', it is virtually certain that this is not plan C.[11] From Aubrey's description, it sounds as if the former may not have seemed worth preserving: but even if it had been given to the King and placed among his rarities, it would probably not have survived, as other scientific drawings presented to him have not.[12] Quite apart from the fact that the endorsement on plan C by Oldenburg makes it almost certain that it had been presented to the Royal Society on 8 July, careful inspection of the document reveals many details, such as the drawing of the Cove, which do not suggest a drawing done from memory (cf. Chapter III, C. 14). Though it is conceivable that plan B was the one presented to the King, a suggestion made in the 19th century (Long 1858b, 66), there is no evidence to substantiate this: the documentation that has come down to us from the 17th century must represent only a fraction of what once existed, and it is much likelier that the sketch done for the King was a different item which is now lost.

Then, we have the meeting at Marlborough and the subsequent visit to the site. After leaving London on 26 August, Charles had spent his first night at Maidenhead and his second at Sir Thomas Dolman's house at Shaw near Newbury; he reached Marlborough on the next day, 28, where he was entertained by the Seymours and stayed overnight at their house. It must therefore have been on Saturday, 29 August, that he visited Avebury, before going on to Sir John Talbot's at Lacock and thence to Bath. Details of the King's progress are given by the government newspaper, *The Intelligencer*, begun by Sir Roger L'Estrange just at this time.[13] Unfortunately, the only details of his sightseeing that this gives are of his visit to the Civil War battlefields at Newbury, but that Charles II had visited Avebury was confirmed by local tradition recorded both by Pepys in 1668 (who also noted that 'most people of learning coming by' visited the site) and by Stukeley in the early 18th century (Pepys 1972–83, ix. 240; Stukeley 1743, 23). The latter noted of the inn yard where the Cove stood: 'King *Charles* II. in his progress this way, rode into the yard, on purpose to view it'.

In 1663, Aubrey still retained estates in Wiltshire, and it was presumably from there that he rode over to meet the royal party at Marlborough. His narrative shows that Charleton was present when the King, the Duke of York and Aubrey visited Silbury; that he was also present at Avebury is suggested by a comment at another point in 'Templa Druidum' where Aubrey noted of a further antiquity to be seen 'on the Downes between Rockley and Marleborough': 'which Dr Charlton shewed his Majestie and R[oyal] Highnesse as we wayted on Them, from Aubury' (Aubrey 24, 90v; Fowles and Legg 1980, 96). The royal visit to Silbury is also confirmed by a local tradition recorded by Stukeley, which claimed that the Duke of Monmouth was also present and that the royal party *rode* up Silbury (Stukeley 1743, 43), while a sequel was recorded by Aubrey in another of his works in connection with the 'abundance of very small snailes' to be found there:

> When I had the honour to waite on King Charles I [sic] and the Duke of York to the top of Silbury hill, his Royal Highnesse happened to cast his eye on some of these small snailes on the turfe of the hill. He was surprised with the novelty, and commanded me to pick some up, which I did, about a dozen or more, immediately; for they are in great abundance. The next morning as he was abed with his Dutches at Bath he told her of it, and sent Dr. Charleton to me for them, to shew her as a rarity. (Aubrey 1847, 67)[14]

It is usually assumed that it was on this occasion that the event occurred that Aubrey refers to in a marginal note to his description of Avebury in 'Templa Druidum': 'His Majestie commanded me to digge at the bottom of the stones marked with the fig. 1 [in plan A], to try if I could find any humane bones: but I did not doe it' (Aubrey 24, 31v; Fowles and Legg 1980, 34). This reference to the Cove has recently been referred to as 'the best opportunity to recover information' about that feature, which, 'ironically, some three hundred years ago John Aubrey may have rejected' (Burl 1988, 8). It is striking, however, that Aubrey's note echoes what Charleton is recorded as having said about 'a certain Triangular Stone' at the Royal Society in July – albeit his interest was almost certainly in the horizontal, fourth cove stone, whereas Aubrey's 'at the bottom' possibly conveys that standing stones were in question. Though Charles may have been prompted by Charleton, who could have repeated his remark during their original discussion and/or on site, it is equally possible that Aubrey confused the two events, since this note was added to the version of Aubrey's account of the site that he recopied twenty-five years later: it is interesting that Aubrey also attributed to the King the comment that he made himself in his draft material for 'To the Reader' about how ''tis strange that our Chorographers tooke no more notice of it' (Aubrey 24, 39; Fowles and Legg 1980, 43).

Another person who appears to have been present during the royal visit to Avebury was Sir Robert Moray. Moray's reference to the discussion of Avebury at the meeting of the Royal Society in July has already been mentioned. This forms part of a paper (printed in full in Appendix I) which comprises observations that were clearly made during the royal progress to Bath in 1663: confirmation of this is provided by the fact that it contains various references to the King's activities and to comments that he made. Moray's paper has nothing to say about the places through which the royal party passed on the first three days of its journey. It begins with a lengthy account of the 'round Mount which may be reasonably supposed to have been an Auncient Tumulus' in the garden of Lord Seymour's house at Marlborough, in other words, the place where the royal party stayed for the night of 28 August: as we shall see, it may not be coincidental that it was a prehistoric antiquity which stimulated him to begin his notes.

27

Moray gave the measurements of the mound, though he devoted more space to describing it as a garden feature. He then went on to describe Silbury Hill, comparing its dimensions with those of the tumulus at Marlborough, and noting two things about it. One was the fact that 'It affordeth store of a sort of snail with a flat shell slender & having 3 or 4 entire turns', a useful corroboration of Aubrey's account of the interest in these shown by the royal party. Secondly, Moray commented on the ditch surrounding Silbury – 'some 90 or 100 foot broad (at a guess) but not above 5 or 6 deeper than the rest of [the] meadow at any place' – speculating that it might have been the source of the earth from which the Hill was constructed, though postulating that, since the ditch was far smaller in volume than the tumulus, the earth must have grown since the monument was erected.

He then proceeded to give an account of what are evidently the Sanctuary, the row or avenue of standing stones descending Overton Hill from the Sanctuary, and then the beginning of the Kennet Avenue: this seems to be how best to construe his description of the stones as going beyond the open downland into enclosed pasture and thence ('opposite'?) to the road. In his paper, Moray gave quite painstaking details about the number of stones that the antiquities comprised and the way in which they were disposed, including measurements. It is interesting that, like Aubrey (Aubrey 24, 34, 63v; Fowles and Legg 1980, 37, 56), he described the avenue as resembling a walk of trees and that, like Stukeley sixty years later, he ran into descriptive difficulties where stones and hedges met. Thus, while the passage in which Moray refers to the avenue as 'being cut off by a hedge' is a little hard to follow, it must refer to the area in which Stukeley was to write of the avenue that it 'marches through two more pastures, all along the quickset hedge-side: so that the quick is planted in the very middle of it' (Stukeley 1743, 31).

In addition, Moray described a tumulus south-east of the Sanctuary, observing how the ditch created when the earth was taken for the erection of the tumulus had now 'grown almost level with the rest of the ground about it', and noting that both this phenomenon and the tumulus itself had been described by Aubrey, who had also 'taken notice of & described' the Sanctuary. In addition, he noted that observations of the Sanctuary had been made by Sir Paul Neile, F.R.S.: if written, these do not appear to have survived.

The remainder of Moray's paper deals with phenomena that he noted at Bath and on the royal entourage's route home through Oxfordshire.[15] Since it forms a single continuous narrative, it was presumably written up after the court's stay at Oxford from 23 to 30 September 1663, probably after the court returned to London on 4 October: the penultimate paragraph refers to matters (concerning tame pigeons and blackbirds) mentioned by Moray at meetings of the Royal Society on 7 and 21 October 1663 (Birch 1756–7, i. 311, 313–14, 320). What is particularly interesting about this document from our point of view, however, is the detail in which it attempted to describe prehistoric antiquities. Although Moray eschewed a description of Avebury itself because of Aubrey's impending description of the site, his lengthy account of associated antiquities may well reflect an interest in monuments of this kind aroused by the discussion at the Royal Society earlier that summer.

Moreover, this interest was not limited to Moray, as is shown by his reference to the similar activity of Sir Paul Neile. Like Moray, Neile was both an active Fellow of the Royal Society and also a courtier, Gentleman Usher to the Privy Council (his seat was at White Waltham in Berkshire, and it would have been easy for him to reach Avebury from there). Both Neile and Moray seem to have belonged to an informal group of court scientists whose deliberations at Whitehall in the presence of the King or the Duke of York are recorded on at least one occasion (Evelyn 1955, iii. 285–6; cf. Bennett 1982, chs. 3–4; Ronan and Hartley 1960). It looks as though, in the summer of 1663, stimulated by Charleton's presentation at the Royal Society, a curiosity about prehistoric antiquities became more widely shared among Fellows of the Royal Society with courtly links. Evidence that such interest continued longer is possibly provided by Pepys' inspection of Avebury in 1668, since Anthony Powell may well be correct in suggesting that it was through his court connections that Pepys was alerted to the significance of the site (Pepys 1972–83, ix. 240; Powell 1963, 109).

Though isolated, the Avebury episode seems to exemplify that link between the new science and the study of archaeological antiquities that is later seen in articles in *Philosophical Transactions* and in the writings of Robert Plot and other natural historians (Hunter 1971; 1975, ch. 3). The earlier episode certainly shares common features with the later. Moray's attempt to give exact measurements, and his clear indication when he was relying on guesswork, shows an attitude similar to that underlying Charleton's and Aubrey's plans and, later, illustrations in *Philosophical Transactions* which can be claimed to include the earliest accurate archaeological plan to be published in this country (Hunter 1971, 116). Equally interesting is the recurrent injunction to excavate, found in Charleton, in the King's instruction to Aubrey as recorded by Aubrey, and yet again in Moray, though in his case it appears in connection, not with Avebury, but with the source of the heated waters at Bath (see Appendix I). Of course, digging had been done before at prehistoric sites, particularly at barrows and comparable sites where treasure might be expected, while, earlier in the century, excavations in 'the middle of Stonehenge' and of 'a Barrowe' nearby had been stimulated by the interest of the Duke of Buckingham and the Earl of Pembroke in that antiquity (this formed part of the episode from which Jones' *Stoneheng Restored* stemmed) (Aubrey 24, 59, 89–90; Fowles and Legg 1980, 76, 92–5). But it is notable that Stukeley, another antiquarian of the Royal Society tradition, was to conduct 'perhaps the first objective barrow-diggings on record' in the early 18th century (Marsden 1974, 4–5), while the 'excavation report' may itself have been another 'scientific' invention of the same period (Hunter 1971, 116).

No less revealing is Moray's interest in discovering the source of materials from which monuments were constructed and the process by which ditches became silted, comparable to the interest in materials and in stratigraphy that was to be characteristic of the archaeological work subsequently done under the Royal Society's auspices (Hunter 1971, 114–15, 119n). On at least one point Moray seems to have influenced Aubrey, who noted of a ditch which he said surrounded the Sanctuary (though he was probably confused as to its location),[16] that it was Moray's belief 'That one might be convinc't, and satisfied by it, that the Earth did growe' (Aubrey 24, 43; Fowles and Legg 1980, 50). This curious notion evidently derived from neoPlatonic ideas about the ability of the earth spontaneously to regenerate itself, which may reflect Moray's familiarity with the writings of the Jesuit natural philosopher, Athanasius Kircher (Rossi 1984, ch. 2; Hoppen 1976, 247–8).

29

v. Aubrey and 'Templa Druidum'

The practical interest in such antiquities stimulated among the scientists at court in the summer of 1663 proved short-lived, however, despite Pepys' visit to Avebury as a tourist five years later. No further evidence of activity of this kind is to be found in any of those involved in this episode, with the one outstanding exception of Aubrey, who was to write up his 'Templa Druidum' in the years immediately following, thereafter revising and adding to it for the rest of his life. It is therefore worth returning to his narrative in 'To the Reader' to comment on his activities in connection with Avebury in the aftermath of the royal visit. After the passage already quoted (at the beginning of section iv), Aubrey went on:

> In September following, I surveyd that old Monument of *Aubury* with a plain-table, and afterwards tooke a Review of Stonehenge: and then I composed this following Discourse in obedience to his Majesties command: and presented it to Him: which he commanded me to put in print. (Aubrey 24, 25; Fowles and Legg 1980, 22)

'In September following' is altered in the surviving draft – itself dating, as we have seen, from the 1690s – from 'Afterwards in obedience to his Majesties command'. The exact date is therefore a recollection of thirty years later, but there is no reason why this should not refer to September 1663, in other words within weeks of the royal visit (in September 1664 Aubrey was in France: Powell 1963, 111–12); moreover this would square with Moray's report of Aubrey's work in progress.

As already noted, it has always been presumed that the surviving results of Aubrey's plane-table survey comprise plan A (Plate 7 and also in folder). Certainly it is true that, in contrast to Aubrey's earlier pencil plan, in which the vallum and rampart had been shown as a regular circle drawn with compasses, he now tried to do justice to the actual irregularity of the ditch and bank surrounding the site, and the verisimilitude of the depiction of these in plan A must have been achieved by the use of surveying techniques (see Chapter III, A.15). In addition, the roads at the centre of the earthwork were now shown staggered, in contrast to the exact cross shown in the earlier plan, while a different field pattern is shown, which bears more relation to what is known of the actual state of the site at the time (see Chapter III, A.8; Chapter IV, d and f). Plan A also differs from the earlier one in that, as Aubrey explains in his text, perhaps referring to plan C or some other plan with houses and other contemporary features marked on it:

> By reason of the crosse-streetes, Houses, Gardens, orchards, and severall small Closes; and the Fractures made in this Antiquity for the building of those Houses; it was no very easy Taske for me to trace out the Vestigia, and so make this Survey. Wherefore I have dis-empestred the Scheme from the Enclosures, and Houses &c.: which are altogether foreigne to this Antiquity, and would but have clowded and darkned the reall Designe. (Aubrey 24, 36; Fowles and Legg 1980, 39)[17]

More significant, he now abandoned the concentricity of plan C, instead showing two separate circles in the north-west and south-east quadrants of the site, the former containing the Cove, though the latter does not clearly differentiate any stone which

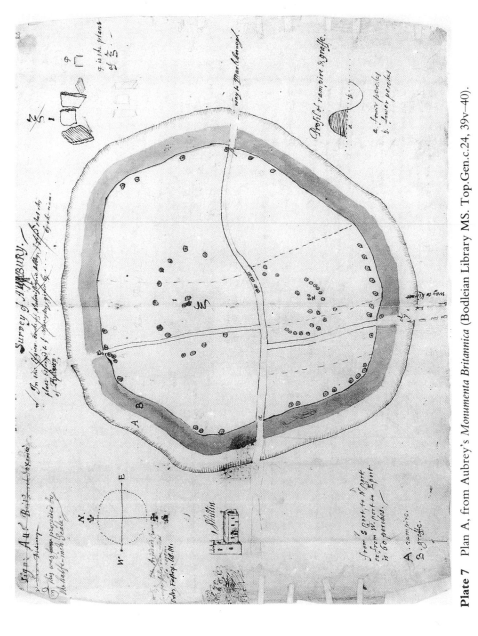

Plate 7 Plan A, from Aubrey's *Monumenta Britannica* (Bodleian Library MS. Top.Gen.c.24, 39v–40).

could be immediately identified as the Obelisk (see Chapter IV, w). Possibly, this recognition of discrete internal circles reflects the influence of Charleton's plan D which Aubrey had seen at the Royal Society earlier that summer. In the margin various details are shown, including a 'Profil' of the bank and ditch and a drawing of the Cove, apparently of three stones only.

The 'Review' of Stonehenge to which Aubrey refers in the passage quoted above also formed part of his 'Templa Druidum', and the date of his work on the better-known antiquity is suggested by the fact that the surviving text includes a manuscript plan endorsed 'The Ichnographie of Stoneheng as it remaines this present yeare 1666' (Aubrey 24, 64v; Fowles and Legg 1980, 80; Plate 18): this was a drawing that Aubrey included to correct Inigo Jones' depiction by indicating which stones were actually standing and by showing the true disposition of the innermost circle of megaliths. This plan has been described – perhaps rather unfairly – as 'a scrappy thing' (Chippindale 1983, 69), and, in contrast to plan A, it is not based on a proper survey, failing to show the ditch accurately. But Aubrey's note of the so-called Aubrey holes and his suspicion that these marked the site of a circle of stones that had formerly stood inside the ditch is clearly based on collation with the monument at Avebury, thus confirming that the Stonehenge review followed his work at Avebury.

More important, the captions to the Stonehenge plan are in similar handwriting to those on Plan A; their layout (particularly the position of the details 'a', 'b' and 'q') is also directly comparable, though the ink in which plan A itself is drawn is lighter than that of the 'Ichnographie' of Stonehenge. In addition, though this 'Ichnographie' is drawn on a standard-sized sheet of paper, it is accompanied by two larger sheets with their edges folded in, presumably derived from an earlier manuscript of larger format. The sheet on which plan A is drawn is similarly folded, while the Stonehenge drawings have jottings on the back which are comparable to those on the reverse of this plan (Aubrey 24, 60–2; Fowles and Legg 1980, 77–84). Such similarities tend to suggest that the surviving plan A also dates from within a few years of Aubrey's survey of Avebury in September 1663.

The same is also true of the third of Aubrey's plans of Avebury, plan B (Plate 8 and also in folder). This, also, is in handwriting similar to that of plan A and the Stonehenge plan, while it too is on a larger sheet that has been folded to fit the format of the current manuscript. Its distinctive intention was to show the mutual relationship between the henge at Avebury, the Kennet Avenue, Silbury Hill and the Sanctuary (of which Aubrey also included a more detailed drawing elsewhere in his manuscript: Aubrey 24, 43av; Fowles and Legg 1980, 51; Plate 27).[18] As we shall see, this may explain why the plan is schematic in certain respects, though, considering its small scale, it is surprisingly accurate. Even more than plan A, plan B was clearly intended to illustrate the text of 'Templa Druidum', as is suggested by its caption – 'The whole view of Aubury with the Walke and the lesser Temple appendant to it' (Aubrey 24, 41v; Fowles and Legg 1980, 48) – and it seems likely that it was prepared in connection with the original writing up of 'Templa Druidum', which evidently occurred in the mid-1660s. From what Aubrey says in 'To the Reader', it seems clear that it was after August 1663 that he began to compose his 'Discourse'; then, his concluding peroration to 'Templa Druidum' is dated '1665', and, though the surviving text of this is a later copy, it is most likely that 1663–5 is the date at which

Plate 8 Plan B, from Aubrey's *Monumenta Britannica*. (Bodleian Library MS. Top.Gen.c.24, 41v–2)

the treatise was first compiled and hence the plans initially executed (Aubrey 24, 80; Fowles and Legg 1980, 129).

It was presumably in the same decade that Aubrey presented his 'Discourse' to the King and was urged to publish it, though no independent confirmation of this survives and neither does the copy so presented (there is, incidentally, no evidence that he presented any version or portion of it to the Royal Society, despite the reminder note already mentioned). Certainly, by the early 1670s, Aubrey regarded 'Templa Druidum' as ready for publication (Hunter 1975, 76–7). But he continued to make piecemeal additions and revisions, and the result was that by the 1680s the manuscripts both of 'Templa Druidum' and of the related treatises to which he had by this time given the collective name *Monumenta Britannica* were in need of complete recopying, a task which Aubrey carried out in 1688–9: Aubrey records how 'The first draught was worn-out with time & handling' (Aubrey 24, 26; Fowles and Legg 1980, 26; Hunter 1975, 87. See also Aubrey 24, 140; Fowles and Legg 1980, 241). Most of the text we have today apparently dates from that point, while some sections – notably 'To the Reader' – were rewritten later still, in the 1690s, when Aubrey continued to make additions to the work. Indeed, although Aubrey entertained hopes in his last years that the work would be printed, even entrusting the manuscript to a putative publisher, the London bookseller Awnsham Churchill,[19] it remained somewhat chaotic. It is thus understandable that when Edmund Gibson saw the work in 1694, he exclaimed:

> There is not in Mr Aubrey's booke what I expected: the accounts of things are soe broken and short, the parts soe much disorder'd, and the whole such a mere Rhapsody, that I cannot but wonder how that poor man could entertain any thoughts of a present Impression. (Bodleian Tanner MS 25, 134; partly quoted in Hunter 1975, 213)

One reason for the disorganized appearance of the manuscript as it survives today is that, in recopying, Aubrey preserved individual pages from his earlier recension, usually because they had on them drawings which he seems to have considered it better to leave in their original state. The idea was evidently that, when engraved as book illustrations, as few stages as possible should separate the original composition from the final product, and the chance of fresh error being introduced would thus be minimized. Specimens of such survivals include Aubrey's plans of the Sanctuary and of the Wedding at Stanton Drew, both of which have on their verso fragments of the original, 1660s recension of Aubrey's text, while, as we have seen, plans A and B also fall into this category (Aubrey 24, 43a, 54; Fowles and Legg 1980, 46, 51, 69, 71). That plan B is taken from an earlier recension is confirmed by the way in which parts have been cut out and replaced. As for plan A, this certainly predates the retranscription of 1688–9, since it has on it various dated notes from earlier in the 1680s, at least one of which – concerning the fall of the great stone at Avebury 'Townesend' in 1684 – was copied into the main text in his retranscription (Aubrey 24, 34; Fowles and Legg 1980, 37).[20] These notes also reflect Aubrey's increasing curiosity about the etymology of the name of Avebury and the possibility that its correct spelling was 'Aubury', which would have meant that he and the antiquity were almost synonymous, a further theme which he incorporated into the main text in its final version (Aubrey 24, 37–8, 40v, 44; Fowles and Legg 1980, 41–2, 47, 57).

The remainder of the notes on the back of plan A are undated, but some – notably the bulk of the material on f.39 – may well be earlier still, not least since, as we have seen, these seem to comprise a preliminary version of material that Aubrey was to use in the introductory sections to his work written in the 1660s. Their handwriting is hard to date precisely: but there is no reason why it should not derive from the 1660s. In sum, a date in the 1660s but presumably after September 1663 seems likeliest for the original composition of plan A, while plan B probably also dates from this period when 'Templa Druidum' was being written up, though it could be either slightly earlier or slightly later than plan A. Further corroboration for this general dating is provided by the fact that it was in the 1650s and 1660s that Aubrey did the bulk of his fieldwork in Wiltshire. Thereafter, the loss of his estates meant that he paid only occasional visits to his county of birth, his activities being more in the nature of revising and consolidating into treatises notes that had principally been made at an earlier date: as he put it concerning the *Natural History of Wiltshire* which he wrote up in 1685, 'I have tumultuarily stitch't up what I have many yeares since collected' (Aubrey 1847, 6).

The very longevity of Aubrey's concern with Avebury and comparable antiquities – in comparison with the brief burst of activity among Charleton and other Fellows of the Royal Society in 1663 – creates a number of problems of interpretation and dating as far as his record is concerned. For one thing, even if the plans in his manuscript which we deal with here were not recopied, he may have added some features to them, as may have been the case in plan A, apart from the deletions in plan B. In addition, the fact that the plans were originally compiled to accompany a text which no longer survives – while the text that we have contains a number of blanks or incomplete cross-references – helps to explain why there are certain discrepancies between what is shown on the plans and the text which they supposedly illustrate. This especially affects plan B, as will be further discussed in Chapters III and IV below. But, despite these complications, it seems likely that all Aubrey's plans of Avebury and its area – like Charleton's – date from the middle decades of the century rather than from later, with plan C dating from c.1650–63, and – despite additions and deletions possibly of later date – plans A and B from between 1663 and c.1666. This means that almost all the 17th-century records of Avebury appear to derive from a relatively short period – of about a decade, or a decade and a half – and the implications of this will be further explored in later chapters.

vi. Enter William Stukeley

Aubrey died in June 1697. Though by this time it was fairly clear that nothing would come of his hopes for publishing his *Monumenta Britannica*, the manuscript of the work was still in the hands of Awnsham Churchill at the time of his death; it remained in the possession of Churchill's descendants and was seen by few until it was purchased by the Bodleian Library in 1836 (Powell 1963, 288; see Chapter III, A.12(d)).[21] Though his book as a whole remained unpublished, however, Aubrey's ideas about Avebury and about the Druidic origins of stone circles *were* at last divulged in print shortly before his death through various brief references to his unpublished work in the new edition of Camden's *Britannia* prepared under the editorship of Edmund Gibson, later Bishop of London, and published in 1695.

For one thing, Aubrey's friend, Edward Lhwyd, made it clear in the sections that *he* wrote that Aubrey 'for what I can learn, was the first that suspected these Circles for *Temples of the Druids*' (Camden 1695, 637; Hunter 1975, 205). Equally important is the reference to Avebury itself, which appeared among the editorial 'Additions' to Camden's original account of the county of Wiltshire. The manuscript of Aubrey's *Monumenta Britannica* was first cited in connection with Stonehenge, where Aubrey's criticism of Inigo Jones' view of its Roman origins was paraphrased (Camden 1695, 108–9). Then, after a note on Silbury and a digression on the numerous barrows in the vicinity, we have the following passage, in which '*Aubury*' and '*West-Kennet*' are accompanied by marginal references to Aubrey's unpublished work:

> About half a mile from *Silbury*, is *Aubury*, a monument more considerable in it self, than known to the world. For a village of the same name being built within the circumference of it, and (by the by) out of it's stones too; what by gardens, orchards, inclosures, and such like, the prospect is so interrupted, that 'tis very hard to discover the form of it. It is environ'd with an extraordinary *Vallum* or Rampart, as great and as high as that at Winchester; and within it is a graff of a depth and breadth proportionable: from which Mr *Aubrey* inferrs, that it could not be design'd for a fortification, because then the Graff would have been on the outside. From the north to the south port are 60 paces, and as many from the west port to the east. The breadth of the Rampart is 4 perches, and that of the graff the same. The graff has been surrounded all along the edge of it, with large stones pitch'd on end, most of which are now taken away; but some marks remaining give one the liberty to guess they stood quite round.
>
> From this place to *West-Kennet*, is a walk that has been enclos'd on each side with large stones, only one side at present wants a great many, but the other is almost, if not quite entire; above which place, on the brow of the hill, is another Monument, encompass'd with a circular trench, and a double circle of stones, four or five foot high, tho' most of them are now fallen down; the diameter of the outer circle 40 yards, and of the inner 15. Between *West-Kennet* and this place is a walk much like that from *Aubury* thither, at least a quarter of a mile in length. (Camden 1695, 111–12)

The text then went on to refer to various other antiquities in the neighbourhood, including 'three huge upright stones, call'd *the Devil's coits*' in 'the plough'd field near *Kennet*', and Milbarrow (which was thought, by analogy with antiquities described by Olaus Worm, to be 'the Sepulcher of some Danish Commander').

The section was probably written by Thomas Tanner, a young antiquary whose assistance with the Wiltshire section of the book was acknowledged in 'The Preface to the Reader'; it is possible, however, that Gibson himself had something to do with it, since, through Tanner, he had seen the manuscript of *Monumenta Britannica*, stimulating the critical comments on it already cited (Camden 1695, sig. a1; Piggott 1976, 46–7; 1989, 113–4). Whoever it was, almost all the information they included could have come from Aubrey's text, some passages of which (e.g. 'one may boldly ghesse, that... they stood quite round about') are quite closely paraphrased. However, as will be seen (Chapter IV, m), the description of the Kennet/Overton Avenue rather misconstrued Aubrey's actual account of it – unless it is based on a separate visit – while the description of the henge at Avebury itself is disappointingly cursory, mentioning as it does only the earthwork and outer circle and ignoring the

*Quamvis obstat mihi Tarda vetustas
Multaq me fugiant Primis spectata sub auuis
Plura tamen memini·* ——— *Ov. met. XII.*

Plate 9 Portrait of Stukeley dated 7 December
1722 which forms the frontispiece to his 'Celtic
Temples' (Stukeley 1722–4b, viii).

inner circles and other features (it is perhaps also worth noting that '60 paces' appears
to be a misreading of Aubrey's '60 perches').

As a result, it was hardly to be expected that this brief passage would do much to
raise awareness of the site, and for this we have to await the activities of the antiquary
whose name is perhaps most closely associated with Avebury, William Stukeley
(Plate 9), the author of the first full study of the antiquity to appear in print, his
Abury of 1743. Stukeley's was not in fact the first publication devoted to the
antiquity, an honour which instead went to a briefer work by Thomas Twining,
Vicar of Charlton, south-east of Devizes, whose pamphlet entitled *Avebury in
Wiltshire, the Remains of a Roman Work* came out in 1723. As his title shows,
Twining believed Avebury to be of Roman date, claiming it to be a temple to the
god Terminus. On the other hand, he said little about the antiquity itself apart from
bewailing the destruction which it had suffered. The bulk of his text was devoted to
an attempt to correlate Avebury and Silbury with what was known of the military
manoeuvres of Vespasian and Agricola in the south of England, together with other
antiquarian speculations which arose 'by the Way' (Twining 1723, 3, 30 and passim).

Twining's work was illustrated by a rather schematic plan (Plate 10) which
depicted the henge itself as consisting of two concentric circles, noting of the
earthwork which surrounded it: 'The Vallum having a Ditch within it Contrary to
the Military Order'. In addition, it showed a wedge-shaped pattern of avenues

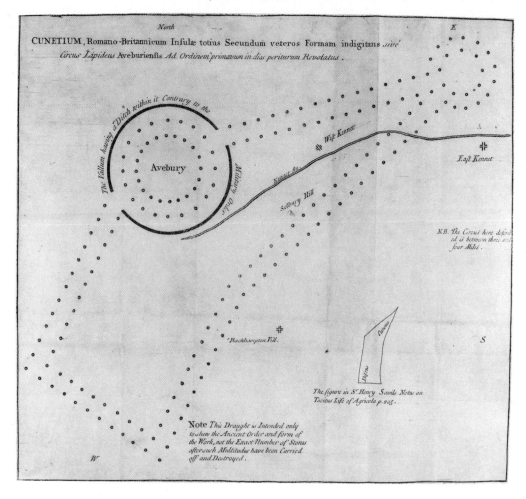

CUNETIUM, Romano-Britannicum Insulæ totius Secundum veteros Formam indigitans *sive* *Circus Lapideus* Aveburienfis *Ad Ordinem primævum in dies periturum Revolatus.*

Plate 10 Thomas Twining's plan of Avebury and its environs: the frontispiece to his *Avebury in Wiltshire, the Remains of a Roman Work* (1723).

surrounding the henge which it was claimed were used for 'Sports and Solemnities' and comprised a representation of the island of Britain as conceived by the Romans (Twining 1723, 6 and passim); these converged on Overton Hill to the east and described a rectangular shape to the west. But Twining disavowed accuracy of depiction, adding the 'Note': 'This Draught is Intended only to shew the Ancient Order and form of the Work, not the Exact Number of Stones after such Multitudes have been Carried off and Destroyed'.

Twining's book may have been stimulated by the extensive fieldwork that Stukeley was by this time engaged in and by rumours of his intention to argue for the antiquity's prehistoric origins: it may be significant that it was dedicated to Stukeley's friend, the Earl of Winchelsea (see Piggott 1985, 56–7). The work was discussed in letters between Stukeley and his friend Roger Gale in the year that it was published, and they dismissed it from the outset as 'a ridiculous performance', in Gale's words, whose argument Stukeley considered 'deserves no answer' (Stukeley

1887, 243–4, 245–6, 252). Certainly he gave it none, and little notice appears to have been taken of Twining's book – though the antiquary Thomas Hearne, for one, shared Twining's view of Avebury's Roman date (Hearne 1915, 187) – until it attracted some critical attention in the 19th century (Long 1858a, 319–22; Lukis 1881–3a, 154).

Stukeley's antiquarian activities and his association with Avebury have been dealt with at length by Stuart Piggott in his widely acclaimed study, *William Stukeley: an Eighteenth-century Antiquary*, first published in 1950 and reissued in revised form in 1985 (Piggott 1985). But, in view of the significance of Stukeley's record in supplementing those of the 17th-century writers, an account of his association with the site must be given here, based on a fresh scrutiny of the extant documentation. In particular, we will devote attention to Stukeley's relationship with the earlier records of the site already dealt with, especially those of Aubrey, a topic necessarily dealt with only relatively briefly in Piggott's book.

Stukeley's interest in megalithic antiquities seems first to have been awakened during the years 1710–17, described by Piggott as 'probably the most obscure in the whole of his extraordinarily well-documented life' (Piggott 1985, 34). In 1710, while on a tour of the West Midlands, Stukeley saw the Rollright Stones, noting: 'I cannot but suppose 'em to have been an heathen temple of our Ancestors, perhaps in the Druids' time' (Piggott 1985, 38; Stukeley 1724, 45). In 1714 his friend Maurice Johnson sent Stukeley reading recommendations on antiquarian subjects, including the Druids, evidently in response to a request by him; among the works he cited was Camden. Then, in June 1716, Stukeley told Johnson how a 17th-century engraving of Stonehenge by David Loggan had stimulated him:

> to make an exact Model of that most noble and stupendous piece of Antiquity, which I have accomplish'd, and from thence drawn the groundplot of its present ruins, and the view of it in its pristine State, and propose from thence to find out the original Architectonic Scheme by which it was erected, together with its design, use, Founders etc and thereby do justice to so wonderful a Curiosity which Mr Camden passes over so slightly (as usual in things ancienter than the Romans) with such a wretched anile account, as tis hard to say whether that or his draught of it be most false and trifling. (Piggott 1985, 35, 40)

The background to these comments can be illustrated from a piece of evidence which has come to light since Piggott published his account of Stukeley: a copy of the 1695 edition of Camden's *Britannia* which is now in the Bodleian Library, which has the ownership inscription 'W: Stukeley M: B: Boston 1714 Novr 3' (cf. Stukeley 1884, 87), together with a portrait sketch 'for Dr Stukeley & very like him', on the verso of the blank flyleaf preceding the frontispiece. In addition, the text bears various annotations by Stukeley, and, though none of these relates to Avebury, other passages in which Aubrey's theories about the Druidic origins of stone circles are mentioned have been underlined and otherwise marked. More significant are Stukeley's comments on the engraving of Stonehenge in the book. Apart from noting beside it in the margin how 'Camdens real picture is 20 times more unlike than this if possible', he wrote underneath:

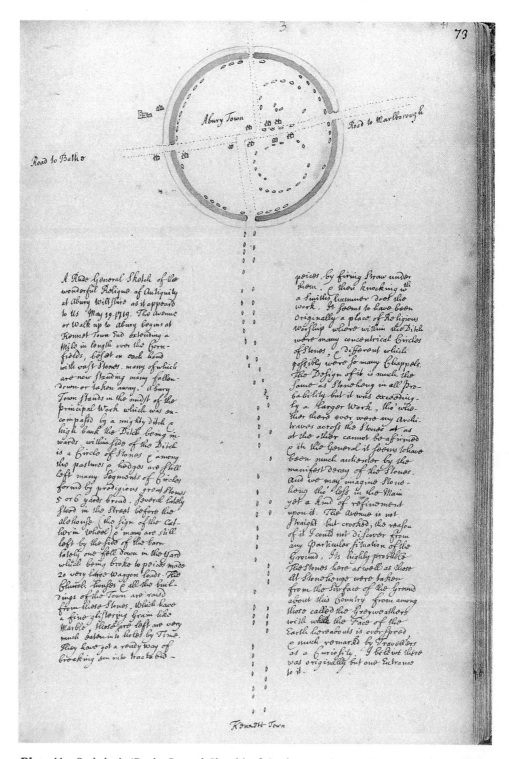

Plate 11 Stukeley's 'Rude General Sketch' of Avebury and its environs, together with his notes, made on his first visit to the site on 19 May 1719 (WANHS, Devizes, Stukeley MS., 41).

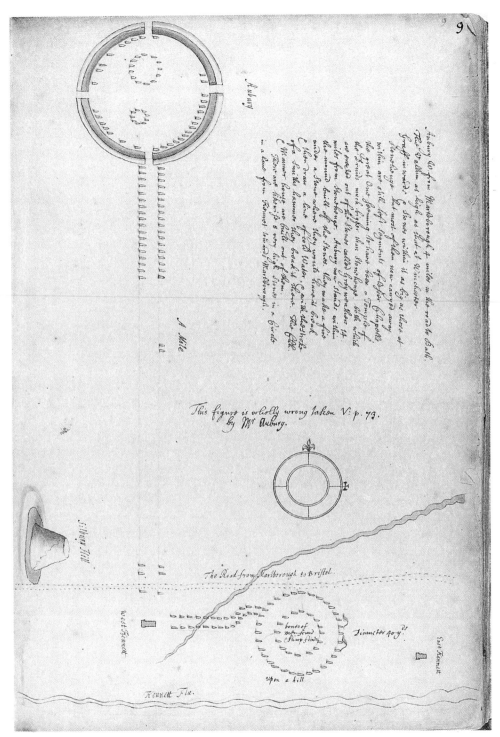

Plate 12 Stukeley's adapted copy of Aubrey's Plan B in his Devizes notebook (WANHS Stukeley ms., 9).

No doubt but this & Rowlright all thos other circular Monuments were the Temples of the Antient Bryttons, for its observable the Persians descended from the same Ancestors made no coverd temples, worshipt upon hills & towers. (Bodleian MS Don.b.33, 95–6, 618, 682)

The background to these embryonic speculations about stone circles on Stukeley's part will be further elucidated in the next chapter.

Also interesting is the fact that at a meeting of the Royal Society on 19 November 1719, Stukeley:

> showed the Society several Curious Draughts and prospects of Stonheng on Salisbury plain which he thinks Inigo Jones, in his Account thereof has in several particulars mistaken: Particularly in his Making the Ambit of the Innermost and largest Stones to have been Hexagonal whereas by a Carefull Examination he finds it to be heptagonal five of the sides being standing, and two Open on the Side of the Entrance which he takes to have been always so, from the first Erecting thereof. (Royal Society Copy Journal Book, xi. 400)

This bears out the reports earlier that year by Stukeley's friend Roger Gale that Stukeley was at work on a new study of Stonehenge, correcting that of Jones, which Gale said would be combined with 'a learned dissertation upon those sorts of Circular Antiquitys' (Piggott 1985, 51–2).

Clearly these reports reflect the fact that on 18 and 19 May 1719 Stukeley had visited Stonehenge for the first time in the company of Roger Gale and his brother, Samuel, making a plan of the antiquity which still survives (Gough Maps 33, 2v): his 'exact Model' in 1716 had, as he later noted, been made 'before ever I had seen Stonehenge, only from Loggans two prints' (Stukeley 1772–4c, 32), though he undoubtedly also drew on Jones' *Stoneheng Restored*, which is certainly the source of a surviving plan of Stonehenge made by Stukeley 'when I lived at Boston' [i.e. 1710–17] (Eng.Misc.c.306, 87; cf. Gough Maps 229, 113 (half only); for Loggan's prints see Chippindale 1983, 64). What is more, it was not only Stonehenge that he saw for the first time on this trip in May 1719, but also Avebury: Stukeley dated his first 'Rude General Sketch' of that 'wonderful Relique of Antiquity' 19 May 1719, and this survives today in his folio commonplace book now at Devizes (Piggott 1985, 48, 165) (Plate 11). It gives a rough impression of the antiquity, including its rampart and ditch with four entrances, the main stone circle around the circumference, two subsidiary circles within – with what is evidently the Cove within the northern one – and a long stretch of the Kennet Avenue running almost straight and due south to 'Kennett Town'.

vii. Stukeley and Aubrey

As Piggott has made clear, by the time Stukeley made his first visit to Avebury on this occasion he had already learnt of Aubrey's unpublished account of the site in his *Monumenta Britannica* through the notes on that work made by Thomas Gale, the learned father of Stukeley's friends Roger and Samuel Gale. Piggott has further argued that 'There is little doubt, I feel, that Stukeley's attention was directed to Avebury by Gale's transcript', which 'must have filled him with the "eager desire" he records to examine the site personally' (Piggott 1985, 46). Interestingly, even Stukeley's plan of Avebury, referred to above, looks as though it owes much to the Aubrey-derived plan which Stukeley had copied into the same commonplace book a few months before and which will be discussed shortly, while the account of the site which accompanies it seems unconsciously to paraphrase Aubrey's account of the antiquity, for instance his description of the 'Segments of Circles' within the main circle, which he compared to 'Chappels'.

If Stukeley's initial discovery of Avebury was stimulated by the writings of Aubrey, this makes the exact nature of his knowledge of the earlier scholar's work crucial. Yet, frustratingly, we cannot now be certain quite how extensive this was. What we do know is that in December 1718 Stukeley transcribed into the commonplace book now at Devizes all or part of the notes from *Monumenta Britannica* that the elder Gale had made.[22] Gale, successively Professor of Greek at Cambridge and High Master of St Paul's School, developed a friendship with Aubrey in his later years, allowing him to use his house as a forwarding address and reading and annotating a number of Aubrey's works, including the *Monumenta Britannica* (Williams 1969, 546 and passim; Hunter 1975, 88). Though the exact date when Gale saw this work is unclear, the fact that he annotated the existing manuscript – as Aubrey proudly noted on its title-page – suggests that it was after Aubrey had retranscribed the work in 1688–9 (Aubrey 24, 20; Fowles and Legg 1980, 3); while, since Aubrey reports that Gale supported the idea of publishing the work in 1692, it seems likely to have been before that (Williams 1969, 529). It was presumably at the same stage that Gale made his own notes from the manuscript, but, since these unfortunately no longer survive, their exact date is unclear (one entry in Stukeley's notes is endorsed 'T. Gale 1697', but this is probably to be taken as an addition rather than as evidence concerning the date of his notes as a whole (Piggott 1985, 45)).

The exact content of Gale's notes is also unknown. On f. 37 of his commonplace book, Stukeley noted: 'Thus far Mr Gales' Notes out of Mr Aubrey's Collections'. But though Piggott observes of the section preceding this that – apart from the notes against which the words 'T. Gale' is written – 'It seems, pending an exhaustive collation, substantially the text of the *Monumenta* as it survives in Aubrey's holograph' (Piggott 1985, 45; cf. 1989, 33, 125), it should be stressed that it amounts only to some thirty sheets, as against Aubrey's hundreds of pages. Further, only two or three of these sheets refer in any way to Avebury or its vicinity: in particular, none of Aubrey's discursive history or description of the site is transcribed, either here or anywhere else in Stukeley's extensive surviving manuscripts. Not only is the Devizes transcript thus highly selective but, curiously, Aubrey's material is often placed in an order quite different from that found in the *Monumenta Britannica* itself. In view of the disappearance of Gale's original, it is unclear whether it was Gale's transcript or Stukeley's notes from it which selected and rearranged the material in this way. There are occasional items which do not seem to appear in Aubrey's original, presumably because Gale or Stukeley added them. Although an alternative possibility would be that Gale made a transcript from Aubrey's 'first draught' rather than the new version he prepared in 1688–9, thus recording information which has not otherwise survived, this would involve the hypothesis that Gale made notes from one copy and annotated a different one, which seems far less likely.

In 1722–3 Stukeley reused a good deal of this material in the work that he drafted at that point entitled 'The History of the Temples of the Antient Celts' (hereinafter 'Celtic Temples'), which is now Bodleian Library MS Eng.Misc.c.323. In the section of this work which gives a topographical survey of such antiquities, he quotes profusely from Aubrey, and it should be made clear that, contrary to the statement that Stukeley used Aubrey's data here with 'no acknowledgement' (Piggott 1986, 116), in fact Stukeley's references to the work of his predecessor in contexts other than Avebury are often full and generous. Sometimes his notes merely indicate their copied status: for instance, 'Mr Aubury informs us of another not far off near Kirk Oswald being a very large circle of great stones as much in diameter as Abury'; or 'The same Mr Aubury speaks of Longstone at Brome near Swindon Wilts' (Stukeley 1722–4b, 35, 55, cf. 49, 67).[23] But on other occasions he defers to the judgment of the earlier antiquary, as in his comment on the Devil's Coits at Stanton Harcourt, 'Mr Aubury thinks them the remains of such works', or in his notes on Kits Coty: 'This conjecture of mine I find much confirmd, by Mr Aubury's account of it who probably saw it in a more perfect state' (Stukeley 1722–4b, 35, 39). Stukeley also included in this section James Garden of Aberdeen's letter to Aubrey of 15 June 1692 about megaliths, which Aubrey had included in the *Monumenta Britannica* (Stukeley 1722–4b, 59f.; cf. Aubrey 24, 117f.; Fowles and Legg 1980, 176f.), while he also used information derived from Aubrey in his accompanying manuscript on Stonehenge, now in Cardiff Central Library (Stukeley 1722–4c, 9, 11).

Stukeley's illustrations, too, were sometimes derived from Aubrey via Gale. We have already suggested that his May 1719 plan may be one instance of this; another is the view of the H-shaped 'monument in the parish of Kynet' copied from Stukeley's original Devizes notes on the *Monumenta Britannica* into an inset scroll labelled 'at Kennet' on a page of illustrations headed 'Temples' (Aubrey 25, 63v; Fowles and Legg 1982, 823; reproduced in Burl 1979, 138; WANHS Stukeley MS., 13; Top.Gen.b.53, 9v, cf. also 8). In addition, and quite separate from the series of transcripts acknowledged as derived from Gale, the Devizes commonplace book includes a modified version of Aubrey's rendition of the Sanctuary: this probably dates from the early 1720s, although endorsed by Stukeley in a later hand: 'Mr Aubry's fig[ure] of the snakes head, or hakpen, on Overton hill. 1660. but he . . .': frustratingly, his annotation breaks off here for unknown reasons, while the status of the date '1660', which does not appear in the relevant section of *Monumenta Britannica*, is also unclear (WANHS Stukeley MS., 77). Perhaps most interesting from our point of view are two Stukeley copies of Aubrey's plan B, one now WANHS Stukeley MS., 9 (Plate 12), the other Bodleian Library Gough Maps 231, 38 (Plate 13), and particularly the former. This modifies the original plan, conflating with it details from other items in Aubrey's *Monumenta* – his drawing of the Sanctuary on Overton Hill, and plan A, in this case notably an attempt to distinguish the ditch from the bank of the henge by a ring of shading which does not appear in plan B and is strongly reminiscent of that in the more detailed delineation (see further Chapter III, B.16).

However, it is important to underline Piggott's observation (1985, 45) that no copy of plan A is to be found in the Devizes commonplace book – nor, for that

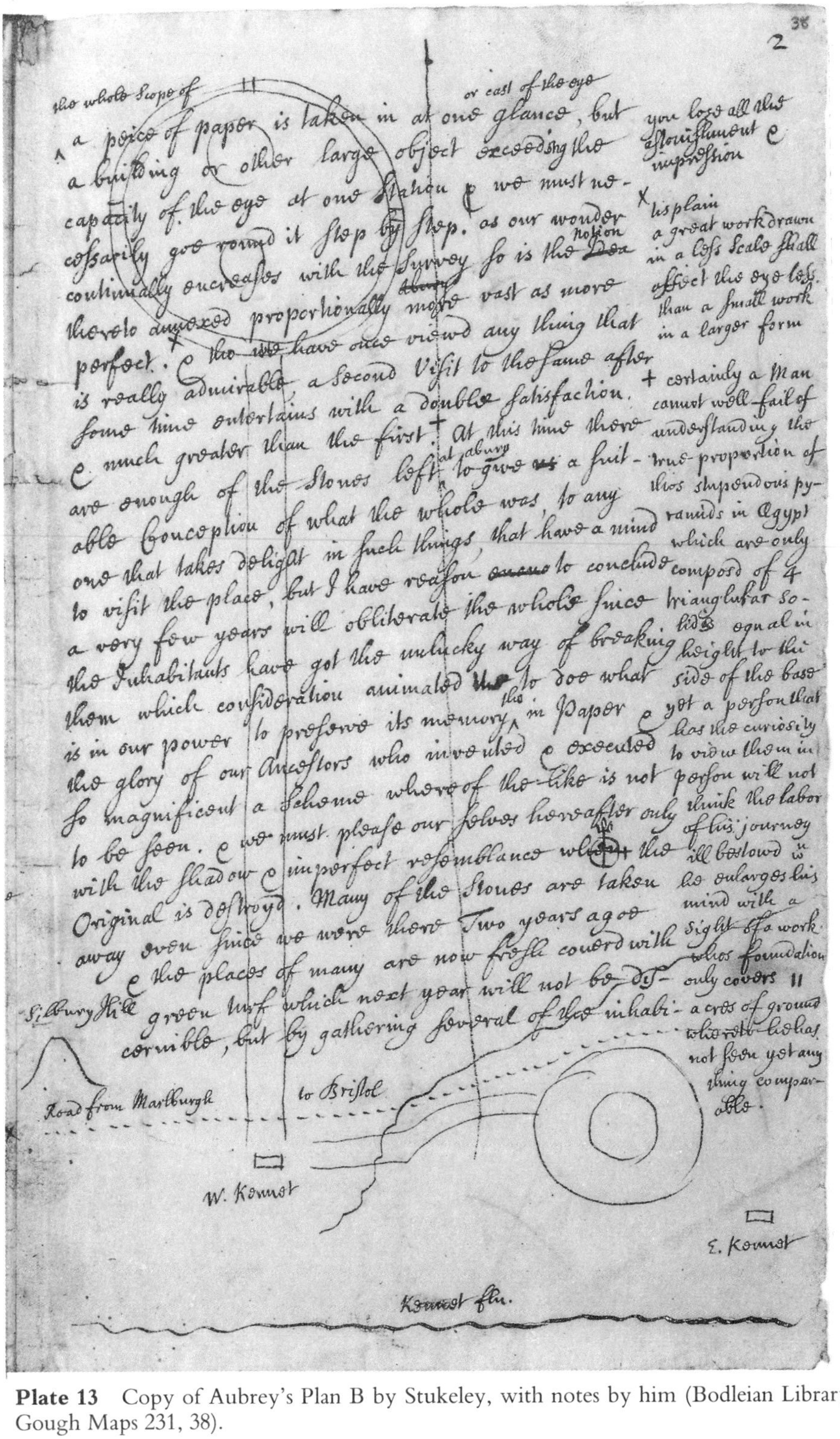

the whole scope of ‖ or east of the eye

a peice of paper is taken in at one glance, but you lose all the
a building or other large object exceeding the flourishment e
capacity of the eye at one station e we must ne- impression
cessarily goe round it step by step. as our wonder x tis plain
continually encreases with the survey so is the Idea a great work drawn
thereto annexed proportionally more vast as more in a less scale shall
perfect. e the we have once viewd any thing that affect the eye less
is really admirable, a second visit to the same after than a small work
some time entertains with a double satisfaction. in a larger form
e much greater than the first. At this time there + certainly a man
are enough of the stones left at saberg to give us a suit- cannot well fail of
able conception of what the whole was to any understanding the
one that takes delight in such things, that have a mind true proportion of
to visit the place, but I have reason enough to conclude those stupendous py-
a very few years will obliterate the whole since ramids in Egypt
the Inhabitants have got the unlucky way of breaking which are only
them which consideration animated the to doe what composd of 4
is in our power to preserve its memory in paper triangular so-
the glory of our Ancestors who invented e executed lids equal in
so magnificent a scheme whereof the like is not height to the
to be soon. e we must please our selves hereafter only side of the base
with the shadow e imperfect resemblance when the yet a person that
Original is destroyd. Many of the stones are taken has the curiosity
away even since we were there Two years ago to view them in
e the places of many are now fresh coverd with person will not
green turf which next year will not be dis- think the labor
cernible, but by gathering several of the inhabi- of his journey
ill bestowd if
he enlarges his
mind with a
sight of a work
whose foundation
only covers ‖
a cres of ground
wherein lies
not seen yet any
thing compar-
able.

Road from Marlburgh   to Bristol

W. Kennet

E. Kennet

Kennet flu.

Plate 13   Copy of Aubrey's Plan B by Stukeley, with notes by him (Bodleian Library MS. Gough Maps 231, 38).

matter, anywhere else among Stukeley's manuscripts – and neither is there any unambiguous reference in his notes either to plan A or to the actual text of Aubrey's description of Avebury. Stukeley would surely have wished to copy plan A had he seen it, rather than conflating details from it into plan B, and this suggests that it was Gale who combined the two in this way. Perhaps, in view of the accuracy and size of plan A, Gale did not try to copy it, instead making do with the more schematic representation of the site given in plan B, which he embellished with elements from the more detailed plan. Hence Stukeley possibly never saw the most painstaking of Aubrey's records of the site: from the extracts in the Devizes notebook we cannot even be sure that he had read those elements of Aubrey's description of it on which almost all subsequent commentators have tended to concentrate, as against a brief epitome by Gale. The implications of this for Stukeley's view of Aubrey as a recorder of the site should be taken into account: for, if *we* lacked not only Aubrey's full text but also plan A, the impression of Aubrey's record of Avebury which would be uppermost would almost certainly be its frustrating scrappiness.

In spite of Stukeley's extensive citation of Aubrey, he was – or became, as he in turn visited monuments noted by his predecessor – far from uncritical of him. Thus the Devizes version of plan B is endorsed 'this figure is wholly wrong taken by Mr Aubury', while a Devil's Coyts comparison is 'very unlike' (WANHS Stukeley MS., 9, 13), and these comments are representative of a number of critical notes. For instance, of the profile of the earthwork at Fripsbury, Stukeley wrote 'very wrong for the rampire is much larger than the ditch'; of Chiselbury, 'erroneously done'; of St George's Hill, 'wretchedly designed'; of Old Sarum, 'This figure is inaccurate' (ibid., 16, 21, 23, 24). This was not a specific prejudice against Aubrey, as is shown by yet another of these captions: 'The Stones called the wedding at Stanton Drew as wretchedly designed by *E. Lhuyd* [deleted] Mr Aubry' (ibid., 10). Aubrey, however, attracted the bulk of this opprobrium, as the chief earlier recorder of this type of antiquity in which Stukeley was interested, and these notes evidently reflect the fact that, after initially being a novice compared with Aubrey, Stukeley later outstripped his predecessor and was increasingly disappointed by Aubrey's work. These marginal critical comments all appear to postdate his original notes, confirming other evidence that Stukeley added to the volume over a number of years (Piggott 1950, 199; 1985, 96).

All this may help to explain a certain ambivalence in Stukeley's attitude to Aubrey. As already noted, Stukeley quoted Aubrey openly and profusely concerning prehistoric antiquities in his unpublished manuscripts. In addition, in his *Stonehenge* he approvingly cited the paraphrase of Aubrey's criticism of Inigo Jones' views on Stonehenge which appeared in the 1695 Camden, while in the account of Stanton Drew which Stukeley wrote in 1723–4 and which was published posthumously in the extended second edition of his *Itinerarium Curiosum*, he flatteringly described Aubrey as 'that indefatigable searcher–out of antiquities' (Stukeley 1740, 3; 1776, ii.169). Concerning Avebury, however, Stukeley's attitude was different. In *Abury* (1743), he gave a history of previous accounts of Avebury in which it would have been natural to include Aubrey, but he there made no reference to Aubrey's work on the antiquity or to the role of this in stimulating his own interest in it (Stukeley 1743, 15). Indeed, nowhere either in *Abury* or in what survives of its predecessor, the manuscript 'Celtic Temples', does Stukeley refer to Aubrey in

46

connection with the main henge – whether bank, ditch, stones or any other feature of it. The main point at which Aubrey *does* enter Stukeley's text is a passage where the description of the Kennet Avenue and Sanctuary in the 1695 edition of Camden's *Britannia* is referred to and two aspects of it are criticized; there are then two further passing references to information recorded by Aubrey (Stukeley 1743, 32, 33, 35).

Even had Stukeley known no more of Aubrey's work on Avebury than is contained in the 1695 *Britannia* and in his Gale transcripts – and we have found little hard evidence to indicate that he did know more than this[24] – his *Abury* treatment of Aubrey would seem both cavalier and disingenuous, though this would not be the only example of Stukeley's lack of consideration for others in his antiquarian work (Evans 1956, 75–6). Perhaps the clearest-cut example of Stukeley's apparent meanness is his suppression of mention of the Aubrey/Gale account of the method of breaking stones by fire and water. Stukeley attributes his knowledge of this method simply to his local informants from May 1719 onwards, despite his having transcribed the clear and concise Aubrey/Gale account some six months earlier. (It is intriguing that Stukeley's dating of the method's discovery by Walter Stretch to 'about 1694' (Stukeley 1743, 25) means that he could, if challenged, have reconciled it with Aubrey's account on the assumption that the latter's Avebury material had been gathered only the year before the 1695 *Britannia* was published.)

Stukeley's lack of generosity to the earlier antiquary has, of course, often been commented on (Long 1858b, 20 n. 3, 58, 61–3; Long 1876, 6 n. 1; Britton 1845, 9; Burl 1979, 50; Piggott 1989, 127). Though sometimes expressed in a rather heightened form, and not seldom incautious in its assumptions about the extent of Stukeley's knowledge of Aubrey's work – as in Piggott's presumption that Stukeley had seen Aubrey's comment that the stone circle at Avebury exceeded that at Stonehenge 'as a Cathedral doeth a parish Church' (Piggott 1985, 46) – such criticism is fundamentally well founded. Since 1695, Aubrey's role as a commentator on Avebury and on Druid temples had been given publicity through Gibson's edition of Camden, and – whether or not he was conscious of it – Stukeley almost certainly perceived Aubrey as a threat to his own role as the discoverer of the significance of the site, writing the earlier author down accordingly.

It is just possible, if unlikely, that Stukeley could also have seen plans C and D, which, for similar reasons, he would have been unlikely to acknowledge. From March 1718 he was an active Fellow of the Royal Society, and would have shared the prerogative of any Fellow to investigate earlier records in its custody. He is also known to have been involved in the reorganization of the Society's repository in the 1730s, a decade during which the archives were also overhauled, and, though this would have been too late for the Royal Society documents to have influenced his work on Avebury in the 1720s, it is suggestive of the opportunities for such access that he had (Simpson 1984, 209n.; Royal Society Copy Council Minutes, iii. 304ff.).

Certainly, some features in Stukeley's plans echo those of plans C and/or D: for instance, these could have contributed to his belief that the Cove once contained a fourth stone, despite the fact that this no longer survived by his time, while his preoccupation with double rings of stones both in the main circle and the inner ones could reflect the influence of plan C. But such connections remain entirely speculative: there is no positive evidence that he saw the plans, and a certain amount of circumstantial evidence that he was unlikely to have done. Such research as has yet been done on access to the Society's records in its early decades suggests that they were not widely used, and that poor indexing would have made it difficult for Stukeley to find the Avebury plans even if he had investigated the Society's archives in search of information on the antiquity (Hunter 1989, 37–8). It is true that by this time an index to the Society's journal and register books existed, the first entry in which under the heading 'Antiquities' pointed to the discussion of Avebury in July 1663 (Index 1660–1695, shelved with Journal Books at Royal Society). But it did not indicate that the plans shown on that occasion had been preserved, and this could only have been learnt from a physical examination of the bundles of miscellaneous papers surviving from the Society's early years, a task which there is no evidence that Stukeley undertook.

viii. Stukeley's record

In any case, whatever the influence of earlier records of Avebury on Stukeley's initial discovery of the site and his perception of it thereafter, what is more important is the profuse recording that he himself carried out in a series of well-documented visits to the site between 1719 and 1724. Indeed, the fullness of our information about Stukeley's fieldwork at Avebury is in marked contrast to the scattered hints that remain concerning the actual visits to the site of Aubrey, Moray and Charleton. In his published *Abury*, Stukeley states that his annual visits were each of a fortnight's duration (Stukeley 1743, 18), but at least in 1724 he appears to have stayed for longer still. References in his published and unpublished writings, together with dates on the illustrations published in his *Abury* and others surviving in the Bodleian Library, make it possible to trace the progress of his studies in detail. Thus he records measuring the outside compass of the rampart with Roger Gale on 16 August 1721, and there is then a sequence of similarly exact datings going through to the beginning of June 1724, when he left Avebury for Stonehenge (Piggott 1985, 165–6; Stukeley 1743, 20; Gough Maps 231, 226). A summary account of such dated references is given by Piggott in an appendix to *William Stukeley*, mainly on the basis of drawings, but this could easily be supplemented from fieldnotes, particularly in 1724.[25]

Cumulatively, Stukeley arguably did more fieldwork than all our other commentators put together. Visually, his record comprised an extensive series of drawings and engravings showing general views and specific details of the site, while he encapsulated his findings into a depiction of 'the whole of this temple', which formed 'the great frontispiece plate' to his *Abury* of 1743. This 'ground-plot representing the true state of the town and temple, when I frequented it', 'done from innumerable mensurations' (Stukeley 1743, 19, 22), is included here as plan E (Plate 14 and also in folder). In it, he gave a bird's eye view of the antiquity, including the fields, palings, houses and roads of the village as well as the megalithic remains they interspersed. In addition to stones still standing at the time when he actually made his record, he also included information on those whose destruction he could date in the decades preceding his fieldwork there. Among these were some stones which had been shown by his 17th-century predecessors, including the most northerly of the three standing Cove stones, which had fallen in 1713, and the Obelisk. On the other

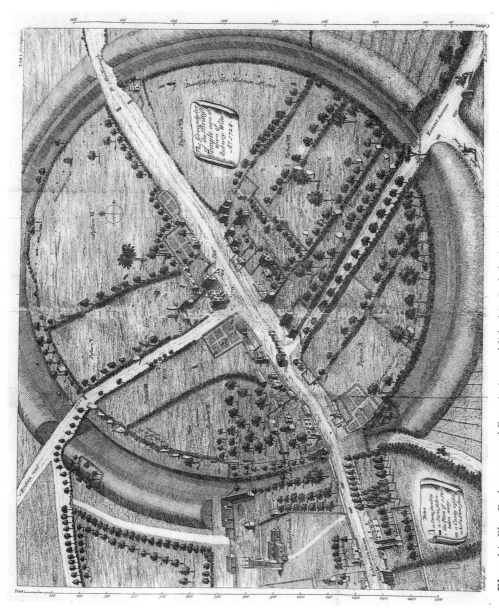

Plate 14 Plan E: the engraved Frontispiece published in Stukeley's *Abury* (1743), State E2.

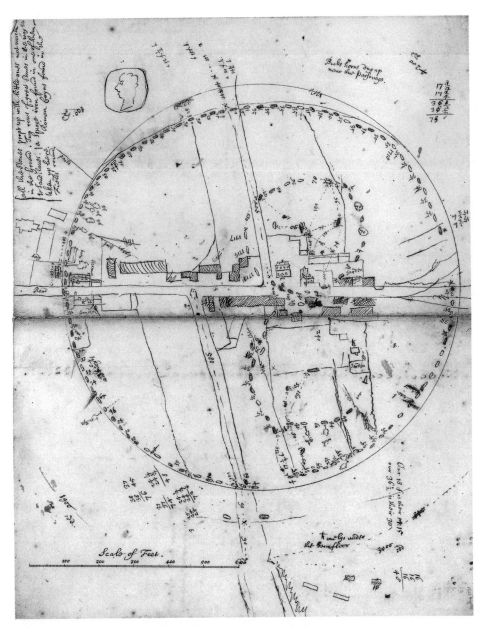

Plate 15 Stukeley's plan of Avebury giving measurements of the distances between the stones and assumed stone positions (Bodleian Library MS. Eng. Misc.c.533, 53v–4).

hand, Stukeley shows no trace of pairs of 'Gateway' stones outside the entrances to the antiquity, although a fallen pair do appear within the south entrance.

Stukeley's published Frontispiece has usually been seen as his definitive record of the site, but in fact it overlaps with a series of nine complete and two half draft plans of the site dating from 1721 to 1724 which survive in the Bodleian Library (Plates 32–42). In addition, the Bodleian holdings include a somewhat cruder map which supplements these by recording the distances between the stones and assumed stone positions (Plate 15). Close scrutiny of all these reveals significant differences both among them and between them and the published version, from which it transpires that the latter is less definitive than has hitherto normally been presumed. Because of the importance of the data available from these drafts, they will be extensively described and compared in Chapter III, while the significance and reliability of the data they provide, especially about stone settings, will be assessed in Chapter IV.

A written commentary on Stukeley's drawings and plans is provided by his extensive fieldnotes on different parts of the Avebury complex, also to be found in the Bodleian, especially those made in his final season on the site (from which the notes which survive seem disproportionately to date). These are now mainly preserved in Bodleian MS Gough Maps 231, and considerable use will be made of them in the pages which follow. A further crucial record of the henge itself takes the form of 'a fine tour' of it which Stukeley wrote in 1722–3 as part of his manuscript treatise on 'Celtic Temples', which will be more fully described below. This seems initially to have acted as a commentary on a version of his 'ground-plot' of the site, but he dispensed with it in his published *Abury*: 'I spare the reader's patience in being too particular about it', he wrote (Stukeley 1743, 22). In this 'tour', Stukeley recorded some crucial information that is not otherwise available, and, in view of its importance for our understanding of the antiquity, a text of it is included as Appendix II. This has had to be the subject of a degree of editorial reconstruction, because, after initially writing a fairly continuous narrative, Stukeley then made piecemeal modifications to this. It seems that the account was first compiled in 1722, as is shown by the fact that at one point Stukeley noted 'theres still left Anno 1722 40 in number' (Stukeley 1722–4b, 121); the bulk of his emendations to it seem to date from 1723, at one point including reference to 'their present state Anno 1723' (ibid., 120). Further additions may date from the following season, though Stukeley seems to have spent less time on the henge itself in that year and more on its outlying components.

Like this written material, it is clear that virtually all of Stukeley's visual records of the site were made in the early 1720s, including the engravings that were to appear in the account of the site that he published twenty years later. Indeed, there is no evidence that he ever returned to the site after his last season there in 1724. In 1722 Stukeley took his then engravers, John Pine and Gerard Vandergucht, to Avebury with him (Piggott 1985, 61–4). Subsequently, he must have had engravings made in London from drawings done *in situ*, proofs of which he then evidently took with him on further visits to Avebury, often endorsing them in ink with corrections which were then incorporated into revised versions of the plates. In one case, an engraving of a prospect 'drawn 8 July 1723' is actually endorsed 'corrected 18 May 1724' (Eng.Misc.d.444, 62), and we may presume that undated corrections resulted from a similar procedure (cf. Piggott 1985, 37).

51

Clearly Stukeley's intention was that the plates thus executed should form illustrations to a book, or rather a series of books, dealing with the class of antiquities of which Avebury formed part, and the nature of this projected work was divulged in his *Itinerarium Curiosum, Centuria I* of 1724. There, Stukeley not only postponed discussion of such relics to his forthcoming book at various points where they appeared in the text (Stukeley 1724a, 45, 95, 141); he also concluded his preface, dated 26 December 1724, with the following announcement:

> What I shall next trouble the reader withal, will be my intended work, of the history of the antient *Celts*, particularly the first inhabitants of *Great Brittan*, which for the most part is now finish'd. by what I can judg at present it will consist of four books in folio. I. The history of the origin and passage of the *Celts* from *Asia* into the west of *Europe*: particularly into *Brittan*. of their manners, language, &c. II. Of the religion, deity, priests, temples, and sacred rites of the *Celts*. III. Of the great *Celtic* temple at *Abury* in *Wiltshire*, and others of that sort. IV. of the celebrated *Stonehenge*. There will be above 300 copper plates of a folio size, many of which are already engraven; and many will be of much larger dimensions. Upon account therefore of the vast expence attending this work, I shall print no more than are subscribed for, the money to be paid to me only. thus much I thought fit to advertise the friendly reader. (Stukeley 1724a, sig. a1)

What he was referring to can clearly be identified with the text which survives today in three manuscript volumes, two of them in Cardiff Central Library and one in the Bodleian. All are bound in uniform vellum, with titles neatly written on both the front cover and the spine: while the Bodleian one is thus entitled 'Celtic Temples', those at Cardiff are respectively entitled 'Celtic Religion' and 'Stonehenge', and they will be so referred to hereinafter. It seems likely that Stukeley had begun to compose these in 1722, probably in the winter season following his visit to Avebury that year. The self-portrait facing the title-page of 'Celtic Temples' is dated 7 December 1722 (Plate 9); the 'fine tour' of Avebury which forms part of the text dates in its original version from 1722, as we have seen; and the date 1722 appears inside the rear cover of 'Stonehenge' (it is possibly significant that he gives 1722 as the year in which 'I began to write' in his published *Abury* (Stukeley 1743, 22)). He then clearly continued work on the manuscripts in the following year: he wrote on the fly-leaf of 'Celtic Temples', 'I came hither (to Abury) 8 July 1723', while the revisions that he made to his 'tour' in that year have already been noted, and a passage on page 175 is headed '17 July 1723'. The date 1723 also appears at the start of the 'Stonehenge' text and at more than one point thereafter (Stukeley 1722–4c, 1, 45, 73, 74), while an appendix to 'Celtic Religion' dealing with celts is dated 24 February 1723/4 (Stukeley 1722–4a, 133).

Stukeley seems to have had two methods of composition. In part, he wrote a continuous text, usually on the rectos of the manuscript, leaving the facing versos blank and filling them up with supplementary material at a later date. Elsewhere, however, he simply wrote a heading at the top of a leaf and inserted relevant notes and paragraphs beneath it, presumably intending to convert this accumulation into connected prose at a subsequent stage (if he needed more than one leaf, he found a further blank elsewhere, usually later in the volume). In both cases, this means that the volumes contain different strata of additions, some of which can be dated.[26] Others cannot, but it should be stressed that virtually the whole text is in handwriting comparable to that in which the manuscripts were originally composed, dating from the early to mid-1720s: additions in Stukeley's later handwriting are immediately distinguishable and few in number. In general, Stukeley's later treatment of these manuscripts seems to have been more negative than positive. In the Oxford volume, particularly, many passages are scored through, presumably because the matter they contained was incorporated in a subsequent recension, while numerous pages have been cut out, leaving gaps in the pagination. This applies to a lesser extent to the Cardiff manuscripts (though a few pages have been cut out, this occurred before Stukeley paginated the volumes), but it clearly complicates reconstruction of the original content of the work.

It is possible that a further volume or volumes is missing, though this is rendered less likely by the fact that the extant volumes contain material on each of the topics to which Stukeley claimed that he intended to devote a published 'book'. 'Celtic Religion' tallies exactly with the relevant part of Stukeley's proposed *magnum opus*, as does the volume on Stonehenge, which included both a detailed description of the antiquity and a critique of earlier opinions concerning its origins. Though there is no full-length treatise devoted to the history of the Celts, a number of pages deal with this topic by way of background, both in 'Celtic Religion' and 'Celtic Temples' (Stukeley 1722–4a, 123f.; 1722–4b, 212–14, 218). Moreover, although Stonehenge had a volume to itself, that on 'Celtic Temples' included not only a general survey of megalithic monuments, but also an extensive description and discussion of Avebury, including the detailed 'tour' of the site already referred to (Appendix II).

ix. Stukeley's interpretation

What the remainder of 'Celtic Temples' comprised, however, was an attempt to explain the meaning and function of this and other megalithic monuments by invoking a mass of speculative and theoretical matter derived from classical and biblical sources and early modern scholarship. This overlapped with comparable material in the volume on 'Celtic Religion', and it will be discussed in full in the next chapter. Here, it will suffice to note that these manuscripts show that, while he was carrying out his fieldwork at Avebury, Stukeley was committed to an elaborate interpretation of stone circles in terms of the rites and symbolism of a learned ancient priesthood which bears a striking resemblance to the views that he was to publish in his *Abury* of 1743. This is also borne out by Stukeley's surviving fieldnotes from the early 1720s. For actually interspersed among Stukeley's observations on the antiquity at Avebury and its surroundings are speculations about ancient mythology, Egyptian symbolism, Pythagorean harmonies, concepts like 'the soul of the world', and even the hieroglyphic of a snake traversing a circle, the significance of which will be drawn out in the next chapter, and all of which he clearly saw as integral to an understanding of the site (Gough Maps 231, 6, 8v, 31v, 33, 40v, 46).

This is important because the leading authority on the subject, Stuart Piggott, has argued the exact contrary to this, both in his original work on Stukeley and in his more recent recensions of it. Piggott has claimed that Stukeley came to hold theories of this kind only after the period of his fieldwork. In the early 1720s, according to this view, Stukeley's work at Avebury comprised 'a purely objective record', innocent of 'the elaborate fantasies of Druids, ancient mythology and patriarchal religion which he had so unfortunately evolved over the intervening years', which were to dominate his published *Stonehenge* (1740) and *Abury* (1743) (Piggott 1985, 87, 89, 153 and passim; cf. Piggott 1989, 10–11, 28, 32–4, 124ff.).

Why did Piggott make this claim? One factor may be that, at the time of his original research on Stukeley, he had apparently not seen the manuscript of 'Celtic Temples' now in the Bodleian (to which it was presented by Alexander Keiller in 1955), though it is more surprising that he overlooked the evidence of Stukeley's early commitment to such theories that is to be found in the fieldnotes which, then as now, were available in Gough Maps 231. In 1950 Piggott also wrongly believed the Cardiff 'Stonehenge' manuscript to date from the 1750s, like other manuscripts with which it is juxtaposed (Piggott 1950, 105n.). By the time he came to revise his study for its 1985 edition, he had seen the 'Stonehenge' and 'Celtic Temples' manuscripts (though he still seems to have remained unaware of the existence of the crucial 'Celtic Religion' manuscript at Cardiff, referring only to 'two' manuscripts: Piggott 1985, 87–8; 1986, 115; 1989, 129). In spite of this, however, Piggott has claimed in this and more recent writings that the Cardiff and Oxford manuscripts bear out his original view of Stukeley, stating that 'our new MS evidence does show us that he did in fact write a book unencumbered by theory and speculation' and that 'the 1723 text scarcely mentions Druids' (Piggott 1986, 116; 1989, 143; cf. 1985, 87–9).

Regrettably, it must here be categorically stated that these claims are incorrect. In both 'Celtic Religion' and 'Celtic Temples', the Druids constantly reappear, perhaps particularly in the former, while the elaborate superstructure of erudite theory which these treatises contain will become clear in the next chapter. Stukeley undoubtedly elaborated his ideas later in life, on this as on other subjects: Michael Hoskin has observed such a tendency in successive drafts of his famous 'Memoir' of Isaac Newton and his cosmological writings, and clearly his work on megaliths and the rites associated with them was no exception to this (Hoskin 1985, 78 and passim). But elaborating ideas is not the same thing as broaching them for the first time, and, by denying Stukeley's interest in such notions in the 1720s, Piggott has imposed on Stukeley's intellectual life a chiasma which has no factual basis, with implications for the reigning view of Stukeley – and his period – which will be more fully assessed in Chapter II.

On the other hand, there was a long delay in Stukeley's preparation of his intended work. Although Roger Gale was hoping that Stukeley had collected enough material for a book even in 1723 (Stukeley 1887, 254), while Stukeley himself announced his work on this subject as forthcoming in 1724, in the event no book was published for nearly twenty years. Hence with Stukeley we encounter some of the problems arising from longevity of concern with the site that we also have with Aubrey. Various reasons may be suggested as to why publication failed to occur as promised. One may have been the difficulty of finding subscribers for as elaborate a work as Stukeley promised the public in *Itinerarium Curiosum*: certainly Stukeley was left with a hearty dislike of publishers in later life, while the books as published had only one plate of more than folio size, as against the 'many' initially promised (Piggott 1985, 108; 1989, 144; Stukeley 1882, 58; 1883, 55). Perhaps more important is the fact that the extant manuscripts suggest that, in the later stages of his fieldwork at Avebury, Stukeley radically altered his views on the site in ways which will be indicated in the next chapter. The result was to leave his text in need of substantial revision and reorganization, and this may have contributed to his initial decision to delay publication. It may also be significant that he more than once apologizes in his manuscripts for being premature in presenting what might have formed a lifetime's study (Stukeley 1722–4b, 266; 1722–4c, 122).

If it was initially so as to consolidate his findings that he postponed publication, however, Stukeley must thereafter have been overtaken by events. Among these were two fundamental changes in his life, the reasons for which have never been fully understood, his move to Stamford in 1726 and his ordination in 1729. A further development of these years which must almost certainly have had an impact on Stukeley's publishing ambitions was the appearance of a work which, though different in subject matter, had a title unnervingly similar to that which he had announced for his own book in 1724, John Toland's 'Specimen of the Critical History of the Celtic Religion and Learning': this formed part of a collection of Toland's writings published posthumously in 1726 (Toland 1726). We know that Stukeley was given a copy of this work by his friend William Warburton in 1729 (Stukeley 1883, 302), and either at that point or earlier Stukeley may well have felt that he had been upstaged by what was effectively the first full-scale publication on a cognate subject. (This is a topic to which Piggott gives only glancing attention, being more concerned with the issue of whether Stukeley might have seen Toland's work and been influenced by it before publication).[27]

Moreover, what is surely crucial is that, in his book, Toland contrived to use material on Celtic religion for ideologically subversive purposes of the possibility of which Stukeley seems hitherto to have been strangely oblivious (Toland 1726; Sullivan 1982, ch. 6). As we shall see in the next chapter, Stukeley had already decided in the early 1720s that a Trinitarian gloss could be placed on Avebury. But it seems likely that this rude awakening to the heterodox use that a thinker like Toland could make of material about ancient religion of the kind that he had spent so long laboriously collecting made him decide to draw out more explicitly the apologetic implications both of his fieldwork in Wiltshire and of his learned researches and thus 'to combat the deists from an unexpected quarter' (Piggott 1985, 104). Indeed, it is even possible that this scenario explains Stukeley's decision to take holy orders, a decision which Piggott tends to see as separate from and antithetical to his antiquarian activity.

It should be stressed, however, that there is no evidence of a radical discontinuity in Stukeley's endeavours. The way in which the ideas in his manuscripts of the early 1720s were to evolve into those of his published *Abury* will be indicated in Chapter II, and it is quite likely that he already had this kind of reshaping of his material in mind when he told Roger Gale in February 1727 how:

> among antiquity matters Abury seems to touch my fancy the most at present, & probably, if business dos not too much encroach upon my time, I shall publish it in a year or two; wherein I shall show somewhat probably that will put the world into a new way of thinking in a matter of some importance. However I shall endeavour to do justice to what I take to be the finest monument in the world, & one of the most antient, which our Country may well boast of, as Egypt of her pyramids & obelisks. (Stukeley 1882, 190–1)

Stukeley's programme of work on Avebury and related topics over the next few years is shown both by correspondence utilized by Piggott – which illustrates his intention of 'reconciling Plato & Moses, & the Druid & Christian Religion' (Stukeley

1882, 220; Piggott 1985, 97–8, 104) – and by prefatory material to a version of his study of Avebury which was evidently compiled in 1731 but was never published. The latter, which survives in the Bodleian Library, comprises a dedication to the Lord Chancellor, Peter, 1st Baron King, John Locke's heir, and himself the author of works on early Christianity, to whose patronage Stukeley owed the living of All Saints, Stamford (Eng.Misc.e.553, 7ff.; Stukeley 1882, 53, 109). In it, Stukeley described Avebury as 'the noblest & most wonderful Religious Antiquity in our Island, perhaps in the world', and he explained his intention to place his study of it in the context of scriptural chronology. Indeed, the strength of his protest of the superior merits of biblical testimony to that of the pagans is perhaps itself to be seen as significant in the light of the developments of the later 1720s described here. He wrote:

> The scheme which I intend to pursue in the following discourse is this. I shall begin with the creation of the world & carry on the Mosaic chronology till we arrive at the latter end of Abrahams life, about which time the first inhabitants of Brittan arriv'd here, who were the authors of this work of Abury, the glory of our Island which I shall describe circumstantially & endeavour to preserve it from further decay. I shall by the bye, add such matters of the Mosaic history as are not commonly remarked, or which are necessary for my purpose. (Eng.Misc.e.553, 7, 9, 10)[28]

The project here outlined bears a recognizable similarity to the 'Canon Mosaicae Chronologiae' which Stukeley announced as the first part of the proposed work on 'Patriarchal Christianity' of which he gave a synopsis in the preface to his *Stonehenge* of 1740 (Stukeley 1740, sig. a1). The intention was that both his *Stonehenge* and his *Abury* should form part of this *magnum opus*, though in the event these two books were all that was ever published, neither the 'Canon' nor any of its other intended components seeing the light of day. Moreover, despite hopes at this time that his work on the subject was imminent (Piggott 1985, 78), even the volumes that ultimately came out took another decade to materialize. From the point of view of the antiquarian discovery of Avebury, however, what is important is that Stukeley's 1743 book, *Abury: A Temple of the British Druids*, drew not only on the elaborate superstructure concerning ancient religion and its symbolism which he had begun to expound in his 'Celtic Religion' and 'Celtic Temples', but also on the description of the site of Avebury which he had given in the latter work and in related manuscripts of the early 1720s. Above all, it gave to the public much of the extensive visual record that he had prepared twenty years earlier, in the form of the sequence of engravings and the 'great frontispiece plate'.[29]

At last, therefore, in 1743 a lengthy and apparently authoritative study of Avebury was available in print, and Stukeley's book for the first time drew widespread attention to the site. For instance, the fourth edition of Daniel Defoe's *Tour of Great Britain* (1724), issued in 1748, contained a reference to 'the stupendous Remains of a *Druids* Temple' at Avebury which had not been present in earlier editions of the book, and Stukeley was specifically mentioned in connection with the religious purpose of this site and of Stonehenge (Defoe 1748, ii.52–3; cf. Defoe 1724–7, ii.51). This is indicative of the way in which Stukeley made the antiquity 'visible' for the first time.[30]

In addition, his influence pervaded perceptions of the site for long after. Thus Sir Richard Colt Hoare's account of Avebury in his *Ancient Wiltshire* (1812–21) was essentially based on Stukeley's conception of it, despite the fact that Colt Hoare carried out his own survey of the site and that, as we saw in the Introduction, he had also gained access to the manuscript of Aubrey's *Monumenta Britannica*, quoting Aubrey extensively and using his evidence to supplement Stukeley's. Colt Hoare even adopted Stukeley's spelling of the placename in preference to that current in his own time (Colt Hoare 1812–21, ii.58n). He accepted Stukeley's claim that Avebury was a 'Dracontium', praising him for seeing the true significance of the site which Aubrey had missed, while also following his views on the date of the antiquity, the nature of its component parts, and their names. Even when sceptical of aspects of Stukeley's interpretation – as concerning Silbury Hill – he still cited them (Colt Hoare 1812–21, ii.65ff.).

The same was true of 19th-century antiquaries who published Aubrey's plans for the first time, whose perception of the site was also inescapably indebted to Stukeley's (e.g. Long 1858a, esp. plate 4), while, in accounts of Avebury in encyclopaedias and the like, the influence of Stukeley's views continued into our own century. Stukeley represents the climax of the early recording of the site, building on – indeed, influenced by – the pioneering work of his 17th-century predecessors, but providing an extensive published record which none of them had achieved. We will return in the next chapter to his elaborate theories about the site, but here his fieldwork and his *Abury* form an appropriate ending to this part of our narrative of the site's discovery.

Notes

1. The date of the incident was 1649 new style, as against 1648 old style, a source of some confusion not only in earlier commentators (e.g. Long 1862, 225–6; Keiller and Piggott 1936, 419) but also in Ponting 1969, v; Piggott 1985, 30; Piggott 1986, 115. We have used new style throughout. In the passage quoted, 'thorough' replaces 'into', deleted; after 'overtooke', 'the' is accidentally repeated. In this and all subsequent quotations from manuscripts, contractions have been expanded and deletions recorded in notes; the fact that words are inserted above the line has been ignored unless it seems significant. We have refrained from giving an accurate text of the whole of Aubrey's description of Avebury here, on the grounds partly that it is scattered in different parts of his text and partly that, when a proper edition of *Monumenta Britannica* exists, readers will be able to refer to that. In the meantime, texts of Aubrey 24, 23–26v and 29–38, will be found in Jackson 1862, 314–23 (the best edited version, superior to that in Long 1858a, 311–18), or Fowles and Legg 1980, 17–26 and 31–42 (though the use of rearranged facsimile in this edition does not make for easy or accurate reading).

It is worth pointing out here that orthography was far less regular in the 17th century than it has become since, much of the regularity to be found in printed texts of the period being imposed by compositors.

Thus Avebury was variously spelt Avebury (Royal Society minutes: see below), Aubury (Childrey 1661, 49; Aubrey, passim), Aveberry (Moray: see Appendix I), Aubery (Hooke: see below), Abury (Stukeley 1743) and Abebery (Pepys: the editors seem wrong to describe this in their footnote as standard: Pepys 1972–83, ix.240). The only significance that should be attached to all this concerns Aubrey's interest in 'Aubury': see below. 'Plan' and 'plant' fall into a similar category, the deletion of the 't' in the Royal Society minutes (see below, n. 3) being a piece of attempted regularization rather similar to what one might expect from a compositor.

2. 'January' is inserted; 'Antiquity' is left undeleted but is duplicated by 'Worke', as is 'Stones' by 'Ruines', 'made bold to lett' by 'did lett', and, in the last sentence, 'was' by 'gave me'. The dots before 'Ruines' are Aubrey's, but those before 'these' denote a word rendered illegible through a portion of the manuscript being torn off; 'way' was inserted between 'that' and 'game' before the longer insertion 'in the country of the Hare' was made; and 'led' is altered from 'ledd' or 'lead'. In the further passage quoted below, 'bignesse' is duplicated by 'largeness'.

3. Royal Society MS 557 (rough minutes, unpaginated): 'that' is deleted after 'suggesting,'; 'the same' replaces 'it,' deleted. Also deleted is the passage which

follows: 'as also into a certain Tombe upon Salisbury plaine'; cf. Royal Society, Original Journal Book, i. 197 (identical except for minor differences of orthography and punctuation, and the fact that the deleted phrase is omitted; in addition, 'Plant' has been spelt with a 't', but the 't' has been deleted), and Birch 1756–7, i.272.

4.   The date 16 July given in Birch 1756–7, i.274, is a misprint. Though, in his edition of Boyle, Birch added to the Hooke letter the date '[July , 1667]' [sic] in square brackets, the reason for this is unclear, since he printed it in juxtaposition with letters dating from 1663. It is just conceivable that it was because he had seen Charleton's plan at the Royal Society and misread the date on it as 1667, as its 20th-century cataloguers did (see p. 19).

5.   Royal Society Domestic Manuscripts 5.72–80. Aubrey's is 80A; Charleton's is 72; Long's is 79b.

6.   See Birch 1756–7, ii.121, 127 (on Aubrey's 1666 task); i.349, ii.109 (on attempts at reinvigoration); see also Hunter 1989, 188–9 (on reinvigoration), 127, 156 (on the disruptions of 1665–6).

7.   In addition, in the journal, the word 'ichnographiam' appears instead of 'Topographiam'. The full text of the relevant part of the journal is as follows:

Visitavi D. D. Walt: Charltonem, a quo haec inter alia excepta: 1. ostendit mihi aliud antiquitatis Danicae monumentum, paene quale, imo grandius, illud Salisburiense, (16 milliar: ab illo *Stoneheng*) quod in *Wiltshire* est, ubi in orbem disponuntur saxa multa 34 pedes alta, in uno latere interiori aliud circulus est saxeus, ut prior in cuius medio saxum aliud eminet caeteris altius ad 40 n. pedes attollitur, et appellatur ab incolis *King-stool*, ichnographiam ostendit, simulque addit illum *Jones*, qui de Salisburiensi illo monimento scripsit multis modis illa Vitruvio adscribere, quae in Vitruvio nusquam leguntur (Borrichius 1983, iii.70).

8.   It is interesting that Stukeley was later to pick up the usage of 'Kingstone' (Stukeley 1722–4b, 24, 26), which is also, of course, associated with the megalithic antiquity at Rollright in Oxfordshire (cf. Lambrick 1988). However, Stukeley thought that such stones lay *outside* the antiquity, not at the centre as in this case.

9.   'King Charles IId' replaces 'His Majestie' deleted; 'one morning' replaces 'once' deleted; before 'Chorographers', 'Chrog' has been deleted; before 'Journey', 'Joye'[?] has been deleted; 'walkt' replaces 'went'.

10.   In fact, the name is erroneously written 'Chareton'; Aubrey subsequently emended this to 'Afterwards my honored friend' before deleting the whole passage.

11.   The suggestion made in Hunter 1975, 158 n.6, should therefore be retracted.

12.   For instance, Wren's microscopical observations: cf. Hooke 1665, sig. g2.

13.   *The Intelligencer*, nos. 1–2 (31 Aug., 7 Sept. 1663). See also *Calendar of State Papers Domestic, 1663–4*, 264 (from Public Record Office SP 29/80, 9,

though Dolman's name is incorrectly given in both the manuscript and published versions).

14.   It should be noted that Aubrey clearly means that it was the Duke of York [i.e. the future James II], not the King, who expressed interest in the snails and who recalled this when in bed 'with his Dutches', contrary to the statement in Chippindale 1983, 68. What is evidently an earlier confusion is to be found in Richard Rawlinson's preface to his adaptation of Aubrey's 'Perambulation of Surrey' (Hunter 1975, 233), in which he records a presumably fictitious meeting between Charles II and Aubrey at *Stonehenge* (Rawlinson 1718, xiii).

15.   See *The Intelligencer*, nos. 5–6 (28 Sept., 5 Oct. 1663). It is possible that not all of Moray's observations were made on 29 August, but that he returned to Avebury during the royal stay at Bath: this could have been on the occasion when he visited James Long's house at Draycot (Appendix I). For a visit to Longleat by the royal party while at Bath, see *Calendar of State Papers Domestic*, 1663–4, p. 271 (from SP 29/80, 53): see also *The Intelligencer*, no. 3 (14 Sept. 1663).

16.   Whereas Aubrey cited Moray in connection with a possible original ditch to the Sanctuary, Moray's speculation in the notes published in Appendix I related to a tumulus and to the ditch surrounding Silbury, though he clearly believed that such growth could occur in any ditch. On the question of whether the Sanctuary had a ditch, see Chapter IV, n.

17.   Before 'Closes', 'Enc' has been deleted; 'to' has been deleted before 'make this Survey'; 'dis-empestred' replaced 'un-pestered', which Aubrey may have intended to reinstate, but we have preferred his revised reading; three words later, 'from' replaces 'of', deleted; 'darkned' is in fact written as 'dakned'.

18.   It should be noted that Aubrey did not use the name, 'the Sanctuary'. He seems to have been unclear about the name of this antiquity. In his text he refers in a cumbersome way to 'On the brow of the hill East from West Kinnet', or 'On the Brow of the hill above Kynet ... such a Monument ... called —— ' (Aubrey 24, 43av, 43; Fowles and Legg 1980, 50, 51). In addition, a note survives in which he prompted himself to ask Robert Toope the name of 'this circular Monument', and Toope's reply, which survives, states that 'the name of the place is Millfield' (Aubrey 24, 44, 45; Fowles and Legg 1980, 55). See also Chapter III, B.5.

19.   On the publication plans see Hunter 1975, 89–90; Piggott 1985, 44–5 (though note that 'Dr Gale's,' which implies that Gale was a collaborator in the project, is a misprint for 'Dr Gale saith').

20.   There are also notes on comparable antiquities in Scandinavia, some of them from John Heysig, one of them dated 1681. In addition, the note which Aubrey has added to his original text on f. 39 – 'I now thinke it a surer way to say, Monuments erected by the Britains [replacing 'British Monuments', deleted]: and so have altered my Title of this Booke' – could date from c. 1680, when he announced this changed title in letters to Anthony Wood (Williams 1969, 337, 343).

21.   At first, its ownership by the Bodleian was not

well known and John Britton was not able to locate it in the early 1840s: Britton 1845, 87–91.

22. Extracts from the Devizes notebook made in 1867, when it was in the possession of W. Tite, are printed in Stukeley 1882, 137–40.

23. In the first quotation 'Abury' is altered from something else, probably 'Aubury'.

24. There is no reason to believe that Stukeley saw the manuscript of Aubrey's *Monumenta Britannica* itself. Such references as we have come across by Stukeley to 'Mr Auburys MS' (e.g. Stukeley 1722–4b, 39) can reasonably be taken to allude to his transcript from Gale. The only clue which could suggest that Stukeley might have seen Aubrey's original rather than Gale's copy is a striking parallel in the way that the two men describe the subsidiary circles within the henge. For while Aubrey wrote how 'Within this circumvallation are also (yet) remaining segments (of a roundish figure) of two (as I doe conjecture) Sacella', Stukeley in 'Celtic Temples' writes 'If we take the whole for a temple, these [two smaller circles] must be esteemd two *Sacella* or chappels' (Aubrey 24, 32–3; Fowles and Legg 1980, 35–6; Stukeley 1722–4b, 123). This term does not appear in the notes on Aubrey in the Devizes notebook; however, Stukeley does discuss it, quoting Festus, in *Abury* (Stukeley 1743, 8).

25. Many of the fieldnotes as well as the drawings in Gough Maps 231 are dated: for instance, of those quoted in Chapter II, the notes on f. 3 are dated 26 May 1724; those on 6, 20, 21 and 31 May 1724; those on 8v, 13 May 1724; those on 15, 20 May 1724; those on 32v, 29 May 1724; those on 46, 31 May 1724; those on 248v, 29 May 1724. In fact, all the dated *notes* are from 1724 except for f. 119, dated 7 July 1723, though more of the drawings are earlier. Dated fieldnotes also survive in MS Eng.Misc.b.65 (109v) and Eng.Misc.c.533 (44b, 45, 48); they also date from May 1724.

26. For alterations to the 1722 text made in 1723, see above. Additions dated 1725 on facing pages are to be found in Stukeley 1722–45, 30, 72. For an addition dated 1729 (in a distinctly later hand), see ibid., 38. For (undated) additions in a still later hand, see ibid., 228, 238–9.

27. The latter possibility is unlikely, partly because, though a note in 'Celtic Temples' shows that Stukeley was aware of the existence of Toland's book, he does not seem to have followed this up, and partly for reasons which will be discussed in Chapter II (Piggott 1985, 84–6; 1989, 140, 144)). It is perhaps worth noting that, in writing of Celtic temples, Toland referred to Avebury as follows: 'There is one at Aubury in Wiltshire, and some left in other places of England' (Toland 1726, 92).

28. Before 'Mosaic chronology', 'Mosaic history & the' has been deleted, as has 'together' after it. The date of this document is shown by the reference on f. 12 to 'the present almanac Anno 1731'.

29. The subscription list to *Abury*, dated 1741, is now Corpus Christi College, Cambridge, MS 552. Two copies of the prospectus for the book, dated 13 May 1741, are tipped inside the front cover of the copy of the published work now preserved as Bodleian Gough Wilts 3.

30. A reprint of Stukeley's *Stonehenge* and *Abury* was issued in 1838: a copy of this edition survives in the Bodleian Library, Vet.A 4 c.193. More recently, both works have been reprinted by Garland Publishing Inc., with an introduction by Robert D. Richardson, jr., as no. 23 in their series 'Myth and Romanticism' (1984).

II *Avebury and the early antiquaries: aims, methods and preconceptions*

i. General

Having indicated the context in which the early records of the site were made, it is now our intention to scrutinize these documents in detail, thereby clarifying various issues that arise concerning their depiction of the antiquity, and to draw broader conclusions by collating their evidence with the findings of archaeology and of non-destructive techniques like resistivity. As we prepared this material, however, it became increasingly apparent that certain prolegomena were necessary, in the form of an analysis of just what the early students of the site thought that they were doing, how they went about it, and how their records of the site may have been affected by their preoccupations. This is an exercise with a double purpose. In part, an understanding of the intentions and presuppositions of these antiquaries may help to throw light on the discrepancies which exist between (and even sometimes within) records made within a relatively short period. In addition, such an analysis is of value in its own right, as a contribution to our understanding of aims and techniques in a formative period of antiquarianism, and as a case-study of how perception and preconception interrelate in the recording of relics of the past in this or any period.

A point worth noting is that all the central records we discuss were compiled by men associated in the first century of its existence with the Royal Society, that symbol of the 'establishment' of the new experimental science of the 17th and 18th centuries. The history of the discovery of Avebury reinforces the claim that has been made more fully elsewhere – that the impact of the scientific movement on the study of the past reshaped priorities, leading to a greater emphasis than hitherto on tangible antiquities, on 'things' as against 'persons and actions', in the words of one exemplar of this tradition, the natural historian Robert Plot (Hunter 1971; 1975, 191f.).

Hence the first thing to be stressed – indeed, celebrated – about these records is that they were made at all, for it is worth remembering how, until the period from which they date, even the most scholarly and enquiring of people were to our eyes surprisingly incurious about the physical remains of the past that surrounded them. Certain special factors may help to explain why most visitors to Avebury failed to recognize the nature of the antiquity, namely its sheer scale and the way in which it was interspersed by the village and its ancillary enclosures (see Chapter IV, b and d). But it is significant that it was Aubrey who apparently first perceived its true nature, for he was a pioneer not only in studying Avebury but also in paying attention to a range of other types of evidence from the past which had hitherto been neglected or which, even when it had been noted by earlier topographers like Leland or Camden, had not been subjected to the sustained study in its own right from which proper conclusions could be drawn (Hunter 1971, 118–19).

Thus, despite the fact that every county in England is full of a rich variety of medieval churches, it was Aubrey who first tried to understand the development of Gothic architecture by building up a typology of dated specimens (Colvin 1968; Hunter 1975, 162, 165–6). It was through a similar use of what he described as 'comparative antiquitie' that he came to the conclusion – the percipience of which we now recognize – that the fact that megaliths were found in areas with no common denominator in the historical period proved that they must be prehistoric (Hunter 1975, 181–3). Interestingly, in his preface to 'Templa Druidum', he justified this by a scientific metaphor:

> the Discovery whereof I doe here attempt (for want of written Record) to work-out and restore after a kind of Algebraical method, by comparing those that I have seen one with another; and reducing them to a kind of Aequation: so (being but an ill Orator my selfe) to make the Stones give Evidence for themselves. (Aubrey 24, 30; Fowles and Legg 1980, 32)[1]

Stukeley's first major publication, his *Itinerarium Curiosum* (1724a), provides evidence of a comparable trend. Described by its subtitle as 'An Account of the Antiquitys and Remarkable Curiositys in Nature or Art of Great Brittan [sic]', it stood in contrast with earlier topographical writings in its greater emphasis on archaeological antiquities, and in the way in which it was illustrated by plans and sections of buildings (Moir 1964, ch. 5; Crook 1968, 108).

Previously, archaeological antiquities had been passed over with little comment in a culture where intellectual enquiry predominantly entailed contact with books. Even when archaeological remains first began to be described, there was a tendency for authors to quote earlier reports of finds rather than to add to them (Hunter 1971, 114). Indeed, an attitude of this kind was still in evidence in one visitor to Avebury in the early 18th century, John Saunders, a servant, whose description of the physical features of the site seems mainly to comprise a paraphrase of that which had appeared in Holland's edition of Camden's *Britannia* a century earlier, though he embroidered this with speculations about the origins both of Avebury and of Silbury. He noted how 'Avebery is compassed about with a wall ditch which was thrown up in wars they say 1000 years before Christ, thare is two large stones as you enter the town which they call gates, there is many large stones standing up as big as those at Stone edge' (Meyrick 1959, 225).

Apart from the significance of the new science in instilling greater interest in such remains, it also had implications for the way in which our observers approached them, for all were imbued with the ethos of careful, empirical investigation championed by Francis Bacon. Aubrey's whole life was dominated by his devotion to the collection of accurate information, whether in his biographical writings or in his natural history. His famous *Brief Lives* contained, as he put it, 'nothing but the trueth: the naked and plaine trueth'; he made similar claims for his records of antiquities, in which he was anxious not to trust others but to rely 'on my owne Eiesight'. His aspiration to accuracy in his biographical writings is shown by his care to change adjectives so as not to be guilty of overstatement, and comparable revision to achieve greater precision is in evidence in the manuscript of his 'Templa Druidum' (Hunter 1975, 82, 180, 75 and passim).

As for Charleton, the seriousness with which his testimony was taken by his colleagues in the Royal Society is displayed by the frequency with which he was asked to investigate topics of interest and the prominent role that he played in carrying out anatomical dissections at the Society's behest. Moray, too, was associated closely with the Society's stress on painstaking experiment and recording in its early years (Birch 1756–7, i, passim), while a generation later Stukeley exemplifies the same ethos: an active Fellow of the Society and the *confidant* of Newton himself, he showed a lively interest in a wide range of natural phenomena and was capable of perceptive astronomical observations which stimulated others to novel theorization (Hoskin 1985). Moreover he echoed this ethos in his writings on Avebury, justifying the pains that he took on the grounds that 'I was resolvd to impose nothing upon the world but what I firmly beleive my self & am fully satisfyd of' (Stukeley 1722–4b, 197). This gives a *prima facie* case for presuming that such men were at least attempting to record what they saw as accurately as possible.

On the other hand, none of them was without his lapses. In Aubrey's case, this was trenchantly expressed by the naturalist John Ray, who criticized him for being 'a little too inclinable to credit strange relations', an evaluation with which posterity may in certain respects concur. In addition, his recording was sometimes executed more haphazardly than might have been wished, with the result that crucial topics, even in his description of Avebury, were dealt with disappointingly briefly (Hunter 1975, 133 and passim). As for Charleton, he too was fallible, as seen in an 'error' that he made in reporting the results of a dissection in 1664, which was 'spread by his very positive affirmations' and, as Henry Oldenburg noted in recording the matter, 'addeth but very little to his credit' (Oldenburg 1966, 280–1). With Stukeley, the acerbic Thomas Hearne was scathing about the value of his work, dismissing him as early as 1722 as 'a very fancifull Man', and adding: ''tis observed by all that I have talked with that what he does hath no manner of likeness to the original ... Though he be a Physician, yet I am informed he knows very little or nothing of the matter'. Moreover Piggott has noted evidence of 'sheer carelessness' on Stukeley's part even in his supposedly 'sound' period (Piggott 1985, 71–2). Simple error, therefore, is one potential explanation of discrepancies in our evidence.

In addition, with the possible exception of Stukeley, it is easy to overestimate the amount of attention that any of our observers gave to the site. This applies even to Aubrey, since, perhaps because of his originality in offering any full account of Avebury at all, some commentators may unconsciously have exaggerated the amount of time that he spent in systematically surveying the antiquity. We have already seen how he did not spend a great deal of time in Wiltshire after the 1660s and the loss of his estates, but even before that he may have devoted less attention to fieldwork of this kind than some have presumed, valuable as are the records that he preserved. 'My head was alwaies working; never idle, and even travelling (which from 1649 till 1670 was never off my horsback) did gleane som observations', he wrote (Aubrey 1898, i.42), and it is significant that he noted of the length of the Avenue from Avebury to West Kennet: 'A showre of raine hindred me from measuring it', thus suggesting that this recording was attempted on only one occasion (Aubrey 24, 34; Fowles and Legg 1980, 37).[2] As for Charleton, we have seen how his record must have been compiled on a visit or visits to Avebury during the months between the time when Aubrey alerted him to the true interest of the site and his presentation to the Royal Society in July 1663, while Moray may only have been there once, or at most twice (see Chapter I, n. 15). Only in Stukeley's case is there evidence of prolonged and sustained fieldwork, though even he felt that the fortnight or so that he spent there annually 'was not a quarter enough to see everything' (Stukeley 1887, 246).

To this lack of time has to be added the difficulties that these men encountered, notably, as already mentioned, the encumbered physical state of the monument. Even when the impediments had been overcome to the extent of noticing that stone arrangements at Avebury existed at all, it is easy to understand how independent observers could misconstrue the overall structure of the antiquity or miss some subsidiary features which others saw. Even of the stones at Stonehenge, John Evelyn complained in his diary how 'To number them exactly, is very-difficult, in such variety of postures they lie & confusion' (Evelyn 1955, iii.116), and the obstacles at Avebury were far greater. This goes far towards explaining some of the discrepancies between the plans, such as the concentric rings which, in plan C, Aubrey construed the internal features of the site to comprise, or the absence of a circle surrounding the Cove in Charleton's plan D. In particular, the impediments clearly encouraged an impressionistic view of the antiquity as a whole, while in cases where greater accuracy *was* attempted – as with Aubrey's plane-table survey, of which more will be said below (ii) and in Chapter III (A.15) – there is reason to believe that the sheer size of the antiquity created difficulties, necessitating sighting from one quadrant of the site to another through gaps in the houses and other encumbrances, a technique which induced an understandable proneness to error.

The result is that we need to find a means of sifting the record that has come down to us, so that we reject the more subjective in favour of the more definitive: certainly, where testimony conflicts, a direct statement or detailed drawing is to be preferred to a vague, small-scale or derivative sketch, or a plan in which features appear to have been extended for the sake of completeness. Thus a number of Charleton's clear statements in the captions to plan D have unambiguous evidential value, to an extent that is not the case with certain rather sketchy depictions of features on the site, and such issues will be taken up in connection with the Cove and other facets of the antiquity in Chapter IV.

ii. Precedents and standards

It is also important to recognize that, for all the good intentions of these men, they had much to learn about the task of recording which they undertook. The tradition of what might be called archaeological draughtsmanship was rudimentary in the extreme, particularly at the time when Aubrey and Charleton made their studies of the site (see Piggott 1965). There were no established standards as to how antiquities should be depicted, what degree of accuracy was desirable, or even whether it was better to show the antiquity exactly as it was – or as it appeared at the time when fieldwork was executed, as against when it was written up – or to attempt to reconstruct its original state. In addition, there was no established terminology to describe such work. Aubrey refers variously to 'surveys', 'plans' and 'reviews', and there does not seem to be any significant distinction between these: insofar as he employed different words, this was not least for stylistic reasons, to avoid re-using the same word too often (see also Chapter I, n. 1). Hence various observations are in order not just about *what* our different authors observed, but *how* they went about it.

The clearest exemplar was Inigo Jones' depiction of Stonehenge in *Stoneheng Restored*, in plans and elevations which seem to show the influence of two-dimensional architectural illustrations like those to be found in the works of Palladio, Barbaro or Serlio (Wittkower 1967; Chippindale 1983, 57–9). Jones was also influenced by his Vitruvian architectural principles, which made him presume that the monument had originally had a regularity which time had eroded. An alternative graphic tradition encouraged a desire for three-dimensional verisimilitude: this was reflected – if crudely – in the earliest engravings of Stonehenge, that by 'R.F.' dated 1575 and the versions derived from this which were included in editions of Camden's *Britannia* from 1600 onwards (Bakker 1979; Chippindale 1983, 33–6; Camden 1600, 219; Camden 1610, 252). Further rather rudimentary engravings of megaliths, which bear some similarity to these, appeared in Olaus Worm's *Danicorum Monumentorum Libri Sex* (1643), a work well known to English antiquaries of the day (Hunter 1971, 117). Charleton was clearly familiar with Worm's book long before he made his plan of Avebury, as we have seen, while Aubrey also knew the work: it was on Worm's title that he based that of his *Monumenta Britannica*, the section in which on 'Danish Antiquitics' included several pages of notes from Worm's text and copies of his illustrations (Hunter 1975, 201–2; Aubrey 25, 75ff.; Fowles and Legg 1982, 854ff.).

Of these precedents, the most important was that of Jones, but his influence was mixed. Aubrey, Charleton and Stukeley were all highly critical of his depiction of Stonehenge on the grounds that 'he framed the monument to his own Hypothesis, which is much differing from the Thing it self', as Aubrey put it in his 'Templa Druidum', in language redolent of the Baconian ethos of the early Royal Society (Aubrey 24, 24; Fowles and Legg 1980, 20; cf. Hunter 1975, 179–80). Indeed, this arguably gave them a shared incentive to accuracy as chroniclers of megalithic antiquities, since each would surely have had his own critique of Jones in mind as he composed his record. In *Chorea Gigantum*, as we saw in Chapter I, Charleton had gone so far in rejecting Jones' interpretation as to adjudge Camden's rather stylized view to be preferable (it is curious that, at this point, it seems not to have occurred to him to do a fresh drawing of his own).

On the other hand, Charleton's plan of Avebury bears quite a close similarity to Jones' of Stonehenge, particularly in the way in which the stones are 'blocked out' in rectangular form and cross-hatched. In addition, Charleton's linking of a commentary to his plan by the use of capital letters is clearly derived from Jones' book, as conceivably may be his use of words like 'Architrave' to describe megaliths (Jones 1655, 56–64). The degree to which Charleton schematized the monument and made it symmetrical bears a close relationship to Jones' technique, despite his criticism of the earlier writer on just this score, while it is even possible that he was influenced by details of Jones' account of Stonehenge such as 'the great stones which made the entrances' (Jones 1655, 57).

The same ambivalence towards Jones recurs even in the 18th century. For

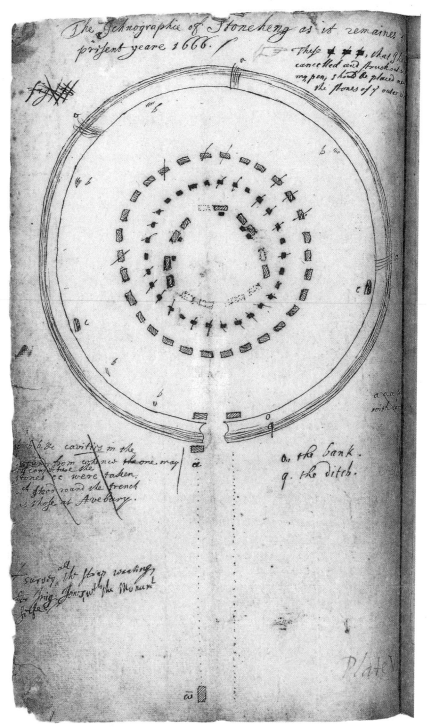

Plate 16 Aubrey's 'Ichnographie of Stoneheng as it remaines this present yeare 1666', based on, and correcting, Inigo Jones' plan in his *Stoneheng Restored* (1655) (Bodleian Library ms. Top. Gen. C. 24, 64v).

instance, Jones' plan of Stonehenge was reproduced virtually unaltered by Stukeley's friend, the German antiquary and Fellow of the Royal Society J. G. Keysler, in his *Antiquitates Selectae Septentrionales et Celticae* (1720) (Keysler 1720, figs. vi–vii; see Piggott 1985, 82). In addition, as we saw in Chapter I, Stukeley's own earliest plans of the antiquity were derived directly from Jones'. Subsequently, Stukeley professed himself critical of these early drawings: the dissatisfaction with Jones' account of the site that he expressed in his presentation to the Royal Society in 1719 has already been cited, and both his published and unpublished writings on Stonehenge were to include lengthy sections criticizing both Jones and his son-in-law and vindicator, John Webb, for their delineation of the antiquity as well as their theorization about it (Eng.Misc.c.306, 87; Stukeley 1722–4b, 85ff., 97ff.; 1722–4c; 1740, passim). Instead, Stukeley compiled more than one plan of Stonehenge, starting with that which he made when he first actually visited the antiquity in May 1719, in which he attempted accurately to indicate the positions and shape of both standing and fallen stones (Gough Maps 33, 2v; Gough Maps 229, passim, esp. 61–2; Top.Gen.b.53, 23v–4). Yet, despite all this, in his published *Stonehenge* he included only a 'Geometrical Ground-plot' together with profiles of the monument when complete, which bear a family resemblance to the earlier antiquary's illustrations (Stukeley 1740, tabs. xi et seq., xxiii).

Aubrey, too, followed Jones in his plan of Stonehenge (Plate 16), insofar as it comprised a corrected version of Jones' own (Aubrey 24, 64v; Fowles and Legg 1980, 80). At Avebury, however, his technique was different (this possibly supports the hypothesis that his recording work at Avebury began before he came across Jones' book: see Chapter I, ii). In his earliest essay, plan C, he attempted, not a two-dimensional plan, but a cross between this and a three-dimensional depiction: thus the stones, houses and other features are shown in profile in spirited sketches which display the talent as a draughtsman that is also in evidence elsewhere among Aubrey's manuscripts (Hunter 1975, 39, pls 1–5). He also tried to give profiles of the stones, while a further air of verisimilitude was given by his attempt to do justice to the imperfection of the surviving circles in his delineation of the irregularity of stone emplacements.

We will assess the accuracy of these details and of the general disposition of the features of the antiquity in this plan more fully in Chapter IV. Here, what is significant is the methodological development which appears to be in evidence in the transition from this plan to plan A. Not only does plan A revise the internal arrangement of the stones, presumably as a result of more careful scrutiny of the site in the light of the conflicting testimony of Charleton's plan D. In addition, Aubrey clearly decided that a plan should be a plan, in two dimensions only, and the stones were depicted accordingly – though, since they were irregular in shape, he did not 'square them off' as Charleton had in his plan. Instead – using a technique which he had evidently devised for himself – he showed them diagrammatically in inked and colour-washed shapes. The profile of the bank and ditch that he included was also two-dimensional, and, though three-dimensional drawings of the Cove, the church and other features appear in the margins, it is quite possible that these were added retrospectively, perhaps derived from the earlier plan C or some intermediate version (see Chapter III, A.5).

In making plan A, as we saw in Chapter I, Aubrey chose in the pursuit of clarity to 'disempester' the scheme of most of the intrusions of the village (see below). More significant, it was now that he decided to use surveying techniques to achieve greater accuracy in delineating the ditch and rampart surrounding the site. The background to this advance in sophistication on Aubrey's part is not entirely clear. Surveying was, of course, widely used for practical purposes in 17th-century England, and in the educational treatise that he wrote Aubrey urged that young gentlemen should be trained to use such techniques; he also understood mathematics and trigonometry and owned various mathematical instruments (Hunter 1975, 50 nn. 6–7, 90 n. 4; Turner 1973; Welfare 1989). But it is not known how expert he himself was as a field surveyor, and hardly any records of such surveying work are to be found among his extant remains.[3] He also says virtually nothing about the methods that he used or who assisted him in the task: indeed, he only gave one hint that it even involved an assistant, when he used the word 'us' in connection with his survey of the Kennet Avenue, a word that he then altered to 'me' (Aubrey 24, 34; Fowles and Legg 1980, 37). His surveying technique will be further discussed in Chapter III (A.15), where we will also assess what can be learnt about the actual execution of his survey from a reconstruction of it.

Stukeley also used surveying techniques. In his *Stonehenge*, he explains how 'I examined their works for several years together, with sufficient accuracy, with a *theodolite*', while in his notes he refers at various points to instruments that he employed, including a chain and an instrument with sights, presumably a theodolite, though it might have been a compass (Stukeley 1740, 64; Eng.Misc.b.65, 83; Gough Maps 231, 3; Turner 1973, 78–9). Stukeley's use of such instruments was particularly important, as we will see later in this chapter, partly because he believed that the layout of Avebury had a geometrical precision over a larger area than could be surveyed with the naked eye, and partly because he thought that the orientation both of the antiquity as a whole and of its component parts might be significant; as a result he preserved very extensive records of compass bearings (Gough Maps 231, passim; Stukeley 1722–4c, inserted leaf). In addition, he recorded measurements within the henge itself, not least in the hitherto unnoticed plan that has already been referred to (Eng.Misc.c.533, 53v–4; see Chapter I, viii) (Plate 15).

Using data like this, together with his skills as a draughtsman, Stukeley drew up the various draft plans which are discussed in full in Chapter III. In all but one of these – in contrast to Aubrey's plan A and going much beyond Aubrey's plan C – Stukeley opted for elements at least of a three-dimensional view, in which the existing village as well as the antiquity were fully depicted. His drawing technique shows the influence of the tradition of topographical engraving which had developed from pioneering efforts of the Elizabethan period like the views of Stonehenge already mentioned. In late 17th- and early 18th-century England this flourished in the work of such artists as David Loggan – whose views of Stonehenge have already been referred to – and Jan Kip in his *Britannia Illustrata* (1707–8), while Stukeley himself made a contribution through the extensive plates that he prepared for his *Itinerarium Curiosum* and other works. But the gain in three-dimensional verisimilitude came at the expense of mensurational accuracy. It was perhaps partly because it was difficult to depict them in any other way in a three-dimensional format that Stukeley showed the ditch and rampart as essentially circular (though see further below), while the inclusion of stone placements in a three-dimensional 'view' also detracted from accuracy in the exact plotting of them.

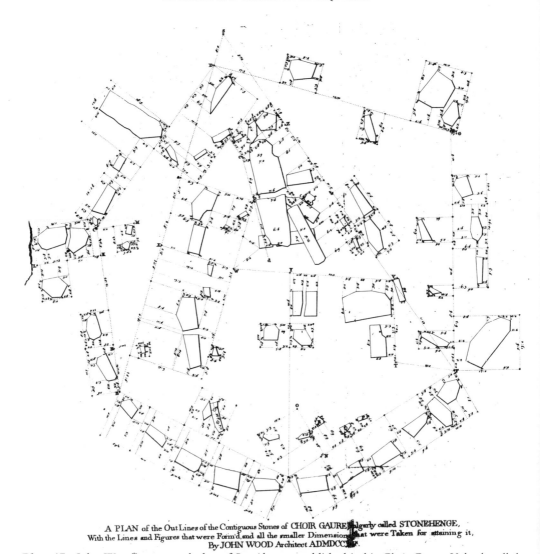

A PLAN of the Out Lines of the Contiguous Stones of CHOIR GAURE vulgarly called STONEHENGE, With the Lines and Figures that were Form'd, and all the smaller Dimensions that were Taken for attaining it, By JOHN WOOD Architect ADMDCC.

Plate 17 John Wood's measured plan of Stonehenge, published in his *Choir Gaure, Vulgarly called Stonehenge, on Salisbury Plain, Described, Restored, and Explained* (1747).

What Stukeley failed to execute at Avebury was an equivalent of the highly exact but purely two-dimensional plan of the disposition of stones at Stonehenge that was made in the early 18th century by the architect John Wood, and published in his *Choir Gaure, Vulgarly called Stonehenge, on Salisbury Plain, Described, Restored, and Explained* (1747) (Plate 17). Wood plotted the dimensions of the base of each stone in the antiquity, relating their positions to a geometrical grid of the site as a means of producing 'as accurate a Plan of the whole Work as the Nature of it can admit' (Wood 1747, 48). He was evidently inspired in this by an exemplar in antiquarian illustration which, since Aubrey's and Charleton's time, had taken the measured description of the remains of ancient buildings far beyond anything that pioneers like Jones had known. This was the work of Antoine Desgodetz, whose *Les Edifices*

68

Antiques de Rome Dessinés et Mesurés Tres Exactement (1682) comprised, as its title promised, a series of plans and elevations of the classical buildings of Rome measured with the utmost precision. But, though Stukeley as well as Wood knew Desgodetz' book, Stukeley claimed that 'Tis not to be suppos'd, that in this work [*Stonehenge*], the minuteness and extreme curiosity of *Desgodetz*, with which he measur'd the remains of old *Rome*, is expected, or even possible' (Stukeley 1740, 11; cf. Wood 1747, 43, 48). Indeed, he criticized Wood for 'mesuring [sic] of the stones, designed to be rude, as if they were the most nice and curious Grecian pillars in any of their capital temples': this, however, perhaps represents special pleading, since it formed part of a vitriolic response to Wood's criticism of his *Stonehenge* (Stukeley 1887, 275; Mowl and Earnshaw 1988, 25), while, as we have seen, Stukeley had himself prepared more accurate plans of Stonehenge than any that appeared in his published treatise.

As all this demonstrates, it was by no means self-evident how an antiquity like Avebury was best depicted, and the intentions of those who made the records need to be taken into account in assessing the evidence provided. Clearly some – like Charleton in plan D – intended only to give a general idea of the site and its component parts, in contrast to others who aimed to furnish an accurately surveyed depiction of all its details. As will be seen in later chapters, a number of apparent discrepancies between the different records can be explained in these terms. Here, we can note a related question, of how far the authors of the plans thought that they should diverge from exactitude of recording in order to reconstruct what they perceived as the original intention of the builders. A case in point concerns the shape of the ditch and bank, for whereas in plan A Aubrey went to the trouble of surveying their irregularities, others showed them as a simple circle, including Stukeley in plan E, as we have seen. Moreover, though Stukeley has often been criticized for this (e.g. King 1879, 378n.), he himself observes:

> 'tis manifest to an ordinary eye that the ditch about Abury is not a mathematical circle owing to the difficulty of getting a rope of sufficient length to strike it withal[:] therefore its done plainly by guess, but the intention is notoriously circular & in such an extent the Cavils are of no consequence & disregarded in my scheme[;] but the lesser circles within the work are very exact. (Gough Maps 231, 48v)[4]

Charleton might similarly have justified plan D or Aubrey plan C on the grounds that the earthwork and the stone settings inside it were clearly meant to be circular – in that they were more like a circle than any other form, such as an oval – while Sir Robert Moray actually observed of the Sanctuary how it comprised '2 Circles or figures intended for Circles as it seemes' (see Appendix I).

Even Aubrey's plan A shows an element of this 'perfecting' tendency. In Chapter I we quoted his commentary in which he justified 'disempestering' the antiquity in pursuit of 'the reall Designe', and this phrase has two possible constructions. One – perhaps the likelier – is that Aubrey meant 'the object of the exercise', in other words that thus the position of the stones could be more clearly seen. But it is also possible that he meant that he was reconstructing the original state of the monument, using the word 'real' in the sense deployed by his friends – John Wilkins and others – who hoped to introduce a 'Real Character': a clear and rational language directly related to what was perceived as the nature of reality, and freed from the obfuscation of existing tongues. Such an aim would echo Aubrey's claim concerning the Druids in another of his antiquarian writings, that 'some of their Temples I pretend to have restored: as Avebury, Stoneheng &c' (Hunter 1975, 60–1, 174–5). If this were the case, however, it is perhaps surprising that he did not omit the 'crosse-street' within the monument, which, as he put it, was not original but 'was made in process of time for the convenience of the Rodes' (Aubrey 24, 36–7; Fowles and Legg 1980, 39, 41) – probably, he retained the streets to assist in orienting the position of the stones, suggesting that clarity rather than reconstruction was his aim.

In any case, even concerning his aspiration to 'restore' these antiquities Aubrey's intentions have to be taken into account, for by restore he meant not so much 'to reconstruct their original form' as 'to return them to their proper ownership', and it has to be remembered that Aubrey's purpose in his 'Templa Druidum' was only partly to give an account of Avebury and Stonehenge. Equally important was his intention to enter into the debate about the origins of megaliths which had been begun by Jones and Charleton, and to indicate 'by comparative Arguments' their prehistoric date. For this purpose, fairly superficial data about stone circles from a wide area were in many ways as important as details about even the most remarkable specimens, and an appreciation of this helps to explain some of the frustrating loose ends that Aubrey left in his description of Avebury, making it easier to understand why his record is slightly disappointing to those looking for clues as to the exact state of the site in his day (Aubrey 24, 25v; Fowles and Legg 1980, 24; cf. Hunter 1975, 158–9, 182).

iii. Preconceptions: Aubrey and Charleton

This raises the still broader question of what it was that these men thought that they were studying, how this may have affected their record of it – including which details they saw as significant and which as insignificant – and how they were prone to interpret what they saw. Here we may recapitulate and extrapolate from some of the material introduced in Chapter I. Aubrey, Charleton and Stukeley were agreed on certain things. All rejected – in Aubrey's and Stukeley's case explicitly, in Charleton's implicitly – the chief earlier hypothesis concerning Avebury, namely Philemon Holland's view that it was a 'Campe'. This was a plausible enough assumption in the light of the nature of most large earthworks in the south of England: but, as Aubrey perceptively deduced (see Chapter I, ii), it was inconsistent with the mutual relationship of bank and ditch, a point which Stukeley elaborated, conjecturing how spectators might have been accommodated on the rampart (Stukeley 1743, 28). In addition, as we have seen, all rejected Jones' theory that Stonehenge – and, by extension, other megaliths – were of Roman origin.

At this point, however, our two earliest commentators, Aubrey and Charleton, disagreed, and this disagreement no doubt provides the background to such rivalry between the two men as there is evidence for, as in Aubrey's criticism of Charleton's thesis of the Danish origins of Stonehenge as a 'gross mistake' (see Chapter I, iv). While Charleton argued for the Danish origins of megaliths, Aubrey saw them as prehistoric: this had clear implications for their perception of Avebury and arguably also for the way in which they approached the site, either initially or throughout their acquaintance with it.

Taking Charleton first, although he included in his book some general reflections on monumental structures and why they were erected, his expectations were clearly formed by his reading of – and correspondence with – Olaus Worm (Charleton 1663, 1f., 59ff. and passim). It was Worm whom he followed in his rather artificial categorization of megalithic antiquities according to the different functions which he claimed that they served – as places of judicature, sites of regal elections and inaugurations, or sepulchral monuments. As we have seen, this was probably the source of his suggestion that Avebury might contain a king's monument, though such a use was apparently not entirely exclusive of other functions, since he seems to have considered that Stonehenge might have had both a funerary and an electoral role. Equally important, parallels between the wording of Charleton's captions and some of his comments about similar monuments in his *Chorea Gigantum* indicate his expectations about the likely function, not only of such antiquities as a whole, but of individual features within them.

Thus, in discussing 'Sepulchres', he associated tumuli of earth with the graves of common soldiers, arguing that, though these had sometimes been used to mark the graves of dead worthies, this had only occurred when stones were unavailable to erect 'Pyramids and Obelisques' 'of the largest size they could possibly get' (Charleton 1663, 39). In a further passage in *Chorea Gigantum*, Charleton noted that such mausolea were usually provided with altars at which sacrifices were offered (Charleton 1663, 40). He cited Worm concerning an antiquity in Denmark which comprised 'an Altar made up of four stones of stupendious magnitude, so as three standing in Triangle, support the fourth upon their heads, which is the greatest of all, and plain or flat' (Charleton 1663, 38 (from Worm 1643, 8), cf. 41). To compare this passage with his caption describing the Cove in plan D appears to indicate that he may have believed that the Cove was at the same time both a king's monument *and* an altar.

It is perhaps more fruitful to take this point in conjunction with the passages from Charleton's book already quoted in Chapter I concerning the Obelisk and its surrounding circle and about 'Kongstolon' at Stonehenge and perhaps also Avebury. It seems clear that Charleton had been alerted by his studies of Scandinavian megaliths to look for particularly large stones with specific functions and for features like smaller circles within the outer one. This may help to explain why – in contrast to Aubrey's initial perception of the arrangement of the antiquity as concentric, with the Cove almost as an anomaly – it was Charleton who made the breakthrough of seeing the inner structure of the monument as focused on particular features. We can be more specific still, since both verbal and visual descriptions in Worm's book would have made Charleton familiar with the idea of a dolmen (for an illustration, see that reproduced from Worm in Chippindale 1983, 63). This does much to explain Charleton's interpretation of the fourth Cove stone as a former capping stone.

As for Aubrey, though he too knew Worm's work, his conviction that Avebury was prehistoric made him look elsewhere for analogues, particularly to types of structure to be found in widely scattered areas with no common denominator in the historical period. Such antiquities might almost be deemed archetypal, and this was arguably separate from the association of them with the Druids, though, as we shall see, the two overlapped, for it is worth noting that Aubrey was more certain that these remains were prehistoric than that they were Druidic. Thus in his preface to 'Templa Druidum', he carefully distinguished the two phases of his argument, separating his conviction on comparative grounds that such monuments were prehistoric, from the '*probability*, that they were *Temples* of the *Druids*' (Aubrey 24, 25v; Fowles and Legg 1980, 24). Moreover, he appears subsequently to have had characteristically querulous second thoughts about the Druid connection, noting at some point on the back of plan A how 'I now thinke it a surer way to say, Monuments erected by the Britains',[5] and hence explaining the title that he gave to the whole of his book dealing mainly with prehistoric antiquities (Aubrey 24, 39; Fowles and Legg 1980, 43).

Though it has not hitherto been recognized, the two components of his attribution gave Aubrey two overlapping sources for his expectation as to the type of monument that Avebury might be expected to represent. The first concerned the origins of buildings in general. Here, we are in a milieu in which – despite the dawning of a scepticism of which Aubrey was aware but the implications of which he did not work out (Hunter 1975, 59) – most people presumed that the early history of the world was accurately encapsulated in the Bible. It was therefore to the Bible and related sources that they went for information on the beginnings of architecture, and this is precisely what Aubrey did. In a passage that he intended for insertion in the preface to 'Templa Druidum', he wrote:

> See Genesis chap.   v. They built an Altar, and then men began to worship the Lord. At first Altars were upon Hills; which after were invironed with stones placed in a circle sub dio [i.e., 'sub divo', under the open sky] as in the following Monuments, and in after ages they grew to be Temples, which were covered. (Aubrey 24, 17v; Fowles and Legg 1980, 27; cf. Aubrey 1972, 149)[6]

Though it is true that the books of *Genesis* and *Exodus* have various references to altars being erected, in at least one case on a hill, while *Exodus* and *II Kings* refer to the erection of pillars, in the former case twelve in number, no reference is there made to their being in circular form. On the other hand, the idea that sacred buildings had originated thus was widely shared in the period. For instance, John Evelyn's view of Stonehenge was very similar: he considered it 'rudly representing a Cloyster, or heathen & more natural Temple' (Evelyn 1955, iii.116). A related belief was that groves of trees had formed the original sacred sites: thus Sir Christopher Wren saw temples with pillars as replacing such groves as the surroundings to 'cellae'; he also saw 'Walks of Trees' as the origins of 'Porticoes of Marble', and it is interesting to compare with this notion Aubrey's and Moray's view of the Avebury/Overton stone avenues, both of whom likened them to avenues of trees (Wren 1750, 354–5; Aubrey 24, 34; Fowles and Legg 1980, 37; Appendix I).

Hence stone circles and avenues could in a sense be seen as primeval sacred buildings. But this was not altogether exclusive of a complementary theory, namely that the temples of the Druids – those intriguing Celtic priests mentioned by Tacitus and other classical authors – were in fact stone circles. Again, this was current in the early modern period, and it overlapped with the former idea in that the Druids were believed, either originally or additionally, to have worshipped in groves. The notion that stone circles were Druid monuments is earliest to be found in 1535, in William Stewart's metrical rendering of Hector Boece's *Scotorum Historiae a Prima Gentis Origine* of 1526, though there is no evidence that Aubrey was aware of this (Owen 1962, 30–1). What he *was* aware of was a connection between the Druids and stones made by Camden in his record of the placename '*Cerigy Drudion*, that is, *The stones of the Druidae*' (Camden 1610, 675). Aubrey saw this as 'the Hinge of this Discourse', and he professed the wish to investigate it further by inspecting for himself the monument to which this name had been given: indeed, he protested in the preface to 'Templa Druidum' that his ambition to fulfil this aim was a contributory factor to the delay in that work's completion. He also gathered further evidence associating the Druids with stone circles (Aubrey 24, 25; Fowles and Legg 1980, 22–3; cf. Owen 1962, 41–2, 105; Hunter 1975, 182–3).

Whether stone circles were archetypal or Druidic, however, this clearly gave Aubrey an expectation of *circularity*, and this may explain why initially he looked for concentric circles in his reconstruction of the site, as seen in plan C. When he revised this in the light of Charleton's assertion of the existence of a circle in the south-east quadrant, his preconceptions are again in evidence, as the text of 'Templa Druidum' shows. For – just as in his collection of folklore Aubrey conflated relics of 'Judaisme' and 'Gentilisme' (Hunter 1975, 169n) – so he combined classical with biblical evidence in interpreting antiquities. Thus he spoke of the inner circles as 'sacella', using the classical word for unroofed shrines (he also conflated antique with more modern experience in his belief that, in the same way that Christian churches could contain many chapels, so there could be several sacella within a single temple). Moreover, in noting that these were 'roundish' rather than exactly circular, he compared them with the constellation of Ariadne's Crown as described by Ovid. He also used the concept of 'Corona' or 'Crowne' to describe the outer circle, and he seems to have seen such allusions, not just as stylistic embellishments, but as genuine elucidations of the antiquities, possibly believing that the circle might bear an intentional resemblance to the irregular constellation so described, of which various depictions existed in the 17th century (Aubrey 24, 32–3; Fowles and Legg 1980, 35–6; Ovid 1931, 154f.; and see Chapter III, A.12(e)).

In addition, it is clear from passing remarks by Aubrey that he visualized the kind of rites which might have taken place at Avebury, evidently on the basis of the knowledge of preChristian religion to be found in the writings of classical authors and Renaissance scholars: thus, for instance, he presumed that avenues were intended as processional ways (Aubrey 24, 34; Fowles and Legg 1980, 37). But he failed to elaborate such ideas in the manner in which, as we shall see, Stukeley was to, the furthest he went towards this being to append to his 'Templa Druidum' extracts illustrating the 'Religion and Manners of the Druids' taken from classical sources and from modern authors, including letters to him from James Garden of Aberdeen and others (Aubrey 24, 94ff.; Fowles and Legg 1980, 131ff.).

iv. Preconceptions: Stukeley

In Stukeley's case, the evidence for his expectations about the nature of the antiquity is even stronger, and it is to be stressed that this dates from the period when Stukeley was at work in the field, and that it was not simply a question of later preoccupations being artificially superimposed on 'hardheaded' earlier fieldwork (see Chapter I, ix). Stukeley's notes in his copy of the 1695 Camden, quoted above (Chapter I, vi), show that by 1714 he had ideas about the nature of the primeval buildings which stone circles exemplified which were quite similar to Aubrey's; thereafter, he greatly elaborated these through further study. By the early 1720s, his surviving manuscripts, 'Celtic Religion' and 'Celtic Temples', reveal him as widely read in such ancient authors as Herodotus, Pausanias and Eusebius, and in more recent ones, both writers of the 16th and 17th centuries like J. J. Scaliger, John Selden and Samuel Bochart, and contemporaries like Bernard de Montfaucon and his friend, J. G. Keysler.

As a result, it is clear that throughout his annual visits to the site between 1719 and 1724, Stukeley's mind was awash with opinions about ancient religion, its structures and symbolism. It is equally clear that he was convinced that such views would throw light on the 'Circles of Stones' to be found throughout the British Isles, 'calld at this time Druids Temples from long continued tradition & without doubt the Druids were their Authors, being the Priests of that vast People which we generally call the Celts' (Stukeley 1722–4b, 21). Indeed, whereas our knowledge of Aubrey's and Charleton's conceptions is based only on scattered hints, in Stukeley's case the available evidence concerning the way in which his ideas developed is profuse in the extreme, and our attempt to do justice to it will inevitably be lengthy.[7] Moreover, though Stukeley apparently began to write his treatises only in 1722, it seems likely that he had started to formulate the ideas contained in them earlier. Thus the notion that the inner temples at Avebury were dedicated to the Sun and Moon, which was elaborated in the original version of these texts, appears in titles to drawings executed in 1721 and 1722: though it is possible that these might have been added after their original composition, it is equally likely that they were integral to it.

In particular, Stukeley seems to have been fascinated – at this time as later – by the mysterious lore of ancient Egypt, as expounded by a succession of Renaissance scholars, reaching a climax with the Jesuit author Athanasius Kircher, whose influence on Sir Robert Moray has already been noted. Kircher's *magnum opus* was his *Oedipus Aegypticus* (1652–4), in which he tried to interpret Egyptian esotericism as an exposition of divine truths of timeless universality (Iversen 1961, 89f.; Godwin 1979, ch. 5; Evans 1979, 433f.; Curl 1982, 65f.). Clearly, this was a work that Stukeley studied and was greatly influenced by. Indeed, he seems increasingly to have taken it for granted that Egyptian antiquities were likely to throw light on Celtic ones. He paralleled the Druids with Egyptian priests and argued that Druidism 'had the same original founder & instructor' as Egyptian religion, the ancient and mysterious figure of Hermes Trismegistus, who was often believed in Stukeley's time to be a contemporary of Moses, although in fact the Hermetic writings are of early Christian date (Stukeley 1722–4b, 217). Nor is it surprising to find such beliefs in Stukeley at this stage, since it has long been known from his diary that in the early 1720s he was taking an interest in Egyptian and other antiquities and the Temple of Solomon, the relationship of which with Egyptian and other temples he was to discuss with Newton in 1726 (Stukeley 1882, 62, 69, 75, 78; cf. 1883, 262).

Though aware of the central role that Egypt played in theories about the early history of mankind, however, Stukeley seems initially to have preferred a view of sacred structures as archetypal, rather like Aubrey's. 'I find most Authors fond of deriving every thing very common in Religion from the Egyptians because the Greeks did but its not to be supposd of our northern nations,' he wrote. Instead, 'All mankind having the same original a great deal of similarity must run thro' their several modes & customs however they were scatterd & dispersd in distant Regions, but especially in what belongd to divine worship a great & universal principle in Nature' (Stukeley 1722–4a, 111, 123).[8] Like Aubrey, he cited the Old Testament together with classical authors in arguing how 'rude unshapen stones' formed the original sacred buildings, claiming that 'all this kind of Manner of building temples of single stones placd in circles perfectly agrees with the naturall notion one would conceive the first rude unpolishd people should practise' (Stukeley 1722–4a, 114).

Rejecting the idea that Stonehenge and comparable antiquities were Roman, he argued that, on the contrary, they were much older. In his view, such open, circular buildings were the prototypes from which classical buildings derived, with covered and rectangular ones being introduced at a later date, either by the Egyptians or by Solomon, the latter 'in imitation of Moses tabernacle which was square in contradiction to the heathen temples': on this topic, as on various others, he expressed at different points in his writings mutually inconsistent views which are not resolved (Stukeley 1722–4b, 210, cf. 229, 233; Stukeley 1776, 177). Moreover the structures which he expected to show similarities due to their common ancestry included those of the Persians as well as the Jews and the Egyptians: he devoted a lengthy section of his 'Celtic Temples' to an account of the ruins of Persepolis, which he believed to be a comparable open shrine built by people who shared the same ancestors, arguing that 'this shows that the notion of building open temples is most antient & probably antediluvian' (Stukeley 1722b, 219–29; cf. Stukeley 1740, 19, 46 and tab. xxxv).

As Stukeley's decision to devote a whole book to the religion as well as to the temples of the Celts shows, he considered it necessary to investigate what the archetypal religion was that was celebrated in such structures, and it was to fertile speculation on this subject that a good deal of his writing in the early 1720s was devoted. At the start of 'Celtic Religion', he set himself a kind of agenda which included 'the origin of religion' in addition to 'the propagation of mankind to which that of religion is annexd' (Stukeley 1722–4a, 1). He was convinced from the outset, on the basis of the synthesizing theories of Renaissance scholars, that monotheism was the original form of religious belief and that this was only later perverted into polytheism. Seeing the purpose of temples as to analogize the operations of God as a means of drawing down celestial blessings, therefore, he repeatedly returns to the idea of the circle – 'round & open' (Stukeley 1722–4b, 203) – as the perfect form for a temple devoted to the supreme being. This was based on man's understanding of nature in his primeval state:

The antient circular form of Temples most expressive of the nature of the deity without beginning or end, the most simple perfect & most comprehensive figure of one dimension

75

only[:] tis an imitation of the earth the heavens the globe of the sun & moon[,] the world. (Stukeley 1722–4a, 117)

Moreover, he believed that the rituals carried out – whether Celtic or Egyptian – were also circular 'in imitation of the celestial sphaeres', being 'but a larger practise of this going round in imitation of the planetary courses especially the sun' (Stukeley 1722–4a, 115, 120).

Although Stukeley considered monotheism archetypal, however, he was aware that early religions had also had a subordinate pantheon of divine agents, and it was to this that he looked for further elaboration of the significance of ancient religious structures and their component parts. In his 'Celtic Religion', Stukeley attempted a comparative analysis of the gods of different peoples, and the leading figures in each pantheon represented the Sun and Moon. It is therefore not surprising that it was to these that he initially presumed that the subordinate circles within the great circle at Avebury were dedicated, explaining:

> The first religion was philosophy, our temple was an epitome of Nature. The sun & moon are the principal agents or instruments of the soul of the world the father & mother, one furnishing heat & the other moisture whence all generation[,] the Liber & alma Ceres of Virgil. (Stukeley 1722–4b, 140)

Indeed, there were some authors who considered 'that all their Theology was reducible to the Sun & Moon', and, though Stukeley thought this 'too strict', he was undoubtedly influenced by these ideas (Stukeley 1722–4a, 3). Stukeley's invocation of such notions in connection with the inner circles is thus not unexpected, and it is worth pointing out that, though Piggott has suggested that his nomenclature might be derived from John Toland's 'Critical History of the Celtic Religion and Learning' (Piggott 1985, 94), it is far likelier that the two men independently derived the idea from the commonplaces of syncretist interpretation of ancient religion in which, as his manuscripts demonstrate, Stukeley was so fully soaked. (It may be added that Stukeley's reading on the ancient Egyptians is also a likelier source than Toland for his use of the concept of an 'obelisk'.)

It was to similar ideas that Stukeley looked in his interpretation of the other component parts of the antiquity, the Kennet and Beckhampton Avenues and the subordinate temples which (at the time he was initially composing these treatises) he believed to be at the end of each. Thus another of the figures whom he discerned in the mythology of the ancients was 'a common Erthus', 'the Mother Earth supposing she is particularly concerned in human affairs & goes from People to people' (Stukeley 1722–4a, 4), and it was to her that he presumed that the temple on Overton Hill was dedicated (see e.g. Eng.Misc.d.444, 62) (Plate 18). On the other hand, the Beckhampton temple he associated with the underworld, describing it as the temple of 'Manes' or 'The Temple of the Infernal Regions[?]' and associating it with Mercury, another of the gods of the standard pantheon, whose task it was to conduct the souls of the dead to Hades (Gough Maps 231, esp. 36v; Eng.Misc.b.65, 109). His view of the subordinate parts of the main henge was equally elaborate, as seen in the following passage concerning its 'Lunar Cove', which (as with many of these early ideas) has no direct equivalent in his published *Abury*. In his view, this represented:

Plate 18 Corrected proof of the engraving published as tab. xxi of *Abury*, showing Stukeley's original title to it of 'Temple of Ertha' (Bodleian Library MS. Gough Maps 231, 235).

no other than the great gate of the gods according to the Egyptian theology, or throne of the supreme mind, or of Isis, nature, the moon. it means the diffusion of the supreme mind to his subordinate ministers, as he is triform so thro' all the triform paths of the triform world we may call it the house of the Moon or of horus the world which from Plato we may show flows from a threefold archetype. (Stukeley 1722–4b, 130)

This shows how Stukeley's view of Avebury was affected by an increasing tendency to correlate Celtic antiquities with those of Egypt, the most elaborate primeval religion with which he was familiar. More and more, he came to see the significance of the stone circle at Avebury and its component parts in terms of the iconography of ancient Egypt, at one point going so far as to claim:

thus what the Egyptian priests many ages agoe contemplated with great devotion, cut on stones on the banks of the fruitful nile, we at home may survey from the top of the southern hills by Wansdike expanded in stones, in much larger dimensions, & I believe of not much less antiquity. (Stukeley 1722–4b, 232)

Perhaps the most extraordinary of all Stukeley's theories in his early manuscripts is to be found in a passage in his 'Celtic Temples' in which he compared Avebury to the Bembine Table, or Mensa Isiaca. This was an elaborate rectangular metal plate engraved with mythological figures and hieroglyphic ornaments surrounding an enthroned Isis, which had come to light in Rome in the early 16th century; though now thought to date from the reign of Claudius and to be a decadent artefact, the maker of which had not really understood the elements used to decorate it, in the 17th and 18th centuries it was frequently seen as 'The general Table of the Religion and Superstitions of Egypt' (Iversen 1961, 55–6; Godwin 1979, 65; Curl 1982, 51–2; Monfaucon 1721, ii.210). Stukeley clearly knew this through the work of Athanasius Kircher, who had published a lengthy commentary on it in his *Oedipus Aegypticus*; later, Stukeley intended that a treatise on the Table should form part of the work on patriarchal Christianity to which his published *Stonehenge* and *Abury* also belonged (Stukeley 1740, sig. a1).[9]

In his 'Celtic Temples' Stukeley drew a direct parallel between Avebury and the Bembine Table: both were 'designed as symbolic pictures of the Theology of their respective priests', the chief difference being that, whereas the Egyptians carved figures and symbols 'on stones & such like lasting materials', the Druids expounded their doctrine 'in the position of the stones, their number & site, which tho rudely yet discovers enough of identity'. The comparison was then elaborated in detail. For instance, the Obelisk in the middle of the southern temple at Avebury was compared to the figure of 'pantomorph Nature' at the centre of the Bembine Table, 'showing how the influx of the supreme mind is expanded & diffused as from a center thro' the universe to all the subordinate classes of Angels, genii, intelligences or ministers'. Similarly, the two sets of twelve genii on the table, representing the signs of the zodiac and the 'patres fontani' of classical mythology, were supposedly matched at Avebury 'by the 12 stones next the two central works or inner circles' (Stukeley 1722–4b, 217; see Chapter IV, w and x).[10]

As this illustrates, just as Stukeley sought a basic dedication to the deity and the two main luminaries, so he believed that other features might be found to reflect other components of the heavens, such as the twelve signs of the zodiac. Equally important was the significance that he saw in number itself, like many Renaissance scholars who – influenced by Pythagoras and other classical thinkers – believed that God had written nature in numerical form, and who saw geometry as essential to attaining knowledge of divine things. That Stukeley should have partaken of such beliefs at this stage is hardly surprising, for in 1720 he had written a treatise on 'The Musick of the Spheres', in which Pythagorean ideas about the harmonic structure of the world were expounded and interpreted (Eng.Misc.c.401, 51ff.). It was to such notions that he now looked, believing that the Druids had much in common with Pythagoras and even going so far as to argue at one point that 'his doctrine is so like our druids that if he learnt it not from there its plain theirs & the egyptian was the same' (Gough Maps 231, 31v).

Clearly Stukeley expected that a sacred structure like Avebury would be deeply imbued with numerical symbolism, and the way in which this interest worked in its application to the site may be illustrated by a quotation which invokes a range of elements in connection with the significance which, as we have already seen, he believed the Egyptians attached to the three-fold power of the deity:

> so the center of the lunar circle is composd of a triad of stones. so are the other coves. so within the ditch there may be said to be 3 distinct temples, each consisting of 3 parts, two circles & the central work or a great circle & two temples. (Stukeley 1722–4b, 216)

He then went on to offer similar comments on the number thirty, believing that each of the outer concentric circles surrounding the Cove and Obelisk had originally comprised thirty stones: he saw significance in the fact that this was made up of 'twice 12 & 6', adding how 'nature consists of innumerable combinations of numbers resolvd or joind being aliquots & having regular ratio's to one another'. If this theme was implicitly Trinitarian, there was also a dualist element, seen when he writes in an adjacent passage:

> and as the Egyptians held an unity or monas of God likewise a trias, & a dyas so we have the dyas here in many respects in the two temples, solar & lunar, in their two component circles, in the two outermost great circles, in the two circles of the temple on Overton hill[,] in the two avenues. (Stukeley 1722–4b, 216)[11]

The number four was significant as 'the fountain of perpetual nature, the idea of all created things', while seven was significant not only because it was the number of the planets (and the days of the week), but also because it was the sum of three, the first 'whole odd number', and four, the first 'whole equal number', the combination of which 'signifys the Universe' (Stukeley 1722–4a, 3; Stukeley 1722–4b, 215, 218). This must have been why he wanted to see the whole antiquity as made up of seven component parts – 'so are there properly 7 temples in our work of Abury', he noted by allusion to the Bembine Table – comprising the great circle with its two inner ones, the two avenues and the two temples at either end of them (Stukeley 1722–4b, 217); it also turned out that the stones in the avenues were generally placed at seventy foot intervals (Gough Maps 231, 8v). On the other hand, these intervals were sometimes 'near 100 foot', while the overall length of the avenue was 1000 foot, both

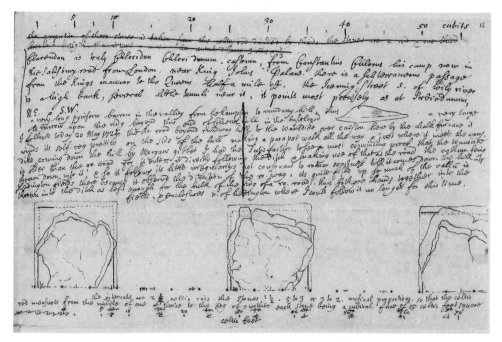

Plate 19 One of Stukeley's drawings attempting to work out the geometrical proportions of the profiles of the stones and the intervening spaces at Avebury, together with fieldnotes (Bodleian Library MS. Gough Maps 231, 15).

of them multiples of another significant number for Stukeley, ten, thought by 'the Egyptians & from them the Pythagoreans' to be 'symbolical of the complement of all things', a topic on which, as on the potency of other numbers, he cited his mentor, Kircher (Gough Maps 231, 8v; Stukeley 1722–4b, 251). Hence he was hardly surprised to find that the main circle of the henge itself comprised 'the compleat number of 100 stones' and that it was 1000 foot in diameter (Stukeley 1722–4b, 132, 216). Moreover, at one point he claimed that the whole monument when complete had comprised 800 stones, analogous to a complete eighth in music (Stukeley 1722–4b, 175).

This was bound up with a further presumption on Stukeley's part, of considerable sophistication on the part of the builders of Avebury. His elaborate theoretical superstructure convinced him concerning this and comparable monuments that 'these antient Philosophers (their founders) seem to have had as much variety in their sacred architecture, as those Nations said to be more polite': indeed, he compared their 'most incomparable dexterity' with that of modern architects like Wren (Stukeley 1722–4b, 23; Gough Maps 231, 248v). Hence Stukeley sought evidence of sophistication such as common measurements in this and other similar antiquities, rather along the lines of more recent attempts to establish a 'megalithic yard' (Piggott 1985, 90–1; Stukeley 1722c, 102–3 and passim). He also took it for granted that care might be expected in the choice of stones, their disposition, and the proportion between the sizes of stones and the spaces between them. Of the stones themselves, he estimated at one point that each was intended as 'a cubical face of 15

80

celtic feet square', though elsewhere – with reference to the stone which survived from the Beckhampton Cove – he claimed that 'they aimd much at a rhomboid as having more beauty than a stone really square' (Gough Maps 231, 15, 32v). As for the spaces separating them, various drawings survive in which Stukeley sought, by framing the stones in squares, to show the harmonious proportions between the width and thickness of the stones and the distance between them. One of these is entitled 'Exemplification of the geometric ratio of the architecture in the outer circle at Abury in the 3 stones still left next the entrance of Kennet avenue', and in it he came to the conclusion that the proportion between the stones and their adjacent spaces was 3:2 (or rather 30.5:22.5) (Gough Maps 231, 245, cf. 15, 214v, 307) (Plate 19). Elsewhere he variously calculated it as 2:1, 1.25:1 or 5:3, and there is evidence of considerable indecision on such matters on his part: for instance, in one case where he initially suggested a space of 'one cube & a half or rather less', 'half' was altered to 'quarter' during the course of composition (Eng.Misc.c.533, 44b). On the other hand, he seems to have thought that various such ratios were 'musical proportions', perhaps particularly 4:3, which represented 'the mysterious & sacred proportion of a 4th in music which Pythagoras held in utmost veneration & made it part of his oath at the initiation of his disciples' (Gough Maps 231, 15; Stukeley 1722–4b, 197). In any case, Stukeley took the view that where a stone was larger or smaller than normal, the method of the builders – 'most consentaneous to reason' – was to vary the proportion accordingly, '& this I find ever observd in all celtic works by which means only they could arrive at the great & simple beauty which is to be found in them all' (Stukeley 1722–4b, 197). His general presumption of regularity is also seen in his view that the stones in the avenues were disposed to form regular parallelo-grams half as long again as they were broad and hence divisible into six squares (Stukeley 1722–4b, 185), while he was also eager to find exact angles between the component parts of the antiquity, for instance of 90 or 120 degrees (Eng.Misc.c.533, 52 (Plate 20); Gough Maps 231, 248v, cf. 314).

Stukeley was also concerned with the orientation of the monuments. In part, he was inclined to see significance in the direction monuments 'faced', as when he noted that Avebury was 'open to the North bec[ause] that is the upper part of the temple & the heavens should appear most free to the eye that way' (Eng.Misc.c.533, 44b), or when he observed: 'there ought to be a free & open prospect to Temples from the East ... both Abury & Stoneheng receive the rising sun' (Stukeley 1722–4a, 159). At a more sophisticated level, he was interested in their exact compass bearings. One surviving page deals with 'the geometry of Abury', showing the main circle with the summer and winter solstice marked on it, and attempting to relate the centres of the inner circles and the terminal points of the avenues to one another and to what Stukeley considered the ten points of the Celtic compass (Eng.Misc.c.533, 52) (Plate 20). This curiosity about alignments is also seen in Stukeley's record of barrows, since, whenever he examined one, he always carefully noted the orientation of the burial within it, hoping to prove that they were aligned in a uniform direction (the alternative was that the axis of the burial might reflect the date of death of the deceased) (Stukeley 1722–4b, 207–8). From his profuse observations of alignments, he came to the conclusion that the Druids observed a standard compass variation of 6 degrees, being confirmed in this view by the fact that an obelisk at Alexandria about which he had read in Kircher 'varys just the same quantity & way from the true

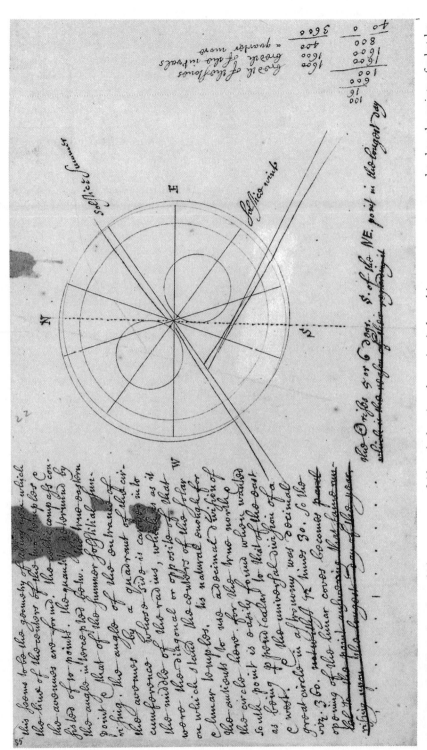

Plate 20 Stukeley's drawing of 'the geometry of Abury', showing the main circle and its component parts related to the points of what he thought to be the Celtic compass (Bodleian Library MS. Eng. Misc.c.533, 52).

cardinal points as our work' (Stukeley 1722–4b, 207). He also decided that 'the celtic works goe much upon quarters of the compass which I fancy they took to be the solstitial points' (Eng.Misc.b.65, 58v).

In addition, he thought that the style of megalithic antiquities deliberately partook of the beautiful simplicity of nature herself. As he put it, 'in my judgment we can scarce in any thing meet with more diversity & greatness, the peculiar & distinguishing characteristics of the Works of the Antients & so nearly copied from the Majesty of Nature, than in these subjects we are treating of' (Stukeley 1722–4b, 37).[12] Himself impressed by the natural beauty of the area, on which he repeatedly remarked in his notes, Stukeley seems to have thought that the choice of site was another manifestation of the art of the original builders. In his fieldnotes he wrote:

> to take in all the beautys of Abury we must widen our imagination & think with the antients & behold the most stately strife between art & nature. (Eng.Misc.b.65, 43v)

Thus he considered the way in which the avenues followed the contours to be masterly; he was especially impressed by the relationship of the antiquity to the surrounding hills at Beckhampton; and it was in this connection that he noted that barrows were often sited on false crests (Gough Maps 231, 3; Eng.Misc.b.65, 43v; Piggott 1985, 68). He also thought that the site at Avebury might have been chosen because of its profusion of springs and natural water. Noting how all three heads of the River Kennet rose within a mile of the antiquity, he continued: 'tis not impossible but that this very thing may have been one regard, that determind the choice of our Ancestors here' (Stukeley 1722–4b, 119). Moreover here again such considerations had a deeper significance. Thus he thought that the temple was 'placd near a spring head to indicate that water is the sustenance of all life', while aesthetics also correlated with meaning when he noted of a view 'where a surprising regularity in nature appears & well regarded by the founders': 'Abury is enclosd on all sides with hills but towards the north, which seems to intimate in their philosophy the immense voyd beyond the works of nature' (Stukeley 1722–4b, 132; Gough Maps 231, 245v).

v. The evolution of Stukeley's ideas

It was this kind of thinking that led Stukeley, during his 1723 visit to the site, to a breakthrough in his conception of the antiquity as a whole. He announced this in a letter to Roger Gale of 22 July that year, claiming that he had 'by great diligence at last gott a full understanding of that most amazing work, of which before I had but a faint glimpse', and that he was 'perfectly satisfyed' about it, 'finding every minute that I had hitt upon the founder's whole intent as I really believe' (Stukeley 1887, 245, 247). Basically, he now decided that 'The Two great purposes in this prodigious Work of Abury is to make a Temple & a mausoleum at the same time' (Stukeley 1722–4b, 175). He had already come to believe that Silbury Hill was the tomb of the founder of Avebury (Stukeley 1722–4b, 158), and background to his further speculation is evidently to be found in his suspicion that there was a link between temples and tombs, perhaps because 'Good Authors have thought that Temples take their origin from sepulchres', or because tumuli 'are really as little temples' (Stukeley

83

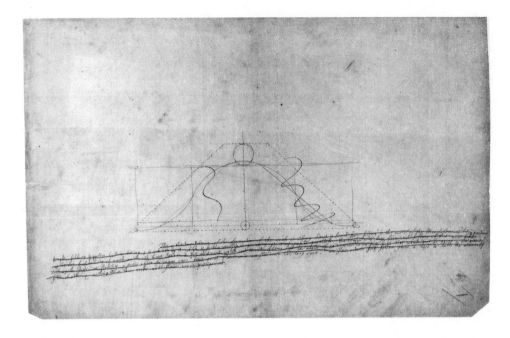

Plate 21   Stukeley's view of the Avebury complex as a symmetrical, two-dimensional depiction of a tumulus based on Silbury Hill (Bodleian Library MS. Eng. Misc.b.65, 18).

1722–4a, 109; Eng.Misc.c.533, 44bv; cf. Piggott 1985, 88). Now, in a passage in 'Celtic Temples' dated 17 July 1723, he announced that Silbury Hill was not the only tomb to Avebury's founder: there was another, fifty times greater, namely 'the whole Temple at Abury with its two avenues':

> which is no other than the most superlative & extraordinary tumulus in the World & this is one chief intent in curving the avenues both ways for so they truly describe an outline the same as one of the tumuli, the Temple being its upper superficies & the line going from Overton hill to Beckhampton at the foot of Silbury hill being the horizontal or groundline. (Stukeley 1722–4b, 175)

In other words, taking for granted at this point that there was a temple at Beckhampton to match that at Overton, he was postulating that the Avebury complex represented a symmetrical two-dimensional depiction of the same outline as Silbury Hill, around which the complex focused: this was the case despite the fact that 'every great part is hid from the other or but obscurely visible & to be found out by trigonometry & such accurate instruments as we use nowadays' (Gough Maps 231, 248v).[13] A drawing demonstrating this layout survives in Eng.Misc.b.65, fol. 18, endorsed: 'This is the true scheme of the formation of the work at Abury' (Plate 21). On it, the way in which Silbury formed at once the model and a part of the whole is described as 'such a curiosity in geometry as is not easily paralleld' (there is then a further elucidatory note) (Eng.Misc.b.65, 18, cf. 109v). It was clearly the same conception that he had in mind when he inscribed a panoramic view of the

Plate 22 Stukeley's view of 'Part of the Solar Temple from the central obelisk. 10 July 1723', on which tab. xvi of *Abury* was based (Bodleian Library MS. Gough Maps 231, 160). See Key to Stones in folder.

Plate 23 Stukeley's corrected proof of his view of the southern temple at Avebury, used as tab. xvii of *Abury* (Bodleian Library MS. Gough Maps 231, 48). See Key to Stones in folder.

whole Avebury complex from a viewpoint south of Silbury as showing 'the original design of this stupendous work & which I found out July 1723' (Top.Gen.b.53, 31b, cf. 31c, dated 19 July; see also below, p. 92, and panorama in folder). Interestingly, it was at this point that he suggested that the reason why the two inner temples were placed asymmetrically within the henge was not only because they stood on a ridge of ground running through the henge as a whole but also because their centres formed an equilateral triangle with the point on a base line rising from Silbury Hill at which the Kennet and Beckhampton avenues terminated: 'this produces a piece of Geometry highly remarkeable', Stukeley commented (Stukeley 1722–4b, 183).

These ideas about the overall layout of the Avebury complex represent the climax of Stukeley's original theories about its symmetrical symbolic structure. That they were superimposed on ideas about the meaning of the antiquity of the kind already outlined is illustrated by captions to drawings and engravings of the site dating from July 1723, in which components like the Solar and Lunar Temples and the Temple of Ertha appear (e.g. Gough Maps 231, 48, 160, 227, 235) (Plates 18, 22 and 23). This is further borne out by a treatise that Stukeley compiled in March 1724 concerning the monument at Stanton Drew, which he had visited in July 1723: this was published in the second edition of his *Itinerarium Curiosum* in 1776, but the original manuscript in Stukeley's early hand also survives (Stukeley 1776, ii.169–77; Eng.Misc.c.321, 17–22). In it, Stukeley postulated that Stanton Drew was a prototype for Avebury, using overlapping explanatory concepts to elucidate it. Here, as at Avebury, he postulated temples dedicated to the Sun and the Moon, which 'claim the highest place in the opinion of all nations', while the Cove was linked to 'the Goddess of the Earth'. All this went with a similar expectation that the disposition of the features of the monument would reflect the 'theology' of its Druidic founders, its orientation to north and east symbolising the creation of the world, while the Cove lay to the west because it was associated with Hell. Equally important was his expectation of circles made up of regular numbers of evenly spaced stones, the whole reflecting the harmonious numerical proportions perfected by 'Pythagoras, the Arch-druid, as I venture to call him'. Stukeley explained:

> Now, what can be plainer than the conformity between this work and Abury? the same situation, near the spring of a river, upon a knoll in a large valley, guarded from severity of weather by environing hills: here is the cove of three stones; the circle of twelve; that of thirty stones, all set at the same intervals of thirty foot: here are the concentric circles. But then Abury is a vastly more extensive and magnificent design; the stones of much larger proportions, and much more numerous. (Stukeley 1776, ii.166–77)

If this was Stukeley's theory in the spring of 1724, however, at some point thereafter, probably during the ensuing summer, he seems to have modified it significantly. This change is reflected in his unpublished manuscripts, while a corollary of it, the implication of which we will explain shortly, was that, in his revised proofs of engravings of the inner circles of the main henge and of the Sanctuary that he had had made in 1723, Stukeley deleted the titles that he had originally given them of 'Lunar Temple', 'Solar Temple' and 'Temple of Ertha' (e.g. Plates 18, 23). That Stukeley abandoned the 'celestial theory' that gave rise to these names has already been noted by Piggott (Piggott 1935, 27–8; 1985, 96, 166), though he was wrong to presume that the deletions necessarily took place in 1724: it is true that one of the proofs that was altered in this way is endorsed 'corrected 18 May 1724', but the change to the title is in a different ink from the emendments to the engraving itself and may well not have been made at that point (Eng.Misc.d.444, 62). What is more important is that the deduction that Piggott drew from this was erroneous, for he postulated that in 1724 Stukeley 'seems to have been in a remarkably clear state of mind': 'his mood of sane, scientific, accurate observation and record was not to be recovered for the rest of his long life' (Piggott 1985, 96). However, it is not very plausible that someone who had devised such elaborate theories on the basis of the cumulative erudition of his day would entirely have abandoned theorization. What is surely likelier is that he had come up with a different theory, and this does indeed seem to be the case.

Up to this point, the reader will have noticed no reference to the interpretation of Avebury as a 'Dracontium', or serpent temple, for which Stukeley is notorious. This lack was also noted by Piggott, who argued that this theory was imposed by Stukeley on his data only later – following his ordination in 1729 and coming to fruition in the 1730s and 1740s. In fact, however, there can be no doubt that Stukeley came to the conclusion that the Avebury complex represented the image of a snake traversing a circle before the end of his fieldwork in 1724. Not only does he say as much in his published *Abury* – where, commenting on the gradual way in which he came to an understanding of the site while his fieldwork was in progress, he writes: 'at length I discover'd the mystery of it, properly speaking; which was, that the whole figure represented a snake transmitted thro' a circle; this is an hieroglyphic or symbol of highest note and antiquity' (Stukeley 1743, 18) – but the arrival of this new interpretation is also borne out by his unpublished manuscripts.

The manner in which the new theory originated is suggested by the evidence of Stukeley's fieldnotes, mainly surviving in Gough Maps 231. These suggest that in 1724 Stukeley's mind was no *tabula rasa* but in a considerable state of turmoil. What one sees is a complex but significant interrelationship between observation and theoretical preconception, and it may not be coincidental that it is from 1724 that the bulk of Stukeley's fieldnotes survive, indicating the extent to which he found himself perplexed by his findings in his final summer at the site. Basically, the problem concerned the putative Beckhampton temple, a crucial component of the increasingly elaborate, symmetrical structure for the antiquity that Stukeley had up to this time postulated, with its numerically important number of seven components, including temples at either end of either avenue, and (since the previous summer) its balanced disposition around Silbury Hill. Many of his drawings of 1723 and others as late as May 1724 took for granted that such a temple existed at the end of the Beckhampton Avenue, despite the fact that he had found no trace of it.[14] What the fieldnotes suggest is that, during the early summer of 1724, Stukeley looked with increasing desperation for the temple which his geometrical preconceptions had led him to expect, until he was ultimately forced to conclude that it did not exist and that his theories needed revision accordingly.

Indeed, a disproportionate number of Stukeley's extant notes deal precisely with the question of just where the Beckhampton Avenue ended and whether or not a temple was located there. He initially assumed that the temple 'was certainly in this vast valley', presumably at the point of 'the termination of the avenue' where he

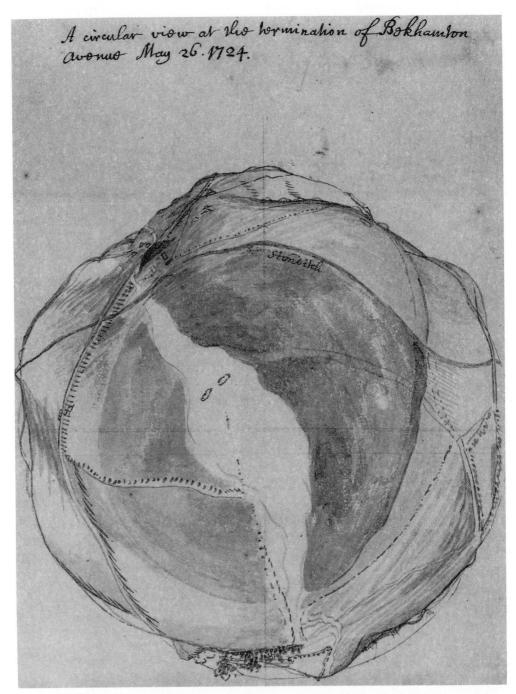

A circular view at the termination of Bekhampton avenue May 26. 1724.

Stondith

Plate 24 Stukeley's 'circular view' executed at the point which he believed marked the termination of the Beckhampton Avenue (Bodleian Library MS. Gough Maps 231, 46).

drew a pair of circular views similar to those that he did on Overton Hill (Plate 24; cf. Gough Maps 231, 46v, 50, 53), despite the fact that there was 'but one stone left standing' at his presumed site. On the other hand, his notes display considerable uncertainty as to exactly where the putative temple stood, exacerbated by the fact that one key location could not be examined that summer because it lay in the middle of a field of ripening corn. Stukeley seems to have been unsure whether the temple was to be found at a spot 6000 feet from Silbury Hill or 7000, 3750 feet from the Beckhampton Cove or 3500. Having claimed that the end of the avenue was 'at the end of the S. cornfield where the London road goes before it crosses the ro[man road] where I have drawn my circular views', he later altered 'at' to 'toward' and inserted 'near' before 'where' (Gough Maps 231, 3, 6, 8v, 25v, 32v, 46, 50v, 217). Further notes reaffirmed the suitability of this location for a Temple to Manes, citing its 'most solemn & melancholy aspect', the number of burials on the adjacent hills, reports of ghosts, and even some strange cavities on the downs which he thought might have played some part in ceremonies concerning the dead: indeed, in a note dated 29 May he wondered if the temple's position could be found from its relationship to that of the barrows on the ridge (Gough Maps 231, 32v, 36v, 226, 248v).

Ultimately, however, he must have decided that it might be more plausible to postulate that no such temple existed after all. What could he do, therefore, but go back to the drawing-board – or rather, to his reading about ancient religions and their iconography – to see what alternative theory he could find which would retain the symbolic significance which he had postulated for the antiquity while sacrificing the exact symmetry on which he had hitherto laid such stress? He came up with the depiction of a circle, representing God's existence, traversed by a serpent, symbolizing his creative power: the Beckhampton Avenue could therefore represent the serpent's tail, a temple at the end of which would be 'absurd in drawing', the avenue instead narrowing 'in imitation of the tail of a snake, and that one stone stood in the middle of the end, by way of close' (Stukeley 1743, 36).

The way in which Stukeley's observations and his reading interrelated at this point is illustrated by the fact that a depiction of this symbol actually occurs among his fieldnotes in Gough Maps 231 (f. 31v) (Plate 25). Though this document is undated, virtually all the other fieldnotes in this volume date from May 1724, and this one almost certainly does too (it in any case cannot be later, since this was Stukeley's last season at Avebury). It is typical of his fieldnotes in the way in which information about antiquities is juxtaposed with reflections, almost in a kind of 'stream of consciousness'. In it, Stukeley drew a symbol of a circle with wings and a snake, rather similar to some of the examples later to be illustrated in his *Abury* (Stukeley 1743, tab. xl), and commented:

> this is the representation of God or the great soul of the world among the persian magi & the egyptian priests & we find it here among the western Druids[,] doubtless tis of vastest antiquity & borrowd by them all from the post diluvian times. (Gough Maps 231, 31v)[15]

The emergence of the 'Dracontium' notion at this stage in his researches is further borne out by the manuscript of 'Celtic Temples', for the repetitive nature of his piecemeal notes on this symbol towards the end of the volume strongly suggests that he discovered the idea and was working it out during the latter part of the time when

At Haradon hill I found the avenue looks directly to long heap hill by Warminst it ranges 16 degrs from the true E. & W. line Northw from the W.

a druids barrow under Haradon hill with an entrance or gap left in the ditch. it looks to the N.W. 3 more barrows close by it inclosd in one ditch thus

coming from Stoneheng to abury. I saw a very large camp hanging upon the side of a hill eastward no determinate figure but a nook northward running down to a valley. it seems to be about upper avon. I take it for British. the ridg of hills parting north & south wills are extraordinary high several barrows at top Wausdike runs along the summit it has a very deep ditch N ward. there are many of the grey weather stones upon the very highest part.

I turned to the left at Wausdike to find the meridian line which abury bringing Silbury hill exactly agt. the circle. & Monklou still in the same line. this is at a gap made thro' Wausdike & at the bottom of a lower depressure thro' two hills. hence a valley runs down with a moderate declivity to Silbury hill but rather trending to the ford at W. Kennet & so to overton hill.

several barrows in this concavity.

this is the representation of god or the great soul of the world among the persian magi & the egyptian priests & we find it here among the western Druids doubtless tis of vastest antiquity & borrowd by them all from the post diluvian times. tis no more wonder we have nothing left of the wisdom of those Sages they kept their doctrin as secret in the east as here & Pythagoras learnt it from the Egyptians. this doctrine is so that our druids that if he learnt it from those its plain theirs & the egyptian was the same. I find the great meridian runs thro' the cove. walking out a good way into Monklou fields upon the elevation there & bringing Silbury & the cove into a line which is the grand meridian you see the horizon open in a very beautiful manner as a visto beyond it. the intervals of 3 stones of out circle at Kennet avenue outrance are wider than I have drawn em what we have of Pythagoras is comprizd in mystical terms orpheus or the egyptians in his roglyphics & symbolical characters & I doubt not but every part of this & like works has such secret meanings tho' now we have no means left of discovering it. every year I come to abury I find more of it demolishd & in a little time the termination of Kennet avenue will be as much obliterated as that of Kennet avenue. if there was not an inner circle at abury the singular stone might possibly be for a starting place but I am inclinable to think there was. the reason why it was first destroyd was bec' they were left & stood more in the way & middle of the pasture the out circle being more on the out side & in some parts in the hedg.

the manuscript was being composed (Stukeley 1722–4b, 246ff.). Its late arrival in the history of the text is also suggested by the number of comments elaborating it which were inserted onto wholly or partially empty pages which happened to exist earlier in the manuscript (Stukeley 1722–4b, e.g. 68, 138, 173, 175): this gives a rather chaotic air to his exposition of the notion, and perhaps made clear to him the need for a complete revision of his work (though it should be stressed that all these notes are in Stukeley's 'early' handwriting as against that of his later years). There is also evidence within the notes of a transitional stage between his original view of the antiquity and his final one, when he spoke of 'our *two* snakes' which 'must be lookd on as chains of Idea's flowing from the divine mind' (Stukeley 1722–4b, 172; our italics).

The source of the symbol lay in Egyptian hieroglyphics, with which Stukeley had clearly become familiar during his antiquarian reading, not least of the writings of Athanasius Kircher. Among the scholars whose study of ancient Egypt has already been referred to, much attention was given to hieroglyphics, which were seen as potent symbols which gave insight into the essences of things: in a culture impregnated by symbolic and metaphorical modes of thought, such allegorical meanings were often rather fancifully elaborated, a process which reached a climax in Kircher (Iversen 1961, 64ff.; Godwin 1979, ch. 5). Indeed, later in 1724 Stukeley himself wrote a treatise on 'The Hieroglyphics of the Egyptians', which shared many of the ideas of such earlier writings on the nature of Egyptian religion and philosophy, and in which he saw the language of hieroglyphics as 'no less remarkable for its excellence than its antiquity' (Stukeley 1724b). What is more, Stukeley seems at this stage to have become more convinced than ever of a direct link between Celtic megaliths and Egyptian tradition. Some of his notes seem to register initial surprise at this, as when he wrote: 'that our temple at Abury is made of this figure is very surprizing bec[ause] tis purely Egyptian'. But he continued: 'it proves undeniably that twas built by some of Thoths disciples' (Stukeley 1722–4b, 230). Moreover it must have been at this point that he drew up a list of similarities between the Druids and the Egyptians, including 'the use of the figure of a globe & serpent signifying pantomorph nature or the platonic anima mundi' (Stukeley 1722–4b, 240 cont. on 194).

Thoth was usually identified with Hermes Trismegistus, and it is interesting that Stukeley cited the mandate of Trismegistus for the hieroglyphic depiction of God in this way (though he also invoked Plato and Moses) (Stukeley 1722–4b, 230–2). His new theory overlapped with his earlier one in that he saw the circle as representing God's existence. But, following Kircher and other writers on the meaning of hieroglyphics, he now laid equal stress on the serpent as the symbol of God's creative role, elaborating in detail on the fascination of the ancients with the serpent and their belief in its God-like quality because of its ability to move without hands and feet, to live by its mouth and to renew itself by sloughing off its skin; these ideas were to recur in chapter XI of his published *Abury* (Stukeley 1722–4b, 173, 249f.; 1743, 54f.).

In elaborating this view, Stukeley also brought to the fore the trinitarian significance of the symbol thus displayed. Already in connection with his 'celestial' theory he had taken the view that 'the supreme being drawn at large' might appear in triadic form, with God acting on the universe 'with a threefold power over the threefold world the archetypal or intellectual the sydereal & the hylarchic or material' (Stukeley 1722–4b, 132). Now, however, he strengthened this side of his argument on the basis of the significance of the serpent hieroglyph. He was undismayed by the fact that, though the Egyptians often added wings to indicate the moving, penetrative power of the deity, these were omitted at Avebury since they 'could not well be expressed in stones'. But, even without the wings, he was convinced that such symbolism 'most plainly shows how antient the notion of the trinity of the deity is' (Stukeley 1722–4b, 230).

Indeed, contrary to Piggott's presumption that this idea was a later gloss postdating Stukeley's taking holy orders, and despite the fact that – as we have already seen (Chapter I, ix) – Stukeley's apologetic intent may indeed later have intensified, he clearly stated in this early manuscript the view that Avebury proved the antiquity of the knowledge of the trinity:

> Tho' the druids by reason of their abhorrence of writing have left us little on record of their principal doctrines of their religion, yet they have left us the largest drought[sic] of the trinity that ever was, whence one cannot reasonably doubt of their faith in that divine truth. (Stukeley 1722–4b, 140; cf. Stukeley 1887, 266)

He had explained in 'Celtic Religion' how 'When God almighty was pleasd to make so large a discovery of himself to the Jews, why should he be thought to make none to the gentiles', denying that the Druids were idolaters (Stukeley 1722–4a, 60–1; cf. Stukeley 1722–4c, unpag. leaf). It was presumably in the context of this revaluation of his ideas that he worked out the implication of this by eliminating his suggestion that the component parts of Avebury were dedicated to the Sun and Moon, with the overtones of antiChristian paganism that this entailed. Hence at some subsequent stage – though, as we have seen, there is no direct evidence when – Stukeley deleted the titles such as 'Lunar Temple' and 'Solar Temple' that he had earlier given to component parts of the antiquity (see above, pp. 86–7).

On the other hand, his basic approach to the site was unchanged, despite his shift in acceptance from one form of symbolism to another. In particular, the 'snake' theory was superimposed on the ideas that he had formulated in 1723 as to how the monument was a vast, two-dimensional mausoleum with its focus on Silbury Hill, and this idea about the general disposition of the antiquity was summarized in his published *Abury* (Stukeley 1743, 49ff., esp. 52). Indeed, the 'Scenographic view' reconstructing Avebury when complete which appears as tab. viii of the published *Abury* is clearly derived from the views showing the general disposition of the antiquity which he drew in July 1723, via an intermediate manuscript recension with a deleted dedication to Lord King (to whom, as we saw in Chapter I, ix, Stukeley would have dedicated the version of his book that he projected in 1731, had it come out) (Plate 26). The principal difference was that the Beckhampton temple which appeared on the original was quietly removed, a transition which occurred between the 1723 version and that dedicated to King (Top.Gen.b.53, 31av, cf. 31b, 31c). Other ideas, however – for instance of numerical regularity, proportion, and landscaping – were retained in the published book, which makes constant allusion to ideas expounded in the unpublished manuscripts. And though there is much material in the 1743 text which is not to be found in the manuscript, it should be borne in mind that many pages from the latter have been cut out, and it is highly likely that this was because they contained material which was reused elsewhere, at least some of it – in a more or less revised form – in the published volume.

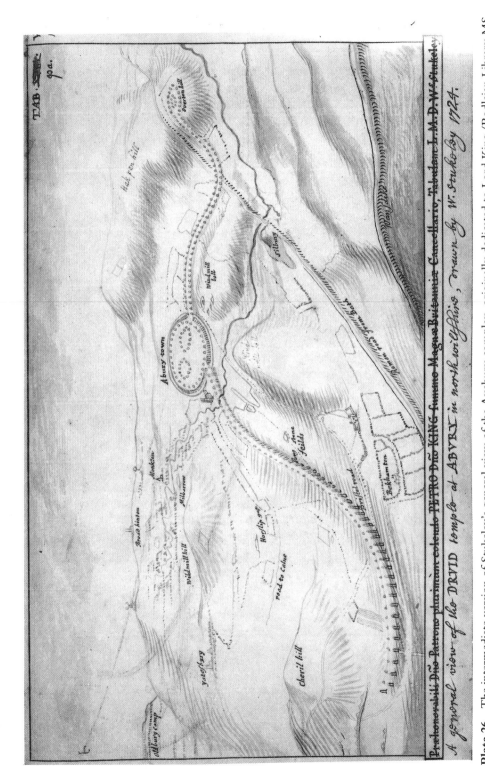

TAB.
90.a.

Praehonorabili Dño Patrono plurimum colendo PETRO Dño KING funeno Magnæ Britanniæ Cancellario, Tabulam I. M. D. W. Stukeley

A general view of the DRVID temple at ABVRY in north wiltshire, drawn by W. Stukeley 1724.

Plate 26   The intermediate version of Stukeley's general view of the Avebury complex, originally dedicated to Lord King (Bodleian Library MS. Top.Gen.b.53, 31av).

vi. Theory and observation

If the alteration of Stukeley's theory of Avebury from a geometrical scheme to a snake may have represented the influence of his observations on his theories, or at least an interrelationship between the two, it is equally important to stress here how his theorization affected his record. Hitherto the most notorious case of this – to which Stuart Piggott first drew attention in an article in 1935 – has been Stukeley's elongation of the shape of the Sanctuary in successive versions of his plan of it so that, as befitted a snake's head, it was of oval rather than circular form (Piggott 1935, 31 and plates; Piggott 1985, 107). This genuinely does seem to have been retrospective, but equally important is the influence that Stukeley's theories had even while his fieldwork was in progress. For, although in connection with the Beckhampton temple his observations in 1724 finally forced him to abandon one set of expectations formed by his preconceived ideas, this was by no means the only case of his record being influenced by his preconceptions.

The way in which his presumption of symmetry affected his record is particularly clearly illustrated in his notes concerning the West Kennet Cove, which show that his 'discovery' of this feature was stimulated by the Longstone Cove in the Beckhampton Avenue (see Chapter IV, m and o). He wrote, in a manner typical of his rather breathless fieldnotes:

> as soon as I saw longstone cove & found it the interval of 50 stones from Abury I conjecturd there must have been another such at Kennet avenue & Measuring with nicety I found at the 50th stone an entire vacancy[:] that its upon an eminence & at that very place the road crosses the avenue whence theres no room to doubt from symmetry &c but that there was a cove too. the stump of the stone on this side is left by the edg of the corn.

He then commented how giving the avenue 'this fine break in the middle' in this way was yet another proof of the skill of the architects. On the other hand, when he later decided that it would be more appropriate for the curves of the snake which this and the Beckhampton Avenue represented to be purely serpentine, he abandoned these ideas, altering the original caption of the engraving of the Kennet 'cove' that he prepared at this stage from 'The Cove of Kennet avenue' to 'Continuation of Kennet avenue' (Gough Maps 231, 3, 236, cf. 25; Stukeley 1743, tab. xix; cf. Burl 1979, 138–9).

More generally, Stukeley's interest in number symbolism certainly affected his expectations as to how many stones might have been expected to make up different component parts of the site, making him prone to presume the original existence of specific – usually round – numbers like 100, thirty or twelve, and the significance of this 'pre-conceived idea' for Stukeley was recognized by W. C. Lukis in the 19th century (Lukis 1881–3a, 151–2). His presumptions of regularity certainly affected his estimates as to the positions of stones no longer extant by the time he did his fieldwork, and the significance of this for his record of the site will be assessed more fully in Chapter IV. At Stanton Drew it was even on the basis of arguments from numerical symbolism that he was led to believe that a whole section of the temple had fallen victim to destruction to make way for 'the manor-house and offices' there (Stukeley 1776, ii.173), and similar arguments are in evidence at

Avebury. A case in point concerns the supposed double circle(s) there: Stukeley clearly started from the presumption that circles were likely to be double – his conviction of the role of the 'dyas' has already been cited – and it is interesting how he was able to provide himself with a rationale as to why, if an inner outer circle once existed, only a handful of stones from it – or even only a single stone – survived:

> if there was not an inner circle at Abury the singular stone might possibly be for a starting place but I am inclineable to think there was, the reason why it was first destroyd was bec[ause] they were less & stood more in the way & middle of the pastures the out[er] circle being more on the out side & in some parts in the hedg. (Gough Maps 231, 31v)

This echoes a further passage which drew a parallel with his hypothesis of an avenue at Stonehenge, in which he commented: 'I dont wonder so much at the 99 which are gone as at the poor one remaining' (Stukeley 1722–4b, 129). Knowledge of destruction was thus juxtaposed with theory to explain what he did and did not actually see, and Stukeley was quite tenacious of this notion despite the paucity of evidence that any such circle existed. On the other hand – as we shall see in Chapter IV, r and w – there is evidence that here, too, he ultimately reconsidered his ideas. For, though this inner circle is marked on Stukeley's published Frontispiece to *Abury*, it is not mentioned in his 1743 text. Moreover, in the Frontispiece one of the two stones which might be construed to be survivors of this circle is identified as a unique 'ring-stone', and a comment on this is included in the book which invokes the sacrifices which he thought would have been carried out at the site, a form of interpretation which he had previously dismissed as 'altogether abhorrent of the Noble Majesty of this Work' (Stukeley 1743, 25; 1722–4b, 129). This probably indicates the direction in which Stukeley's ideas were moving in the years after he left the site.

As instances like this confirm, Stukeley was not uncritically influenced by his reading in ancient sources and more recent scholarship. Rather, an interrelationship existed between this and his fieldwork. While Stukeley was certainly in many ways conscientious in his recording, he was inescapably influenced by the theories with which he approached the site, and we ignore this at our peril if we are properly to understand what he recorded. His case illustrates with particular clarity how preconceptions must be mastered if perceptions are to be properly understood, and, as should by now be clear, an attempt to make sense of Stukeley by separating the two is a recipe for disaster.

Yet the interpretation of Stukeley which is currently generally accepted – that of Stuart Piggott – does just this, and it is worth concluding this chapter by exploring the reasons for this and examining their implications. To modern eyes, much of the elaborate superstructure of Stukeley's theory concerning Avebury seems fanciful. It was clearly for this reason that, in his 1935 article and 1950 monograph on Stukeley, Piggott was inclined to postulate a dichotomy between a 'hard' early period in Stukeley's life, when he did his best fieldwork – 'The Doctor and the Field Archaeologist' – and a later, more speculative phase, when these 'hard' findings were put to whimsical uses, warped by Druidic fantasies (Piggott 1985, esp. ch. 7). In fact, however, such a distinction cannot be sustained: the findings laid out here concerning the continuity in Stukeley's writings on Avebury bear out suspicions already entertained concerning his antiquarian work more generally (Hunter 1971, 190). What is more, the implication of this is that the broader picture of 18th-century antiquarianism and intellectual life that Piggott has sketched on the basis of this false dichotomy is also flawed. We doubt whether it is either useful or correct to talk of a 'decline' in antiquarianism, as Piggott has done not least on the basis of his reading of Stukeley (cf. Hunter 1990). There were undoubtedly changes in intellectual life in the early 18th century, but the notion of deteriorating standards is more likely to obscure than to elucidate what actually occurred and why, as the example of Stukeley suggests.

Why did Piggott misinterpret Stukeley in this way? For this there are two reasons. The more prosaic is that Piggott began his research by looking in the wrong place. His view, as stated in his original, 1935 study of Stukeley, was that:

> prehistoric archaeology in England was not the product of the classical lore so eagerly absorbed from Italy in the 16th and 17th centuries, but originated in those eccentric gentlemen of the 18th century who perambulated the countryside studying at first hand the antiquities of their own forefathers. (Piggott 1935, 22)

Subsequently, he came to see that Stukeley's speculations were not original, but drew after all on the intellectual inheritance of his period – in other words, the legacy of antiquarian erudition which English scholars shared with their continental counterparts, which has been expounded here (Piggott 1985, 100; 1986, 116; 1989, passim). But even then, the date at which Stukeley took up these ideas was wrongly construed, with the result that Piggott continued to regard the fanciful super-structure as separate and distinguishable from the objective study 'underlying' it.

A more fundamental reason, however, was surely one which has bedevilled the study not only of antiquarianism but of intellectual life in Stukeley's period as a whole, namely a Whiggish reluctance to admit that scholars who were admired for their pioneering contribution to some areas of knowledge could have combined such concerns with others that to us seem backward-looking. This is well exemplified by 19th-century views of Aubrey: thus John Britton wanted to separate Aubrey's positive qualities from his participation in the 'appalling and degrading fanaticism, with the frivolous superstition' of his age (Hunter 1975, 230). Such attitudes can easily be paralleled elsewhere in the historiography of the ideas of Aubrey's time – for instance, in the difficulty in accepting Newton's alchemical studies to be found not only in Sir David Brewster in Britton's day but also in his successors well into the 20th century (Fauvel et al. 1988, 149–50).

Today, we are able to accept Newton's alchemy, not as an aberration on his part but as an integral aspect of his view of nature, and this is part of a broader awareness that it is impossible to do justice to such thinkers unless their preoccupations are studied as a whole. Only by considering what seem to us the weaknesses of intellectual enterprise as well as what we retrospectively applaud as its strengths will we understand the nature of scholarly activity at the time. Here, a particularly interesting parallel to the case of Stukeley is provided by J. M. Levine's study of his fellow F. R. S., John Woodward, of the 16th-century shield that he acquired, and of his contemporaries' misconstrual of it as a classical antiquity of immense importance, which in our eyes seems extraordinary. This interpretation was underwritten by the inappropriate application of a mass of classical learning, exacerbated by what Levine calls 'an overwhelming predisposition to believe'; it illustrates the difficulties of interpreting such items in a scholarly context which lacked the 'systematic archae- ology' which we take for granted and by which the plausibility of such connections between written sources and the relics of the past could be tested (Levine 1977, 156, 158 and passim).

With antiquities like Avebury, the problems were if anything greater, since the relatively short historical timescale to which most thinkers of this generation subscribed meant that they were prone to find plausible connections which we would dismiss out of hand. Wherever one looks in the antiquarian literature of the period, one encounters attempts to correlate physical finds with events in historical sources, which in retrospect seem to us fanciful: Thomas Twining was far from unusual in his attempt to link an antiquity like Avebury with Roman military manoeuvres, while other examples of the same tendency include Thomas Hearne's identification of bronze age socketed axes as '*Roman Chissels*' used to prepare the '*Stones* in their *Tents*' and for other purposes (Hunter 1971, 190; cf. Piggott 1989, 97). In a sense, all that Stukeley was doing was using the resources which his contempo- raries presumed would throw light on primeval antiquities in a resourceful and erudite way.

Indeed, we should be aware that, when we praise those who 'simply' recorded and criticize those who went beyond this in supplying an interpretative structure according to the criteria of their day, we are often engaging in an anachronistic value judgement, in that those who refrained from such interpretation were showing a lack of proper erudition by contemporary standards. Though we know in retrospect that a correct understanding of prehistoric antiquities was to be reached through removing them from their anchorage in written sources and making a comparative study of them in their own right, and though we obviously respect those who began to make such a study, we need to be careful that we do not artificially modernize them in doing so. Even a man like Aubrey, who went further than most in the study of 'comparative antiquitie', was not immune from influence by the commonplace presumptions of his day, as we have seen here: parts of his 'Templa Druidum' and some of his other antiquarian writings indulge in speculations which were recogniza- bly similar to those which Stukeley was so fully to elaborate, suggesting that Aubrey's restraint from these was only partially conscious (Hunter 1975, esp. 188).

It is equally important for us to recognize that we will only understand records of a site like Avebury if we fully appreciate what those who were studying it thought they were looking at, and acknowledge how inescapably their observations were influenced by their theoretical preconceptions. Moreover, the implications of this are wider. An analogy to the findings laid out here about the notions underlying Stukeley's view of Avebury is provided by recent work on Newton's theory of colours. For it now seems clear that Newton's 'empirical' observations were preconditioned by the belief that he shared with Stukeley in the Pythagorean harmony of the spheres, and that 'the British tradition of the seven-coloured rainbow stems directly from Newton's conviction that "the Spaces which the several Colours . . . take up" were "divided after the manner of a Musical Chord"' (Henry 1990, 593; cf. Fauvel et al. 1988, 118–20). What we need to remember is that, hard as they may try, no-one can entirely divest themselves of their preconceptions in their empirical work. The implications of this sobering thought for the understanding of Avebury in the centuries since Stukeley will be further explored in Chapter V, after we have scrutinized the exact details of each of the early plans and collated them with archaeological knowledge of the site.

Notes

1. In this quotation, 'the Discovery whereof' replaces 'the which', deleted; 'endeavour' is duplicated with 'attempt', and 'those' with 'them', but neither is deleted; 'in some degree' is deleted after 'restore'; 'method' replaces 'manner', deleted; before 'reducing', 'so' is deleted; before 'being', 'so' replaces 'and'; 'give Evidence' replaces 'to speake'.

2. See also his note in Aubrey 24, 36v; Fowles and Legg 1980, 40: 'The Area within the circumvallation of this Monument would easily be found: but it little concerns this matter', to which he added: 'but doe it'.

3. For a possible example of a survey by Aubrey (of Deepdene, Surrey), see Aubrey 4, 49–50.

4. 'not' replaces 'far from', deleted. Subsequently, the whole passage was deleted. Elsewhere (Eng. Misc.c.533, 48), Stukeley writes: 'tho the ditch of Abury be not a mathematical circle yet nearer than one would imagine for I frequently found the eye is deceivd & thinks it turns with an angle where it is bounded both ways tho' it really is not [:] this is owing to the excessive grandeur of it. the ark that is visible from the bank appearing like a strait line becaus you are on the convex side'. See also Stukeley 1743, 20.

5. replacing 'British Monuments', deleted.

6. Before 'stones', 'circ' is deleted; after 'Monuments', 'sub dio' is deleted. 'Genesis' is hastily written 'Gensis'. The blanks are Aubrey's.

7. For a brief exposition of such ideas based solely on Stukeley's 'Stonehenge' MS, see Owen 1962, 119–20.

8. 'se' is deleted before 'distant Regions'. For an alternative view of the origin of architecture (as deriving from trees), see Stukeley's MS on the 'Creation', Freemasons Hall MS 1130 Stu (1), 31f.

9. For expositions of the Bembine Table by Stukeley, see Freemasons Hall MS 1130 Stu (3) (loosely inserted at end) (n.d.); Cardiff Central Library MS 2.369 (1761). For a series of engravings by Stukeley which may have been intended to accompany a treatise on this subject, see Gough Maps 230, 466f.

10. Before inner, 'cir' is deleted.

11. Immediately after the passage cited here, 'in the avenues and circular works' is repeated and this has not been reproduced in the text. Previously, 'solar and lunar' is deleted after 'temples': there are a number of such deletions in this MS, reflecting Stukeley's revision of his ideas after he originally composed his text, and these have generally been ignored here.

12. 'of' has been altered from 'from'.

13. Before 'hid from', 'entirely' has been deleted.

14. It should be noted that Piggott was wrong to assert that it was on 19 July 1723 that Stukeley altered the title of the Beckhampton Avenue view from 'spot of the Temple at the end of Bekampton avenue' to 'spot of the Termination of Bekampton avenue' (Piggott 1985, 166; cf. Stukeley 1743, tab. xxv). In fact, this appears to be the date when the original drawing was executed; fieldnotes in Gough Maps 231, passim, show that the notion that there was a temple in this location was still entertained by Stukeley well into May 1724, and the alteration to the title must have postdated that. It should be stressed that it is in general difficult to date alterations made to engravings: see Chapter I, viii.

15. Before 'the egyptian priests', 'from' is deleted.

III   *The plans and their annotations*

Preliminary

The Introduction has listed the five plans on which this book is centred, and Chapters I and II have set them in context. Now we describe the plans in detail. Our primary concentration here is on each plan as a self-contained document, in order to assess how far it is also self-explanatory; but we refer to other sources when necessary. A number of inter-plan comparisons thus incidentally arise, but the main work of comparison and analysis is reserved for Chapter IV.

There are five sections, covering plans A to E; each is designed to be read with frequent reference to the appropriate plan(s), loose copies of which are therefore supplied in the accompanying folder, as well as those in the book. In addition, special transparencies have been produced of some of the plans, to assist in comparison: these are designed to be superimposed in any position the reader desires.

At first we found the plans to be so distinct and individual that each suggested a different form of treatment. This has remained so to some degree, particularly in the case of what we call the Plan E complex, since we are there dealing with eleven variants. However, we have evolved the set of headings listed below, under which plans A–D are treated. The same sequence of topics is followed, so far as it fits, in Chapter IV.

1–5:   General and Archival

  1:   Title/heading
  2:   Orientation and scope
  3:   The document
  4:   The verso of the document
  5:   Annotations

6–9:   'Modern' and natural features

  6:   Buildings & foliage
  7:   Highways & roadways (external/internal)
  8:   Boundaries
  9:   River

10–14:   Ancient artificial features

10:   Bank and ditch
11:   Entrances
12:   Key-letters and keyed features
13:   The stone depictions
14:   The stone settings

15–16:   Supplements

A.15:   Surveying
B.15:   Kennet Avenue and Sanctuary;
B.16:   Stukeley's versions of plan B
C.15:   Sketches and words on the verso

Plan A: Bodleian Library MS. Top. Gen.c.24, fols 39v–40 (Plate 7, also in folder)

A.1–5:General and archival (see also Chapter I,v)

A.1   Title/heading
This 'Survey of Aubury' is also headed 'Plate I', reflecting its intended use for engraving as an illustration for Aubrey's long-unpublished *Monumenta Britannica* (see Chapter I; A.5(a)). Plan B is similarly headed, 'Plate IId' (see B.1).

A.2   Orientation and scope
Oriented with N at the top, the plan shows the bank and the ditch ('rampire & graffe') and stone settings in the area thus enclosed; also one within the S entrance, and beyond it the beginning stones of the Kennet Avenue, but no other entrance stones. Topographical features outside the bank include, to the W, Avebury church, and an enigmatic 'foliage' feature beyond it; to the E and W, the external roads. We have discovered also a near-invisible vertical feature which may be an abandoned attempt to show a river (see A.9).

A.3   The document
Plan A is in ink and wash, with one or two probably contemporary pencilled features (see A.10; A.12(h)); it also bears later pencillings by Sir Richard Colt Hoare (see A.12(c)). The plan is on a sheet of laid paper measuring 310 × 400 mm. (12.2 × 15.75 in.). The chainlines run vertically, about 1 in. apart; a single watermark appears in folio 40, the righthand of the two leaves into which the plan has been folded. This mark is a 'coat of arms' – orb, crown, double-lined shield with three vertical x-crosses, and supporters – similar to some of the examples 342–437 given by Heawood 1950, but not identical with any.
    Aubrey's re-transcription of the *Monumenta Britannica* (see Chapter I,v) was on to sheets giving the openings of the MS. volume a typical dimension of some 310 × 360 mm. However, as its old folio number (16, plan B being 17–18) confirms, plan A is one of those preserved from the previous recension. The greater width of these older sheets meant that both outer edges had to be folded in: in the case of plan A this was done to a width of some 40 mm. A number of short tears on the outer edges have been repaired, not recently, with narrow strips of paper pinched over both sides of the sheet.
    To the back of the plan, at the inner edge of fol. 39, is affixed a vertical strip, some 50 mm. wide, of paper of another stock; it has been there since Aubrey's time, for his notes are written over it. Along the straight-torn inner edge are a few marks interpretable as the edges of needle holes; we assume the strip to be the remains of a guard, through the edge of which the folded plan would at one time have been sewn up by Aubrey as part of an earlier set of papers (the 'first draught' or some part of it). A similar strip remains on the back of plan B (see B.3).

A.4   The verso of the document
On the back of the plan, and filling each of its folios (i.e. Aubrey 24, 39, 40v; Fowles and Legg 1980, 43, 57) are drafts of passages found in re-worked state elsewhere in the volume (see Chapter I,ii,v). All have been cancelled by Aubrey's crossings-out, and all are undated

100

except for the two notes at the foot of 40v. The upper of these two is dated 1681; the following and final note is that 'the great Stone at Aubrey's Townesend, fell down in Autumne 1684 . . .'.

All but the last of these drafts begin at, or extend across, the full width, rather than the folded-in width, of the folios on which they are written. This clearly implies that they pre-date the incorporation of plan A into its present volume, and makes more significant the fact that the final note is placed at the new folded margin. It seems likely that this sheet, and presumably the other larger ones, was incorporated with sheets of the smaller size – probably as the present *Monumenta* volume, but possibly as some intermediately revised predecessor – between the addition of the penultimate note, referring to 1681, and that of the last note, referring to 1684.

The 'π [pi] Aubury' written on the verso is discussed in the following paragraph (A.5(a)).

A.5   Annotations
In addition to the key letters and keyed features (see A.12), Aubrey's notes written on the face of plan A comprise:

(a) the headings already mentioned (see A.1): 'Plate I' (or possibly '1st'), and 'Survey of Aubury' (altered from 'Avebury'). This alteration, found also on plan B, reflects Aubrey's developing theory that 'Aubury' was the true spelling (see Chapter I, ii, v). His recorded speculations about this appear to date from the 1680s and 1690s, engendered by references such as those cited at A.5(b–c), below. Simply as a spelling, the 'Aubury' form will not have been novel to Aubrey, since it had been used in Childrey (1661, 49), a work to which he refers in other connections, both within the *Monumenta* (Aubrey 25, 60; Fowles and Legg 1982, 810–11) and elsewhere (Roy. Soc. Cl.P.VII(1).28, 93, transcribed in Aubrey 1972, 325).

This preferred spelling also appears prominently on the verso, as 'π Aubury', the phrase's inking and slightly bold style seeming to associate it with writing found on the face of the plan rather than with the notes surrounding it on fol.39. Since, further, the phrase is placed right of centre and somewhat isolated – the quotation from Ovid's *Fasti* appearing to have been appended later – we suggest that this 'π Aubury' may have been the first thing written on the reverse, perhaps to serve as finding-title for the folded plan.

(b) a deleted note below the title-heading, added in a later hand, being a revised version of a passage, also deleted, on fol.42v: 'n. In the Legier-booke of Malmisburie Abbey, I find that this | place belonged to that Monestrey, givin by . . . by the name | of Aubury' [Aubrey's ellipsis].

(c) a lined-through note at top left (inked over a slightly sprawling pencilled original): 'sign: Au? Brit. ref Saxonice | v. Saxon Dictionary'. This also appears to be a later addition.

(d) below this, top left, an uncancelled note, the initial preceded by Aubrey's 'memorandum' contraction: 'This was [surv, *del.*] projected by the halfe-inch Scale.' This, in Aubrey's running hand, appears to be an original or early note.

(e) below this, top left, a conventionally oriented compass-rose, lettered, at the end of cross-lines, N, E, S, W. At the head of the vertical a fleur-de-lys or trident; at its foot a Maltese cross, this latter and the letter 'S' both blotted (the blot perhaps cause of a pair of ink smudges, below it, which on some reproductions of the plan could appear a meaningful feature). The compass has a decorative dotted circle, between its quarters, containing some 70 dots.

(f) below and to the left of the compass, a deleted quotation, its ξ referring it to the northern circle (rather than to the Cove: see A.12(d)): 'π ξ   like Ariadne's Crown: | Aurea per stellas nunc micat | illa novem. | Ovids Fastoru. lib. III.' This insertion appears to be in a later hand.

(g) above the sketch of the church, centre L, a boldly written 'shillin', preceded by what appears to be a figure '1' (or 'I': cf. the verticals of the 'III' appended to the Ovid tag at A.5(f)

101

– though it could possibly be a letter 'I', or a vertical feature. The word's placing may indicate that it refers to something connected with the church, but it need not.

The handwriting of this word looks contemporary with the body of the plan, while its confidence, its inking, its nib, seem particularly akin to those of the ξ on the plan. However, we cannot rule out the possibility that it was written later.

This word is perhaps the most puzzling minor feature of the plan. It has been ignored by many previous commentators, though Fowles & Legg (1980, 44) suggest 'possibly the old dialect *shilling* or *skilling*, meaning "shed, outhouse"' (see (iii) below).

The options for interpretation of 'shillin' appear to be the following:

(i) *Name* It could be a personal surname with I as an initial, though the uncapitalized 's' makes this unlikely.

(ii) *Money* It could be a note of the amount paid for some service in connection with the plan. One shilling was an amount paid by Samual Pepys, on 15 June 1668, to an Avebury man ('a countryman of the town') who had shown him round (Pepys 1972-83, ix. 240); it might have been rather poor pay for, say, a plane-table survey assistant.

Or, conceivably, the reference could be to a tithe valuation. (In Domesday Book, 'Rainboldus, a priest ... holds the church of *Avreberie*, to which belong 2 hides, that are worth 40 shillings').

(iii) *Dialect* As suggested by Fowles and Legg, it could be a dialect word. We have considered additional OED entries such as 'shieling' and 'sheeling-stone', but the shed/outhouse/lean-to cluster of meanings does seem the most likely. However, its specific reference is unclear, unless it is an (disparaging?) appellation for the church. Or, an equally unlikely possibility is that 'shillin' refers to the tithe barn – erected in a levelled part of this area not later than 1695 – which would make the word a late addition by Aubrey in the light of these and other developments at Avebury Manor by the 1690s, to be dealt with in Chapter IV,e.

A.6–9: 'Modern' and natural features

A.6 Buildings & foliage

(a) Church The church is drawn neatly and in some detail, yet, as was remarked in the last century (King 1879, 380), it does not appear to be an accurate depiction of the actual 17th-century building. In particular, it shows no separate chancel (a feature correctly present in Aubrey's plan C) and no S aisle (but that is similarly absent from plan C). This might suggest that the church was added to the plan after it was originally compiled, or that plan A as a whole was drawn away from the site, and without an accurate sketch of the church to hand. Either way, however, this does appear to be an early component of the plan, since the drawing style, including that of the hatching used, is similar to that of the rampart.

(b) Church beneath bank Curiously, remains of an earlier drawing of the church appear (about its nave's length away) to the eastward and slightly (about its nave's height) to the S. This earlier drawing has been partially erased, so vigorously that the paper is thinned over that entire area and some holes have appeared in it. The vestiges now fall largely under the bank and ditch as depicted immediately N of the W entrance, but most of the old drawing of the tower, apparently founded on a dotted outline, is clearly visible against the line of the bank to the W of that entrance, its base formed by the roadline.

The size and shape of this erased, and therefore earlier, version seem to be identical with those of the later – however, what we take to be the top of the erased tower might by some be seen as the remains of a heavy 'W'. In the roadway below is a further erasure, which could be of a capital letter, possibly an 'L': it does not appear to have been another 'W'.

Of this phenomenon, Fowles and Legg say (1980, 45) 'Aubrey has drawn the parish church of Avebury, having correctly re-positioned it after rubbing out an earlier version which was placed too close to the bank'. Although in itself this comment is not entirely clear, it raised for us the question, whether the need for the alteration came about as a result of Aubrey's surveying techniques? This and related queries (see A.7(b); A.10) prompted the simulated survey reported on at A.15.

(c) The 'foliage' feature   At the centre of the L edge of the plan, above the roadway W of the church, is an enigmatic feature taller than the church tower and longer than its nave. A first glance is likely to interpret it as the foliage of trees, with verticals that could be their trunks. On closer examination, and after allowing for the horizontal line of a repaired edge-tear at this point, these verticals are seen to be part of a pattern more like a sketch (partly crossed out) of a building or buildings. This does not look like yet another version of the church. Because of the feature's placing, Avebury Manor must be a possible candidate: the whole feature could be intended to convey the proximity of the Manor's planted grounds, and/or the 'building' elements could be a sketch of the Manor's southern aspect (cf. the 1720s Stukeley sketch reproduced in V.C.H. 1983, 92).

If this feature was begun as a sketch of buildings,. the 'foliage' swirls and scribbles could represent a later effort to cover up or conceal them. This possibility, however, is made less likely by the presence on the earlier plan C of a similar feature, identically placed, from which such 'building' elements appear to be absent (see C.6(b)). Perhaps both plan-features are connected with Aubrey's mention of 'a watery place' (see A.16; Chapter IV,g).

A.7   Highways & roadways

(a) External   No roadway is shown emerging to the N, although there is space enough, but each of the other cardinal points has one. To the E, the beginning of the 'way to Marleborough' is indicated by a few short dashed lines. To the S, the road is defined solely by the first three or four pairs of stones of the West Kennet Avenue, labelled 'way to Kinnet'. Both of these 'way' names appear to be later additions. To the W, the road is unnamed, but its edges are clearly shown, most of the way to the edge of the plan, by long but discontinuous lines.

(b) Internal   The internal roadways are shown by double (i.e. 'parallel') ink lines, continuous except at the road junctions. The E–W road is shown as first following a line continuing the N-of-W orientation of the eastern entrance, then curving pronouncedly (and inaccurately) southward to a point, some halfway across the circle, immediately beyond the westernmost of four stones depicted close together in the roadway. From there it runs straight to its junction with the southern road, then to the western entrance on a slightly N-of-W course conformable to that entrance's orientation. Roads from the S and N entrances are depicted running to T-junctions with the E–W road, the southern road the more westerly, to form a markedly staggered 'cross-roads'. The southern road again appears to follow the orientation of its entrance, but the relation of northern road and entrance is less definite.

The strange curve shown in the E–W road provides another reason for our interest in Aubrey's surveying (see A.15), since it is an error that might have arisen during an effort to fit together four quadrants separately surveyed.

A.8   Boundaries

Three lines of dashes extend from the southern ditch northwards to the E–W road; the two westernmost of these lines run roughly parallel with the southern road, one to its W and one to its E. The latter, central, line of dashes meets the E–W road at the centre of its T-junction with the northern road (the line of which it might seem to continue, like a footpath). The easternmost line runs obliquely, W of N, to a point on the E–W road just E of the place where the four stones are depicted in the roadway. Here, on the other side of the road, begins a fourth, corresponding, line of dashes, curving slightly to run N across the NE quadrant to the northern ditch: about halfway across it appears to bisect a stone. In isolation these four features might all be interpreted as footpaths or tracks, but we accept them as field or 'close' boundaries (see Chapter IV,d).

A.9   The vertical feature (river or stream)

Some 3¼ in. (85 mm.) from the L edge of the plan runs a very faint vertical feature, impressed with some hard blunt-pointed instrument. A similar technique is used by Aubrey in his 'hawking' drawing (Plate 2) – in which it looks as though he first sketched out the main components with the blunt instrument.

This feature is best visible on the original when the document is held with strong light falling across, not down, the page. It may not have been noticed since Aubrey's time, since it is so faint that it is not made visible even by ultraviolet/infrared photography. Our account of it must therefore be detailed.

The feature begins as a minute circle some 2½ in. (60 mm.) from the top of the plan A sheet. Down from within this circle runs a single line, which soon opens into double 'parallel' lines (actually, diverging for some distance): these terminate about 1¾ in. (45 mm.) from the foot of the sheet. The beginning is about level with the top of the vertical of the compass-rose, and is placed between that and the bank. Its opening into double lines is opposite the NE quadrant of the compass-rose. Where they run between the compass letter 'E' and the end of the compass cross-bar, these lines are about 1 mm. apart; opposite *shillin*, some 4 mm. apart; below the W roadway, some 5 mm. apart. The lines then maintain that 5 mm. spacing until they tail off a little below the words *E port*: this width places the 'rt' of *N port*, and the 'or' of *E port*, between the two lines.

It will be noticed that the alignment described takes this feature down the length of the W side of the half-erased tower of the 'church under the bank'; the feature is therefore presumably later than that tower.

Our treating this intriguing feature as significant is entirely attributable to plan C, since that shows an indubitable 'river', running vertically down the plan on a very similar alignment which makes it 'flow' just outside the W entrance (see C.9). Whereas the plan C river 'rises' somewhere to the N of the plan area – for it is of even width from top to bottom of that plan – the present plan A feature 'rises' within the plan area. Aubrey therefore must have revised that among other plan C opinions by the time he came to make plan A.

Of course, plan A has been through its vicissitudes, so it is conceivable that these lines result from some casual damage or doodling in later time. To us their alignment would make that seem too great a coincidence. If this feature be accepted as Aubrey's, it provides additional evidence tending to suggest that plan A is in part based on features re-sketched from a preceding plan: C or another.

A.10–15: Ancient man-made features

A.10   Bank and ditch

These are depicted as an irregular 'circle': so irregular that it can equally easily be seen as, for example, a rough hexagon with smoothed-off corners (cf. Fowles and Legg 1980, 45: 'a series of short straight sections with rounded corners'). The bank is defined by a firm outer ink line, with short hatching (feathering) within; the ditch is similarly defined by a firm inner ink line, while its breadth is indicated by a broad band of grey-brown colour-wash. The internal border, between bank and ditch, is defined only by the edge of the colour-wash. The lines defining both inner and outer edges display various small irregularities (e.g. at the inner edge above, and the outer edge below, the E entrance), but the overall effect is to convey that bank and ditch are of equal breadth, and that their combined breadth is consistent, around the whole 'circle'. This unrealistic symmetry became another factor prompting us to ask questions about Aubrey's surveying procedures (see A.16).

It should be noted that a few faint traces of pencil, which could be surmised to be remains of an original pencilled outline, appear at two or three points around or within the bank/ditch: outer edge of NW quadrant, inner edge of SE quadrant, and (perhaps) above E–W roadway in NW quadrant.

A.11   Entrances

Four entrances are shown: to N, E, S, W. All are of similar dimensions, except that the S appears somewhat broader than the others, particularly at its outer end. Broken ink lines edge the entrance to the E, solid ink lines that to the W, while those to N and S appear as apertures without clear internal edges: these differences correspond in each case with peculiarities of treatment of the respective external roadways (see A.7(a)). Each entrance is shown as canted slightly away from a simple compass bearing: N and S entrances both a little W of N; E and W entrances both a little N of W. The E and W entrances are shown as roughly in the centre of those halves of the bank/ditch, but not as diametrically opposite, the W being shown as more southerly than the E. The N and S entrances are both shown as appreciably W of centre of their halves; again they are not exactly opposite, the N being the more westerly.

A.12   Key-letters & keyed features

(a) In the bottom right-hand margin is a neat 'Profil of rampire & graffe', the bank to the left, dark-shaded. The depiction is not quite symmetrical, since the height of the upcurved bank is about 25% greater than the depth of the downcurved ditch. Rampire and graffe are marked 'a' and 'b' respectively: these letters are not directly keyed to the main plan but to the caption: 'a. fower perches | b. fower perches' (i.e. about 22 yards or 20 metres), and thus indirectly to the plan via the capital 'A. rampire. | B. graffe' noted at (b) below. The present headings, in Aubrey's 'caption hand', appear to be, like the 'profil' itself, early in date.

Slightly confusingly, this sketch is 'the wrong way round' in relation to the bank/ditch closest to it: perhaps it was designed for the opposite corner, next to its capitalized key letters just noted.[1]

(b) On plan A's NW bank and ditch a capital 'A' and 'B' relate to a note in its bottom L corner: 'A. rampire. | B. graffe.'. The running hand in which these words are written is clearly distinguishable from the 'caption hand' of the same words (see (a) above); all the present examples seem to be early in date.

Above this note is another 'from γ [gamma] S port to δ [delta] N port, | or from W. α [alpha] port to E β [beta] port is 60 perches.' (i.e. about 330 yards or 301 metres). The alpha (or 'a') and the beta, are at W and E entrances respectively, set at the inner edge of the ditch. The gamma appears toward the outer end of the S entrance, in mid-bank, but immediately above it is an unexplained letter 'd' – in black ink: the alpha-delta are in orange-brown wash. We accept this as a 'd' although, perhaps because it is written as a separate 'word', it is not of Aubrey's characteristic shape for that letter.

There is a wash δ in the N entrance, toward its inner end, but it is not easy to resolve because it is overwritten by an unexplained 'c' (in black ink). It seems likely that Aubrey began by lettering the four entrances 'abcd', but then decided to use Greek characters instead – possibly because he was using 'ab' for his rampire/graffe inset (see (a) above) – and, in making the change, reversed the sequence of the characters attached to N and S entrances.

Other marks within the S entrance are puzzling. On the L, below the gamma, is a vertical mark with a comma-like mark, separate but very close, half-way down its length to its R. Viewed as one entity, these two marks could possibly be yet another Greek letter: perhaps a λ [lambda]. On the R, slightly farther in, is a dot-like mark. Conceivably all three marks could be bases for uncompleted depictions of stones, but that seems unlikely in view of the presence of a proper stone-depiction at the inner end of this S entrance (see A.14).

(c) Immediately above the Cove appears a figure 1 (or I) in brown, and immediately below it a bold ξ [xi], both of which key-characters (the ξ now with an orange-brown ink line drawn through the black character, diagonally top L to bottom R) appear above a perspective sketch of the Cove in the top R corner of the sheet. Three upright slabs are shown, the two outer ones apparently obliquely set – at up to 45 degrees to the central stone (but see (d) below); this bay-shape being viewed from its open side.

Behind the R stone is an oblong shape that could possibly be taken to be a fourth stone lying flat on the ground, but which, being unedged, is more likely to be intended as a shadow: the inner face of the L stone is hatched in a way perhaps intended to convey that it is in shadow, while a narrow horizontal band is drawn from this stone's base toward the centre of the Cove. A mid-morning sun shining from the L might be inferred; the sketch seems to offer no other clue to orientation, unless the diagonal drawn through the Greek letter xi above be intended as a directional line: S–N perhaps? However, we think it more likely that the diagonal represents a crossing-out, reserving the ξ as key for the whole northern circle and 1/I for the Cove itself – if so, the key to the 'plant', (d) below, should have been changed also, but was not. These key-characters are discussed further at (e) below.

It is worth noting that the hatching of the stones is coarser than that of the rampart and the church. Though such hypotheses are tricky, it may be that this should be taken to show that the sketch is a later addition. Conceivably, detail of the Cove – perhaps in the form of a copy of or from plan C (see C.14) – was recorded on a separate sheet in the 1660s 'first draught' text of 'Templa Druidum', then copied again, on to the present plan, during Aubrey's re-transcription in 1688/9.

(d) Immediately to the right of this marginal sketch of the Cove is a right-angled three-sided ink figure, with a φ [phi] above it and a caption below: 'φ is the plant of ξ'. Faint orange-brown inner lines indicate the breadth of the three stones.

This plan seems clear in its intention to convey that the two outer slabs were set at right-angles to the central slab, although at first sight the sketch to its left seems equally clearly to convey the message that they were set obliquely outward. However, it is possible that this apparent obliqueness is an accidental by-product of an effort at extreme perspective depiction. We should also recall that Stukeley and later close observers on occasion record one or more of the Cove stones (among others) as leaning at various degrees: if they were leaning in Aubrey's time, as seems likely, this also may have complicated his perspective, whether or not he was actually trying to show the lean.

Below Aubrey's two Cove-sketches appears a further sketch of the Cove, in pencil: this is attributable to Sir Richard Colt Hoare, who studied the *Monumenta* MS during the preparation of his *Ancient History of North Wiltshire* (1819–21) (see Introduction). As Colt Hoare explained, in a note dated at Stourhead, 1 February 1811 (WANHS Aubrey Wilts MS, fol.70):

> Having, after some difficulty, discovered that the manuscript Volumes entitled MONUMENTA BRITANNICA were safely lodged in the Library of WILLIAM CHURCHILL Esqr. of Henbury in the County of Dorset; in the Autumn of the year 1810, I applied to him for the inspection of these curious Volumes, and he obligingly granted me the Loan of them.[2]

(e) Below the close pair of stones within the southern semi-circle is a figure '2', in brown – apparently written over a black 'c', though it is difficult to be sure about this. This 'c' is not keyed on the face of plan A, but is presumably, together with the figure 1 (or I) against the Cove (see (c) above), to be explained from Aubrey's text (Aubrey 24, 32–3; Fowles and Legg 1980, 35–6):

Within this circumvallation are also (yet) remaining segments (of a roundish figure) of two (as I doe conjecture) Sacella. one, the fig.1, the other fig.2. and their ruines are not unlike Ariadne's Crowne; and are no neerer to a perfect circle than is that Constellation. So within our Christian churches are severall Chapelles respective to such, or such a Saint: and the like might have been here in the old time.[3]

To the margin opposite his mention of Ariadne's Crown, Aubrey has transferred the quotation from Ovid's *Fasti* concerning that constellation (the Corona Borealis, also known as the Corona Septentrionalis) originally inscribed on the face of the plan (see A.5(f)). We imagine that the quotation is not coeval with the plan, but occurred to Aubrey later, on newly seeing the patterns his stones made; however that may be, the whole Ariadne's Crowne parallel is even more appropriate than perhaps Aubrey intended, in drawing attention to the possibilities of multiple confusion to which it itself contributes. Ovid refers to nine stars, whereas the Corona Borealis in Aubrey's time had long been accredited with only eight; however, the eye of an inexpert observer can easily draw into the coronal 'circle' additional stars from the edges of neighbouring constellations. The analogy seems clear, in particular with Aubrey's S inner 'circle'.

Further ambiguities are introduced by Aubrey's seeming changes of mind, over the years and drafts, as to the referents of his key-letters. On the one hand, the term 'Sacella', in the quotation above ('Sacellum ... a small roofless temple ... attached frequently to the larger temples': OED) goes appropriately with Aubrey's references to 'remaining segments' and to the absence of 'a perfect circle' – inasmuch as all are clearly applicable to the whole inner 'circles', N and S. On the other hand, the term could reasonably be applied also, or alternatively, to the Cove and to its possible counterpart in the S circle – seen as sacella within sacella.

The foregoing considerations arise because of Aubrey's placing of his key letters close against the innermost features – Cove and Obelisk – and his use of them on occasion unambiguously to refer to these. An example important to us is the oft-quoted note (Aubrey 24, 31v; Fowles and Legg 1980, 34) keyed by a lozenge-star to the phrase 'two ... Sacella. one, the fig.1 ...': it reads 'His Majestie commanded me to digge at the bottom of the stones marked with the fig.1. to try if I could find any humane bones: but I did not doe it'. Without this note, the reader would have no reason to suppose that the sentence to which it is appended could refer to anything less than the entire (remains of the) N and S 'circles'.

The stones

A.13 Stone depictions

The depictions of stones within the bank and ditch appear at first as blobs of orange-brown wash: they are not uniform in size or shape, but neither are they sharply individualized. Underlying each blob is an inked irregular shape – circular, squarish, or oblong – having at its centre an ink dot. A sole exception, the easternmost of the three depicted 'Cove' stones in the NE quadrant, contains two dots. The oblong shape seems to be confined, within the bank and ditch, to the three Cove stones and to four stones in the E–W street; however, all the Kennet Avenue stones shown (three and a half to the E, three to the W) are oblong, but with undotted centres.

We can identify no obvious common feature of the stones shown by these oblongs. It is momentarily tempting to assume that they were fallen (presuming all the rest to have been standing) – and indeed those 'in the roade' very probably *were* fallen – but the inclusion of the Cove stones rules that out (see also Chapter IV, x and y).

These central dots, which do not appear to have been remarked until now, may reflect some aspect of surveying procedure (see A.15). However, they are not 'pinpricks' such as might be produced on an actual survey-sheet, for the paper under them is unblemished.

A.14   Stone settings (Transparency 1)

Problems arising from the nature both of the depictions and of the arrangements of stones are dealt with further, and related to archaeological evidence, in Chapter IV. However, for the purpose of the following enumerations, we speak as though each blob represents a definite stone.

Stones of the outer circle are shown as heavily concentrated in the SW and SE quadrants – nine stones in both, with seven of the SE ones in a row in its SW corner – with only six in the NE quadrant (two close to the N entrance) and seven in the NW (four close to the N entrance): a total of 31 survivors.

Within the northern half, 12 stones (four in the NW quadrant, eight in the NE) are depicted in an arrangement which might be perceived as an irregular semicircle open toward the S – we must be conscious, however, that such a description invokes the ubiquitous expectation of circularity (see Chapters II, V, VI). This arrangement embraces, at its centre, a separate group of three 'oblong' stones – the Cove – apparently oriented so as to have an open 'side' to the NE. Perceptible as a quite separate group are the four 'oblong' stones in the eastern part of the E–W road; the erroneous southward kink of the road, remarked on at 7(b), contributes to the disconnection of these stones from the northern circle.

We have once again to turn from Aubrey's plan to that part of his text already quoted and discussed at A.12(e), if we wish to justify our perception that these particular northern features are, most probably, 'remaining segments (of a roundish figure)' of one of his conjectured 'Sacella'. Here it is necessary to recognize that neither plan A nor any passage in Aubrey's surviving text explicitly connects the four stones in the roadway with the 12 to their N, as parts of one 'roundish figure ... no neerer to a perfect circle'. That he could indeed see these northern groupings as a single coherent feature can be confirmed only by turning to plan B (see B.14; Chapter IV, x). The *Monumenta* text does not even mention the stones in the roadway until four or five pages later (Aubrey 24, 37; Fowles and Legg 1980, 41): the ellipses and the square brackets are Aubrey's:

> One of the Monuments in the Street <that runnes East and West, fig ...> [like that above Holy-head, pag ...] is converted into a Pigstye, or Cow-house: as is to be seen in the Roade.

To a lesser extent, similar considerations apply to our perceptions of the southern groupings we are about to describe: it is again necessary to look beyond plan A if we are to justify the supposition that regular shapes are being shown.

We have so far noticed 50 stones depicted. Within the southern half, 13 stones are shown in another (presumable) 'remaining segment', apparently open (or, for the perfecting eye, incomplete) toward the NE, with six stones within it – two of these in a close pair – and one outside it to the S. To the N of the eastern end of this semicircle, toward the E–W road, are a further three stones. Finally, this plan's one within-entrance stone: it is shown at the eastern side of the inner end of the S entrance (i.e. at the corner of the ditch) bringing the henge total depicted to 74. Apart from the Kennet Avenue stones, none are shown outside the entrances.[4]

A.15   Supplement on surveying (see also Chapter II,i)

The presence of the 'church under the bank' (see A.6(b)) helps raise a question as to the status of plan A. Is it the actual plane-table survey, subsequently annotated and colour-washed, or is it a version resulting from the survey and specially prepared for publication? In other words, was this original church an integral part of the survey, but inaccurately plotted, or was it simply drawn in first on the version intended for publication, and then found to get in the way of the bank/ditch? In order to choose between these alternatives, we would need to know whether Aubrey's survey, 'in obedience to his Majesties command', was purely a plane-table one, whether it was by plane-table combined with other instrumentation, or whether it was a theodolite survey. We have not been able to trace any notes of readings which might derive from a theodolite-based survey, while plan A shows no signs of traced lines nor of pinpricks, which would be necessary for the drawing up of a plane-table survey carried out in the field (cf. Welfare 1989). It seems most likely that plan A was made by combining the results of a plane-table survey, quadrant by quadrant (as noted at A.7(b), the curve in the E road may be evidence of this). In an effort to simulate such a survey, and to examine the possibility that the church had been essential to Aubrey's survey, Mr R. J. Fitz-Gerald (Royal Commission on Historical Monuments; formerly Department of Archaeology, University of Southampton) has been able to elucidate some parts of what may have been Aubrey's field surveying techniques at Avebury. We are grateful to him for the following:

'Report on a plane-table error-simulation survey of the Avebury henge
monument, Wiltshire' (1989)
On the assumption that only a plane-table was used, it would have taken Aubrey and one assistant at least three and probably four days (September daylengths) to carry out a survey of the degree of accuracy of Plan A. Even so, the survey has attempted only to delimit the actual features of the *ditch* – presumably by placing a sighting rod at the points of angle change (perhaps regularly where long curved sections occur) along the inner ditch line, which is the easiest point of access. In drawing up the plan into its A version, Aubrey seems simply to have measured the bank profile and to have used it as a standard width for ditch and bank: two features which are not in fact regular, whether in prehistory, the 17th century, or today (Smith 1965, 193–7).

It seems clear that during his surveying Aubrey did little checking of his measurements – if he did indeed take measurements at all. His statement that the monument measured 60 perches from N to S and 60 perches from E to W is an underestimate of 30 m. (5.9 perches) and 48 m. (9.5 perches) respectively. Such under-estimates might suggest that the distances were not measured in the field, but were derived from the scale of the finished plan. For whatever reasons, plan A is grossly distorted (according to modern standards); thus, for example, the S inner 'circle' would have had an actual diameter of some 340 feet (Smith 1965, 198), whereas Aubrey's rendition is approximately one-third too small. In fact, when one attempts to compare plan A with a modern survey (Transparencies 1 and 17), the distortion is such, and so spatially uneven, that if the causeways are aligned the Cove stones and N and S circles are displaced to the W, while similarly if the Cove stones are aligned the entrances and bank/ditch are shifted to the E. However, if each quadrant of the site is compared separately, the individual quadrant lines of bank/ditch, although disproportionate, are not dissimilar from those of a modern plan: this strongly supports the hypothesis that Aubrey used a plane-table, and separate sheets of paper for each quadrant or station.

The hypothesis receives further support if it is assumed that a plane-table only was used, and that plan A itself represents the first bringing together of the whole survey. The critical point at issue concerns the partly erased church, and why it was erased at all. The fact that there is space on plan A between the more recent church and the W side of the bank suggests that the church's location had indeed been an integral part of the survey, perhaps a reference point. The essence of a plane-table survey is that it is composed while in the field; if Aubrey had been using only one sheet of paper for the whole survey, he would have known immediately that errors were occurring, since each radiation would have been annotated. The first church would, therefore, have been erased at the time of planning the NW quadrant in order to avoid continuing confusion. That the confusion did continue, creating the distortions noted above, suggests that Aubrey did not discover the error at the time(s) of surveying, and thus, if it was a plane-table survey, that he had used separate sheets of paper for each quadrant.

The church tower is almost the only feature that can be clearly seen from almost all parts of the monument: it might, therefore, have been used as an initial reference point – if only when setting out the base-line to tie in and orientate other reference points. The consequent possibility that the church had been the first item to be drawn in, when Aubrey had begun to construct plan A from a compilation of data, led to the following simulation.

Whenever direct measurement was used between stations, it was entered on the same sheet of paper because the distance was known. Where it was awkward to measure distance, the church tower and previous station, plus a chimney on one of the houses, were used as three reference points on a fresh sheet of paper, which was then added to the other sheets after completing the survey. Where the same sheet was used, errors were immediately apparent. When joining sheets, the effect was often a reduction in the true scale distance between stations, with the result that the plan of each quadrant was distorted. It was found to be possible to correct this distorting process by measuring the distances to the stones and ditch from just one station in each quadrant. Interquadrant radial intersection proved to be only reasonably accurate when the distance between stations was measured: a 5m. mismatch as a result of spiralling. The plan produced when no measurements were taken resulted in extreme distortions: a triangle-of-error spiral of between 10m. and 70m.

At Station 2, in the NW quadrant, an assumption that the point was 30 m. W of Station 1 on the base line by measurement was checked tacheometrically: it was shown in fact to be 29.7m. W and 4cm. S of the base line. At a scale 1:100, that would amount to 3mm. on the plan. When radiation to the stones in the quadrant was carried out, a 4 degree clockwise displacement of stone location was produced, and also resulted in the church being located in the bank, almost exactly where Aubrey had placed the partially erased one on plan A, purely as a consequence of the 4 degree rotation. The explanation was simple. Only 14 minutes of error was attributable to the combination of measurement errors. The remaining error occurred because the centre of the table was displaced 4cm. SE of the mark on the ground. To test this error, it was repeated at Station 3, without the station measurement error, and the church again appeared (slightly) W of the bank, a 3 degree error resulting from off-centring 2cm. to the SE. Radial intersection from Stations 2 and 3 shifted the stones on average 3–4cm. clockwise and brought them closer to the stations, foreshortening the arc of the quadrant.

If any of the above results applied to Aubrey's procedures, it seems likely that he used no control network to check the reliability of his plan, since the simulation also suggests that the errors of plan A could have been avoided by the use of radial intersectioning combined with the measuring of distances between stations. It appears that Aubrey may not have used measurements at all to move between stations, nor to establish distances to objects.

It seems, in sum, that plan A was the result of a plane-table survey, carried out by at least two people over several days. It is possible that Aubrey paced out the E-W axis of the monument and also the distance between the church and the W bank or causeway, thus providing the scalar distances for the plan. His actual survey apparently incorporated an error in the NW or SW quadrant of such magnitude that spiralling was produced. In correcting this spiral when drawing up plan A, which he must have started from the E side, Aubrey had not only to erase the first version/location of the church, but also to distort the line of bank/ditch and thus the locations of all objects marked on his plan.

110

Plan B. Bodleian Library MS. Top.Gen.c.24, fols 41v–42 (Plate 8, also in folder)

B.1–5: General and archival (see also Chapter I,v)

B.1   Title/heading
Headed 'Aubury', and subtitled 'The whole view of Aubury with the Walke, and the lesser Temple appendant to it', plan B also bears the heading 'Plate IId' (plan A being 'Plate I': see A.1; A.5(a); B.5(a)).

B.2   Orientation and scope
Oriented with N at the top, this plan, alone of the five, covers an area extending much beyond the henge itself – which appears as a roughly circular bank/ditch, with features within. Also shown are the Kennet Avenue, in two lengths set at right angles – from the henge to West Kennet, and from West Kennet to the Sanctuary – the Sanctuary itself, and two barrows close by; none of these features is named (see B.15). 'Selbury o̶r̶ Silsbury hill' is surrounded by a heavily emphasized ditch, and has a steep, slightly wandering diagonal line, representing a footpath, rising to the flat top from R to L across its S face. Other topographical features, all toward the foot of the plan, are the villages of 'West Kynnet' and 'East Kynnet' (spellings altered from 'Kinnet') both indicated simply by the name and a conventionalized sketch of a church, and the 'Rode from Marlborough to Bristoll'. Lastly, running along the foot of the sheet, and with its name at the very foot, centre of fol. 41v, is 'Fluvius Kynet' [sic], shown by three or four 'parallel' wavy lines. This river, Silbury Hill, and East (but not West) Kennet church are emphasized by a grey-brown wash, similar to that used to indicate the ditch on plan A.

We must note at once that the depiction and positioning of the Kinnet/Kynnet/Kynet features (the single 'n' may be Aubrey's preferred latest spelling) introduce several problems and confusions. The course of the actual river is not a simple W–E, for just E of West Kennet it curves southward, around the base of Overton Hill: even so, the village of East Kennet, with its church, is in actuality not to the N of the river but to the S (see also B.9). Further, the village of West Kennet appears never to have had its own church, being part of the parish of Avebury; at most, and long before Aubrey's time, there may have been a chapel there (cf. V.C.H. 1983, 101–2).

B.3   The document
Plan B is in ink and wash. There are also some pencillings that may or may not be contemporary, and few or none of which are likely to be visible in reproduction (see B. 10; B.13). It is on a sheet measuring 310 × 387 mm. (12.2 × 15.25 in.). The chainlines of its original laid paper run vertically, about 1 in. apart; a single watermark appears in folio 42, in the form of a 'horn in shield' somewhat similar to example 2694 in Heawood 1950. To the back of the plan, at the inner edge of fol. 42v, is affixed a vertical 'guard' strip, some 47 mm. wide, similar to that on the back of plan A; and again Aubrey has written notes over it (see A.3–4; B.4.). As with plan A (see A.3), short tears on the outer edges have old repairs with narrow strips of paper pinched over. These outer edges have been folded in, to some 30 cm.; the old folio numbers 17–18 (plan A being 16) confirm that plan B too is preserved from an earlier recension.

The cuttings-out   Unlike plan A (or C), plan B lacks substantial pieces of the original whole sheet, these having been cut out later. The cut edges are not straight, so dimensions of the three pieces must be given approximately: at the top right some 112 × 162 mm. (i.e. over one-third of the leaf), at top left some 250 × 184 mm. (about four-fifths of that leaf), toward bottom left a long narrow strip of some 10 × 180 mm. (almost the whole width of the leaf), below the western part of the 'Rode', and running up to just short of 'West Kynnet'.

Each cut piece has been replaced with backing paper of another stock. All three replacements are probably by Aubrey, and the largest (top L) certainly is, since it bears his writing. On the R leaf (fol. 42v) the 'guard' strip has been cut into, confirming not only that the guarding preceded the cutting-out, but also that the versos of the original guarded papers had already been annotated – and, probably, the set of papers had already been disbound – before the pieces were removed. The backing piece here, of some 135 × 195 mm., is affixed partly over the guard, thereby concealing some of the remains of Aubrey's notes (see B.4.).

The cut-outs and backings of the L page are more complicated. The large piece appears to have been cut out first, then replaced by a backing sheet originally almost as large as the page itself. The long narrow horizontal strip seems to have been cut out later, through the two thicknesses of paper, this aperture being filled by a second full-width backing piece, some 60mm. high, affixed to the foot of the first.

Aubrey's procedure in cutting out large sections of this plan is not unique: he similarly removed the top L corner from one of his Stonehenge plans (Aubrey 24, 60v–61; Fowles and Legg 1980, 78–9). Although the present *Monumenta* MS. does include occasional fair copies of plans – their recopied status evident since they are preserved along with earlier versions (e.g. Fripsbury 'camp'[1]) – no doubt the recopying of even comparatively simple plans was something which Aubrey tried to avoid when possible. Moreover, the excisions from the present plan are so extensive that Aubrey's preservation of it must be largely attributable to the factor mentioned earlier (Chapter I,v): his knowing that this original incorporated first-hand or on-the-spot elements which could only tend to become corrupted if copied.

B.4   The verso of the document

No unconcealed notes remain on fol. 41 (which, being apparently blank, is not reproduced by Fowles and Legg). Efforts to read the upper and more substantial of the note-fragments concealed under its backing paper, and cut short by the scissors, have yielded us, on successive lines: 'but what re [*or* ne, *or* he] | 'st not have | Borough mu | Pryo[r?]'. Further down is a handful of one- or two-letter beginnings of lines.

Unconcealed in the centre of 42v is written 'π [pi] Sepulchres', lightly underlined. In style and inking this is similar to the 'π Aubury' of fol.39 (see A.4; A.5(a)), so may also have been intended as a finding-title – for this sheet alone, or for a group of sheets of sepulchral interest. Fowles and Legg (1980, 47) reproduce a portion of 42v, containing this 'π sepulchres' and two unconcealed notes below it. However, above this portion, concealed under the backing paper, is a further note, preceded by Aubrey's swash-q 'quaere' sign, which we read as 'Mr Ashmole de mon[umen]t[a] juxta Whitehor[se?] [*illegible word*]'.

All notes surviving on these versos begin, like all but one of plan A's (see A.4), close to the true edge of the paper, not the fold edge. This again suggests that they date from a time when the sheets were part of a gathering in larger format than the present *Monumenta* volume.

B.5   Annotations

(a) The title and headings mentioned at B.1. Although plan B may appear the least finished of the five, the 'Plate IId' heading confirms that, like plan A, it too was intended as basis for a book illustration (see A.1). This heading and the subtitle are the only two items written on the replacement paper of this plan rather than on its original sheet.

The title 'Aubury' has been altered from 'Avebury' (like that of plan A: see A.5.(a)). The subtitle includes an unaltered 'Aubury', which would indicate that it was written later even did it not appear on replacement paper. It also contains a deletion of two letters, apparently the beginning of a word, made the more suggestive because we cannot be sure what the second character was intended to be: 'The whole view of Aubury with the Walke, and

[Sa?/Sc?/Se? *del.*] the lesser Temple appéndant to it'. Aubrey may have begun to write 'Selbury', which has warrant within this plan, or 'Sacella' or 'Sacellum', not far away in the *Monumenta* text, but 'Sanctuary' remains a teasing possibility, albeit it is a name first definitely used by Stukeley and sometimes suspected to be of his invention (Piggott 1985, 49; and see Chapter I, n.18; Chapter IV).

(b) Names already noted at A.3 above are almost self-explanatory. In 'Selbury or Silsbury hill', the second 's' of 'Silsbury' looks like a later insertion. The spelling of the two 'Kynnets' is carefully altered from 'Kinnet', in ink of a lighter colour. (No such alteration has been made to the 'Kinnet' at the head of the drawing two sheets farther on (our Plate 27), while text relating to this, on the sheet between, uses the river's spelling, 'Kynet'.)

The 'Rode' is discussed at B.7 below.

(c) An elementary compass-rose, near the centre of fol. 42, gives initials of the four cardinal points; the ring linking its cross-pieces is a single line, not dotted as in plan A (see A.5(e)).

(d) *Deleted annotations?*[5] The cutting out of the long thin strip, running from the L edge of the plan almost up to West Kennet 'church', is particularly striking. It suggests removal either of a single sentence of description or comment – this explanation perhaps supported by the presence immediately above the cut of a number of tiny dots, irregularly spaced, which could be the tips of rising letters – or of a depiction of some lateral feature about which Aubrey had changed his mind: road?, avenue?, spring?, river? Whatever it was seems to have been confined within the strip, for we find no trace of erasure on the remaining original paper in the area of the plan around West Kennet 'church' (see Chapter IV,g).

Otherwise, only two fragmentary areas directly related to the cut-outs now survive on the face of the plan: both tend to indicate verbal content (text or notes) rather than further plan elements.

One such area appears to the R of the northern part of the Kennet Avenue: it includes a 'pointing hand' directed toward the cut-out area, followed by what looks like a contracted 'memorandum' sign (cf A.5(d)).[6] Below these appears the 'quaere' sign followed by a ' + ' sign, while about halfway along the foot of the cut-out section is a part-curve, possibly the foot of a descending letter such as an 'f', a 'g' or Aubrey's capital 'I'.

The other fragment appears halfway down the Avenue, where is an enigmatic double-dot feature in the centre of the Avenue: what appear to be the ends of two cut-off words run up to it: 'ly' above and 'con' below, with, below the 'n' of the latter, an inverted 'v' shape touching its second vertical. The inking of the avenue and of the letter 'n' appears distinctly darker than that of all the rest of these items: if the difference means anything it presumably is that the lighter items are later, since we must take the avenue to have been put in first.

Two main interpretations of the double dots seem possible. One is that they represent a feature, presumably of two stones, about halfway down the Avenue – this is one of the areas within which the controverted Kennet Avenue 'Cove' may have been located (see Chapter IV, o). The other interpretation is that the dots belong to the words cut off by Aubrey, as marks of contraction which might for instance show that the lower cut-off word ended in 'tion'; the inverted 'v' would then be interpreted as a caret of insertion of those dots.

B.6–9: 'Modern' and natural features

B.6.   Buildings & foliage
None shown, apart from the conventional 'churches' at East and West Kennet.

B.7   Roadways
If we except the Kennet Avenue (see B.15) no roadways are shown in relation to the henge circles. It is possible that E and W roadways toward the henge appeared on the cut-out portions, but this does not seem likely, since there are no traces remaining on the surviving original paper immediately outside those entrances.

As it is, the only road on this plan is the 'Rode from Marlborough to Bristoll' already mentioned (B.2). This, indicated by a double line of dots and dashes, runs almost due E–W across the plan, bearing slightly S after passing the Sanctuary on Overton Hill but straightening again before it reaches West Kennet. Aubrey's name for this 'Rode' is echoed, as 'the high-way which goes from Bristow to Marleborough', on the following leaf (Aubrey 24, 43; Fowles and Legg 1980, 50), in text relating to his 'Plate III' (the detailed plan of the Sanctuary). Thus, interestingly, of four Aubrey plans not one actually names a Bath road (see Chapter IV, f).

B.8 Boundaries
Plan B indicates no boundaries.

B.9 River
Problems arising from the depicted course of the river in relation to the Kennet villages have already been discussed (B.2). Its style is like that of some other river drawings in the *Monumenta*, e.g. the 'Avon fluv.' at Amesbury (Aubrey 24, 159; Fowles and Legg 1980, 293), as well as resembling that of the puzzling N–S river of plan C (see A.9; C.9). The river's placing at the extreme foot of plan B could indicate that it was an afterthought – perhaps added after the cutting out of the long thin strip above its westward half (see Chapter IV, g).[7]

B.10–15: Ancient artificial features

B.10 Bank and ditch
Plan B's undifferentiated bank/ditch is indicated by a double circular line, with portions of hatching extending from the inner line a short way toward the outer; with the exception of a small area S of the W entrance, this hatching appears only along the easternmost third of the circle. Unlike those of the Sanctuary (see B.15), the circles are freehand, not compass-drawn, but their irregularities are no greater than any eye-drawn circle is likely to exhibit. No explanation of this feature remains within plan B: in particular, there is no hint that it comprises two different elements. A naive reading could thus easily misconstrue these circles as intended to show a single high bank or broad ditch, or a pair of narrow banks or ditches. Traces of pencilled lines of arc can be found within and without the W entrance; the outer line leaving no entrance gap. While these could well represent remains of an original rough double ring done by Aubrey – broader at the W than the present inked ring – it is equally possible that they are by a later hand such as Colt Hoare's (see A.12(d) & n.2). Also, written vertically up the plan in pencil outside the E entrance, and now largely erased, there appears to have been a three-word phrase of which only a central 'to', not definitely in Aubrey's hand, remains legible: perhaps it was 'way to [London?; Marlboro?]' (see also B.13).

B.11 Entrances
Four entrances are shown. Ink lines edge those to E and S; those to W and N appear as unedged apertures. N and S entrances are centrally placed and diametrically opposed; E and W entrances are shown as a little S of central and not quite opposite, the E entrance appearing the more southerly.

B.12 Key-letters
The portions cut from plan B could have included an explanation of the φ [phi] and σ [sigma] inscribed within the N and S inner 'circles' respectively. No key to these has been identified in Aubrey's surviving text – although the *phi* is of course used on plan A, in similarly close connexion with the N circle/cove complex, to key the 'plant of *xi*' (see A.12(d)). Since the S circle contains no internal features, the *sigma* must have keyed the whole of it. In the case of

the N circle, however, there may originally have been scope for ambiguity (cf. A.12(e)), arising from the placing of the *phi*, within the inner circle to the W, almost equidistant between 'cove' and circle: i.e. it could key either the N circle as a whole or just the feature within it.

B.13   The stone depictions

Stone arrangements within the bank and ditch are indicated by ink dots, all heavy in the outer 'circle', some heavy and some light, with two or three borderline cases, in the more complete-looking S and N inner 'circles'.

Within the bank/ditch, mainly in the western portion of the outer circle, are partial arcs of pencil dots. These partly overlap, but are not identical with, the arcs indicated by the existing ink dots, but pencilled dots also appear in places where there are no inked ones, mainly in spaces in the NW quadrant. In the inner circles there are no separate pencil dots, but a few of the ink dots may again overlap earlier pencillings.

As with the other pencilled features on this plan (see B.10), it is not clear whether some or all of these dots are to be attributed to Aubrey, to Colt Hoare, or to another. Even if these dots and lines are Aubrey's, both their own appearance, combining roughness and symmetry, and the trend of our other evidence (see Chapter IV, q) would lead us to view them as indicative only: a quick dotting-in of the fact of an outer circle, not an attempt to show its actual stone settings. We shall accordingly not be including these pencillings in our counts in the following paragraph, nor using them for comparisons in Chapter IV. However, their presence does remind us not to overlook the possibility that, despite appearances, the ink dots of this plan may also have been placed casually (rather than carefully): if so, the various apparent accuracies of the latter dots (established in Chapter IV) would have to be attributed to chance: a striking coincidence.

B.14   The stone settings

The outer circle   This shows nine stones in its SE quadrant (the same number as in plan A), eight in its SW (nine in plan A), eight in its NW (seven in plan A), and four in its NE quadrant (six in plan A). The total of 29 is two less than that of the outer circle of plan A, although the distribution shown in plan B is considerably more regular – except in the largely blank NE quadrant. Since the count of these outer dots is so close to that of plan A, we speak in the following enumeration as if all such heavy dots in plan B are, like the 'blobs' in plan A, intended to convey the presence of 'actual' stones, not just past stone-positions. It may be further noticed that the patterns of heavy dots in plan B's N and S inner circles look close enough to those of the corresponding circles in plan A to suggest that the light dots may be intended to convey something different: past stone positions, perhaps, either known to or surmised by Aubrey? However, such speculations only arise from comparing one plan with another: once we bring the monument itself into the analysis, our detailed comparisons in Chapter IV will confirm that dots of all sizes must be evaluated equally and without preconception.

An additional stone (light dot) is shown, about halfway between the E side of the S entrance and the southern inner ring. Due W of this is a small mark which could possibly denote another stone, but has more the character of a tiny accidental smudge: which is what we take it to be.[8]

Stone within entrance   Finally, before itemizing these inner circles, we must note that in plan B, as in A, one additional stone is shown within the E side of the S entrance, but that this one appears almost centrally placed whereas that in plan A is clearly at the inner edge of the ditch.

The inner circles   The N inner circle is shown as larger than the S by about half the latter's diameter; these relative proportions are very similar to those shown in plan A – and thus seem to repeat the distortion of Aubrey's plane-table results (see A.15). Both inner circles of plan B are depicted as regular; both are centrally placed on the N–S axis of the bank-and-ditch circle – so that, if a due N–S road were shown, it would 'inaccurately' bisect both circles. At the same time the S circle is centred, slightly but distinctly, W of the N circle, thus repeating in a subdued form another message of plan A. It is of interest that, if a due E–W road were shown, there would be found in its track the bottom four stones (or stone positions) of the N inner circle, corresponding to the four stones 'to be seen in the Roade' of plan A (see A.14; Chapter IV, x).

This N inner circle is of 17 dots (some might be seen as doubles), of which we count seven heavy. Within the circle are five heavy dots, the northernmost being in a very close, perhaps a touching, pair (which may appear as one in some reproductions). It is possible to read these as a 'cove' of four stones with an isolated stone slightly N of E, between them and the inner circle (see Chapter IV, y).

The S inner circle is of 12 dots (one, in its NE, smudged but definite), of which two (the easternmost) are certainly heavy, and five more (the westernmost) could be called heavy. Notably, its centre is empty of dots, containing only the σ [sigma] character (see B.12).

B.15 The Kennet Avenue
This is depicted as running in a straight N–S line from the S entrance to West Kennet 'church'; its length appears as something over three diameters of the Avebury circle. The E limb is virtually ruler-straight all the way (down the centre fold of the plan); the W limb is equally straight for its upper two-thirds or so, after which it is angled very slightly SE, narrowing the avenue. The W limb is made up mainly of long dashes, some 34 in number; the E limb of dots or short dashes, some 40 or more. The total arrangement seems more regular than is suggested by the Aubrey-based Camden description, with its 'one side at present wants a great many [stones], but the other is almost, if not quite entire' (Camden 1695, 111–12; quoted in full in Chapter I, vi).

The Sanctuary and its avenue   Plan B depicts the avenue from West Kennet by some eight pairs of dashes (actually nine to the N, eight to the S), set at a right-angle to run due E, for a length less than one diameter of the Avebury circle, to a concentric pair of circles toward East Kennet and just S of the Marlborough–Bristol road. A northward curve or kink in this Avenue, immediately before it meets the outer 'Sanctuary' circle, is shown clearly – this detail echoed by a N-and-then-W Avenue kink in Aubrey's detailed plan of the Sanctuary (not named by him: see Chapter I, n.18) (Plate 27).

Unlike plan B's main henge, the Sanctuary is based on compass-drawn circles, the central point-hole still clearly discernible. The inner circle is in pencil, while the outer is simply impressed by compass-point. Whereas the detailed 'Plate III' plan distinguishes fallen from standing stones, no such attempt is made here, stones and/or places being indicated by very short dashes or elongated dots, regularly spaced. The inner circle of the Sanctuary is shown by 14 dots, close in number to the 15 stones shown in the detailed plan – on which Aubrey also wrote, in confirmation, 'inner O 15 stones | outward O 22 do | [total] 37'. However, the outer circle in plan B has 29 dots, as against 22 stones (shown as well as stated) on the detailed plan.

A symmetrical pair of barrows – tops to the E, their S sides hatch-shaded – is shown immediately E of the outer Sanctuary circle, in a depiction similar to that of the detailed plan.

B.16 Stukeley's versions of Aubrey's plan B
It is convenient briefly to describe here the three Stukeley MS plans related to plan B, and already mentioned in Chapter I,vii. The first is explicitly derived from Gale's transcript, and

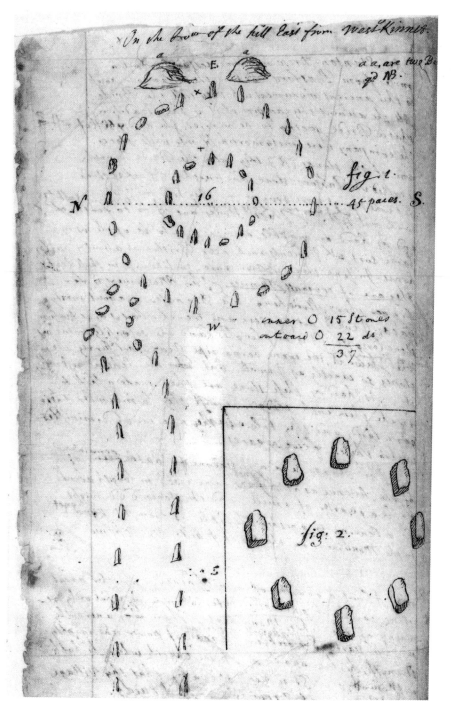

Plate 27 Aubrey's plan of the Sanctuary (Bodleian Library MS. Top.Gen.c.24, 43 av).

the other two are presumably so. These are WANHS Stukeley MS. 9 and 77, and Gough Maps 231, 38.

(a) Folio 9 (Plate 12) is that noted by Piggott (1985, 45) as 'a copy of the small-scale plan of the stone circles and Kennet Avenue', and its layout is indeed obviously based on that of plan B. That said, however, there are many dissimilarities, several stemming from apparent elements of conflation with plan A and with the 'Plate III' detailed Sanctuary plan (our Plate 27).

The main differences from plan B are as follows:

—Plan largely turned sideways, to be viewed from W: this entails the turning of Silbury Hill, and the showing of all stone-depictions as pointing E.

—Henge bank (unshaded) distinguished from ditch (shaded): as in plan A but not B.

—Outer circle: five more stones shown in SE quadrant; one less in NE and SW; spacing different.

—Inner circles: both set more westward; both smaller proportionally, and S circle more obviously smaller than N; nothing within N (i.e. no Cove).

—West Kennet Avenue: shown by 18 regular pairs of stones, then a long gap to a single pair (in the E limb) above which are the words 'A Mile', then a much longer gap to three pairs of stones leading down to West Kennet 'church'.

—The Sanctuary (not so named): Aubrey's dotted plan B version replaced by one based on his 'Plate III' detailed plan. Stone numbers different: one more stone in S limb of avenue, one more in inner ring, and (remarkably) 10 more in the outer (32, as against Aubrey's shown and stated 22). Pronounced kink almost in middle of avenue from West Kennet to Sanctuary.

—Rivers: 'Kennet Flu.' remains at foot of sheet (with East Kennet church still to N of it), but a novel, and surely fantastical, river is shown rising to the N of the Kennet but S of West Kennet 'church': this flows, broadening, as it were *up* the shoulder of Overton Hill, across the Avenue about halfway between West Kennet and the Sanctuary.

Apart from Stukeley's note that 'This figure is wholly wrong taken ... by Mr Aubury', all the writing on the face of this plan appears to derive from Aubrey. In addition to the possibly conflated elements discussed in Chapter I,vii, we may point out here that it includes a version of Aubrey's note referring to the inset plan on his 'Plate III' page, of '8 very high stones in a circle'.

(b) Folio 77 is captioned by Stukeley 'Mr Aubrys fig. of the snakes head, or hakpen, on Overton hill. 1660. but he' [sic], while at the head of the plan an 'A[nn]o' date, probably 1660, has been crossed out (see Chapter I,vii). This is a bare version, of stone settings only, but again their numbers vary, both from those shown in Aubrey's surviving plan and from those in the Gale transcript just discussed. This time the inner ring has only 13 stones, while the outer has 28.

(c) Gough Maps 231, 38 (Plate 13). A simple outline plan, mainly done in continuous ink lines, although the 'Road from Marlburgh to Bristol' is shown by a single line of dashes. At first glance it could appear to be a direct simplification of plan B, but it actually incorporates two of the most striking features of the Gale transcript ((a) above): the additional 'river', and the pronounced kink in the avenue to the Sanctuary.

As Plate 13 shows, Stukeley re-used this sheet, writing over the rough plan a set of comments, dated August 1721, on the apparently imminent destruction of Avebury as an antiquity.

Plate 28   Plan C detail (W entrance, Church and river) (Royal Society MS. 131, 67).

Plan C. Royal Society MS.131, 67 (Plates 6, also in folder, and 28–31, 50–51, 57)

C.1–5: General and archival (see also Chapter I.iii)

C.1   Title/heading

The title 'Avebury', in capitals, is set close to the L edge of the sheet, centrally. The characters composing this word are carefully lettered – as are the capitals NESW (see C.5) – in a style similar to that of the MS. title- and dedication-pages of the *Monumenta Britannica* and 'Templa Druidum' (Aubrey 24, 20, 27, 28; Fowles & Legg 1980, 3, 14, 15) (Plate 28).

The ink note, top R centre, 'By Mr Awbrey | july 8. 1663', is in the hand of Henry Oldenburg, Secretary of the Royal Society 1663–77. The inked and parenthesized numbers 60–61 (the (60) being written on the verso), indicate the plan's place, immediately preceding the Charleton plan D (62–63), in a formerly existing sequence of illustrations, plans, and short papers from the Society's early years. A list survives, in Oldenburg's hand (Roy.Soc. Cl.P.XXIV.78), showing this to have been a gathering, some 110 pages in all, of about forty items, none of them 'ordered to be registered', but apparently having little else in common. This sequence will have been broken up, and its contents redistributed, before or during the major re-sorting of the Society's archives which occurred in the 1730s.

C.2   Orientation and scope
Oriented with N at the top, the plan shows the bank/ditch, symmetrical roadways within, and four concentric circles of stone settings or places. Two sketches of the Cove appear, one in place within the NE quadrant, the other a supplementary depiction in the top L corner of the sheet. Additionally, outside the henge, the broad W margin shows the westward roadway with buildings on its S side, and on its N side the church and a 'foliage' feature beyond. A 'river' is shown immediately outside the W entrance. Pairs of stones are shown in the narrow margins outside N and S entrances, and in the broad margin outside the E.

C.3   The document
Plan C is on a sheet of wove paper, not watermarked, measuring 272 × 386 mm. (10.7 × 15.2 in.). It was folded in half, vertically, and then in half again in the same dimension, at some early time. Since the sketches and notes by Aubrey which appear on one half of the verso (see C.4; C.15) are clearly contained by the fold line, the folding was presumably done by him.

   This plan is executed throughout in pencil. The surface is evenly and well preserved overall, the only slight loss of pencilling appearing to be at the very foot of the centre, mainly to the R of the fold-line. However, the pencilling is in general very faint, only the main ring being at all heavily emphasized. A first glance might take in little more than that ring, divided into equal quarters by an exact cross of roads, and therefore give a misleading impression of sketchiness. The full extent of detail depicted, and the seeming care of its execution, reflected in the neatness of the lettering, emerges only gradually and by close examination. Fortunately the original faint contrast can be enhanced photographically, and perception of detail is then easier: thus a reproduction such as ours (Plate 6) may well be more legible than the original.

C.4   The verso of the document (Plate 31)
Faint sketches and pencil notes in Aubrey's hand appear on the verso of the L half of the plan. In the hope of sharpening these, and perhaps revealing more detail, a multispectral photographic examination was undertaken (in February 1989); the results, however, improved only slightly on conventional bromide prints. The sketches and notes are described in detail at C.15.

   To the R verso, at its centre edge abutting on the fold line, was vertically affixed a long thin strip of paper, some 204 × 14 cm. (8.0 × 0.5 in.), of which the bottom three inches or so has later been torn off. The inner edge of this strip, running along the centre, is uneven as if it too has been torn; and indeed 'bay-and-headland' irregularities attributable to a sideways pull-tear remain on the face of the strip.

   The strip's paper looks early; perhaps it is the remains of a small guard, or possibly a strengthener – rather than a repair, since wear at the centre fold does not appear to have been heavy. The only obvious repair is probably 20th-century: a small internal tear in the top L corner has been closed by a small piece of material stuck to the verso, which shows through on the face of the plan. Unfortunately this slightly affects the legibility of the bottom L corner of the supplementary Cove sketch (see C.14(d)).

C.5   Annotations
Plan C is the only one of the five entirely unaccompanied by author's explanatory text, beyond its title, 'Avebury', and the single key-letter 'A' (see C.12). The neatly drawn capitals NESW, for the four compass points, appear outside the four entrances, close to the edges of the plan; the letter S, being in the rubbed area of the plan, is not easily legible.

C.6–9: 'Modern' and natural features

C.6   Church, foliage, other buildings (Plate 28)
(a) Church   In comparison with that of plan A, this depiction is more accurate in showing a separate chancel and the pinnacles of the tower, and in the height of the tower relative to the nave; it is less accurate in showing no S porch. Neither A nor C shows the lower-roofed S aisle which is such a clear feature of the church in Stukeley's Frontispiece and at the present day.

As with the plan A church (A.6(a)) the juxtaposition of small church and great rings can be seen as having a dramatic or rhetorical effect – reminding us that, in Aubrey's view, these were temples new and old. This effect is generated in a perhaps subdued form by plan C.

(b) The 'foliage' feature   In describing plan A we noted (A.6(c)) the 'trees or foliage' shown beyond the church to the W, at the very edge of the plan; that feature was apparently partly underlain by a set of vertical lines with some diagonals. A similar-looking depiction appears in C, but in this latter there is no perceptible 'underlying' element: the verticals are few, short, and freehand, and ask to be interpreted simply as tree-trunks. (Trees are one of those impediments from which all three Aubrey plans are otherwise 'disempestered', within the henge.)

While we are not inclined to interpret the present feature, either in plan A or here, as directly depicting the 'watery place' (see C.9; Chapter IV, g), the trees or foliage could of course be surrounding such a place. In any case, it is interesting that Aubrey made sure to include such a feature in both.

(c) Other buildings: presence, distribution, style   Plan C is the sole 17th-century plan to depict buildings within the circle. Both N–S and E–W roadways are shown as lined with sketched shapes interpretable mainly as dwellings – houses, cottages, and perhaps inns – some with and some without out-houses. Along the E–W axis these extend the full width of the circle and out beyond it to the W, on the S side, of the road; here the church (see C.6(a)) is the lone building on the N side. Along the N–S axis the buildings extend about half the width of the circle, in a slightly staggered pattern extending more to the N on the W side of the road, more to the S on the E. All buildings along the E-W axis are depicted as if observed from the S; all those along the N–S axis are as if observed from the E. It is interesting that several buildings to the W of the N road appear to be shown by their roofs only, as though behind an obscuring bank or fence.

(d) Other buildings: numbers, significance, analysis   The total number of buildings shown within the circle is at least 39, and could be argued to be up to 50 (see analysis below). The depictions are probably conventionalized, but are certainly not standardized: we have found no two identical. They are shown as varying in shape, size, relation to out-houses, and spacing. This variety seems clearly intended to convey the impression that the circle's centre, and particularly the E–W road, was heavily and almost continuously lined with obscuring village buildings.

C.7.   Roadways
Plan C shows the circle divided into equal quadrants by ruler-straight roadways, drawn some 5/16 in. wide, meeting as a perfect cross at its centre. It is not known whether this symmetry could have implied at the time, for Aubrey, that cruciform roads had been part of the original design (see further Chapter IV, f).

The ruled lines of the E roadway tail off into dotted edges, about 12½ in. from the far side of the sheet: it may be that Aubrey used a foot-rule and did not bother to move it across.

Road/side			Buildings	Shapes[a]	Total
E–W :	W :	N	8	2[b]	10
	:	S	6	3[c]	9
	: E :	N	6	2[d]	8
	:	S	6	1[e]	7
N–S :	N :	W	4	2[f]	6
	:	E	4	–	4
	: S :	W	2	–	2
	:	E	3 or 4	–	3 or 4
Totals			39 or 40	10	49 or 50

Notes (for ring numbers, see C.13)
[a]: We call 'shapes' those we are not confident of identifying as buildings or outbuildings, as follows:
[b]: Two ?stones?: on ring 1, & between rings 3–4.
[c]: Two ?stones?: on ring 1, & between rings 3–4; oblong shape between rings 1–2.
[d]: A ?shape? at inner crossroads corner?; ?stone? on ring 1 (partly in street).
[e]: Oblong shape between rings 1–2?
[f]: Two shapes: between rings 3–4 (S of northernmost building), & just above inner crossroads corner?

Where they cross roadways, the lines of the divider-drawn circles have generally been erased. However, the line of the inner edge of the ditch remains at the W entrance, and ring 3 remains where it crosses the S roadway. The dotting of ring 4 is carried across the W roadway.

The edges of the N–S roadway, where not lined with buildings, are not left as plain ruled lines but have squiggles and/or curlicues all along them. We take this to be a convention representing hedges, as explicitly used by Aubrey elsewhere, e.g. in his depiction of Stanton Drew (Aubrey 24, 54; Fowles and Legg 1980, 69) (see also C.8). We are again reminded of the hedges and trees shown as lining the N–S road in Stukeley's frontispiece, plan E (Plate 14).

C.8 Boundaries and hedges

The clutter within the circle is completed by a network of fine lines wandering over it. At least some of these are presumably intended to indicate divisions (e.g. in the SE quadrant) into fields or enclosures. Few of these lines are straight. Some, such as those in the NE quadrant, are single sinuous lines; others, as in the SE quadrant, are treated in the curlicue convention we take to signify hedges (see C.7). Those two quadrants appear to contain 5 and 7 enclosures respectively; the number possibly intended to be shown in the two W quadrants is more difficult to determine, since some of the lines are particularly faint (see further Chapter IV, d).

Thus, what with buildings, roadside hedges, and hedged enclosures, plan C seems to call attention to almost all those obstructive features of 17th-century Avebury 'which are altogether foreigne to this Antiquity, and would but have clowded and da[r]kned the reall Designe'. This probably demonstrates the literalness of Aubrey's associated remark as to the usefulness of his having 'dis-empestred' plan A 'from the Enclosures, and Houses &c.' (Aubrey 24, 36; Fowles and Legg 1980, 39): he must have had in mind the experience of drawing up this rather congested plan (see also Chapters I and IV).

C.9 River

A distinctive feature of plan C is its unambiguous depiction of what we can interpret only as a river, oriented due N–S, from top to bottom of the plan, and presumably flowing S, passing immediately to the W of the circle between the W entrance and the church (Plate 28). The convention employed is similar to that used to depict 'Fluvius Kynet' in plan B: a series of up to 10 'parallel' wavy lines.

Although this 'river' may at one time have had an analogue on plan A (see A.9), it remains one of the most puzzling features shown on any of the plans. It has no direct historico-geographical warrant, for the contour of the land seems always to have prohibited such a flow, while the only remark of Aubrey's which might account for his showing *some* stream in the area is so phrased as clearly to exclude *this* one. In an undeleted aside (Aubrey 24, 38; Fowles and Legg 1980, 42) he says: 'At this Townes end (sc. Aubury), by the church, is a Watery place, which (I thinke) is the source of the River Kynnet.' (see further Chapter IV,g.)

C.10–14: Ancient artificial features

C.10 Bank/ditch

The plan is based on a series of concentric circles, drawn with dividers, the central point-hole being clearly visible. The ring of bank and ditch, drawn some ⅜ in. wide, is based on four such circles: a central pair, about 1/16 in. apart, with inner and outer circles equidistant from these. The close central pair serves as guide for the pencilled emphasis, done probably freehand and perhaps with a softer pencil. An uninstructed eye might interpret this as indicating some tripartite feature: a central bank/wall with ditches or causeways on either side, or a central ditch with ramparts or causeways. The emphasized circle is of 9 in. diameter.

C11 Entrances

The E and W entrances are ruler-edged; the S entrance appears almost edgeless, but again this is in the somewhat rubbed area. The N entrance is treated differently, the road-lines having been ruler-drawn only as far as the circle at the inner edge of the ditch. The short remaining stretch of roadway, through the entrance and out beyond it, is angled distinctly E or N; its edges are equally firmly lined, but freehand not ruled.

C.12 Key-letters and keyed features

The single key-letter 'A' links the depiction of the Cove within the NE quadrant with the supplementary sketch in the top L corner of the sheet (see C.14(b-c)) (Plates 29–30).

C.13 Stones: the rings and their depiction (Plates 6, 29)

Four concentric rings of stones are depicted; the three inner circles are of 7 in., 4⅝ in., and 3 in. respectively. The drawing of the outermost, immediately within the circle of the inner edge of the ditch, was evidently guided by that circle; the other three rings are drawn directly on to the lines of the divider-drawn circles. Counting from the outermost, we refer to these as rings 1 to 4. None of the four shows stones regularly spaced around its whole circumference, but all except ring 2 include sequences of stones closely and regularly spaced (see list below). The shapes and sizes of the stone-depictions are varied: sufficiently so to suggest an intention to convey, at the least, a general impression that the actual stones were equally varied, and possibly, beyond that, to convey the shape and size of each surviving stone. Two main kinds of depiction are employed: a minority of closed circlish or oblongish shapes, mostly unshaded and a majority of shapes resembling gravestones, unclosed at one end, and mostly shaded. The open end could be seen as the foot or base: if this is so, these latter shapes all ask to be interpreted as erect, and thus as depicted outwards from an implied viewpoint at the centre of the plan. The former shapes, which suggest no particular viewing-orientation, could be recumbent stones. These interpretations may be strengthened by reference to Aubrey's plan of the Sanctuary (Plate 27), in which what looks like a similar set of conventions is used in a more refined way.

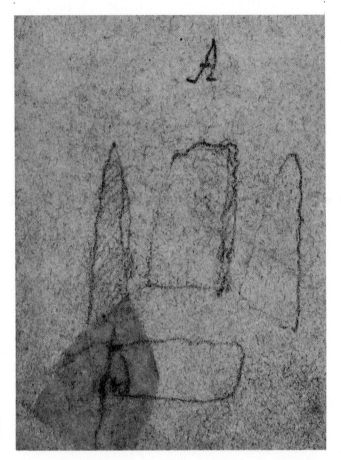

Plate 29 Plan C detail (Cove from margin of plan) (Royal Society MS. 131, 67).

Between the stones, each ring is emphasized by a series of pencil-point dots: their pattern is not entirely regular in any ring, but the dots tend to be closely spaced, especially in rings 3 and 4. The effect is simply to confirm the shape of the ring, not to convey an intention to indicate actual positions or spacings of missing stones.

Our count of depictions of stones in these rings totals 76, plus 3 possibles, made up as follows:

Ring 1: 24 definite plus 3 possible[*] (two inside the W entrance, on either side, one inside the E, on the N side, partly in the street); regular series of 3 and 6 stones included.
Ring 2: 18 definite; no regular series.
Ring 3: 22 definite, excluding Cove stone (including one in E–W street, E section[**]); regular series of 3 & 7 stones included.
Ring 4: 12 definite (including one in E–W street, E section[**], and one on edge of N–S road, S section); regular series of 2 & 4 stones included.

We have not included in the analysis above and the table on p. 126 the remaining seven of the ten 'shapes' itemized at C.6(d), being forms possible to interpret either as stones or as buildings. If these were stones, they would be the only ones within the circle, apart from the Cove stones, not placed on a ring. These shapes include a possible pair on the E–W road, W

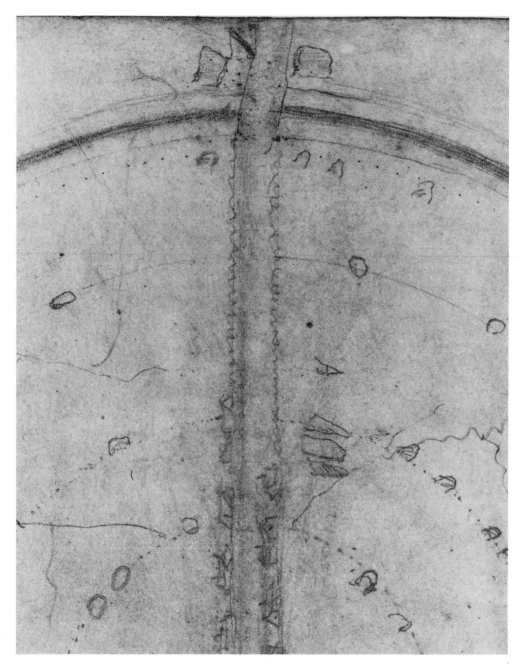

Plate 30 Plan C detail (Cove within NE quadrant) (Royal Society MS. 131, 67).

Ring	NW	SW	NE	SE	Total
1	3+1)	5(+1)	6(+1)	10	24(+3)[*]
2	3	5	4	6	18
3	3	7	7(1s)[**]	5	22
4	3	3	4(1s)[**]	2	12
Total	12(+1)	20(+1)	21+1)	23	76(+3)

Notes

[*] The 'possibles' constitute three of the ten 'shapes' noted in the analysis at C.6(d).

[**] The presence of at least two stones in the E–W street is thus again attested.

half, between rings 3 & 4, and a single on the N–S road, W side, just above the crossroads; the final four, oblongs, we think the most likely to represent buildings.

C.14   Stones: entrance and Cove

(a) Entrance   Of the three Aubrey plans, C is alone in showing pairs of large stones outside three of the four entrances; these are on either side of the roadways, to N, E, and S. Outside the W entrance there is no such clear and squarish pair, but the first shape on the S side of the road, immediately beyond the 'river', is more like a stone than like the buildings beyond it (Plate 28). Also, within the outer end of the W entrance on its S side is what could be a stone of the 'gravestone' shape; another of these may be similarly placed within the E side of the S entrance – it is rubbed, so we cannot be sure. The pair outside this S entrance are clearly shown, but we see no depiction of a beginning Kennet Avenue beyond: however, this area is close to the foot of the plan, so there would have been space to fit in at most a single pair of Avenue stones.

(b)–(e) Stones: the Cove (Plates 29–30)

(b) Cove within circle   Within the NE quadrant, a setting is shown of three 'upright' stones with individually characterized shapes. This Cove's 'open' side is oriented due E, but the setting is depicted as if viewed from the W, so that its 'back' is toward the observer; the key-letter 'A', N of the Cove, is also aligned to be read from the W.

Thus viewed, a central slab, its N shoulder sloping or bevelled, is flanked by two tall triangles, angled away from the observer, apparently standing at some 30°–45° to it. The N stone, on the line of ring 3, appears slightly broader at its base than the more heavily shaded S stone.

The viewing-orientation, being opposite to that from which the buildings in the adjacent road are viewed (see C.6(a)), helps emphasize the Cove as a distinctive feature. Both this sketch and that in the corner (c) appear to have been carefully executed.

(c) Cove in the corner   The shapes, and the relative dimensions, of the three stones are confirmed by the supplementary drawing of the Cove, in the top L corner of the plan. Although also positioned to be 'read' from the W (a viewpoint called for by no other features of the plan), this is clearly intended to show the opposite face of the setting: that is, as seen from the E. Both side-stones are here angled toward the observer, again apparently at some 30°–45°, while the diagonally shaped, narrower, and more pointed stone is moved from the R to the L of the central slab. Oddly, however, the sloping upper corner of the slab has not been reversed, and thus now asks to be read as its S shoulder. This seems to be an error – inasmuch as the present-day central stone shows its main shoulder-slope to the N – and may indicate that the Cove-depiction within the rings was drawn first and the one in the

126

corner partly copied from it. Nevertheless, other features of the corner drawing, such as its shading and its implied angle of view, could suggest that it is a fresh sketch.

(d) The fourth stone
Perhaps the most striking feature of this corner-drawing of the Cove is its depiction of what asks to be interpreted as a fourth stone, large and oblong, lying flat on the ground to the E, broadside-on to, and just outside, the setting formed by the other three. The L 'vertical' line of this simple four-line feature has a curvature to the R which may or may not be significant. In either case, although this curved line is within the area of the small repaired tear mentioned earlier (C.3), its shape does not seem to have been distorted thereby. These four lines taken in isolation might possibly suggest, rather than a stone, the outline of a pit, or of a place where a stone had formerly been. Since the presence of this fourth stone is the main additional information provided by the corner-sketch, and since depicting the three stones from a W viewpoint 'naturally' conceals whatever is on the ground immediately to their E, the question arises, why Aubrey did not from the start simply select an E viewpoint from which to show this whole feature in its place within the circle? Answers are likely to remain speculative. One possibility is that the supplementary sketch was fruit of further visit or study, after the main plan had been drawn: if so, it might have been made at the same time as the faint sketches on the verso (see C.15). Or, the W aspect of the Cove may have held some significance or use in Aubrey's eyes outweighing its hiding the fourth stone; or he may simply have wished to avoid running his sketch up to the road-line, which showing the E aspect there might have entailed (see Chapter IV,y).

(e) Cove-plan comparisons   It is noteworthy that both plan A and plan C emphasize the Cove by according it corner sketches keyed to the main plans. Only plan A provides both a sketch and a 'plant'; only C provides two sketches. All three sketches convey that the outer stones are set obliquely to the centre one; thus all apparently contradict the 'plant' in A, which shows them set at right-angles. Another divergence is between plan A's showing the three stones as block-like, almost square, and C's twice showing the outer two as tapering, the centre as slope-shouldered. Although our relating of these four plans to Stukeley's, and to archaeological information, is mainly reserved for the comparisons and analysis of Chapter IV, it is helpful at this point to remind ourselves of Cove-stone dimensions recorded by Stukeley (1743, 24) set alongside those measured by Smith (1965, 202 & n1). The northernmost stone of the three, recorded by Stukeley as having fallen in 1713, was then said to be some 21 feet tall (including its sunken base), and narrow: 'of the same shape as its opposite ... We measur'd this 17 foot above ground ... 7 foot broad, two and a half thick' (Smith 16 ft. high, 8.8 broad). Stukeley goes on 'That [stone] on the back, or in the middle, is much broader, being 15 foot, as many high, 4 thick; but a great piece of one side of it has been broke off by decay of the stone' (Smith 14.4 ft. high, 16.8 broad). Since any lean of the stones may have affected their depiction, we note further from Smith (1965, 202 & n1) that in 1881 the narrow southernmost stone was leaning 27½ in. from the perpendicular, a figure unchanged in 1961. The 'central' stone, in 1881, leaned 15 in., a figure which had increased to 23 in. by 1961 (see also Chapter IV, y).

C.15   Sketches and words on the verso (Plate 31)
As noted above (C.4) Aubrey's use of the verso is confined to its L half. This appears to have comprised the outer surfaces of the doubly folded sheet, so the pencilling will have been subjected to a good deal of rubbing. One result is that, even after the advanced photographic techniques already mentioned have been brought to bear, some of what was recorded on the verso remains at or beyond the border of legibility. We indicate our degree of uncertainty as each item is mentioned. (Orientations are to the half-sheet viewed longways on, original centre fold at top.)

Plate 31   Plan C verso (Royal Society MS. 131, 67: Band 7 C imagery; photo: C. J. Brooke).

Words   The clearest word is certainly 'Littleton' (lower L quarter). This is preceded by a now-faint word, almost certainly of four letters, the erasure of which may have been intentional: it could be 'fair'.

In the lower R corner, faint but almost entirely legible, is written 'Stones neere Kinnet | within a mile of Aveby': we are confident of this reading except for the spelling of the last word, which runs up to the affixed margin of the sheet – but it does appear to be 'Aveby'.

In the top L quarter of the sheet, and written downwards at right-angles to the other words, is what appears to be a name consisting of two words and ending in 'Mill' or 'Hill'. It begins with what is probably a B or a P, possibly an R, followed by some five letters. We have checked this against the British names in the printed index of *Monumenta Britannica* (Fowles and Legg 1982, 1080–97) without finding a useful lead. However, the first part may possibly be 'Beckap': the implied 'Beckhampton' makes this a tempting reading, but we are not confident of it. Another possibility is 'Barrow Hill': see next paragraphs.

Sketches   Immediately above the last-mentioned, uncertain, word appears a straight line, about as long as the word, with, based on it, the remains of a small sketch. This could consist of two short double-line uprights bearing a large oblong cross-piece, taller than its supports; alternatively, the R upright may appear as the trunk of a bushy-top tree.

Above the word 'Littleton' appears the shaded long side of an oval feature, having a straight vertical line as its left end. Two small shaded uprights with rounded tops rise from this line as from a base. We are indebted to Professor Stuart Piggott for the suggestion that this may represent the Lugbury long barrow at Littleton Drew – of which a depiction does appear in the *Monumenta Britannica* (Aubrey 25, 42; Fowles & Legg 1982, 805). Aubrey's account of Lugbury appears on the same sheet as a sketch and account of the Lanhill long

128

barrow ('Hubba's Low'), which is at Barrow-hill, beyond Chippenham – offering, as just noted, another possible interpretation of the above uncertain word.

Above the 'Littleton' sketch, and above the conspicuous fold-line of the document, appear the faint remains of a sketch of what could be a large conical hill. The pencilling at the top has virtually gone, but the lower part is reminiscent of the sketch of Silbury Hill, with its emphasized ditch, on Aubrey's plan B. A horizontal line appears to extend to L and R of this 'base', and to be interrupted by it. Upon the R end of this line appear to be placed at least three shaded and pointed vertical features, probably stone-depictions. These can be viewed as a discrete feature, or they can be seen as the topmost items of a faint and irregular circle of such pointed stones. The lowermost items of this circle are on a curved portion of line, immediately above the 'Stones neere Kinnet' phrase. There are at least two shown here, and at least three more, above and to their L, rising in a curve toward the top three. Some possibly analogous sketches of stone circles survive in the *Monumenta Britannica*: compare particularly the circle of 'eight huge stones' 'In a Lane from Kynet towards Marleborough' (Aubrey 24, 43, 43av; Fowles and Legg 1980, 50–1) (Plate 27) – although these are coffin-shaped, not pointed (cf. Piggott 1948).

Plan D. Royal Society MS.Cl.P.XVI.18 (Plate 5, also in folder)

D.1–5: General and archival (see also Chapter I, iii)

D.1   Title/heading

The plan is headed, in Walter Charleton's hand, 'The Plant of the admirable Stone Antiquity, | at Avebury, neer Marleburgh in Wiltshire; | whose general Diameter is neer 400 paces.' The ink note, top R, 'By Dr Charlton | july 8. 1663', is, like that on plan C, in the hand of Henry Oldenburg. The inked and parenthesized numbers 62–63 (the (62) being written on the blank verso) indicate the plan's place, immediately following the Aubrey plan C (60–61), in the former sequence of items described at C.1. The small pencilled 102 in the bottom R corner is a modern archival leaf-number relating to the whole volume in which D is bound.

D.2   Orientation and scope

This Charleton plan is reverse-oriented, with N appearing at the foot and E to the L of the sheet. It also differs from each of the other four plans in at least two other major respects: it immediately strikes the reader as schematized and indicative – and indeed seems to have at most one representational or naturalistic feature (see D.14) – and it is the only one to bear extensive explanatory text on its face.

The plan covers only the henge itself – bank/ditch and a uniform outer ring – shown with pairs of stones outside each entrance, and two stone features within. These are the Cove (not named), in the NE quadrant, and a southern inner circle, in the SE quadrant, with a single stone (the Obelisk, again not so named) at its centre. The only other feature shown – and the only 'modern' one – is 'the high way from Marlburgh to Bath'. These features within the main ring depart from simple symmetry, but, being equally firmly and schematically drawn, still serve to emphasize a strong formal regularity in the entire representation.

D.3   The document

Plan D is executed in ink and pencil, on a sheet of laid paper measuring 240 × 357 mm. (9.5 × 14.0 in.). Chainlines run vertically, 1 in. apart. In the centre of the R half of the sheet appears a single watermark, consisting of the capital letters F D and measuring some 10 × 20 mm. overall. These capitals are thinly single-lined, the 'F' having pronounced vertical cross-pieces ending its horizontals, the 'D' being shaped like a circle with a short flattened L side.

Plan D was folded in half vertically, and then in half again in the same dimension, at some early time. The folding may have been done by Charleton himself; in any event it almost certainly dates from well before the 1730s when the present series of Classified Papers was brought together. The outer folds slant slightly, being some 95 mm. from the edges of the sheet at their head, some 87 mm. at their foot. This brings them, on both sides, to be just touching the edges of the depiction of the main stone circle.

D.4   The verso of the document

Blank. The exposed faces of the folded document (which form the L verso) are discoloured, darker than the protected faces. Some wear has taken place on the outer folds, resulting, on the L fold, in light holing which has been lightly repaired on the verso. Both side edges of the sheet have sustained light fraying, which has been similarly repaired. Both varieties of wear are visible in our reproduction (Plate 5), together with some discolorations at the R margin of the face of the plan: it will be seen that none of these blemishes reduces its legibility.

D.5   Annotations

It is convenient to transcribe here the series of lettered notes which are all we have of Charleton's direct word on Avebury.

A.   the circular Earth-work, or | Circumvallation, about 20 foot high.
B.   the Trench, about 30 foot broad.
C.   the great stones at the four Entrances,
D.   the greater Circle of huge Stones, immediatly | within the Trench.
E.   the lesser Circle of the like stones, in the South-east | quadrant of the whole work.
F.   the greatest stone of all, in the Centre of the lesser Circle.
G.   the three high stones, standing in the North-east quadrant of | the greater Circle, in a Triangle.
H.   the high way from Marlburgh to Bath.
I.   a Triangular stone, of vast magnitude, | lying flat on the ground; but, (probably) | at first imposed on the heads of the other three, | in manner of an Architrave.

There is an interesting flavour of the *aide-mémoire* or fieldnote about this series of observations: the immediacy of their detail is such that it seems valid to read them as written on the spot to accompany the making of the plan.

D.6–9: 'Modern' and natural features (no buildings, foliage, boundaries or rivers)

D.7   The highway

This is shown by a single carefully and closely dotted line. It runs straight from the inner edge of the trench circle, opposite the centre of the E entrance, almost to the centre of the plan. A short diagonal section, oriented SW–NE, takes the dotted line just across the centre: this slight staggering was done, presumably, to avoid running the rest of the dots down the centre fold of the plan. The result is that this remainder, running due S, up to ring B within the S entrance, is a little offset from the centre of the entrance. While his highway is as firmly patterned as all the rest of his plan, Charleton's choosing to show only two of the four road-sections, and to represent those by a dotted line, tends to imply that he did not view the roads as a basic feature of the monument (see further Chapter IV, f).

D.10–14: Ancient artificial features

D.10 Bank/ditch
Like plan C, plan D is based on a series of concentric circles, drawn with dividers, the central
point-hole being clearly visible. The outermost two circles, lettered A and B, remain in
pencil: representing bank and ditch ('Earth-work, or Circumvallation [and] Trench'), these
are respectively of 7¾ in. and 7¼ in. diameter. Another ½ in. within is the outer edge of
the 'greater Circle of huge Stones', this lettered D, and ⅛ in. wide. Like most of the rest of
the plan, this circle is now in ink; it appears at no time to have been pencilled. It seems to have
been based originally on a ring drawn with a divider-point, stretches of the circumference of
which are still visible to close scrutiny: this is one of the few features of plan D which may
not be perceptible in reproduction.

D.11 Entrances
At each of the four compass-points a gap of some 7/16 in. has been left in the outermost
pencilled ring A. From the open ends, pencilled lines, some ¾ in. long, extend outwards at
right-angles; presumably these indicate roadways, although no corresponding gaps appear in
the inner pencilled circle B, even where the 'high way from Marlburgh to Bath' is shown
running right up to it at E and S. The compass letters SWNE – with S at the top, as already
noted – are placed centrally within each extension.

D.12 Key-letters and keyed features (see also D.5)
The guide-letters ABCD are repeated in pairs on either side of all four entrances,
emphasizing the symmetry of the overall large-circle arrangement. This repetition would
have been of practical help to viewers from different angles, if the plan was indeed shown to
a small group, as at the Royal Society meeting (see Chapter I, iii). With the plan held so that
Charleton could read from his notes, viewers would have seen the conventional N
orientation restored.

D.13 Stone depictions and settings
(a) Entrance stones Outside each of the four entrances, to their L and R, a pair of stones,
lettered C, is shown; these are in ink, and are depicted by conventions similar to those used
for the stones of the main circle (see (b)). A standardized effect seems to be aimed at although
the dimensions of the depictions vary somewhat: in this case, most are from ⅜ to ½ in. long
and ⅛ in. wide or a little narrower. No stones are depicted *within* the entrances.

(b) Outer ring The sides of each stone-depiction are stongly lined, particularly the outer
sides (this perhaps owing to ink-run into the divider-drawn ring); both sides show
irregularities consistent with freehand lining. The sides are connected at right-angles by short
vertical strokes, typically some 16 per depiction. Of these, the end strokes are no more
strongly marked than the others: this gives a slightly open-ended effect.
   The stones, and the gaps between them, vary in length: most are between ¼ in. and ⅜ in.,
though the largest gap (S of the E entrance) is over 9/16 in, one less stone being shown on the
E side than on the W: 14 and 15 respectively, giving a total of 29 stones. Again, given the
overall strong formalization, these variations do not seem intended to be significant.

(c) Inner ring This small ring, in the SE quadrant, is again based on divider-drawn circles.
Once more a point-hole is at its centre; there is another, eccentric, point-hole close by. The
outer diameter is 1⅞ in., the inner some 1⅝ in., the width of the stones being about ⅛ in.,
like those of the main ring. The outer circle shows some remains of pencilling; the inner
circle shows only a divider-point line. The 13 stones of this ring are depicted by the same

131

conventions as those of the main ring, except that these stones are shorter, between 3/16 and ¼ in. long. In this case the inner edge of the ring, rather than the outer, is the more strongly marked. The central 'greatest stone of all' is shown as a perfect circle, of just under ½ in. diameter.

D.14   The Cove

This appears a little above the centre of the NE quadrant. The 'three high stones' are represented by conventions similar to those of the rings, but each is over ½ in. long; again they are about ⅛ in. wide. The three are shown oriented due E-W, with the central one the most northerly. The inner ends of the two outer stones are shown due S of the respective ends of the central stone, at about half its length (i.e. ¼ in.) away. The orientation of the 'open' side is thus represented as due S. Within this side is shown the 'Triangular stone, of vast magnitude, lying flat on the ground'. Its point, rounded like the top of a beehive, is shown as due S; its long straight base is parallel with the other stones, and less than ⅛ in. away from the S face of the central stone. In view of Charleton's description, this stone is the one feature of the plan that might be taken to be representational (cf. D.2). Its shading or hatching is also distinctive.

The 'Plan E' complex: Stukeley's 1743 frontispiece for 'Abury', its illustrations and its variants (see also Chapter I,vi,viii; Chapter II,i,ii)

Plan E (Plate 14, also in folder)

E.1

What we here call plan E, the birds-eye panoramic Frontispiece compiled and drawn by William Stukeley, engraved by Elisha Kirkall (d.1742), and finally published in 1743, is captioned 'The Groundplot of the Brittish [sic] Temple now the town of Aubury Wilts. A[nn]o. 1724'. Its place in the English tradition of topographical engraving has been briefly discussed in Chapter II,ii; since adequate and inexpensive reproductions have long been on sale at Avebury and elsewhere, this plan must by now be one of the best-known 18th-century examples of that tradition. Its compact conveyance of varied information, and its engaging period and human detail, are deservedly admired.

Because of this, readers can easily fall into the assumption – as we ourselves initially did – that plan E must represent Stukeley's definitive view: his most considered synthesis, either at the time of the end of his Avebury fieldwork in summer 1724, or as evolved in ensuing years up to the preparation of *Abury* (1743). It is equally natural to make similar assumptions about the book's text, especially in view of its apparently long period of gestation. However, comparative scrutiny reveals enough points of disagreement between the testimonies of plan and of text to make it certain that they cannot both be complete and coherent wholes. A number of such conflicts are identified here and in Chapter IV, and there are probably more. Doubt about the final authority of the Frontispiece can only be reinforced by comparison of it with elements of the supplementary material discussed below (E.3.; E.6–8) and further in Chapter IV.

E.2

Although we might at this point provide detailed description of plan E, on the lines of our treatments of plans A–D, this seems unnecessary for three main reasons:

(a) Considered in isolation, plan E is largely self-explanatory: most of the problems related to it arise when it is compared with other records or with the site itself. A few strictly internal problems do appear, which we list and comment on below (E.5).

(b) Since its 'original' form is that of a published engraving, there is no problem of limited access to plan E, while it is also unlike the others in presenting within itself few problems of legibility, and none of physical deterioration, or palaeographical or archival interpretation. This holds good despite our finding, at a late stage in our researches, that the published engraving exists in two variant states. We call these E1 and E2: the differences between them are noted below (E.5ii(b); E.5.v(d)).

(c) Perhaps most importantly, as soon as we look away from plan E's persuasive appearance of self-sufficiency, we find that it is further unlike plans A–D in being part of a large mass of potentially relevant material. To deal with all this in the same detail as we have accorded the comparatively scanty background of plans A–D would demand a book in itself. We do, however, draw on it extensively for particular comparisons (e.g. the discussions of stone positions in Chapter IV).

E.3

What is this supplementary material? Physically closest to plan E are the *Abury* text, with which it sometimes conflicts (cf. E.5,iv), and the book's 39 other plates – eight of which feature parts of the area covered by plan E, and so may be used to confirm or to question its depictions. Archivally, these plates are in turn supported – and often brought into question – by a number of surviving sketches, and variant and proof engravings. These latter, the existence of which has already been noted (Chapter I,viii and II,v), usually bear Stukeley's notes, alterations, or instructions to the engraver. Similarly, the published *Abury* text, while itself showing signs of hasty editing (e.g. see E.5.iv(b)), emerges as the organized apex of a disorderly pyramid of fieldnotes, learned jottings, and extended drafts (see Chapter I,viii). Notably, these include an almost complete stone-by-stone 'fine tour' of the henge, in Stukeley's 'Celtic Temples' MS., of which only a few phrases survive in the published text: these are about the 'southern temple' (1743, 24). A reconstruction of this account and its context forms our Appendix II.

E.4

This 'tour', comparable in detail with the Frontispiece itself, is virtually the verbal equivalent of a plan (Transparency 19). Additionally, however, and crucially for any serious investigation of what plan E appears to be telling posterity, there are not only a detailed measurement plan (Eng.Misc.c.533, 53v–54) (Plates 15 and 72, Transparency 20) but at least eleven actual surviving draft plans of the henge itself – and even this number excludes the several more plans, from that dated 19 May 1719 onwards (Plate 11), in which henge depictions figure as part of larger schemes including avenues, Sanctuary, Silbury and so on (e.g. Plate 26 & panorama; Eng.Misc.b.65, 38). We refer to the 11 'versions' hereafter also as 'variants', 'draft plans', or, occasionally, 'draft frontispieces'.

No two of the versions are identical, and each one proves to include some data unique to it. Further, most of them appear not to be products of a single time: they bear evidence of having been gone back to, revised and modified – particularly in relation to the status and position of stones – over or after more than one season. Several of the variants can be seen as trials of different conventions of plan-making; perhaps also Stukeley was noting new observations on whatever version he had with him at the time; and, again, sometimes trying out alternative understandings, either of the site itself or of what was worth recording about it, on different drafts. Whatever the reason, the result is that there may well be no absolute sequence or overall progression to be established among these drafts; they can be grouped or sequenced by a number of criteria, but each criterion yields a different result. These problems are discussed below (E.6) before we offer (E.7) our own necessarily tentative working sequence, lettering the versions from N to X.

E.5

First, however, it is necessary to detail those few internal problems presented by plan E itself. Our descriptions are based on what we have called state E2, since this appears to be the later and the more perfect: its differences from state E1 consist in variations of treatment of some of these problems (see E.5.ii(b); E.5.v(d)).

E.5.i.   Vallum incompletely shown   The outer edge of the vallum is cut off by three of the four margins, with least loss at the S, more at the E, and most at the N, where much of the N ditch is forfeited too. Such cutting-off, to varying degrees of severity, is found also in most of the drafts (see E.7). Apparently no significant data are thus lost, but the reader may nevertheless wish that the full breadth of the 'circle' had been depicted.

E.5.ii   Missing key-symbols   The 'Notes' cartouche lists four symbols for different categories of stone or position (standing, fallen, taken away, cavity), but at least four further symbols are used without explanation:

(a) An open rectangle, of dimensions similar to those of the shaded key-symbol for 'a Stone fallen', is used in the outer main circle (4th position S of the W entrance) and again in the outer circle of the 'northern temple' (2nd position in from the N road) (see further Chapter IV,s,x).

(b) Small roundels seemingly indicate the centres of both N and S 'temples': the N one is positioned between the two Cove stones, on the former 'Silbury meridan' line (see E.5.v(d)). The S roundel is larger, while, in state E2 only, it surrounds what might be the oblong shadings of 'a stone fallen': if so, presumably the Obelisk. In state E1 of the Frontispiece there is no sign of this oblong, while both roundels, but particularly the N, appear considerably fainter. (It is of interest that a roundel, for the Obelisk and/or the centre of this circle, appears in eight of the drafts – T has a pencil cross, N has nothing, and U does not cover this area – but none of these appears to contain the oblong shading; a hatched oblong is, however, used here by Stukeley in his measurements plan (Plate 15).)

(c) Within the S 'temple', and apparently forming part of its inner circle insofar as that is shown, are at least three very small open circles. These could simply be dots (for 'Place of a Stone taken away') which were accidentally not blacked in, or they could possibly have some special meaning. However, their status is so debatable that we have not taken them into account in Chapter IV's comparisons and analyses.

(d) Finally, just E of the N entrance are two distinctively irregular 'stone' symbols. These are not shaped like the isolated 'stone standing' immediately to the E of the roadway, and presumably represent projecting parts of stones 'tumbled into the ditch' (see Chapter IV,r).

E.5.iii   Pastures   Clockwise numbering is provided on the Frontispiece, beginning at the S entrance, from 'Pasture I' to 'Pasture X', but the reader may feel that the total, even excluding the three gardens on the outer circle, could more usefully be at least 11, if not 12, since pastures I and II are both subdivided into two by fences ('pails') across, and both halves of the latter contain stones. The implication must be that Stukeley took only hedges and roadways to constitute pasture boundaries (see further Chapter IV,d). It is of interest that, in all draft versions in which they are given numbers, Stukeley adheres to the total of 10 pastures, although his numbering in several was anti-clockwise, both on drafts and in the written tour: he went over to the familiar clockwise sequence only for the drafts dated 1724 (versions V, W, X: see E.7) and for published plan E.

E.5.iv   Incompletely indicated stone-settings   There is surprising scope for uncertainty as to the intended shapes and numbers of most of plan E's settings, and this is enhanced if we permit ourselves to check against Stukeley's analytical list in *Abury* (1743, 37). The list calls for 100 stones of the outer circle, and 30 and 12 respectively in the outer and inner circles of both northern and southern 'temples', besides three of the Cove, the one 'ring stone', and 'the ambre or central obelisc' (of the S temple). Only these last two single settings can be said definitely to be confirmed by plan E. Otherwise:

(a) The outer circle is almost completely depicted, but it yields a count only of between 96 and 98 positions – depending on interpretation of slightly obscured series at the S end of pasture I and the N extremity of pasture VI – even though some draft versions (e.g. N and R: see E.7) do show the stated 100 places.

(b) The intention to depict an inner concentric circle seems clear: although it is shown as containing only two actual stones it evidently is intended by Stukeley to consist of about the same number of places as the outer circle. However, an accurate count appears impossible except by inferring, via assumed regularity of spacing, a number of dot-'places' not clearly shown. This problem is particularly evident round about the S roadway, and in pasture III to the N of the W roadway.

The retention in plan E of this concentric main circle constitutes a major contradiction of the accompanying 1743 text – and of its tab.viii, 'A Scenographic view of the Druid temple' (cf. Plate 26) – in which Stukeley tacitly abandons the idea of such a feature. Further, he explicitly assigns the stone which he appears for long to have identified as either its sole survivor or, possibly, one of two survivors, to a unique new category, as the 'Ringstone'. The presence of that name on plan E's inner circle epitomizes the contradiction (see further Chapter IV,w).

(c) The intended shapes of the two 'temples' are not quite clear. The outer circle of the S, after 22 regularly spaced stones or places, goes blank on either side of a northern arc of four or five (one of these using the symbols both for 'fallen' and for 'taken away'), leaving the reader to infer three or four more. The inner circle here would be patchy even were we to include in it the three or more unexplained open dots (E.5.ii(c)), with an arc to the SE left unindicated. Again the last three or four places, at the least, must be inferred (see further Chapter IV,w).

Of the N 'temple', the outer circle looks regular, but has one or two almost illegible marks, presumably for 'stones fallen', in its northernmost arc: the count of this circle is rather problematic, but looks like 29 rather than 30 places. The inner circle here appears to be of a complete 12 places. For the Cove, however, no special attempt is made to show the place of the former third, most northerly, stone: at best, its position has to be inferred from the removal-date '1713'. Yet Stukeley had shown this place clearly in several preceding drafts (E.7), while in the book itself it is carefully added to tab.xiv, 'Prospect of the Cove Abury 10 July 1723' (see further Chapter IV,x,y).

E.5.v. Miscellaneous problems (a) The name 'The Cove' is oddly placed, so that its referent could be unclear to uninformed readers. (The eccentricity results from Stukeley's late decision to delete 'Lunar': see E.6(b); E.7, draft X.)

(b) Other written information given is variable: the range is from 'Demolished by Tom Robinson A[nn]o. 1700' (for the 9 places shown in Pasture VII), through 'taken away 1718 [1719; 1720]' at three different points, to a number of bare year-dates – e.g. in the N temple – before each of which 'taken away' has to be inferred. Apart from names of roads and of buildings (Vicarage, Aubury Church, Meeting house, The Inn), the other notes are 'Broke 1722' (of a 'stone fallen' within the S entrance, at its E side, beside the ditch), and 'broke off to the Stumps' (of three 'Stones fallen' at the N end of Pasture III).

(c) In the garden to the N of the W entrance are four beds of a shape and size that might lead to their being taken as stone symbols.

(d) Finally, traces of what looks like a vertical flaw or join run close to the centre of the plan: these become especially visible as a kind of seam across the S ditch and bank. This is evidence of (Kirkall's?) re-working of the engraving to remove the vertical 'Meridian line thro' Silbury', which appears on four of its extant predecessors (S, V, W, X: see E.7), presumably in response to Stukeley's MS. instruction, on draft X, to 'omit the line drawn across' (see further E.6(b)).[9]

The difference between states E1 and E2 consists mainly in what appear to be two different re-workings of this meridian[10]. In state E1 the removal has been more crudely done, resulting in an obvious lighter-coloured strip from top to bottom of the sheet. This affects, for example, both a triangular portion at the N end of Pasture X and the enclosed garden immediately S of that portion. Again, in E1 though not in E2, the 'seam' across the S ditch and bank, and across the wall just NW of the Inn, clearly consists of remains of the meridian line itself.[11]

The draft plans

E.6(a) Survivors and fragments   All 11 draft plans mentioned above (E.4) are now in the Bodleian Library. Six (respectively our Q, O, P, U, R, X) are to be found in one volume: Gough Maps 231, 22, 23, 24, 34, 58, 304; the other five (our S, V, W, T, N) in another: MS. Eng. Misc. b.65, 19, 23, 28, 31v, 33. (The latter volume, probably from the Stukeley MSS. sale of 1924, was among those in the possession of Alexander Keiller during the period of his Avebury excavations: see Chapter IV.)

Even Stukeley's surviving record shows itself to be incomplete, in more than one way. For instance, fragments exist of what appear to have been yet further draft henge plans, e.g. in Gough Maps 229, 55v, 56v, 105 and in Gough Maps 231, 255v, 306v. Again, as is noted in Appendix II, the written 'fine tour' appears to describe a draft plan which does not conform with any surviving version so far identified.

Further, the 11 main drafts include two vertical-half plans, an eastern (Plate 38, Transparency 12) and a western (Plate 39, Transparency 13), both appearing to be survivors from plans originally whole. These two cannot be the separated halves of a single plan, since they are drawn on sheets of different sizes, and to different scales. However, similarities of graphic concept and execution suggest that both halves may date from the same season – July 1723, according to the date on the much more finished western plan – and this is reflected in our placing them as T and U, respectively, in our list (E.7).

E.6 (b) Problems of sequencing and grouping: general (for problems related to stones see E.8)
Our list below (E.7) letters the 11 versions as N to X, in a pragmatic sequence based firstly on their stated dates, secondly on the way in which the bank S of the W entrance is depicted (the relevance of this will be seen shortly), and lastly on graphic and MS. features. Selection by the first criterion yields us a sequence closing, for example, with a group of three versions dated 1724, but it happens that the second criterion is of no help in distinguishing between these three. We therefore order them as apparent steps toward plan E, the 'final' Frontispiece. Draft V comes first, because it is drawn not engraved, X last because it is not only (like W) engraved but also bears instructions and notes found executed only in plan E.

Typical difficulties of grouping and sequencing begin to appear when we turn to draft S, the only one dated 1722. It groups with V, W, and X in showing the vertical 'Silbury meridian' (deleted from plan E), and both by date and by style appears to be the earliest of these four. On it, the name 'Circus' is crossed out, as are 'Lunar' and 'Solar' in the temple names, 'Northern' and 'Southern' being substituted: it 'must', then, surely be later than versions in which those older names stand? Yet the old names are still in place on draft V, dated two years later; while, although all three names have gone from the engraved versions, W and X, even these still show 'The Lunar Cove' – though 'Lunar' has been crossed through on the latter. On the other hand, 'Solar' and 'Lunar' are erased even from version O, one of the group of four (O, P, Q, R) dated 1721, albeit these are all so 'early' as not to record the levelling on the S side of the W entrance.

If we look outside the plans themselves for help in resolving such puzzles, the impression of disorder will not necessarily be banished. For instance, in the present case we have seen (Chapter II, v) that the 'Silbury Meridian' is likely to have been conceived only in 1723, while Stukeley's reasons for deleting both it and the 'Solar' and 'Lunar' descriptions arose during summer 1724. Conceivably this could indicate that during or after that year Stukeley considered still active only those plans on which he bothered to make the deletions – thus already excluding the 1724-dated version V – but any such hypothesis would need testing in its turn by yet further comparisons.

The apparently otherwise unrecorded second levelling episode, S of the W entrance (see further Chapter IV, e), has seemed to us significant enough to use as our second criterion for sequencing. Remarkably, the transition itself is recorded in draft R ('August 1721'), almost like a double-exposure snapshot: the pre-levelling conformation first drawn in, then the alterations superimposed on it. Since the new state of the W entrance is firmly established by draft S ('1722'), this second levelling episode would appear to have taken place between the summers of 1721 and 1722. If caution demands further confirmation, we have to look to (half-)draft U, on which the later state of the bank and ditch again appears. Since this draft is dated July 1723, and appears to belong all to one time, is seems safe to say that the destruction must have been carried out within the previous two years at longest.

From the titles given in the lettered listing (E.7), it will be noticed that, while the earlier 'Abury' becomes 'Aubury' for all plans with dates after 1721, and remains so through to plan E – albeit thus at variance with both the text and the very title of the 1743 book – the place's status veers from 'town' to 'village' and back again, in terms of the plan dates. However, the spelling 'British' does not change to 'Brittish' until the '1724' group.

The list also cites the range of stone-removal dates found on each draft. It emerges from these that one of the group dated 1721 (version R) contains the latest removal date of all: a '1723', in the outer circle of the northern temple: this appears in none of the '1724' versions, nor even on plan E itself. We think this apparent anachronism a useful warning that the nominal dates of the drafts should be treated with great caution. We deal with other grouping or sequencing features relating to stones at E.8, and more of these will emerge in Chapter IV, in relation to particular quadrants and stone settings, Apart from these, some further features noted in the lettered listing (E.7), but not commented on in detail here, are: the graphic treatment of the title-cartouche, and the presence of any other cartouches; the manner in which buildings are represented (i.e. block plan, 2- or 3-dimensional); the treatment and numbering of the pastures; the manner of representing the ditch/bank, and on how many sides it runs off plan; and the naming and treatment of Temples, Cove, and Obelisk.

Whatever the further criteria chosen, however, it appears to be inescapable that the attempt to apply any two or more of them to refine a sequence will produce conflicting results, just as have those already discussed. This is the basis of our conclusion that no one coherent sequence can be established within this rich and teasing collection of surviving drafts, and that neither can plan E be a summation of all that is valid in them.

E.7   The versions in detail
* = Listed feature unique to that plan

Version N. Eng.Misc.b.65, 33   18.75 × 23.0 in.
(Plate 32; Transparency 6)
Date: undated.   *Removal dates*: 1702 only.   *Title*: untitled.
Buildings shown: All 3-dimensional.   *SW bank*: Up
Pastures: [VIII–X] only: no names/numbers.
Ditch/bank: Compass-drawn circles still evident. Ditch shown (full circuit) by *flat wash.   *Cut off*: No.

137

There is Stone was demolisht by The Solution

Plate 32 Stukeley draft frontispiece – N (Bodleian Library MS. Eng. Misc.b.65, 33).

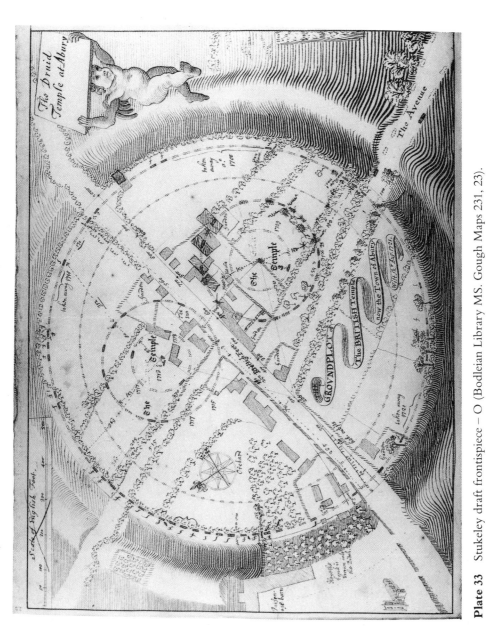

Plate 33 Stukeley draft frontispiece – O (Bodleian Library MS. Gough Maps 231, 23).

Circus: No.   *Temples*: Unnamed.   *Cove*: Unnamed; two stones.
Obelisk: Pencil cross   *Ringstone*: No.
SE Robinsons: * 'These 12 [sic] Stones were demolished by Tho. Robinson' [no date].
Miscellaneous: *Overall least detailed of any whole draft. Measured double scale (three line) SW–NE along street.

Version O. Gough Maps 231, 23   12.00 × 15.00 in.
(Plate 33; Transparency 7)
Date: August 1721.   *Removal dates*: 1700–20.
Title & cartouche: *'The Druid Temple at Abury' [top R cartouche upheld by putto]; 'The Groundplot of The British Temple now the Town of Abury Wiltshr. Aug. 1721.' [*ribbon within SW quadrant].
Buildings shown: All block-plan, except church 3-dimensional.   *SW bank*: Up.
Pastures: 10, unnamed, except for 'Orchard' (pasture III of Plan E), & unnumbered.
Ditch/bank: 3-dimensional.   *Cut off*: N & S.   *Circus*: No.
Temples: 'The [Lunar *del*.] Temple' & 'The [Solar *del*.] Temple'.
Cove: Unnamed; two stones & position of third shown.
Obelisk: Unnamed; dark circular blob.   *Ringstone*: Yes.
SE Robinsons: 'taken away A[nn]o 1700' [Bracket covering 8 positions].
Miscellaneous: Measured double scale (single line) SW–NE along street. SE outside road named 'The Avenue', on this and draft P only. Compass-rose within henge on this and P only: here in 'Orchard' in NW quadrant.

Version P. Gough Maps 231, 24   12.00 × 14.5 in.
(Plate 34; Transparency 8)
Date: August 1721.   *Removal dates*: 1700–20.
Title: 'Groundplot of Abury made Aug. 1721' [no cartouche: ★written vertically up R margin]
Buildings shown: All block-plan.   *SW bank*: Up.
Pastures: unnamed, except for 'Orchard' (pasture III of Plan E), & unnumbered.
Ditch/bank: 3-dimensional.   *Cut off*: N, S, *W.   *Circus*: No.
Temples: 'The Lunar Temple'; 'The Solar Temple'; * written diagonally N–S down plan.
Cove: 2 Cove stones & *2 places shown (*4 in all, arranged in a circle, open toward NE).
Obelisk: *Two symbols: open circle, lined through; dark blob to its W. Unnamed.
Ringstone: Yes; unnamed.
SE Robinsons: '1700' [*bare date] [Bracket covering 8 positions].
Miscellaneous: Several features shared only by this and draft O. Compass-rose here in 'pasture I'. *Stone-positions of 'The Avenue' numbered (1–6), beginning centre ditch. *Full name of inn given: 'The Catherin wheel Inn'.

Version Q. Gough Maps 231, 22   13.00 × 16.75 in.
(Plate 35; Transparency 9)
Date: August 1721 (possibly altered to 1722 &/or 1724)   *Removal dates*: 1694–1720.
Title & cartouche: 'The Groundplot of the British Temple now the Village of Abury in Wiltshire designed & ad-measur'd by W. S. Aug. 1721'; top R cartouche upheld by putto.
Other cartouches: 'Penbrochiae' top L, similarly upheld.
Buildings shown: All open block-plan.   *SW bank*: Up.
Pastures: 10, unnumbered; four called 'Pasture', one (as before) 'Orchard'.
Ditch/bank: 3-dimensional (except in N quadrant).
Cut off: Slightly, at N & S.   *Circus*: Yes.   *Temples*: 'Lunar Temple'; 'Solar Temple'.
Cove: Unnamed. Two stones, position of third shown.
Obelisk: Dark circular blob.   *Ringstone*: Yes, unnamed.
SE Robinsons: 'demolishd A[nn]o 1700 by Tho. Robinson' [covering 9 positions].

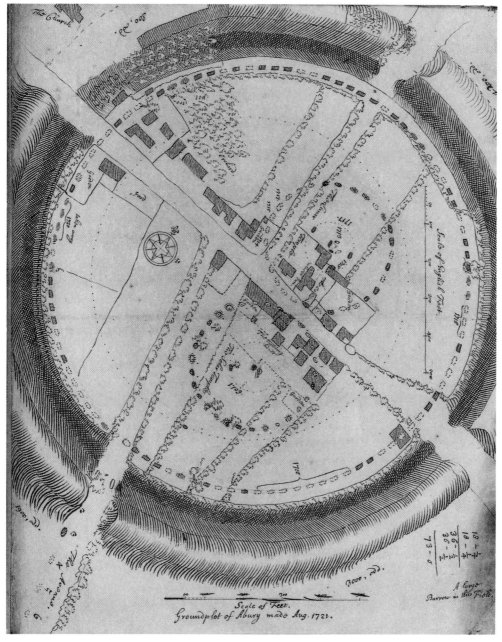

Plate 34 Stukeley draft frontispiece – P (Bodleian Library MS. Gough Maps 231, 24).

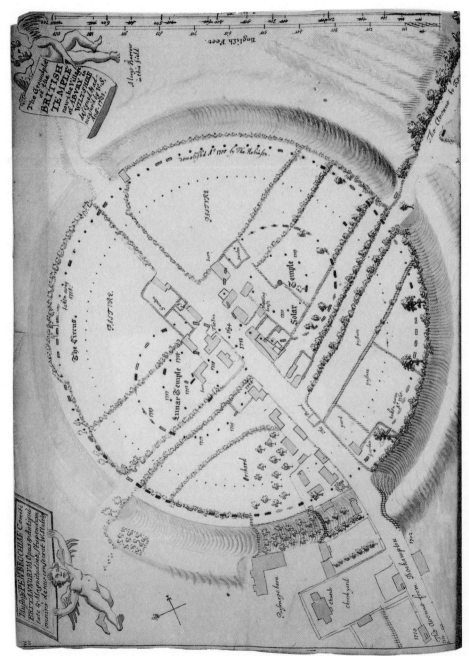

Plate 35 Stukeley draft frontispiece – Q (Bodleian Library MS. Gough Maps 231, 22).

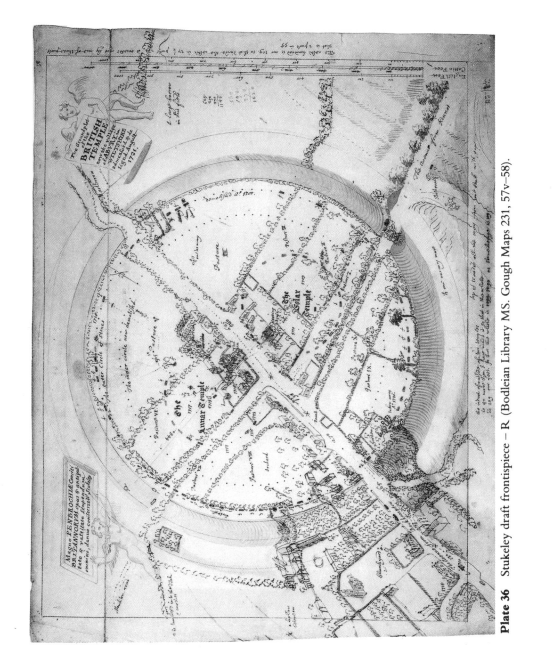

Plate 36 Stukeley draft frontispiece – R (Bodleian Library MS. Gough Maps 231, 57v–58).

Version R. Gough Maps 231, 57v–58   14.75 × 18.5 in.
(Plate 36; Transparency 10)
Date: August 1721.   *Removal dates*: 1700–23 [sic].
Title & cartouche: 'The Groundplot of the British Temple now the village of Abury in Wiltshire admeasurd & designd August 1721'; top R cartouche upheld by putto.
Other cartouches: 'Penbrochiae' cartouche top L, similarly upheld.
Buildings shown: All 3-dimensional.
SW bank: *Originally 'up', but 'down' topography entered over this.
Pastures: Named/numbered I–X, anti-clockwise.
Ditch/bank: *3-dimensional in S & E quadrants, flat in N & W; remains of compass-drawn circles still evident.   *Cut off*: No.   *Circus*: *'The Outer Circle of Stones'.
Temples: 'The Lunar Temple'; 'The Solar Temple' [*On three lines vertically].
Cove: Unnamed; position of third stone shown.
Obelisk: Unnamed; unfilled roundel.   *Ringstone*: Yes.
SE Robinsons: 'demolishd A[nn]o 1700' [covering 9 positions].
Miscellaneous: Blank spaces outside henge bear scribbled calculations; notes in most margins. *Stone oblongs all marked 'f' or 's' (fallen or standing).

Version S. Eng.Misc.b.65, 18v–19   18.5 × 23.00 in.
(Plate 37; Transparency 11)
Date: 1722.   *Removal dates*: 1694–1722.
Title & cartouche: *'The Remains of the British Temple in the Village of Aubury Wilts. A°. 1722, dedicated to the most Illustrious Thomas Earl of Pembroke &c. by Wm. Stukeley' [*strip along foot of plan]
Buildings shown: All 3-dimensional.   *SW bank*: Down.
Pastures: Named/numbered I–X, anti-clockwise.
Ditch/bank: 3-dimensional.   *Cut off*: N (entire width), E, S.
Circus: Named & deleted.
Temples: 'The [Lunar *del.*] <Northern> Temple'; 'The [Solar *del.*] <Southern> Temple'.
Cove: 'The Cove'; position of third stone shown.
Obelisk: 'The [Solar *del.*] obelisc', shown as dark roundel.
Ringstone: Yes.
SE Robinsons: 'demolishd by Tho. Robinson A[nn]o 1700 [covering 8? positions].
Meridian: 'The Meridian line of the whole Work passing thro' Silbury hill southward' passes vertically between the two standing Cove stones.
Miscellaneous: *Instructions to engraver in SE quadrant (pasture IIII). Diagonal N–S line passes through Cove, Obelisk, Ringstone (as on draft X). *Trees & bushes in green wash.

Version T. Eng.Misc.b.65, 31v   17.5 × 11.5 in.
(Plate 38; Transparency 12)
Date: undated.   *Removal dates*: None.   *Title*: untitled
Buildings shown: Block plan: few faint outlines only.
Pastures: Two divisions only.
Ditch/bank: Faint wash along SE ditch (n.b. S entrance). Outer pencil ring shown.
Cut off: N & S (W not shown).
Circus: No.   *Temples*: unnamed.   *Cove*: off plan.
Obelisk: unnamed; marked by X.   *Ringstone*: Yes.
SE Robinsons: [8 places (?); no words]
Miscellaneous: *E half-plan. Unfinished: abandoned?

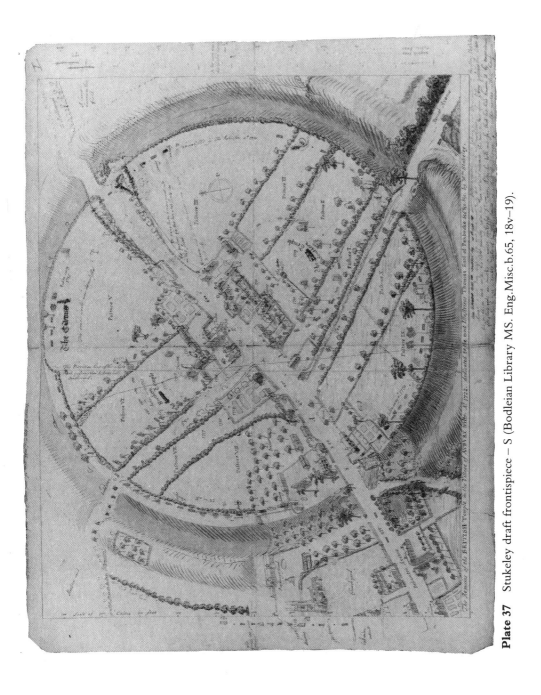

Plate 37 Stukeley draft frontispiece – S (Bodleian Library MS. Eng.Misc.b.65, 18v–19).

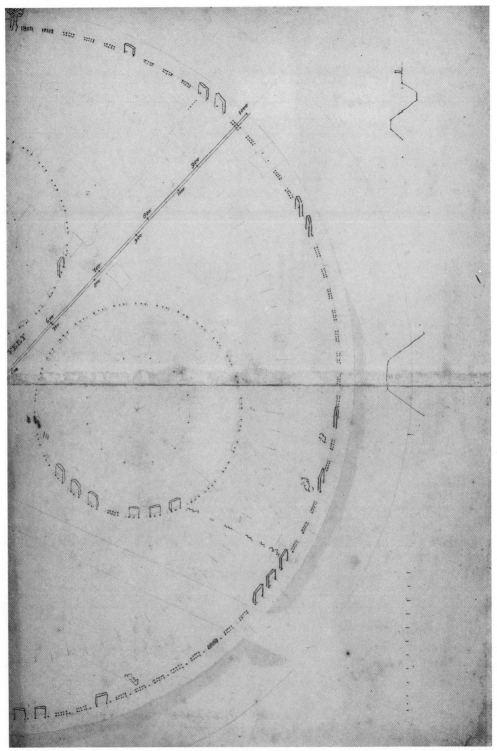

Plate 38 Stukeley draft frontispiece – T (Bodleian Library MS. Eng.Misc.b.65, 31v).

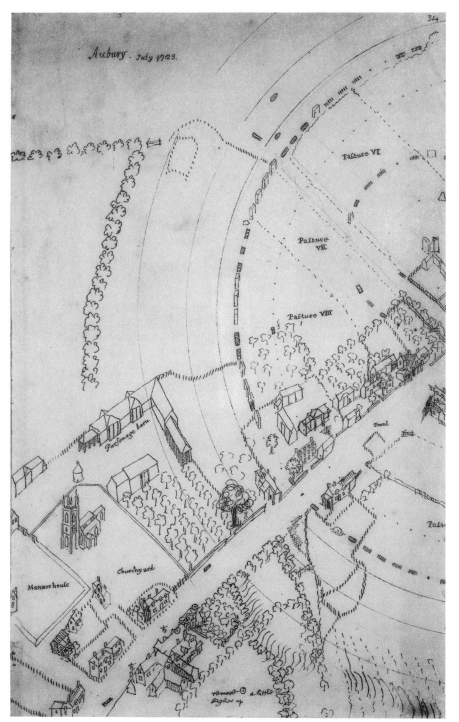

Aubury. July 1723.

Pasture VI

Pasture VII

Pasture VIII

Parsonage barn

Pound

Pasture

Churchyard

Mannor house

Romond ⊙ a little higher up

Plate 39 Stukeley draft frontispiece – U (Bodleian Library MS. Gough Maps 231, 34).

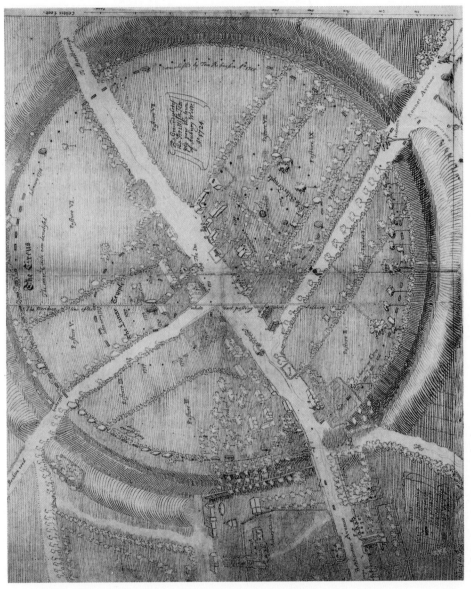

Plate 40 Stukeley draft frontispiece – V (Bodleian Library MS. Eng.Misc.b.65, 23).

Version U. Gough Maps 231, 34   12.25 × 7.75 in.
(Plate 39; Transparency 13)
Date: July 1723.   *Removal dates*: None.
Title & cartouche: 'Aubury. July 1723' [*only title not framed].
Buildings shown: 3-dimensional.   *SW bank*: Down.
Pastures: VI–IX, numbered anti-clockwise.
Ditch/bank: Almost unshaded; remains of compass-drawn circles evident (centred off sheet to E).   *Cut off*: N only (E not shown).
Temples: N only on plan, unnamed.   *Cove*: Two standing stones only.
Obelisk & ringstone: off plan.
Miscellaneous: *W half-plan only, tear-line just E of Cove stones, and just W of W corner of junction of N road with E–W road. Instruction (to engraver?) at foot.

Version V. Eng.misc.b.65, 23   17.25 × 22 in.
(Plate 40; Transparency 14)
Date: 1724.   *Removal dates*: 1694–1722.
Title & cartouche: 'The Groundplot of the Brittish [sic] Temple now the town of Aubury Wilts. A[nn]o 1724' [cartouche within SE quadrant (Pasture VII)].
Other cartouches: 'Notes' cartouche, botttom L.
Buildings shown: All 3-dimensional.   *Pastures*: I–X, clockwise.
Ditch/bank: 3-dimensional.   *Cut off*: N, E, S.
Circus: Yes.
Temples: 'The Lunar Temple', 'The Solar Temple' [sic *1724].
Cove: 'The Lunar Cove' [sic]; two stones, position of third faintly shown.
Obelisk: 'The solar obelisc' [sic, *1724]; open roundel with dot in centre.
Ringstone: Yes.
SE Robinsons: 'demolishd by Tom Robinson A[nn]o 1700 [covering 9 positions].
Meridian: 'Silbury meridian' in, with centre-dotted roundel between Cove stones.
Miscellaneous: * 'Stukeley del.' in bottom L corner.

Version W. Eng.Misc.b.65, 28   19.5 × 23.0 in.
(Plate 41; Transparency 15)
Date: 1724.   *Removal dates*: 1694–1722.
Title & cartouche: 'The Groundplot of the Brittish [sic] Temple now the town of Aubury Wilts. A[nn]o 1724' [cartouche within SE quadrant (Pasture VII)].
Other cartouches: 'Notes' cartouche bottom L.
Buildings shown: 3-dimensional.   *SW bank*: Down.
Pastures: I–X clockwise.   *Ditch/bank*: 3-dimensional.
Cut-off: N, E, & S (slightly).   *Circus*: No.   *Temples*: unnamed.
Cove: 'The Lunar Cove' [sic]. Position of third stone not marked, unless by '1713' removal date.
Obelisk: Unnamed; shaded roundel.   *Ringstone*: Yes.
SE Robinsons: 'Demolishd by Tom Robinson A[nn]o 1700 [covering 9 positions].
Meridan: 'Silbury meridian' in, with open roundel between Cove stones.
Miscellaneous: Engraved: 'Stukeley del.' in bottom L corner; 'E.Kirkall sculp.' in bottom R corner.

Version X. Gough Maps 231, 304   19.5 × 23.0 in.
(Plate 42; Transparency 16)
* In most respects identical to preceding draft (W), but bears diagonal N–S line similar to that on draft S (but differently oriented). *'Tab. I. frontispiece' written in top R corner; *'ring

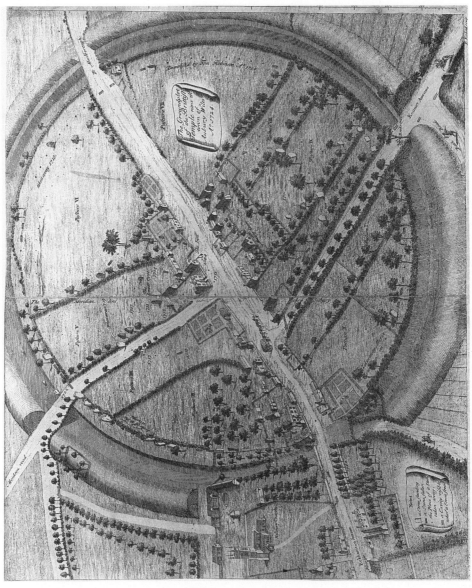

Plate 41 Stukeley draft frontispiece – W (Bodleian Library MS. Eng.Misc.b.65, 28).

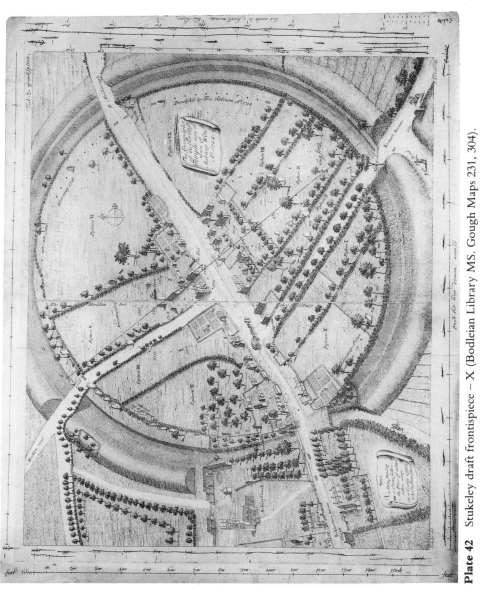

Plate 42 Stukeley draft frontispiece – X (Bodleian Library MS. Gough Maps 231, 304).

stone' written in; *instruction at foot 'omit the line drawn across' (probably the 'Silbury meridian', but possibly the diagonal). ★Compass-rose in Pasture VI, drawn in. ★'Lunar' deleted from 'The Cove'. ★Revised scale up R margin, with note 'this scale is a small matter too large': see E.8.

E.8 Stones and settings: sequencing and other problems

Of stone positions, our E.7 list records only two representative variables: the number and description of 'Robinson' removals from the SE quadrant of the outer circle, and the status of Cove, Obelisk, and ring stones. Both of these are analysed under the appropriate headings in Chapter IV.

Before selecting for mention a few of the many other stone-related criteria by which attempts to group and sequence the drafts might be made, it is relevant to note a parallel between the relation of these drafts to plan E, and that of the 'fine tour' to the published *Abury* (including plan E). In both cases the transition to the published form seems to have entailed not only a perhaps necessary tidying up of earlier data and views, but also a 'firming up', to a degree we may suspect not always justified. A slight but representative example is the conversion of the tour's 'I beleive all those [stones] in the pastures were standing within the memory of Man' (Appendix II) into the book's flat '[a]ll those in the pastures were standing within memory' (1743, 24).

More examples emerge if we compare 'tour' information with plan E key-symbols (see E.5.ii). For instance, the dot signifying 'the place of a stone taken away' appears to blanket a remarkable variety of specific evidence, some of it of a kind from which modern archaeology might attempt to draw conclusions: a 'visible' stone 'lodgment and a young ash tree planted in its room'; a 'little rising above the level of the ground'; 'a great cavity left and a young elm tree planted therein'; a 'hollow'; a 'perfect vacuity'; 'a very deep hole and a great bredth' (Appendix II). It is all the more fortunate that Stukeley's decision to represent the 'true state' of Avebury in 1724 so largely by plan E alone, has now at last – however belatedly – proved reversible.

Categorizing the drafts according to the manner in which standing stones are represented yields three groups. The largest, consisting of versions N, S, T, U, V, W, and X, is that in which standing stones are represented three-dimensionally as standing. Then there are plans P and Q, in which standing stones are shown only by filled rectangles (heavily hatched and solid respectively), and O and R, in which *all* actual stones appear to be shown by hatched rectangles, but accompanied by the letter 's' (standing) to distinguish these from 'f' (fallen). This last pair, O and R, incidentally, have something in common with Stukeley's measurements plan, which indicates both standing and fallen stones by infilled oblong shapes.

Like other grouping criteria, this one, of the depiction of standing stones, could be used in an attempt to sequence the plans. The result would have little better chance than any other of proving generally applicable, but it would tend to put draft N alongside T and U, which also looks right by the criterion of graphic technique.

Another criterion could be Stukeley's variable positioning of the inner N and S circles in relation to the outer circle(s), as well as variations in the oft-stated inaccuracy of the diameter of the S circle(s). We have not attempted a sequence on this basis, but must note the extreme case of draft O, where the diameter of the S outer circle is shown as on plan E, but the proposed inner circle is larger, and the location of both is greatly different from those shown on all the other drafts and from that of plan E itself. Possibly this is related to Stukeley's quest for significant angles of measurement in his overall view of the site, as seen in Plate 20 (Chapter II,iv); certainly one of his 'triangles' in the SE area of his measurement plan (Plate 15) has one side with a self-evidently impossible measurement. It may thus be relevant that plan O (Plate 33) includes triangles which do not appear to be part of survey nor triangulation, but rather some attempt to work out the relations of stones to one another.

Plate 43 Stukeley's watercolour view of Avebury from the north (Bodleian Library MS. Gough Maps 231, 326). See Key to Stones in folder.

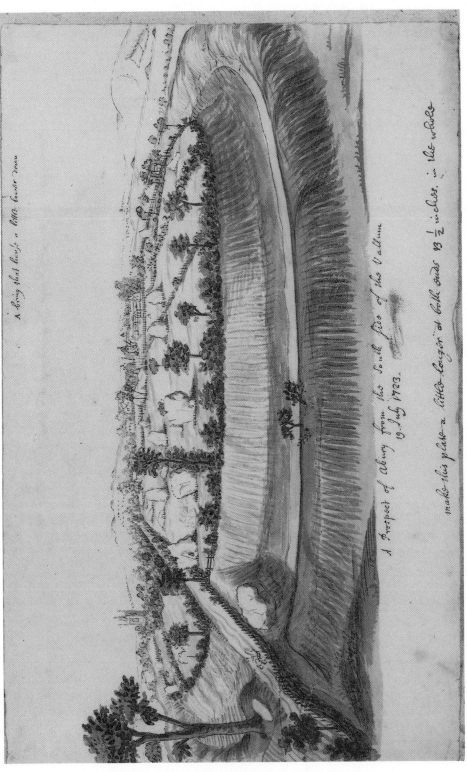

Plate 44 Stukeley's 'A Prospect of Abury from the South Side of the Vallum' (Bodleian Library MS. Top.Gen.b.53. 57). See Key to Stones in folder

Groupings based on Stukeley's handling of stones within the S entrance are of particular interest. Plan E itself clearly shows two 'stones fallen' here, one on either side, and this could be the best plan-confirmation we have of Holland's vivid report of 'huge Stones as jambes' *in* two 'gates' (see Chapter I,i). The plan appears borne out by some of Stukeley's illustrations, for example Top.Gen.b.53, 57 (Plate 44), which, however, shows the stone on the E side as much more substantial than that on the W side. Some 'firming up' may be reflected in the groupings we identify: versions N and Q show only the E stone, O has the W stone also, as a dotted outline, and this becomes firmer on P (which may additionally be attempting to show *two* E stones rather than one). On version R the relative bulk of the two stones may even be shown, while on S, V, W, X the fallen pair familiar from plan E are established, the E stone recorded as 'Broke 1722'.

Lastly, we may end by noting that the scale of feet used on plan E is itself incorrect. This came to light when it (Transparency 2) was being drawn to the same scale as Transparency 17 (i.e. Smith 1965, fig 70). Various 'known' measurements were taken from both plans, and Stukeley's 'feet' were calculated to be 4/5 imperial feet. The fact that this is a simple fraction suggests that it may be an engraving error made when the plan was scaled for the plate: one of Stukeley's unpublished drawings has a note to the engraver asking for it to be enlarged (Top.Gen.b.53, 57), and another has the instruction, 'Make this plate a little [wider *del.*] longer this way' (Gough Maps 231, 326v (Plate 43); see also Eng.Misc.b.63, 103).

Although this suggestion gains support from the realization that some of Stukeley's plans (e.g. draft Q) show the scale correctly, it is far from clear when the error(s) may have occurred. Draft frontispiece X – which must presumably be almost the last version of plan E before publication – is accompanied by various scales. All of them are incorrect, but those not crossed out were used on plan E. Whatever the cause, Stukeley himself seems to have used the incorrectly scaled plan for the measurements in his published text. Subsequent commentators have noticed the inaccuracies in the measurements given by Stukeley, and have scaled-off his plan, but do not appear to have appreciated the reason for these.

Notes

1. Useful comparison can be made between this sketch and the similarly proportioned one of a rampire/graff at Fripsbury 'camp', later transcribed in fair copy (Aubrey 24, 157–8; Fowles and Legg 1980, 285, 289). Both examples are 'the right way round', but the key-letters are swapped: 'a. ditch | b. rampire'.

2. Colt Hoare's other light pencillings on the face of plan A appear to comprise the (Stukeleian) names 'North Temple' and 'South Temple', and an intermittent series of stone-numbers for the outer ring, arranged clockwise beginning with '1' to the W of the N entrance and ending with '31' to the N of the W entrance. The other pencilled features, which we deal with in their places, we attribute to Aubrey.

3. In the first sentence, 'the fig.1' replaces '1. the', deleted; before 'Ariadne's Crowne', 'the Constillation of' is deleted. In the second sentence, 'within' replaces 'in', deleted; 'the old time' replaces an undeleted 'those dayes'.

4. *'Ghost' stones* For the sake of future students, we must note than even good reproductions of plan A can seem to show an extra stone, centrally placed within the inner end of the N entrance: it is in fact an unedged and uncentred blob, the foot of the Greek letter delta placed there (see A.12(a)). Further 'ghost' stones, in the N and S circles, may be created by overlap in reproductions printed on a double-page spread, such as that in Fowles and Legg (1980, 44–5).

5. The variant of plan B copied by Stukeley from Gale (see Chapter I,vii; B.16(a)) has a number of notes about Avebury written on it (Plate 12). Whether these in any way reflect items once written on the cut-out portions of plan B itself has to remain matter for conjecture.

6. The 'pointing hand' is a device often used by Aubrey, e.g. on the verso of plan A (Aubrey 24, 40v; Fowles and Legg 1980, 57).

7. The reproduction in Fowles and Legg (1980, 48–9) unaccountably stops short of the foot of the sheet, and thereby leaves out both the river and its name – an omission all the odder since these features do appear in the reproduction of plan B used in the book's prospectus.

8. 'Ghost' marks that could be thought to be stones are liable to crop up on reproductions of this plan. A particularly plausible-looking example appears in Fowles and Legg (1980, 48), a little to the NE of the genuine light dot just mentioned: this mark, on the centre line of the original, is in fact that of a sewing-needle hole.

9. The ambiguity must be noted, however, that draft X bears another 'line drawn across', in the form of a diagonal linking Cove, Obelisk and 'ring stone' (name written in), and that this line too was removed. Such a diagonal is found otherwise only on draft S, in which the ring stone is shown but not named.

10. State E2 is found in both of the Bodleian Library copies of *Abury* (1743) (Folio Godwin 158; Gough Wilts 3), as also in its copy of the 1838 reprint (Gough adds Wilts c.19); the modern reprint of plan E sold at Avebury is likewise of state E2. State E1 is represented by, for example, the copy in the Newberry Library, Chicago, used for the 1984 Garland reprint, and by a copy in the Alexander Keiller Museum, Avebury, reproduced by Pitts (1986, 63). Wider bibliographical examination of extant copies of the first edition of *Abury* would be of interest.

11. As with plans A and B, imperfect reproductions of the Frontispiece may introduce additional difficulties. For instance, while all four internal roadways are engraved showing a verge on either side, it is easy for the verge-lines to become whited-out in reproduction (e.g. Dames 1977, 111; Pitts 1986, 63). This gives the impression that the stones (misleadingly) shown by Stukeley inside the E and N entrances are supposed to be lying across the carriageway: the plan E originals clearly represent them as across the verges.

A different problem in one recent reproduction, that placed at the end of the Garland reprint of *Stonehenge and Abury* (1984) (from copies in the Newberry Library, Chicago), is that the original appears to have been torn and imperfectly repaired. This shows up as a vertical flaw (quite distinct from the re-worked meridian described at (d) above), about one-third of the way across from the L margin of the reproduction, which for instance affects the legibility of the scale in the L margin, creates the misprint 'Psture [sic] IIII', makes Pasture III read as another 'Pasture II', and divides and vertically displaces the halves of the first of the unshaded 'stone' rectangles (E.5.ii(a)).

IV *Analyses and comparisons*

a. General

These, then, are the plans. Together with the unpublished drafts of Stukeley's frontispiece and the associated documents introduced in Chapter I – such as the notes of Sir Robert Moray (Appendix I) and Olaus Borrichius, and Stukeley's hitherto unknown detailed written account of the site (Appendix II) – they provide a flood of information on the state of the antiquity at Avebury and various aspects of its surroundings in the late 17th and early 18th centuries. On the other hand, valuable as this information is, it is far from unproblematic. Though there is a striking degree of congruence in what the plans reveal, a number of puzzling anomalies exist between the different records.

Of these the most important are: the conflict over the number of stones in the Cove; the failure of Charleton to note a northern circle; Aubrey's failure to indicate the unusually large size of the Obelisk; the issue of whether or not there were pairs of stones outside and/or within each or several of the entrances; the fact that on some plans an exact crossroads is shown, as against the staggered one on plan A; the different (field) boundaries shown on various versions of Stukeley's plans and on plans A and C; the concentric rings of stones shown on plan C; and Stukeley's recording of the outer circle of the henge, as well as the two inner circles, as double circles of stones. In addition, plan C shows some unique details, such as houses on both of the cross-streets and a river positioned between the church and the earthwork (the latter a feature which may be echoed in plan A), while plan B may include evidence of a West Kennet Cove, and plan E marks the existence of a Beckhampton Avenue which is also postulated in other Stukeley sources. Lastly, our scrutiny of Stukeley's overlapping draft frontispieces of Avebury has revealed a substantial degree of discrepancy even within the record of one author as far as the detailed location of stones is concerned.

As has already been indicated in Chapter II, and as will be further considered in Chapter V, some of these anomalies can be explained in terms of the different intentions of their authors. The antiquaries involved may also have exaggerated features which fitted their preconceived ideas, or deleted those which did not. Others, however, present difficulties of a different kind, and in order to assess these – and to evaluate the significance of features which are now not visible on site but on which two or more of the documents appear to agree – it seems essential to collate them with the extant physical evidence.

Having briefly introduced the latter, and especially the evidence of geophysical survey, we will then deal with Avebury feature by feature, beginning with the 'modern' use of the site – as represented by buildings, (field) boundaries, roads, and the destruction of stones. We will then work from the outside inwards – from features like the waterways to the stone avenues and their appendages; the earthwork; the main outer circle; the inner circles; the Obelisk and the Cove. In concentrating on these particular features – and excluding others, such as Silbury Hill, which are just as important – we have followed the bias of the newly discovered plans C and D. To have dealt in equal detail with all the monuments and features in the area, such as the Kennet Avenue, would have led to a publication three times the size of this one.

Chapter I concluded at the moment when Stukeley's *Abury* first drew general attention to the site. The Introduction indicated how this was followed up by Colt Hoare (1812–21), and by Long (1858a) and others in the mid-19th century, and it was at this point that excavations were first undertaken. Such activity coincided with fierce debate about the relative accuracies of Aubrey and Stukeley, much of which focused on the likelihood or otherwise of there having been a second avenue of standing stones leading from the west causeway of the henge to Beckhampton, as Stukeley had claimed.

It is interesting that this debate included not only general accusations about the nature and quality of the work of Aubrey and Stukeley, but also attempts to interpret the local environment as it might have been at the time of the construction of the monuments. While the quality of the excavations at the time was by modern standards unscientific in the extreme, an important innovation was the probing for buried stones – a technique which, quite extraordinarily, has not been systematically repeated to date. Despite such intense interest in attempting to check the reliability of the early records, it does not appear to have occurred to any of the 19th-century investigators to examine the Royal Society's archives to see if relevant material existed there.

Just as surprising, perhaps, is the relative paucity of more recent archaeological research against which such earlier records may be assessed. When it comes to details about the stones, the archaeological evidence which can be compared to the record of Aubrey, Charleton and Stukeley comprises little more than the results of Keiller's work, as reconstructed by Smith (1965), together with the records of later limited excavation published by Piggott (1964). More recent excavation at Avebury has been strictly limited to very small exploratory examinations of areas under 'threat' from development, or capable of resolving problems about the environment (e.g. Harrington 1986). Such restraint has been inspired by the best of intentions, to avoid compounding the damage done by excavation in the 19th century: but it is important to recognize that this means that 'virtually none of the ground between the Outer and Inner Circles has been explored. Indeed, the whole of the excavations covers less than two acres, mainly in the vicinity of the ditch, leaving ninety-four percent of the interior untouched' (Burl 1979, 75). All in all, therefore, the available archaeological evidence from Avebury remains haphazard, almost incidental, and focused on the standing stone monuments and earthworks alone (and see Chapter V). Dates of the construction phases of the Avebury monuments remain rough estimates only (but see Pitts and Whittle forth-coming, for a date of c.2100 BC), and nothing is really known about where the people who built the sites actually lived (Smith 1984).

What is more surprising is that this major site, of archaeological significance not only for Britain but for World Heritage as a whole, appears until now not to have had a word published about it from the point of view of modern non-destructive archaeological pros-pecting techniques – despite the evident success of much earlier attempts to locate buried stones by non-destructive probing. Even modern techniques of field walking and surface collection have only just begun in the area (Holgate 1987). This extraordinary situation is at least in part due to the structure and perceived priorities of archaeological investigation in Britain in the 20th century (see Chapters V and VI). It is significant that the present book at last incorporates results of modern non-destructive resistivity surveys in addition to the analysis of historical documents and the reinterpretation of archaeological evidence.

Both the potential and the limitations of non-destructive scientific exploration of sites such as the Avebury monuments should be noted. Techniques of remote sensing, such as ground-penetrating radar, need to be fully exploited at this site in conjunction with elaborate landscape and palaeoenvironmental survey. In the present study, where the emphasis has necessarily been on the recognition of stone settings, it has been the techniques of magnetometry and resistivity surveying which have been applied. The areas thus surveyed, which are discussed in detail later in this Chapter, are indicated on Plate 45.

The physical remains indicative of the former positions of stones which should be detectable by one or other of these latter techniques are as follows:

1. a pit in which a stone has been buried,
2. a burning pit containing burnt soil and stone fragments,

158

N ←

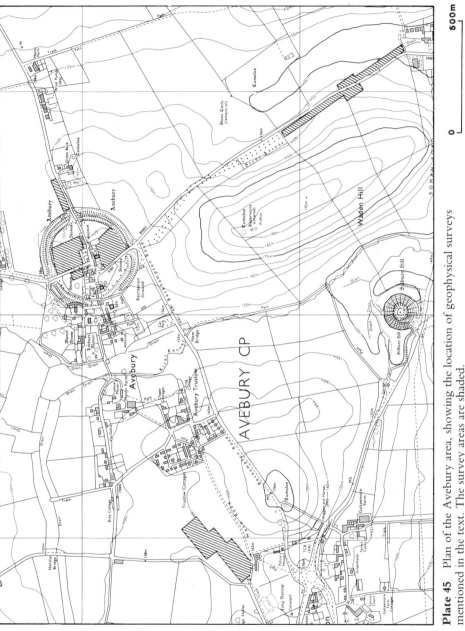

Plate 45 Plan of the Avebury area, showing the location of geophysical surveys mentioned in the text. The survey areas are shaded.

0   500m

3. the base of a stone with or without associated burning pit, or
4. a stone hole with packing stones.

The special circumstances presented by the presence of buried stones (as well as other sub-surface features) at Avebury present a considerable challenge to conventional archaeological prospecting. Of the two non-destructive techniques tested at Avebury resistivity has proved to have the more potential. Since chalk and sarsen (the silicified sandstone of which all the Avebury monoliths are composed) are normally inert for the purposes of magnetic detection, the latter technique is only of use in locating burning pits, where accumulations of burnt soil and sarsen chips can be expected to create anomalies in the local magnetic field. The individual magnetization of each stone fragment scattered within these pits results in a magnetic pattern of equivalently distributed minor anomalies localized as an aggregation of magnetic 'noise'. Unfortunately, such magnetic noise is often indistinguishable from that generated by ordinary iron litter in the soil (such as that commonly found near buildings), thus limiting the effectiveness of this type of survey for many of the questions being posed here.

Buried stones or pits containing stone fragments should be detectable by conventional resistance measurements (Clark 1975), yet the clarity of this response, if present, will depend on an interaction between variables such as local moisture levels, surface topography, the degree of disturbance from adjacent features and natural background variability in soil and geology. Stones have been found to have been buried at varying depths within the solid chalk, up to 2.4m. from the surface (Keiller 1939, 225); the pits were then filled with rammed chalk leaving a surface scarcely distinguishable from the solid geology (Smith 1965, 177). Both the depth of burial and the muting of physical contrast caused by the encapsulation of the stone within solid chalk act together to diminish the production of either resistivity or magnetic anomalies.

Wherever such geophysical methods were applied, a 30m. grid was established and tied into local features. Instrument readings were taken along successive 30m. traverses across each survey grid and the data stored in a portable computer for later processing at the laboratory. Readings were taken at either 1.0m. or 0.5m. intervals across the pre-surveyed grid using a Geoscan RM4 meter and DL10 data-logger. The probe configuration used was the Twin Electrode, with a mobile probe separation of 0.5m.

Magnetometer survey, applied more sparingly, made use of a Geoscan FM18 fluxgate gradiometer, logging readings at 25cm. intervals along 30m. traverses spaced 1.0 and 0.5 metres apart across each grid.

The data accumulated in these ways were processed using the Ancient Monuments Laboratory's Sequent minicomputer and graphics system. Images of the data can be built up on the graphics screen as colour or grey-tone displays, manipulated if necessary by numerical enhancement routines, and then plotted as graphical traces, contours or grey-tones, as appropriate.[1]

We make no pretence that such up-to-date technology is not affected by the interpretative preconceptions of the operator/investigator (and indeed we shall explore this point in Chapter V). We do, however, maintain that such 'objective' techniques should be of value in discriminating between some of the varying, and often conflicting, evidence and claims of over 300 years of enquiry into what existed at the prehistoric site of Avebury.

Armed with interdisciplinary tools and approaches, and, we hope, fully conscious of the various factors which may have influenced – and possibly still continue to influence – those whose aim is the interpretation of the archaeology of the Avebury region, we may now turn to the nature of the site(s) itself.

'Modern' use of the monument·

b. 'Modern' use: general

We have noted earlier the difficulties presented to those seeking to record the state of the antiquity of Avebury by the extent to which it had become entwined with the village. In contrast to Stonehenge, standing unencumbered on Salisbury Plain and hence impossible to overlook, the fact that the stone circle at Avebury was interspersed by cottages, inn, hedgerows, closes and orchards greatly complicated its elucidation. Well into the 18th century this was one of the principal factors which made the antiquity easy to miss, despite the fact that a main road traversed the site. As Stukeley put it in a manuscript draft of August 1721 (Gough Maps 231, 38):

> It is really Matter of Surprize that such a place in the Bath road from London should have escapd the Survey of the Curious when Travellers & stage coaches every day pass thro the very midst of the Town & cannot but see many of the Stones that compose this Work which are enough in my Apprehension to astonish the most vulgar Beholder.

In actuality, generations of travellers had passed through Avebury without leaving record of ever noticing the stone circle at all, though Charleton's remark about the grey wethers, that 'these stones I my self have often seen, in journeys to *Bath* from *London*' (Charleton 1663, 58), reminds us that, close by in the North Wiltshire countryside, there were many scattered sarsen stones which were clearly of natural origin, and a casual glance could have suggested that those interspersed through the village at Avebury might simply be more of these.

Even when the antiquity was noted, it was easy to mistake its nature. 'The prospect is so interrupted, that 'tis very hard to discover the form of it' (Camden 1695, 111). Indeed, William Stukeley claimed in the 18th century of the local inhabitants that 'the great stones of the great circles of *Abury* were not by them discern'd to stand in circles' (Stukeley 1743, 32). Even when the encumbrances had been overcome to the extent of noticing that stone formations existed, they make it easy to understand how independent observers could misconstrue the overall structure of the antiquity or miss some of its subsidiary features which others saw. This goes far towards explaining some of the discrepancies between the plans, especially the concentric rings of Aubrey's plan C, and the absence of a circle surrounding the Cove in Charleton's plan D. They also compounded the difficulties of making an accurate record, a state of affairs not wholly unfamiliar in more recent times, as in the 1930s, when Keiller had physically to dismantle modern rubbish dumps and rusty pig wire in order to conduct his investigations (Keiller 1939, 223). We shall therefore shortly look further at the history of these encumbrances, on which the evidence of the plans is not entirely consistent.

c. Estate maps

Before doing so, it is worth noting a class of evidence which has not hitherto been explored by those interested in prehistoric Avebury, namely that from local historical sources. Documentation concerning land tenure and the like provides fragmentary information, but, in addition, three maps showing the monument exist in the Wiltshire County Record Office, which have not previously been reproduced. None of these record the megaliths, which were presumably seen as irrelevant to the purposes for which they were compiled, and they are hence unhelpful for a consideration of the antiquity itself. But they throw considerable light on questions concerning field boundaries, land ownership, buildings and roadways. They are as follows:

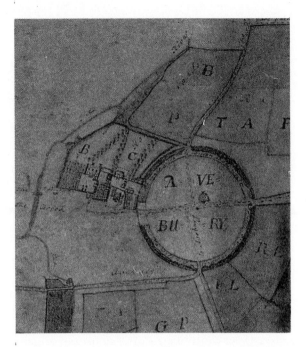

Plate 46 Estate map of Avebury Great Farm, surveyed by Thomas Alexander in 1733 (WRO 1553/71).

WRO 1553/71 (Plate 46). An estate map of 'Avebury Great Farm belonging to Richard Holford Esquire who is Lord-Royal of Avebury', surveyed by Thomas Alexander of Avebury in 1733, a coloured ink map on parchment. This clearly depicts the earthwork and the intersecting roads within it, but it has no field boundaries, and it includes only one building, at the SW corner of the NE segment. This was evidently included because it was the only building within the earthwork which belonged to the home estate of Richard Holford, as did the Manor House and associated buildings to the W, which *are* shown: other buildings, which did not belong to the estate, therefore fell outside the surveyor's brief. The following words are written around the different segments of the ditch: 'Wall Ditch' (NW segment), 'Common Wall Ditch' (NE segment), 'Spansicks Wall Ditch' (SE and SW segments). 'Spansick' is evidently a corruption of the proper name 'Spanswick', presumably that of the man who owned or leased these plots of land.

WRO E/A 95. Inclosure Map, 1794 (Plate 47). In this map, drawn by B. Haynes, the earthwork is shown clearly, as are the buildings and enclosures within it. In addition, the fields are named, and in some cases the owner's name is also given; the ditch is inscribed 'Wall Ditch' three times. The numbers refer to the accompanying inclosure award, which gives details of the plots in the possession of each landowner.

WRO T/A Avebury. Tithe Map 1845 (Plate 48). The depiction of the area enclosed by the earthwork is incomplete on this map. The whole of both segments to the N of the E–W road through the site are shown, but of the SE quadrant only the E half is shown, while the SW quadrant is omitted altogether; of the earthwork, only the NE segment is marked. Within the parts that are surveyed, buildings and land-holdings appear to be accurately delineated and keyed to the tithe apportionment.

A further relevant item is an earlier sketch map of the Manor House and gardens accompanied by 'Instructions to Farmer Skeate' dated 27 September 1695, for the removal or planting of trees – 'syccomores', 'elmes' and 'oakes' – and for repairs to stonework, etc. (WRO 184/4) (Plate 49). The absence of any indication of sarsen stones both from the

162

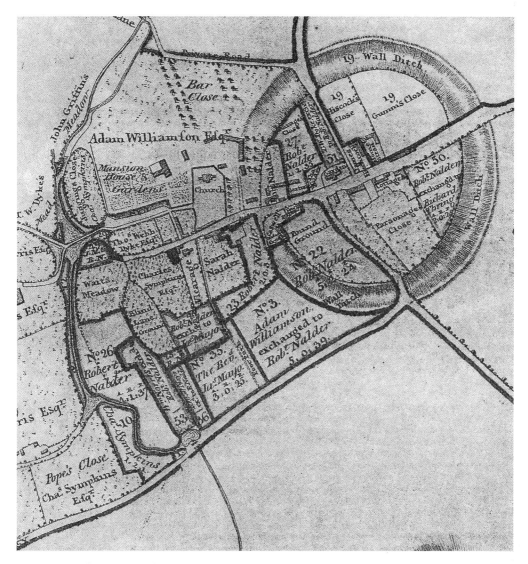

Plate 47   Inclosure map of 1794 (WRO E/A 95).

instructions and from the plan could reflect either that stones were not shown because they were not relevant to the gardening objectives in question, or that ancient stones had long since been removed. Like Aubrey in plan A, the 1695 plan-maker had trouble with his depiction of the church, first inserting it upside down! More significantly, the map provides useful information about the topography of the churchyard and the adjacent area, including the question of at which point the bank was levelled (see e below).

d. Buildings, fields and boundaries

The first issue raised by plans A–E, and particularly Aubrey's plan C, is the extent to which 'contemporary' uses had intruded into the antiquity in the early modern period. The evidence suggests that for several centuries prior to the 17th the ancient monument had not

163

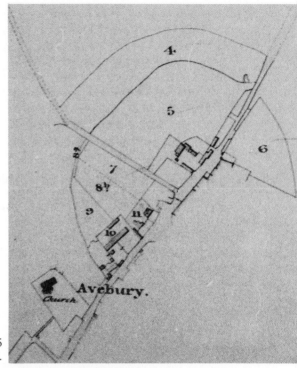

Plate 48 Tithe map of 1845
(WRO T/A Avebury).

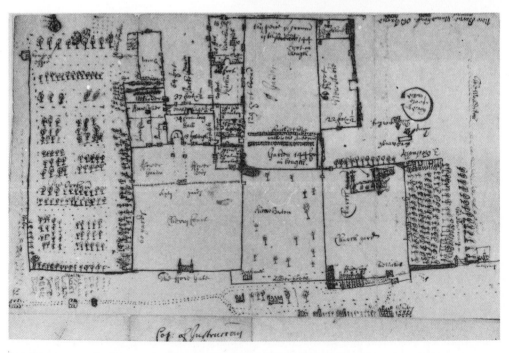

Plate 49 1695 sketch map of Manor House and gardens (WRO 184/4).

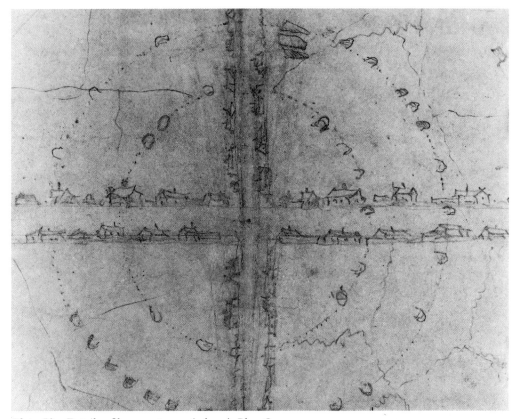

Plate 50 Details of houses etc. on Aubrey's Plan C.

been seen as a particularly special place: the land encompassed by the earthwork had long been used for farming, while the living village had grown first towards and then into it – though the exact period over which this took place is unclear.

Of the 17th-century plans only one, plan C, makes any attempt to illustrate the village (Plate 50): in plan A Avebury consciously ignored the buildings so as to show the prehistoric antiquity more clearly, and the same is also true of Charleton in plan D. Plan C, if accepted at its face value, would appear to show at least thirty-nine buildings on both the N–S and the E–W roads across the monument. On the other hand Stukeley spoke of there being 'about thirty houses' in the early 18th century (1743, 25), although a conservative count direct from plan E shows only some 13 more or less obvious dwelling *blocks*, including the inn, the other buildings looking more like barns, outhouses and so on. While this may be the basis for Burl's unreferenced observation (1979, 46) that 'by the early eighteenth century there were at least *thirteen* homes inside the earthwork as well as ten pastures' [our italics], it is evident that the 13 blocks might well have contained, by subdivision, 30 'houses' or 'homes'. The 1794 inclosure map (Plate 47) may be collated with plan E: the former shows a layout fairly similar to Stukeley's, although a few buildings appear here which Stukeley did not show, while some that he did show are not present: in view of the differing scale and degree of detail, however, these slight discrepancies are trivial compared with the overall similarity of the two. This suggests that the bulk of the extension of the village into the monument had already occurred by 1724 and that not much more such expansion took place after that.

As to when the houses shown by Stukeley were built, his statement that 'most of the

165

houses, walls, and outhouses in the town are raised from these materials', in other words the spoil from the destruction of stones (1743, 25), relates their construction directly to that destruction, which appears to have been at its height in the generation around 1700 (see below). Aubrey too thought that the houses of the village were 'built with the Frustrum's of the Stones of this Monument: for hereabout are no other stones to be found (except Flints). The Church is likewise built of them: and the Mannour-house ...: and also another faire House not far from that' (Aubrey 24, 36; Fowles and Legg 1980, 39). On the other hand, material for building was also available from the natural sarsens. Stukeley records that: 'They have sometimes us'd of these [demolished] stones for building houses: but say, they may have them cheaper, in more manageable pieces, from the gray weathers' (Stukeley 1743, 16). Either way, that building activity in Avebury should have been at its height in the late 17th century is plausible; it was at this time that building and rebuilding reached a peak in the English countryside generally, in contrast to previous claims that this climax had come a century earlier (Machin 1977; Hoskins 1953).

How, in the light of this, should we interpret Aubrey's plan C (Plate 50)? The answer seems clear. Since even by 1794 there were fewer houses than Aubrey there shows; since there is no other evidence at all of houses on the N–S axis as depicted by him; and since there is no reason to suppose extensive depopulation in the period c.1660 to c.1720, the likeliest explanation of the discrepancy between plan C and the 18th-century evidence is that plan C was intended only to represent schematically the fact that there were houses on the roads,

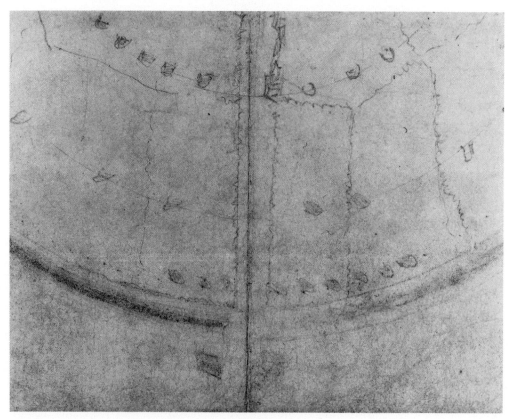

Plate 51 Details of 'boundaries' etc. on Aubrey's Plan C.

rather than to give an accurate depiction of exactly how many there were and where they stood. The fact that the 1733 map (Plate 46) shows only one building has already been accounted for above.

As for boundaries, the most striking discrepancy is between plan C and plan A, the former apparently showing a network of concentric, vaguely rectangular but highly irregular enclosures (Plate 51), the latter a simpler and more regular pattern of, presumably, field boundaries running N–S across the NE, SE and SW segments of the site. In this, plan A (Transparency 1) bears a recognizable similarity to plan E: Aubrey's plan A has four of the pasture boundaries shown in Stukeley's plan (transparency 2), perhaps indicating that they were the major ones. Comparison between the two is, however, complicated by the fact that, since he ignored the houses, Aubrey incidentally also deleted most, if not all, of the enclosures surrounding them. The 1794 map shows a similar pattern, though it lacks a few of the boundaries shown by Stukeley, for instance that subdividing the SW quadrant of the site. Frustratingly, the 1733 map shows no boundaries inside the 'Wall Ditch', though it does show that at least part of the bank and ditch remained common land right through to the mid-18th century: the NE segment of the ditch itself is captioned 'Common', and this is confirmed by a release dated 4 April 1754 which also refers to 'the Common Called Wall-ditch' (WRO 212A/31/4; cf. V.C.H. 1983, 87). The two southern segments of the ditch, on the other hand, already appear to have been privately owned (see above), and by the time of the Inclosure Map of 1794 this fate had overcome the NE segment as well (Plate 47).

Such evidence as is available from archaeology tends to bear out the same pattern, though such post-prehistoric activity within the Avebury monument has often been seen by field archaeologists as an encumbrance to their work or, at best, as of secondary interest (Keiller 1939, 224, 229). Twentieth-century excavation reports tend to give brief and generalized mention of field boundaries, as in Keiller's (1939, 229) remark that 'a positive network of medieval and more recent ditches intersected the entrance area'. In the SW and NW sectors of the monument parts of such features were picked up by Keiller's excavations, along the inner edge of the main ditch, as well as two parallel ditches traversing the N causeway in a northerly direction (Isobel Smith, pers. comm.), and a medieval field-boundary consisting of 'a low turf-covered dry stone wall connecting many of the stones' and covering four of them (Keiller 1939, 224). An unpublished plan of the SE sector prior to excavation in the 1930s (Plate 52) appears to confirm the regularity of field strips, and the significance of this for the interpretation of Stukeley's record will be seen below.

Recent resistivity coverage at Avebury has revealed distinct anomalies in the plotted data deriving from existing or former field banks and/or ditches. In the NE sector of the monument (Plate 53) the field bank running around the N perimeter of the field is clearly visible as a positive resistivity anomaly, as is that running N–S; both are recorded by Stukeley in plan E and the latter by Aubrey in plan A. Other alignments shown in the plot include two further N–S field boundaries, neither of which is shown by Stukeley, but the easternmost of which is visible from the air (Keiller 1939, pl. I). A linear *negative* anomaly entering the northern circle from the E is possibly a former trackway (and see discussion of Plate 58, section k, below).

The SE sector is the only one for which we have reliable archaeological evidence pre-dating the excavations in the 1930s (Alexander Keiller Museum, G5785 10384; Plate 52 and Transparency 3). Whereas most of the main boundaries are on alignments consistent with Stukeley's plans, there are some discrepancies. That seen running N–S near the E margin of the resistivity plot (Plate 54) existed on the surface until recently, but does not show the deflection shown in Stukeley's plan E. The others, detected only in part by the survey, have left no surface trace. In Stukeley's pasture X (Plate 14 and Transparency 2) there is an E–W division visible in the resistivity data which does not represent a corresponding

167

Plate 52 Plan of field (pasture) boundaries in the SE quadrant of the Avebury henge (Morven Institute of Archaeological Research, 1939).

feature on plan E, as is also the case in the N part of his pasture IX. Unfortunately, more than half of the S parts of pastures VIII–X have suffered such physical disturbance that resistivity survey has produced no useful results. Nevertheless, as will become evident below, it is important to recognize that the boundaries indicated in this quadrant in Aubrey's plan A are likely to have been the same as those between the road and Stukeley's pasture X, and between Stukeley's pastures VIII and VII (Transparencies 1, 2).

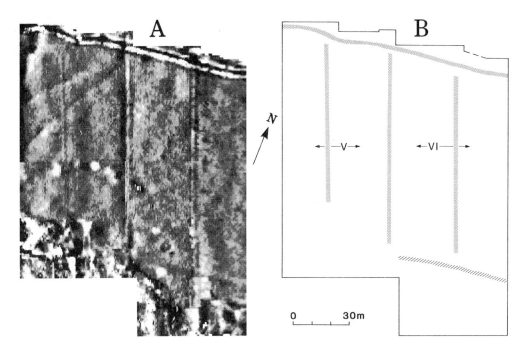

Plate 53 Resistivity survey of the NE quadrant of the Avebury henge, illustrating the location of former field (pasture) boundaries: (A) grey-tone plot, and (B) interpretation. The linear anomaly shown by diagonal shading may be the response to a former trackway.

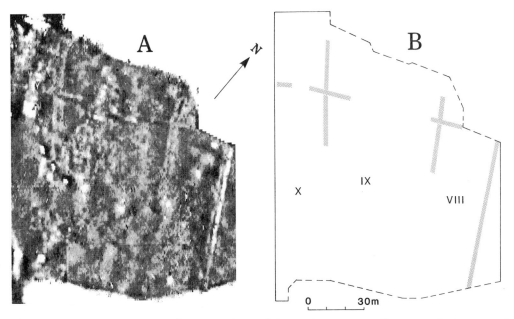

Plate 54 Resistivity survey of the SE quadrant of the Avebury henge, illustrating the location of former field (pasture) boundaries: (A) grey-tone plot, and (B) interpretation.

We are left with plan C and its apparent discrepancy with the pattern revealed by virtually all the other evidence available concerning boundaries within the earthwork. How is this to be explained? One possibility, especially if plan C refers to a period a decade before plan A, is that the plan records a phase when there were numerous smaller holdings which were combined into fewer larger ones in a process of consolidation of late 17th-century date, but there is no independent evidence to corroborate this. Alternatively, could Aubrey in plan C have been intending to show a network of pastures, gardens, orchards, closes and palings? A comparison of plan E with the 1794 map shows that the latter omits several shown in Stukeley's record, suggesting that within the basic pattern fences or hedges were erected or removed from time to time, perhaps as land ownership changed. That this was so is confirmed by a close study of Stukeley's draft frontispieces (Chapter III, E.7): he did not accept palings as constituting pasture divisions, and, except where there were established trees, it does indeed appear that gardens, fences, and possibly other boundaries at Avebury formed a confusing and changing mosaic of interconnecting and irregular patterns. It is not inconceivable that Aubrey's plan C is an attempt to depict such a mosaic. On the other hand, the divergence of the pattern shown here from the broad physiognomy shown in common by plan A and the 18th-century plans renders it likelier that the boundaries on plan C are schematic rather than realistic.

A last conceivable possibility is that what Aubrey was showing in plan C were not field or other boundaries but irrigation channels, perhaps because, at the point when he drew it up, local interest – and their implications for co-operative endeavour – made them more significant, for the time being, than any pattern of gardens, orchards or fields. Here, it is worth noting Aubrey's own observation in his *Natural History of Wiltshire* that:

> The improvement of watering meadows began at Wyley, about 1635, about which time, I remember, we began to use them at Chalke [i.e. Broad Chalke in South Wiltshire]. *Watering of meadows about Marleburgh and so to Hungerford was, I remember, about 1646.* [italics added] (Aubrey 1847, 104)

The practice, therefore, clearly interested Aubrey: had it indeed been in use at Avebury, he might well have wanted to convey its implications to his Royal Society audience, and this could explain the discrepancy between plan C and other records. On the other hand, though there is environmental evidence for the channelling of water from the Winterbourne (Susan Limbrey, pers. comm.) and though quite a broad irrigation channel – of unknown date – led from the Winterbourne to the NW gardens of the Manor (C. Gingell, pers. comm.), it seems highly unlikely that water from this source could have been taken all the way to meadows/pastures within the henge. There is also no physical evidence for channelling from the springs. However, such superficial channels would not be expected to show up in resistivity data.

On balance it is most likely that – on this point as in the case of the buildings – plan C was schematic, reflecting Aubrey's lack of expertise in the art of giving an accurate as against an impressionistic view of a site's topography in this, his earliest attempt at a representation of Avebury.

e. Avebury Manor and its environs

A subsidiary question relates to the Manor House and the way in which works done to this impinged on the antiquity, particularly the westerly segment of the bank and ditch. Sir John Stawell had re-acquired the Manor at the Restoration, and at some later point a considerable stretch of the bank was levelled to the N of the W entrance and the ditch filled. This appears to have been done after Sir John's son and heir Ralph was created Baron Stawell in 1683, since Stukeley's reference to the episode, noting finds made at the time, attributes the work to 'lord Stowell' (Stukeley 1743, 27, but cf. Welfare 1989, 19). Burl simultaneously fills out and confuses the story, in two unreferenced passages, saying both that 'around 1685, Lord Stawell had part of Avebury's western bank removed to make space for a barn' and that 'John, second Lord Stawell, who had inherited Avebury Manor, levelled a great length of the bank north of the West Entrance to make room for a barn before selling the manor-house to Sir Richard Holford in 1696 for £7500' (Burl 1979, 46, 57). In fact, genealogical works show that John, who had become 2nd Baron on his father's death in 1689, himself died 'at the early age of twenty-four, in 1692, and was s[ucceeded] by his half brother William Stawel' (Burke 1883, 504–5). William lived until 1742, so the sale to Holford must have taken place under his auspices; yet, strangely, this 3rd Baron goes unmentioned not only by Burl but by Knowles (1956, 366) and even by the otherwise well-referenced Victoria County History (V.C.H. 1983, 91). The exact relationship of the levelling of the rampart to the complex history of the ownership of the manor (which during 1693/4 involved a private Parliamentary Bill dealing with the confused affairs of the Stawell estate) remains obscure (but see below). What *is* clear is that the levelling occurred at latest by 1695, when the map (Plate 49) already referred to was made. Indeed, in its depiction of the area between church and ditch N of the entrance, almost every detail which is shown is identical with those delineated in Stukeley's plan E: not only is the area already levelled, but even some of Stukeley's mature trees are present as saplings.

However, while the 'Old Barne' and the 'Warme house' – the two outbuildings aligned with the new barn – are similar in both plans, the 'New Barne' itself is quite small in 1695: it apparently occupies only part of the northern arm of the L-shaped barn shown by Stukeley. The accepted name for the whole earthwork, 'The Wall Ditch', runs down the E edge (opposite the 'Round poole walled'), creating the impression that both bank and ditch were still there: we have to refer to Stukeley's plans to see that only the ditch, or part of it, could have remained.

It looks as if the September 1695 map accompanied a flurry of activity preceding the sale of the Manor, which followed an earlier phase which had not only destroyed the bank and filled part of the ditch, but had been succeeded by colonization of, and tree-planting in, the reclaimed area. Such activities could have begun to take place at any time after the 2nd Baron's succession in 1689, with each year that passed making them more likely – either as one of the causes, or as one of the effects, of the financial embarrassments documented during the House of Lords hearings (HMC, *MSS of the House of Lords*, 1692–3, no. 682; 1693–4, no. 801). It seems likely that the destruction would, at latest, have been initiated by the passing of the *Lord Stawell's Estate Act* in Spring 1694, just over three years before Aubrey's death. Aubrey, who visited Avebury Manor, probably in the 1680s or later (Knowles 1956, 366), may well have known of some or all of these events (see Chapter III, A.5(g)(iv)).

This same sketch map (Plate 49) also provides valuable information about the Avebury Manor grounds as they appear along the W road – valuable in the context of possible interpretations of several of the features indicated on plans by both Aubrey and Stukeley. The 'Church yard' (no trees shown) has 'The Wicket' giving on to the road, and 'Fivens house' in its W road corner. W of the churchyard are successively three large enclosures: the 'Sheerhe Barton', containing a scattering of trees and having a 'Ladder hovel(?)' against its S wall and the 'Dog Kennel' in its W road corner, the 'Cherry Court' (no trees), stretching back to the flower gardens in front of the Manor, and finally the 'Old Orchard', shown as heavily planted with regular groups of trees. 'The Ford Gate' is shown, apparently an elaborate main gate of the Manor, giving on to the road in the centre wall of the Cherry Court not far from the present-day westward path and footbridge over the Winterbourne. In view of all this detail it may possibly be significant that no stones are shown anywhere in this map, either within the Manor grounds or in the W road.

This is an appropriate place to note a further instance of levelling of the bank and ditch, this time to the S of the W entrance (a third instance, when the bank W of the S entrance was quarried, took place in 1762: cf. Burl 1979, 53). A sequence of details in Stukeley's draft plans (see Chapter III, E.7) clearly conveys that the second destruction took place between 1721 and 1724. The bank S of the W entrance is shown as whole both in version N (Plate 32) and – carefully edged with a fence – in version Q (Plate 35). Version R, however, records that a stretch of bank is down, the ditch filled, a gated track curves into the area, and a small enclosure is planted with trees (Plate 36). Variants of these features appear also in .'A Prospect from *Abury* Steeple' (Stukeley 1743, tab. xxiii). We have found no written reference by Stukeley to this episode; but it seems likely that this second levelling followed a further change in the ownership of Avebury Manor in 1722, when it passed to Sir Richard Holford's son, Samuel (V.C.H. 1983, 91).

f. The road network

The first question that needs to be clarified about the network of roads is the route of the road from London to Bath in the Avebury vicinity. For the last two centuries or so, the only proper road between Marlborough and Bath appears to have been that following the line of the present-day A4, passing immediately to the N of the Sanctuary and immediately to the S of Silbury Hill. For some but not all of its course through the Avebury region, this line follows that of the Via Badonica, the Roman road from Cunetio to Aquae Sulis. From the A4 at West Kennet, a lane strikes NW, often within sight of the route of the Kennet Avenue, to enter Avebury by the S entrance.

However, throughout the century from Aubrey's 'discovery' of Avebury to the publication of Stukeley's book on it, another important route from Marlborough toward Bath was in use: this was a coach road over the downs, entering Avebury by the E entrance. Both Aubrey (plan A) and Charleton provide entrance-names confirming this, despite the fact that Aubrey's plan B equally clearly confirms the southern (A4) route as the 'Rode from Marlborough to Bristoll'. At separate points in his *Abury*, Stukeley notes the functioning presence both of the 'direct *Bath*-road from *London*' for travellers 'from *Marlborough* hither', and of the 'common road from *Marlborough* to *Bath*', passing through the 'inclosures ... of *West-Kennet*', and meeting, at the W foot of Overton Hill, the (at that point) slightly divergent line of 'the *Roman*-road from *Marlborough* coming down the hill' (Stukeley 1743, 14, 30).

Though it seems odd that none of the contemporary sources so far cited takes explicit note of the fact that there were two Marlborough–Bath routes in use simultaneously, this was presumably because it tended to be taken for granted. Modern commentators, in ignoring one or other route, have created possibilities of confusion or ambiguity (e.g. Piggott 1985, 47; Burl 1979, 12, 42; V.C.H. 1983, 89). Contemporary sources appear to suggest that the S rather than the W entrance was the main way to and from Bath – perhaps because the fords at the 'Watery place' W of the church was unsuitable for major traffic. When Aubrey reported that 'his Majestie left the Queen and diverted to Aubury', it seems likely that the royal party came up the lane from West Kennet, down which, five years later, Pepys was to take his departure (by coach), glimpsing the Sanctuary as he went (Pepys 1972–83, ix. 240). Thus travellers from and to London could arrive and depart both by the S and by the E entrances.

The only contemporary account known to us which both acknowledges in one place the presence of these two working roads and offers an explanation for it is an interesting passage in Stukeley's *Itinerarium Curiosum* (1724a, 132–3). Since this was published while his field-work on Avebury was still in progress, Stukeley may have felt no need to repeat the detail in the *Abury* volume itself:

172

I shall begin my journey from *Marlborough* ... and from [there] pursue the *roman* road, which we have before trac'd from *Newberry* hither, and lately discover'd its whole progress toward the *Bath* ... Its course is east and west. It goes hence all along the north side of the *Kennet* river, between it and the high grounds; and is the present road, but highly wants a *roman* hand to repair it ... it proceeds directly up to the famous *Overton*-hill ... this ridg is a little to the north of the present road, somewhat higher up the hill, it points directly east and west, one end to *Marlborough* the other to *Silbury* hill. 'Tis perfect for some space over the down, but upon descending the hill westward, they have plow'd it up ... At the bottom by the corner of the hedg, it meets again the common road near the *white hart* alehouse, and so they go together above *west Kennet* to *Silbury* hill. This was the post and coach road to the *Bath*, till for want of reparation they were forc'd to find a new one, more northward upon the downs, and farther about thro' the town of *Abury*. When on the south-side of *Silbury* hill, it goes very strait and full west thro' the cornfields on the south of *Bekhamton* ... They have of late endeavor'd to exclude travellers going upon it, by inclosing it at both ends with ditches, but the badness of the lower road has defeated their purpose, and made people still assert the public right. Beyond *Bekhamton* it again enters the downs, and marches up the hill in a very plain ridg and beautiful to behold; the pits and cavitys whence the earth was taken on both sides, being conspicuous all the way.

The words above about the convergence between the routes of the Roman and the 'common' roads, added to the fuller description in *Abury* (Stukeley 1743, 30–1), incidentally help to account for the difficulty – encountered by Aubrey and Moray as well as Stukeley, and not yet resolved by modern archaeology – of identifying the course of the Avenue down Overton Hill.

Moving to the roads within the henge itself, Charleton in plan D picks out only 'the high way from Marlburgh to Bath', presumably because it was the main road at the time. The other plans all show a cross-roads, but Aubrey at first (in plan C) stylized this into a perfect cross, in contrast to his plan A, in which the road junction is shown as staggered, just as in plan E and other 18th-century plans. It is interesting that the first of Aubrey's three relevant statements in his commentary – that 'the Village of Aubury ... stands *per crucem*,' as is to be seen by Scheme the 1st' (Aubrey 24, 35; Fowles and Legg 1980, 38) – is most readily comprehensible in terms of a plan resembling C, since this does show not only a village but a cruciform one, whereas plan A shows none. It is conceivable that the two following mentions of 'crosse-streetes', in the text on the next page, could signal Aubrey's move away from a simplistic cruciform perception, apparently so evident between plans C and A themselves.

While there may be temptation to seek deep significance in Aubrey's rendition of plan C as a uniform cross, especially in view of his use of the Latin 'per crucem' (see further Chapter VI), this should not be laboured. As we have noted (Chapter II, ii), an advance in plan-making technique is certainly part of the reason for differences between plans C and A, and it would be justifiable to conclude that their changes in treatment of the main roads are simply an instance of the greater accuracy of the latter. However, the marked S-bend in plan A's eastern street is certainly inaccurate (Welfare 1989, 20): in that particular respect plans C and D happen, however schematically, to be the more accurate.

g. The river(s) and the Kennet Avenue

Aubrey's plans C and (possibly) A indicate a 'river' running N–S between the church and the W entrance, a position which is clearly in error. However, a lower part of the river's actual course, running E–W, is more credibly shown in the extreme S of Aubrey's plan B. In addition, it is worth noting Aubrey's undeleted aside (Aubrey 24, 38; Fowles and Legg 1980, 42) which is clearly relevant to his perception of water-related features in the vicinity of the site:

> At this Townes end [sc. Aubury], by the church, is a Watery place, which (I thinke) is the source of the River Kynnet.

This quotation may even point to an explanation of the 'foliage features' of plan A and plan C (Chapter III, A.6(c), C.6(b)), which could possibly represent such 'a Watery place' or, conceivably, water meadow irrigation.

It is tempting to explain away the river of plan C by suggesting an error, perhaps through Aubrey having made notes on different occasions and on different scraps of paper and then wrongly collating them. The similar mistake on plan A would presumably have derived from the use of plan C as a starting model, since it seems unlikely that it could derive from errors in Aubrey's surveying (see Chapter III, A.15). There are alternative, albeit unlikely, possible explanations. One extremely improbable suggestion would be that Aubrey was trying to record a change in the river's characteristics since antiquity, a suggestion which was in fact made in the 19th century (Lukis 1881–3a, 155). This possibility seems remote and may be discounted, but examination of it does demonstrate a complex hydrological situation at Avebury, and may cast light on Aubrey's plan B, as well as on some of his textual statements, including that just quoted.

The main monument of Avebury has recently been described (Harding and Lee 1987, 284) as lying some 300m. E of the Winterbourne stream and c.1km. N of the River Kennet. The most recent detailed scientific analysis of environmental change in this area shows that there must have been considerable flooding of large areas beside both the Winterbourne and the Kennet in the late second or early first millennium BC, but that such flooding did not last for long (Susan Limbrey, pers. comm.). Certainly by the medieval period these large areas had reverted to dry ground with cultivated arable land. At some time subsequent to the medieval period, water-meadows with distributory channels were probably introduced to produce deliberate flooding to warm up and fertilize the meadows in spring (Kerridge 1954; Evans et al. 1988, 102). Susan Limbrey's (pers. comm.) study states that 'the Winterbourne acquires greater and more continuous flow and assumes the name of Kennet at the Swallowhead Springs close to Silbury Hill; though it does not dry up for such long periods in the summer as does the water course above the springs, it is still essentially a winterbourne [as it flows E towards Marlborough]'. Very recently, results from a 1m. hand-dug test pit in West Kennet (Allen and Carruthers 1989) have suggested both that narrow strips of land along the Kennet course (and therefore probably the Winterbourne also) were very marshy and commonly inundated in the medieval period, and that the river may have not existed in its present course during the later parts of the Neolithic.

The question which now arises is, could the 'river' in plan C (and plan A) be an attempt by Aubrey to depict a seasonal feature which he either saw or had been told about by locals? Matters are complicated by the fact that the Winterbourne is not always distinguished from the Kennet by its own name (e.g. V.C.H. 1983, 87), but it appears that neither Leland nor Camden (even in Holland's 1610 recension) (Chapter I, i) was aware of the existence of the Winterbourne. Holland reports how at Rockley, 'there breaketh out sometimes at unawares water in maner of a streame or sudden Land-flood, reputed the messenger, as it were, and forerunner of a dearth, and is by the rusticall people of the countrey, called *Hungerborne*' (Camden 1610, 255). However, this phenomenon, still 'occasionally experienced nowadays (i.e. about once every ten years)' (Isobel Smith, pers. comm.), is quite distinct from the annual cycle of the Winterbourne, which runs (N–S from Winterbourne Monkton) each winter.

The evidence of Stukeley is more promising. In contrast to Twining, who believed that the Kennet itself rose actually within the Avebury monument (Twining 1723, 34; cf. Long 1858b, 13), Stukeley claimed that the river had two or three heads (Stukeley 1722–4b, 119; Stukeley 1743, 19). The third of these, which is mentioned only in his 'Celtic Temples' but not in his published *Abury*, was said to be 'coming from *Bekampton*'. On the other hand, of the other two, one was claimed to rise from the 'plentiful spring' at Swallowhead, flowing E to '*Marlborough, roman Cunetio*, which has its name from the river', while the other existed only in 'wet seasons', deriving from Monkton and running S to Silbury. In addition, in discussing the possible derivation of the name Avebury from 'water', Stukeley refers to 'the brook running by' (Stukeley 1743, 19; King 1879, 382), and this may well have been the local Avebury term used for the Winterbourne as it passed to the W of the church, as stated for instance on the map of 1733 (Plate 46), before it flowed farther south towards Silbury when it is called 'river'. As was seen in Chapter II, iv, at an early stage in his 'Dracontium' theory of Avebury, Stukeley saw considerable symbolic significance in this 'brook running thro' & crossing the tail of the serpent' (Stukeley 1722–4b, 132).

In the light of this corroborative evidence, we may assume that Aubrey's N–S depiction on plan C – and what may have been an initial attempt to reproduce it in plan A, albeit modified with a 'spring-head' (see Chapter III, A.9) – probably represented the Winterbourne, but that he misplaced it too far to the E. Whether this was due to some technical mistake, or was based on local hearsay at a time when the Winterbourne was not actually flowing, it certainly presents confusion, and it is unclear how the 'foliage feature' nearby, which has already been alluded to, should be seen to relate to this.

If Aubrey was confused about the position of the Winterbourne and the source of the Kennet, so he was also by the river's location in the southern valley. In his text, he wrote that the Kennet Avenue 'turnes with a right angle eastward crossing the River, and ascends up the hill to another Monument of the same Kind (but less)', (Aubrey 24, 34; Fowles and Legg 1980, 37) in this repeating almost verbatim a deleted passage elsewhere (Aubrey 24, 63v).

On the other hand, as many commentators have pointed out (e.g. Colt Hoare 1812–21, ii.63; Cunnington 1932, 301 n. 5; Fowles and Legg 1980, 56), plan B (plate 8) does not show the Avenue stones actually crossing the river. Hence Aubrey let an erroneous statement stand in his latest text, which contradicted the illustration to which it explicitly refers, as well as topographical actuality. Indeed, if Aubrey's text is taken literally, so that one insists on a due N–S Avenue, a right-angle at West Kennet, and then a further straight stretch to the Sanctuary, as shown in Aubrey's plan B (and as demanded by topography), the resulting line has to cross the (present-day) river *twice*: this would still hold good even with a straight Avenue of anything like the actual (SE) orientation, since Aubrey nowhere suggests that the Sanctuary was itself on the far (S) side of 'Fluvius Kynet'.

The likeliest explanation of this confusion about the river is that it derives from Aubrey's own simplified plan, and here the circumstances in which the record was composed need to be taken into account. We must remember the short time that Aubrey may have spent on his Avebury work and the possibility that his detailed survey was confined to the henge monument itself. In plan B, it appears that the river (while shown stylistically in a similar way to that of plan C) may have been a later addition: its placing right at the bottom of the sheet tends to suggest this. Other late alterations could have included the caption referring to 'Aubury', the names and details of the villages of 'Kynet', and possibly the cutting-out of the very narrow strip of paper (see Chapter III, B.5(d)) which might have indicated the supposed source of the river or its course from a spring. Such last-minute additions and corrections would explain why the river was misplaced; they might also explain the inaccurate placement of 'East Kynet' on the wrong side of the river, and the indication of churches at both villages although only one church actually existed.

In the passages cited above, Aubrey clearly states, with slight variations, that the Avenue stones 'turne with a right angle crosse the river and goe uphill'. It was at this 'right angle' at West Kennet, 'where the Walke from Aubury hither; and that from the top of the hill, did joine', that Aubrey identified the possible place of 'Habitations' of priests (Aubrey 24, 34–5, cf. 43; Fowles & Legg 1980, 37–8, cf. 50). Moray's newly discovered description (Appendix I) can also be read as suggesting that the Avenues met at right angles to each other in the vicinity of West Kennet village (but cf. Stukeley 1743, 30–1). On whichever side of the river, this spot is close to the recently discovered site of a huge palisaded structure or enclosure of large timbers: a structure claimed to be prehistoric in date and to have extended over both sides of the present-day river (Whittle 1988; Smith and Trott 1989). It is again tantalizing that Aubrey did not give details of the actual relationship of the Avenue to West Kennet village. Even today we do not know the precise nature of the turn that the Kennet Avenue may have made towards Overton Hill (see below and Smith 1965; Borthwick 1989).

Finally we must consider Stukeley's position in relation to Aubrey's record of the Kennet Avenue. Several authors have accused him of dissimulation in claiming to have been the first to realize that the Sanctuary and the main Avebury monument had been connected by the Kennet Avenue, and they have attacked him for his criticism of Aubrey on this score – he wrote that the latter 'did not see that 'tis but one avenue from *Abury* to *Overton-hill*, having no apprehension of the double curve it makes' (Stukeley 1743, 32). Such attacks (e.g. Cunnington 1932, 301; Burl 1979, 50) have seemed all the more justifiable since Piggott's demonstration (1950; 1985) of Stukeley's possession of extensive transcripts from Aubrey via Gale: indeed, as we saw in Chapters I, vii, and III, B.16, Stukeley had certainly made a copy of Gale's transcript of plan B before his first visit to Avebury in May 1719. However, although the main plan B transcript (Plate 12; WANHS Stukeley MS., 9) bears a number of brief notes on various aspects of Avebury, none of these are about the Avenue, while the plan itself clearly shows the right-angle at West Kennet. Equally significant is the fact that, since November 1714, Stukeley had possessed a copy of the revised *Britannia*, with its new Avebury description, much of which is derived from, and all of which he could reasonably have assumed to be by, Aubrey (Camden 1695, 111–12): it is this that Stukeley criticizes in the passage cited above. Since the Camden description is couched unambiguously in terms of two walks – one, mentioned at the start of a paragraph, from the henge to West Kennet, the other, from West Kennet to 'the brow of [Overton] hill', mentioned at its end – any reader with no other information to go on would naturally interpret plan B as showing two walks not one. Ironically, Stukeley's own first plan (Plate 11), dated 19 May 1719, strikingly reflects such an interpretation, visually echoing the straight Avenue of Gale's version of plan B, and verbally confirming that '[t]he Avenue or Walk up to Abury begins at Kennet Town End'.

Criticism of Stukeley for this interpretation is based on the tacit assumption that he had access either to the full *Monumenta* text or to some other means of knowing Aubrey's full writing about the Avenue; however, common as such an assumption is, it appears to be false (see Chapter I, vii). Moreover, even the full *Monumenta* is not as clear on this point as Aubrey's defenders might wish or Stukeley's detractors assume, since all three of the pertinent passages insist on the right-angle at West Kennet (Aubrey 24, 34, 43, 63v; Fowles and Legg 1980, 37, 50, 56), while, as we have seen, the second clearly refers to two distinct walks meeting there.

As noted in Chapter III, B.15, in both versions of Stukeley's plan B transcript (Plates 12 and 13), while 'Kennett Flu.' remains at the foot of the sheet, with both West and East Kennet to the N of it, a 'river' rises N of it and appears to flow up Overton Hill, across the Avenue about halfway between West Kennet and the Sanctuary. Though it is possible that the extra river could have been supplied by Gale, it is likelier that it represents Stukeley's own attempt to understand and unravel the confusions in Aubrey's various textual and plan B versions of the relationship between river(s) and Avenue(s).

The humanly constructed site of Avebury

h. Destruction of stones

Observers like Aubrey were acutely aware of the damage to the monument that was being done by their contemporaries. At one point in his text he altered his wording concerning stones no longer present from 'gonne' to 'taken away'; elsewhere he referred to 'the Fractures made in this Antiquity'; and in a further passage he detailed how the megaliths were broken up:

> Make a fire on that [side of the, *del.*] line of the stone, where you would have it crack; and after the stone is well heated, draw over a line with cold water, & immediately give a knock with a Smyths sledge, and it will break, like the Collets at the Glass house. (Aubrey 24, 32, 35, 36; Fowles and Legg 1980, 35, 38, 39)

He also noted how the stones were being adapted to contemporary needs, 'One of the Monuments in the Street that runnes East and West ... is converted into a Pigstye, or Cow-house: as is to be seen in the Roade' (Aubrey 24, 37; Fowles and Legg 1980, 41).

A similar awareness of how interpretation had been made more difficult by recent destruction was shown by Sir Robert Moray, in this case in connection with the Sanctuary and the Avenue leading to it. Moray noted:

> diverse of the stones are entire, others broken and others it seemes have been carried away for use yet leaving sufficient Vestiges to discern where they stood. (Appendix I)

Similarly, Stukeley wrote (1743, 16):

> Every year that I frequented this country, I found several of them wanting; but the places very apparent whence they were taken.

He, too, observed contemporary use of the stones, remarking that the stone in the NW quadrant 'at the corner of the lane ... was us'd as a stall to lay fish on, when they had a kind of market here' (Stukeley 1743, 24). Uniquely, however, Stukeley also set out systematically to document the details of the contemporary history of destruction of individual stones, partly from oral information that he was given about destruction and partly from the evidence of depressions in the ground which he deduced must mark their former locations.

Unfortunately, it has to be said that Stukeley's account of the chronology of such destruction is unreliable on two counts. He wrote 'Just before I visited this place, to endeavour at preserving the memory of it, the inhabitants were fallen into the custom of demolishing the stones, chiefly out of covetousness of the little *area* of ground, each stood on. First they dug great pits in the earth, and buried them... After this, they found out the knack of burning them' (Stukeley 1743, 15). This makes it sound as if the practice of burning had only just begun at this time; indeed, Stukeley went on to claim that it was Walter Stretch, the father of one of his 1720s informants, who 'found out the way of demolishing these stones by fire', dating this to 'About 1694' (Stukeley 1743, 25). Yet the latter cannot be true in view of Aubrey's testimony – one version of which had been in Stukeley's hands since 1719 – that burning was already going on in his time (see also Chapter I, vii).

Equally misleading was the idea that burial, too, though older than burning, was of relatively recent date, at least if the implication was that this was true of all buried stones at Avebury. At one point Stukeley seems himself to have been aware of the likelihood of much earlier downthrowing and burial of stones at Avebury, which he appears to have forgotten

177

by the time he wrote his 1743 text. In his 'Celtic Temples', he wrote that Romans had probably 'thrown down' an Avenue stone near West Kennet over a burial (with accompanying Roman coins), as a memorial to the deceased (Stukeley 1722–4b, 132: Appendix II). Furthermore, Stukeley had at that stage been aware that many more buried stones might exist than his reliance on oral testimony and physical depressions revealed, since he speculated that other stones might have been removed, 'but the tumor not apparent, because they might disperse the superfluous mold to render the pastures level', thus leaving no 'hollows left in their stations' (Stukeley 1722–4b, 121, 129) – and hence negating his claims that oral history or depression in the soil allowed him completely to reconstruct the pristine state of the prehistoric site.

Stukeley's presumption that destruction was due to the need to clear the land – and hence was likely to be related to intensification of the use of the site in the early modern period – had a long life. The view that the stones were an inconvenience was apparently prevalent even before the realization that they had been part of an *ancient* site (and no doubt the same objection applied to naturally occurring sarsen stones too): thus Inigo Jones had noted earlier in the 17th century of the grey wethers how they were 'no small prejudice to the bordering inhabitants' (Jones 1655, 30). A similar view was strongly represented in the 19th century when it was posited that the removal of such stones had been in the interests of ploughing, the definition of pastures, and/or the construction of buildings (e.g. Long 1858b, 52; Long 1876, 5). In the early 20th century, Cunnington still assumed that, where burial of stones at Avebury had occurred, this had been carried out by farmers 'to get them off the land' (1914b, 13) – having presented evidence for it not being possible to plough quite up to the sides of stones, the ground immediately around unremoved stones often being dug over by hand (1914a, 4). Hence in 1936, when Keiller and Piggott favoured this utilitarian view that any destruction or removal of stones had been due either to attempts to facilitate ploughing, or to the provision of materials for the building of houses, walls, etc., they were following a long tradition of observation and/or assumption about the way in which the stones interfered with local Avebury life.

This functional explanation of the burial of stones changed on June 29, 1938, with the discovery of 'a skeleton ... found pressed up against one side of the [stone's] burial pit' (Keiller, quoted in Coupland 1988). Keiller reported that under the newly discovered skeleton's head 'was a sherd of medieval pottery ... in the pelvis (we found) three coins, lightly joined together'. Young (1938) is very clear about the archaeological association of skeleton, pottery and coins:

> Directly underneath the head was a large fragment of 12th century ware, and close to the left femur, – between it and the side of the burial pit were three silver long cross pennies of Ed: I. The latter, which were stuck together, occurred in a pocket of soft dark mould – apparently all that remained of a leather pouch ...
>
> That the death of the individual was contemporary with the burial of this stone is perfectly obvious, both from the fact that – apart from a small amount of a dark mouldy substance around the skeletal remains – the filling above was entirely of the same character as that which occurred elsewhere in the pit, namely pure chalk rubble, and the fact that it would have been absolutely impossible to have buried a body in such a confined space, and in the position in which it was actually found.
>
> There can be no doubt that we have here evidence of a tragic accident which happened during the early years of the 14th century when [this] stone ... was being buried.

Although the precise dating of such coins (Plate 55) (Fox and Fox 1909–13, 91) has varied (e.g. Keiller 1938; Keiller 1939, 231; Jope n.d., 15–18; Smith 1965, 177–80; Dolley 1968, 250; Mayhew 1983, 120–1; Stewart 1984, 81–5), the date of this group is now clearly seen to be c.1320–c.1350, with the earlier date being likelier (P. H. Robinson, pers. comm.). Such a

Plate 55   Two of the coins found near the 'Barber-Surgeon's' skeleton under stone 9 (Smith 1965, 178) in the SW quadrant of the Avebury henge (Alexander Keiller Museum, Avebury).

date-range in no way conflicts with the possible dates for the iron buckle, iron pointed instrument, and hinged iron scissors (Plate 56) found with this individual (Jope n.d., 12a–14) – while Jope's report (n.d., 25) that 'the burial pit contained sixteen small sherds of XII century type and only one XIII century piece', although differing from Keiller and Young, does not materially affect the arguments regarding dating.

As realization grew of this example of medieval interference at Avebury, so arguments were advanced (Chapman 1939; Keiller 1939, 231; Smith 1965, 176–80) that the burial of stones was unlikely to have been necessitated by ploughing practices. As Young put it (1938, 29):

> There is no evidence whatever to suggest, let alone prove, that any of these stones were buried in order to get them out of the way of the plough, and the latter belief, which is becoming alarmingly widespread is to my mind utterly unreasonable since stones above ground, whether standing or fallen are far less likely to obstruct the plough than those buried or partly buried under the surface. Where they could be seen they could easily have been ploughed around, with the loss only of the small space of ground they occupied ... as the West Kennet Avenue was in the Early Iron Age, when all the stones were present, and above ground, standing or fallen.

Yet the actual state of our current knowledge regarding medieval activity at Avebury remains rather unsatisfactory. Attempts to explain medieval burial, or throwing down, of stones (e.g. Burl 1979, ch. 2) remain unconvincing. Various references to the proscription of the worship of stones by the ecclesiastical authorities of the day have been cited, but any link with sites like this remains entirely speculative (Piggott 1985, 94, 178, 261). As Smith notes

179

(1965, 179), 'In the absence of any known medieval reference to the Avebury stones the circumstances surrounding the burials must remain largely conjectural'.

The evidence from modern excavation is sadly deficient. Despite Stukeley's assertion, quoted above, that the burial of stones was a 17th-century practice (information presumably derived, like that about burning, from oral evidence from local Aveburians), most archaeological commentary appears to have ignored this, instead claiming all such burial – as distinct from the burning and breaking up of stones – to be medieval (e.g. Malone 1989, 90). Thus, although it is claimed that 'at least 40 stones were buried at Avebury during the middle ages and probably many more' (Jope n.d., 28), that some may have been knocked down when medieval boundary banks were built up (Keiller 1939, 225, 229), that many others had been thrown over and left lying on the ground (Smith 1965, 186, 197, 199, 201–2), that the stones involved were both large and small ones (Smith 1965, 179, 199) and that such activities appear to date from the 12th to the early 14th centuries (Smith 1965, 177), specific evidence giving convincing dates to individual stone burials is all but lacking (Annable 1959, 229–30; Young 1961, 30). Within the henge, almost all the medieval 'sherds were found littered through the top-soil all over the site', 'almost all in small fragments' (Jope n.d., 18, 23): at most five burial pits (perhaps two from within the henge) could actually be shown to have derived from medieval activity (E. M. Jope, pers. comm.; Jope n.d., 23–5). Currently, therefore, we lack substantive archaeological evidence for 'association' between stone and

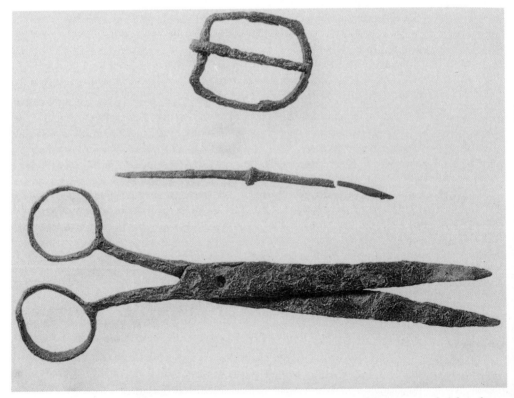

Plate 56 The (recently conserved) iron buckle, hinged iron scissors and 'lancet or probe' found near the 'Barber-Surgeon's' skeleton under stone 9 (Smith 1965, 178) in the SW quadrant of the Avebury henge (Alexander Keiller Museum, Avebury).

180

cultural debris which would allow us to confirm major medieval interference with the Avebury monuments.

A further complication in the archaeological evidence is seen in those cases of stones which are claimed to have been 'buried' *and* then 'burnt' (some four henge stones as well as stones i, ii, ix–xi in Smith's 1965 terminology), the archaeological evidence for the dating of either of these practices remaining somewhat obscure in any case (Smith 1965, 186 ff, 197, 201–2, and see above). The potential confusion grows when we recognize that the term 'burning pits' (Smith 1965, fig. 70) has been applied in advance, *inter alia*, to unexcavated hollows in the ground. About this, Smith only says, 'Unlike the pits in which stones were buried, those in which they were burnt were not levelled' (Smith 1965, 180). In fact, relatively few of the so-called burning pits have been excavated – some 16 within the henge, of which only nine (including the Obelisk and 'ring-stone') had archaeological evidence to support this interpretation of their function (Smith 1965). Thus, the majority could as well have been buried stones, or the result of stone removals, as burning pits. It must be admitted, therefore, that the archaeological evidence here has proved largely incapable of dating the original destruction of stones at Avebury.[2]

Unfortunately all this is more than merely an academic exercise regarding dating. If stones at Avebury *were* buried in significant numbers in medieval times, then Aubrey, Stukeley and others were studying an already highly depleted monument. If, on the other hand, there had been no major medieval impact, and the burial of stones was rather, as claimed by Stukeley, a relatively recent practice, then the 17th- and 18th-century records grow in significance. Moreover, added importance accrues to our assessment of the reliability of the oral evidence recorded by Aubrey and Stukeley regarding the date, and circumstances, of stone destruction.

Whatever the nature and rate of destruction prior to the 17th century, there is little doubt about the intensity of such interference from then onwards. For example, it appears that, as Aubrey's text and plan both convey, the Sanctuary was still largely intact when he and Moray saw it (though most of the stones had already 'fallen downe'); and that, as Stukeley records, it was depleted of all or most of the remaining stones during one year, 1724 (see also Piggott 1946). In the previous twenty years, at least 13–20 stones had been destroyed at Avebury itself. Indeed, if Stukeley's oral history can be believed – though this will be further discussed below – Tom Robinson alone was personally responsible for the destruction of 40 stones, Farmer Griffin for the breaking of nearly 20 of the Avenue stones and another person, in 1700, for 10.

Thus the sheer rate of destruction of stones in the early 18th century, as also at times in the 17th, may be one valid explanation of discrepancies between the different plans, particularly between the mid-17th-century ones and Stukeley's plan E. In addition, some of the discrepancies between Stukeley's versions may be able to be explained thus, for Stukeley records on several occasions that stones had been demolished since his previous year's visit to the area (Stukeley 1722–4b, 121, 124, 131; Appendix II). Indeed, here the combined intensity and relative longevity of Stukeley's record adds further complexities to the decipherment of his surviving materials.

This accelerating rate of destruction invests the detailed information in Stukeley's published Frontispiece with great significance. In it, he keyed in standing stones, fallen stones, 'the Place of a Stone taken away', and 'a Cavity visible where a Stone stood'; it also sometimes provides additional details regarding such events (e.g. 'Taken away Anno 1720' or 'Demolished by Tom Robinson Anno 1700') as well as remarks on the nature of remaining features (e.g. 'broke off to the Stumps'). The draft frontispieces have overlapping infor- mation, and it is also worth noting that Stukeley's unpublished 'tour' already foreshadows the major categories of plan E: 'The Place[s] of a Stone taken away' (shown by a dot), and 'the places of such as are carryd away the turf leveld thereupon: which the report of the

Inhabitants of their own memory the Symmetry of the work sufficiently demonstrate' (Appendix II, shown by a 'point'/dot).

As this shows, and as was freely acknowledged in his *Abury*, Stukeley was reliant on oral history for much of his information. By comparing Stukeley's various draft frontispieces and his manuscript text (Appendix II), we are afforded a unique insight into the reliability of such oral historical evidence, as well as a chance to monitor changes in Stukeley's understanding as derived from it. Though many antiquaries were by the early 18th century more reluctant to use oral sources than had been the case a century earlier (Woolf 1988), Stukeley showed no such restraint, presumably because he perceived such evidence as providing data which would not otherwise be available at all. In consequence, his own record illustrates some of the difficulties involved in the employment of oral sources. For instance, his information was not always derived at first hand: the local tradition that Charles II had visited Avebury (Chapter I, iv) was recorded not as ascertained directly by Stukeley from a witness to the event but from a hearsay report concerning the recollections of his informant's mother (Stukeley 1722–4b, 124). Moreover, though in this case there is no reason to doubt the accuracy of the account, the same is not true of the comparable tradition which he also recorded about an earlier visit by James I (Chapter I, i). Insights of this kind are crucial to any attempt to evaluate the nature and reliability of plan E, particularly if Stukeley was prone to presume that the destruction of stones was more recent than was actually the case. Both this, and the general difficulties associated with oral evidence, may help to explain the discrepancies we encounter, and thus shed a degree of doubt on the reliance that has often been placed on Stukeley's published record.

The initial question before us is, how much can we rely on Stukeley's evidence for the removal and/or burial of stones? Despite his claim (Stukeley 1743, 16) that stone-destruction 'is so late, that I could easily trace the *obit* of every stone; who did it, for what purpose, and when, and by what method, what house or wall was built out of it, and the like', the answer unfortunately already seems unequivocal: very little. In several examples the textual descriptions and/or the positions indicated in his manuscript 'tour' (Appendix II) do not coincide exactly with those of plan E. In some cases it is likely that Stukeley was in possession of further information by the time he compiled his Frontispiece; in other cases, it is possible to surmise that he discovered that his own notes – gathered over five seasons – were either inadequate or self-contradictory. A comparison of his text (in 'Celtic Temples') with both text and Frontispiece to *Abury* reveals that 'vacancies' in one source are often equivalent to 'fallen', 'taken away', or 'hollow' in the other; 'broke off by the root' in one is equivalent to 'taken away', and 'fallen' in the others. Worse still, in plan E, as in its earlier states, critical discrepancies may have crept in between recording, drawing and engraving. Since we increasingly cannot assume that plan E should be taken as Stukeley's final, definitive judgment of the site (Chapter III, E.1), we have to remain undecided when a critical area of the SE quadrant of the Avebury outer circle is shown in plan E as having only 9 dots representing 'the Place[s] of a Stone taken away', 'Demolished by Tom Robinson Anno 1700', whereas the printed text (1743, 22) says categorically that '*Ten* ... all contiguous, were at once destroy'd' (our italics) (and see below).

In fact, we are forced to conclude that Stukeley's famous published Frontispiece, and accompanying text, is often less full and sometimes less accurate than his initial recording. In addition, and perhaps not surprisingly, the consequence of the innovatory conventions of recording which plan E embodied is that it often represents a set of compromises. These defects may be illustrated by two striking cases, but further examples will be provided by the detailed examination, quadrant by quadrant, which follows. Inaccuracy is illustrated by the fact that *Abury* (1743, 22) records the existence of a large stone in the N entrance of the henge which is reported to have been standing during the memory of Reuben Horsall 'clerk of the parish' and to have been seen by both Stukeley and Lord Winchelsea in a fallen state with 'three wooden wedges driven into it, in order to break it in pieces'. In his 'Celtic Temples' (Stukeley 1722–4b, 120, 122; Appendix II), however, Stukeley provides the detail that the stone supposedly 'fell down at noon time of day a loaded cart going by which probably shook it being almost undermind by wearing away of the road', and says that 'three or 4' wedges had been employed to 'rend it in pieces'. As for compromises, Stukeley appears to take the easy way out in his plan E by showing two stones as definitely fallen across the road within the E entrance, when he actually had no evidence for this other than his ubiquitous assumption that 'the Symmetry of the work sufficiently demonstrate[s]' regular placement of stones: he was simply *presuming*, on that basis, that the two stones 'are no doubt thrown into the ditch when they filld it up to make this road' (Stukeley 1722–4b, 121, 120; Appendix II).

j. 'Entrances' and 'Avenue'(s)

One of the most striking unanimities between all five plans is that each shows four entrances to the monument. They disagree, however, as to how many of these were ancient. Plans C and D appear to make it explicit that all these entrances were ancient ones by placing stones outside them, while A and B both show only one (the S) entrance as self-evidently ancient by this criterion.

Aubrey's and Charleton's recognition in plans C and D of four *ancient* entrances to Avebury was presumably unknown to Stukeley, who, though showing four entrances, presumed first three then two to be modern. Certainly the possibility of there having been four ancient entrances was at no point mooted by him: initially, he had postulated only one entrance – again the S (Plate 11; Long 1876, 6 note 1; Piggott 1985, fig. 3) – and, later, two (S and W) (Stukeley 1743, 28–9), the 'North Entrance' (Top. Gen.d.13,7; Plate 43), like the E one, being thought to be modern. Observers in the 19th century (e.g. Hunter 1829, 3) and archaeologists of the 20th century similarly postulated only these two, until Keiller's excavations in the 1930s (cf. Keiller and Piggott 1936; Keiller 1939) established the antiquity of a third, N, entrance/causeway (Smith 1965, 195). Today, 'although the eastern entrance remains uninvestigated, the conformation of the bank on its northern side indicates that this, too, is an original feature' (Smith 1965, 195; Chapman 1939, 9).

As we have just noted, both plans C and D indicate the presence of two large stones *outside* the Avebury bank on either side of three of its four entrances (N, S and E) with Charleton showing a further pair, and Aubrey one (or possibly two) outside the W entrance also. It is of course easy to assume that such depictions were simply inaccurate, or the result of the imposition of a false 'symmetry'. On the other hand it is possible that Aubrey (in plan C) and Charleton were correct in their independent recording of such stones. Here it is worth recalling Holland's evidence (Chapter I, i) that in two of Avebury's entrances 'stand huge Stones as jambes', which may constitute further confirmation (though we have seen, in the discussion of plan A in Chapter III, the necessity of distinguishing between evidence about stones *within* entrances and those *outside*).

If we *do* assume the correctness of plans C and D with respect to these particular stones, we are left with the question why Aubrey, in his plans A and B, should have 'removed' them from outside all the entrances except the southern, with its Kennet Avenue. In the case of plan B it can be argued that Aubrey's primary intention was to show the relationship between the Circle, the Avenue and the Sanctuary, and that other details of the monument were largely irrelevant to his purpose. This cannot, however, be the explanation for the absence of such stones from plan A, which is generally taken to be Aubrey's attempt at a definitive record. On the other hand, here we may extend the suggestion made in Chapter III concerning additions to the plan after its initial composition, and suggest that the discrepancy may be explained by the fact that it was his intention to define the monument by its

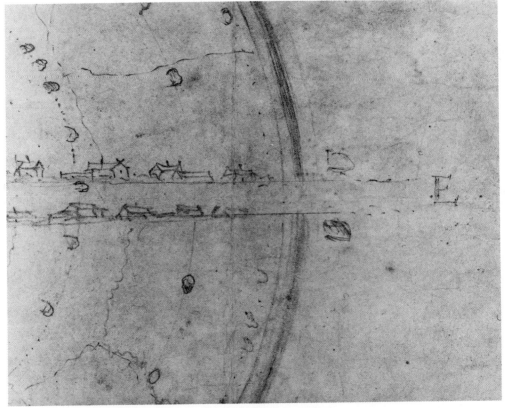

Plate 57 Detail from Aubrey's Plan C (E entrance).

circumvallation, so that he initially deliberately refrained from showing anything outside it, and was haphazard about which features he later reinstated.

There is, therefore, good reason seriously to investigate any evidence which might confirm Aubrey's (plan C) and Charleton's plans indicating four entrances with stones outside each, and the consequent possibility that ancient Avebury might have had portals facing in four directions, and conceivably might even have been the centre of a complex of radiating influences and 'avenues' very different from that imagined until now.

k. The E entrance and road

Unfortunately, later landscape changes severely limit the ability of geophysical survey to identify possible former stone settings outside the henge entrances, and we have made no such surveys in and around the N or W entrances and roads. The most appropriate location for such a search was identified as at the present roadway leading from the E entrance. This E entrance was also of especial interest since not only was it shown with outer portals on plans C (Plate 57) and D (Plate 5), but it was almost certainly the entrance from London and Marlborough used by the visitors to Avebury (see section f above). An area 30m. × 150m. was surveyed parallel and as close to the roadway as possible in the hope that this might encompass any settings on an E–W alignment, such as the N limb of an avenue.

The resistivity plots (Plate 58, A and B) are dominated by a single swathe of low resistance, about 5m. wide, running the length of the survey from E to W. From the henge it

184

A

B

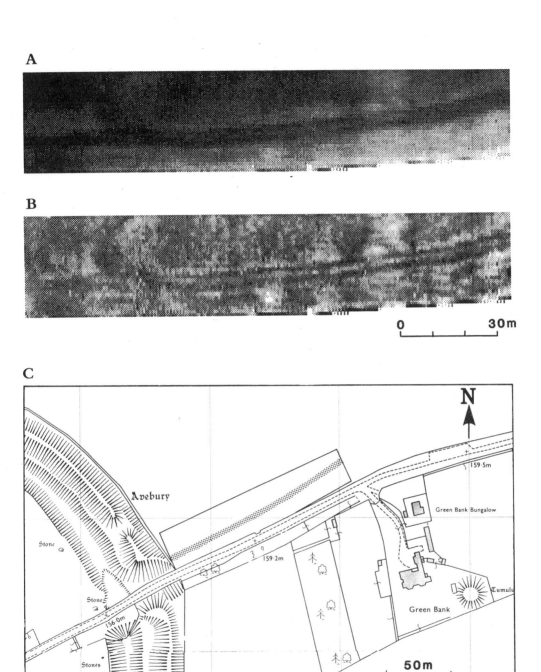

C

N

Avebury

Stone

Stone

Stones

156·0m

159·2m

159·5m

Green Bank Bungalow

Green Bank

Tumuli

0   30m

50m

Plate 58 Resistivity survey outside the eastern entrance to the Avebury henge: (A) grey-tone plot of the raw resistivity data, (B) grey-tone plot of the enhanced data, and (C) interpretation and location of the survey.

follows a course parallel to the road for some 100m. before gently curving away to the NE. This feature, unobserved on available aerial photographs, is clearly an early road into Avebury. It meets the henge to the N of the gate in the SW corner of the field (Plate 58, C).

The direction of the road from the NE cannot be established without extending the survey, but it must at least be a possibility that it is a route that once led through Avebury up to the Ridgeway. The character of the resistivity response suggests that the track is unmetalled and deeply eroded, with a central ridge preserved in places (Plate 58, B), indicative of severe rutting by coaches or carts. These features suggest that the track was not necessarily a simple droveway, although this is a further possibility.

If this roadway is a relatively early (medieval) feature we may go on to speculate whether it followed still earlier routes, such as a prehistoric avenue, should one ever have existed. The geophysical evidence unfortunately does not lend support to such a hypothesis, in the absence of conclusive evidence within the data for either subsidiary ditches or buried stones (cf. section m, below). However, the fact that the road anomaly appears to abut onto the bank – as opposed to entering the causeway – raises the question as to the real configuration of the E entrance whose details, as we have just seen, are unknown. A further intriguing possibility may be that this road alignment connects with the linear anomaly running W–E in the S of the NE quadrant (see section d above, and Plate 52).

m. The S entrance and the Kennet Avenue

We now move to a consideration of the S entrance: here all plans agree, and Charleton and Stukeley (1743, 28–34) also state, that stones stood outside it. Aubrey's plans A and B, and Stukeley's plan E, show these as the beginning of an ancient avenue of stones, the Kennet Avenue, a 'solemne Walke' which was still evidently intact (although with some stones fallen) when Aubrey first saw it and whose N course, at least, has since been well established archaeologically (Keiller and Piggott 1936, 419; Smith 1965, fig. 71). Aubrey's plan B shows some 30 marks defining each limb of the Kennet Avenue and at least 8 on either limb leading to the Sanctuary (see Chapter III, B.15), totals which if translated into stones are at sharp variance with Stukeley's, who claims to have seen and counted 72 in 1722 (Stukeley 1743, 29–30). It is perhaps worth noting that this claim may have been affected by Stukeley's preconceived idea that the Avenue leading from the Avebury henge to the Sanctuary was likely to have comprised 100 stones (on each side of the Avenue): despite statements to the contrary (Burl 1979, 186–7), Aubrey does not seem ever to have claimed 100 stones for either limb of the Avenue and its continuation to the Sanctuary. Archaeologically, however, the number of Avenue 'stones' shown on Aubrey's plan B appears to be impossibly low; as with plan C's depiction of houses, Aubrey's intention here must have been to give an impression of rows of stones rather than an accurate record of their number.

Both Aubrey's plans A and B clearly show one stone in, or by, the E bank-ditch within the S causeway of the henge, more or less where Stukeley (1743, 30) records the first of his Kennet Avenue stones (said by him in plan E to have been broken in 1722). Aubrey, however, does not show the one which Stukeley has indicated as immediately opposite; on the other hand he does indicate 'paired' stones immediately outside the bank, where Stukeley shows only the W placement. Once again there are considerable difficulties in interpreting the Stukeley record – which are compounded the more his plan E and text are compared with their drafts. For example, according to plan E key, these first two stones (one or both broken in 1722) were fallen stones; the published text, however, states that the westernmost 'stood where at present a sycamore tree [clearly shown in Plan E] is planted' (Stukeley 1743, 30; Plate 44). The notation which should have been adopted here was, therefore, either a dot (denoting the place of a stone taken away) or a sign indicating 'a cavity visible where once a stone stood'. Such inconsistencies abound: thus the next Kennet Avenue stone is said

186

(Stukeley 1743, 30) to be 'standing, by the turning of the *Bath*-road', yet it too is shown on plan E as fallen.

Given the disturbances that have taken place in this part of the monument and the difficulties of making sense of the subsequent archaeology (Smith 1965, 185–7, 195, 206–10), it is understandable why the details of the placements within the S causeway, as well as at the beginning of the Avenue, still remain obscure today. Certainly there is nothing, either in plan A or B or in Stukeley's plans, to indicate that their authors had appreciated the 'anomaly at the approach to Avebury' revealed by 20th-century excavation, whereby there is 'a sharp, awkward turn ... but no satisfactory junction ... with the four pairs [of stones] at the actual entrance' (Smith 1965, 208).

Moving to the Avenue more generally, it might at first sight be tempting to see in the opposition of long dashes and dots/short dashes of the Avenue stones in plan B an Aubreyan anticipation of Keiller's and Piggott's (1936) claim – subsequently accepted by Smith (1965, 197) – that two types of stones 'are consistently paired in the Avenue'. The two types are claimed to be 'a tall stone whose height considerbly exceeds its breadth', and a stone whose 'breadth is proportionately greater, and may nearly equal the full length'. However, their further claim as to the nature of this pairing in the Avenue militates against any such interpretation of Aubrey's dots and dashes, for, 'Either type [of stone] may occur on one side of the Avenue or the other' (Smith 1965, 206), and this contradicts Aubrey's depiction in plan B (Chapter III, B.15). It might alternatively be tempting to suggest that Aubrey was using a dot and dash distinction to anticipate the observation in the 1695 Camden (Camden 1695, 111) that one side of the Avenue still had stones standing but that many on the other side had disappeared. However, since this information does not appear in Aubrey's surviving *Monumenta* text – although it is attributed to Aubrey by the Camden editors and therefore by Stukeley, who seems mistakenly to have taken the description to refer to the stones leading to the Sanctuary (Stukeley 1743, 32) – it would be dangerous to read too much into this observation. It is also impossible to assess whether the absence of dots in Aubrey's depiction of the 'oblong stones' in the Avenue in plan A (in contrast to their presence in all the stones within the henge) could be related to any feature such as pairing.

A crucial piece of evidence from the 'entrance'/'Avenue' area exists which shows that, in one case at least, Aubrey did not update a stone-depiction on plans A or B in the light of evidence which comes into his hands later: it also tends to confirm that he did not alter his depictions to reflect the exact contemporary condition of any particular stone after he initially made them. He notes that he was told by the attorney Walter Sloper of Winterbourne Monkton that 'the great stone at Aubury's Townes end, where this Walke begins, fell-down in autumne 1684, and broke in two, or three pieces: it stood but two foot deep in the earth' (Aubrey 24, 34; Fowles and Legg 1980, 37; quoted by Smith 1965, 206 n.1; other versions of this note, not including the phrase 'where this Walke begins', are in Aubrey 24, 40v, 63v; Fowles and Legg 1980, 56, 57); however, there is nothing on plans A or B to distinguish this ill-fated stone from the others.

This is also the one case where Aubrey appears to have recognized a particular stone as especially large – although Smith (1965, 206 n1) claims that all the stones at this entrance 'were larger than average'; yet there is nothing to suggest any such differentiation on plans A, B or C.

It appears that here we have confirmation of a difference in intention between Aubrey's plans A and B and Stukeley, the latter consciously recording what he found to be a living and changing monument, while Aubrey, in these plans at least, was predominantly concerned with the remnants of the ancient site as he imagined it once had been. It is also interesting to note the possible unreliability of the oral testimony available to Aubrey and Stukeley respectively; if this is indeed the same entrance stone, it is variously affirmed to have fallen and broken in 1684 and in 1722, though this may favour the view that Stukeley's 1722 note

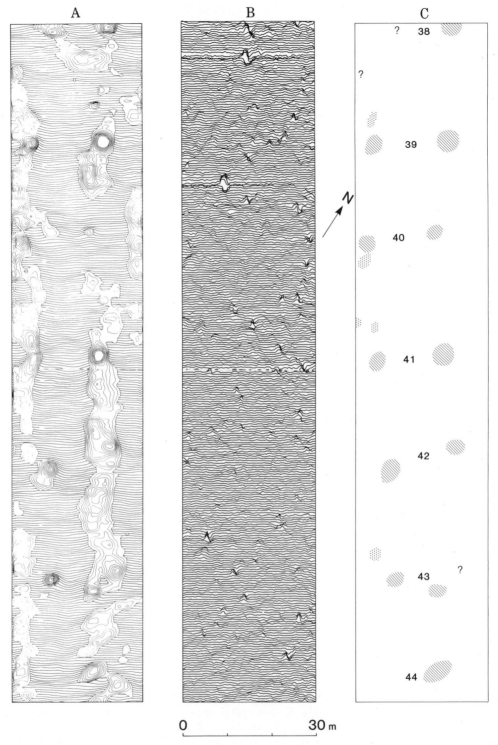

Plate 59 Geophysical survey of part of the West Kennet Avenue (covering stone pairs 38–44): (A) raw resistivity data, displayed as a combination of graphical traces and contours, the latter outlining areas of highest resistance; (B) magnetometer data displayed as a series of graphical traces; and (C) combined interpretation of both sets of data drawing attention to anomalies of potential archaeological significance (diagonal shading = resistivity anomalies; stipple = magnetic anomalies).

applied only to one of the two stones, and that this broke forty years after the other (see further below).

Towards the S end of the Kennet Avenue, archaeological enquiry fades away. Evidence for the existence of some stones derives from the Ordnance Survey of 1883 (published 1887); from Crawford's(?) annotation of the 1925 edition of the O.S. with a 'stone uncovered 1931 in road widening' opposite the second most northerly of the above stones, as well as from his unpublished manuscript (Crawford MS.); from probing by Passmore in 1921 (Passmore 1926); from 19th-century observations (Long 1858a; Smith 1885); and from investigations by Young and Smith (Annable 1959, 229–30; Young 1961, 30). We have already reviewed (Chapter I, iv) the evidence for the Avenue's problematic course as presented by Aubrey and Moray and, in the light of the difficulties they experienced in seeing clearly how the Avenue connected with the double row of standing stones leading to the Sanctuary, it is remarkable how firmly Stukeley felt able to depict its curving course as part of his snake's neck (see also Smith 1885). This controversial route between the Sanctuary and West Kennet may prove to be less than two hundred metres from a possible causewayed enclosure, which has not yet been investigated (Palmer 1976).

We now turn to the response of 'known' stone settings to resistivity and magnetic survey, both methods having been applied to part of the 'gap' in the Kennet Avenue following on directly S from Keiller's restored section. An area 30m. by 150m. was aligned on the course of the projected line of the Avenue and surveyed with both methods at a traverse spacing of 0.5m.

The resistivity plot (Plates 59A and 62A) clearly indicates isolated areas of high values spaced at intervals fully consistent with the expected pattern of the Avenue. Anomalies corresponding with members of up to seven pairs of settings can be seen, equivalent to stones 38–44 in Smith's 1965 fig. 71. The strength of the resistivity response over each setting is extremely variable, however, and in places barely exceeds background levels, or coalesces with adjacent areas of high readings: indeed, without foreknowledge of the probable arrangement of stones, several settings could not have been distinguished with certainty. This variability in response no doubt partly results from the depth at which stones are buried, the stronger anomalies occurring over shallower stones, the weaker anomalies over stone holes, pits or very deeply buried stones.

The magnetometer survey (Plate 59B), by contrast, reveals next to nothing. There is no apparent magnetic response over buried stone positions and the lack of any specific concentrations of magnetic 'noise' would seem to rule out the presence of burning pits (whether of prehistoric monoliths or naturally occurring sarsens). Almost all the magnetic variation across the survey area can be explained as minor background 'noise', interspersed with occasional anomalies caused by iron litter in the topsoil. In only two or three instances are there anomalies (Plate 59C) which might represent shallow pits containing magnetically enhanced deposits of archaeological significance.

The primary result of the resistivity survey then was to determine the course of the Avenue for a distance of 150m. S of the restored section (Plate 62A), but, in addition, an unexpected and interesting observation arises from the resistivity data, namely that high readings over stone positions on either limb of the Avenue are often linked to form linear anomalies running longitudinally between the stones (Plate 59A). This suggests that the chalk bedrock may be less eroded along the two limbs of the Avenue than it is either 'within' the Avenue or to either side of it. The resistivity result seems to conflict in part at least with Keiller's observation (MS., 1934–5), that 'looked at on the surface, prior to excavation, the Avenue appeared to have a slight depression on either side; that on the right being directly in line with the original stone holes, while that on the left was definitely outside of the Avenue. This gives the impression – which afterwards proved to be correct – of a raised surface down the centre of the Avenue of convex form'.

What both these observations *may* suggest, however, is that the two lines of stones did not contain the only route towards, or away from, the henge. At present, all interpretations known to us seem automatically to follow Aubrey's assumption that the prehistoric 'walke' took place *between* the two rows of Avenue stones. Stukeley, too, spoke of the 'road' as seen from the top of Overton Hill, his view perhaps being reinforced by the idea which he gathered from some local inhabitants that the Avenue(s) had served to direct offenders or fugitives from the 'Sanctuary' towards Avebury temple itself (Stukeley 1743, tab. xxi; 1722–4a, 131).

To the S of the above area we cannot at present even be certain of exactly *what* features Aubrey and Stukeley were recording. For example, there is still no general agreement today as to whether Aubrey's 'Devil's Coytes' formed part of the Kennet Avenue, as he clearly suggests (Aubrey 25, 63; Fowles and Legg 1982, 823), or whether, rather, they could have been Stukeley's 'Beckhampton Cove' (Plate 60) (see section o below). Certainly, as Burl pointed out in 1979, they look nothing like the Adam and Eve complex as interpreted by Stukeley (Burl 1979, 138–9): indeed, it is hard to accept claims that Aubrey's West Kennet Cove represented a confusion on Aubrey's part with Stukeley's Beckhampton Cove (Burl 1988, 3, 14; King 1879, 379); had there been such a confusion, Aubrey's failure to recognize, or to mention, a connecting western stone avenue – a feature which he neither mentioned nor depicted in any plan – would appear truly inexplicable.

There is also confusion about the status of Stukeley's claim for such a West Kennet Cove, Burl's recent interpretation representing a revision – indeed almost a reversal – of his earlier opinion (Burl 1988, 14). Stukeley certainly took 'The Cove of Kinnet avenue' seriously enough at one stage of his enquiries to find its site, to take bearings from it (Stukeley 1722–4c),[3] and actually to plot it on various of his plans and depict its position relative to other Avenue stones and to meadows (Eng.Misc.b.65, 39, 44, 48); it also appears in his panorama of c.1723 (which is included in the folder to this book; Piggott 1985, pl. 13). In addition, Stukeley indicates the nature of the stone arrangements there – a three-stone Cove opening out from the E limb of the Avenue opposite one recumbent stone, two vacant stone positions and three fallen stones. Furthermore, at this point in the Avenue, which he called

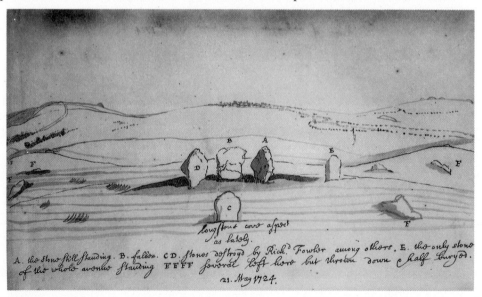

Plate 60 Stukeley's drawing of the Beckhampton Cove, dated 21 May 1724 (Bodleian Library MS. Gough Maps 231, 42).

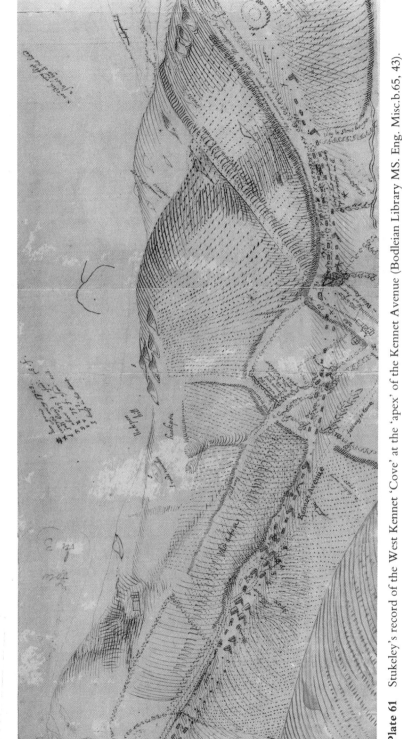

Plate 61 Stukeley's record of the West Kennet 'Cove' at the 'apex' of the Kennet Avenue (Bodleian Library MS. Eng. Misc.b.65, 43).

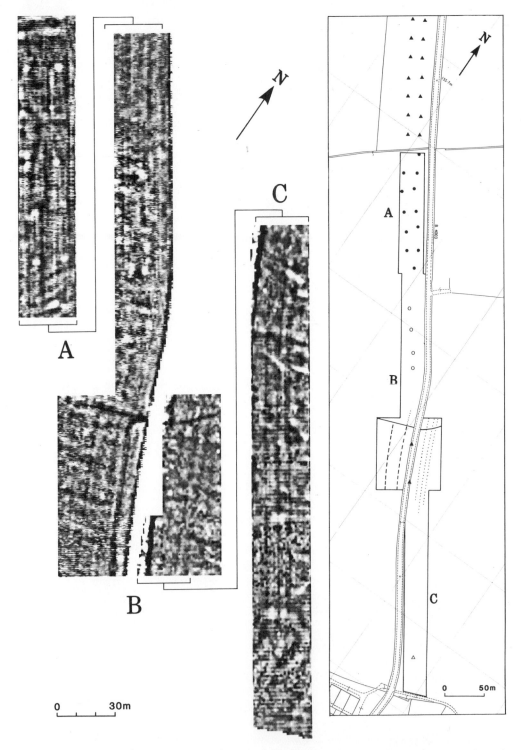

Plate 62 Resistivity surveys (A–C) of part of the Kennet Avenue (covering approximately stone pairs 38–64): grey-tone plots of the data, and location and interpretation of the surveys (right). Key: ▲ established stone positions; ● stone positions apparently established by resistivity survey; ○ selected resistivity anomalies aligned on established stone positions; ---- and ······ linear resistivity anomalies; △ stone located by Ordnance Survey, 1883.

the 'Apex' (Plate 61), he records that one of these Cove stones was 'carryed away 1723' and another 'just buryed' (see panorama in folder). As we shall see shortly, it is exactly this kind of apparently detailed evidence that has made it so dificult to discount Stukeley's claim for the existence of a Beckhampton Avenue – although Crawford did just this for the West Kennet Cove, attributing its claimed existence 'solely to Stukeley's love of symmetry' (Crawford MS., 11–12; and see Chapter II, vi). The possibility remains that Stukeley may have received some hint of a West Kennet Cove from Aubrey's work, probably from the 1695 Camden. On the other hand, this is not a necessary hypothesis, since we have already seen how the existence of such a cove fitted into Stukeley's overall concept of the site at the stage when he sought a purely symmetrical structure for it (Chapter II, vi).

In September 1989 the earlier resistivity survey was extended S along the Avenue alignment and to the SW of the intersection of the Avenue with the road, beyond the estimated positions of stone pair 50a and 50b (Plate 62B) in the hope (admittedly remote) that geophysical data might be able to throw some light on the quandary of a West Kennet Cove. Any special optimism was limited, however: according to Stukeley's plans, the site of the conjectured cove lies close to the intersection of the road and the Avenue (at approximately SU1101 6881); because of the shallow angle of the intersection, as much as 125 metres of this critical stretch of the Avenue may therefore have been interfered with, both by the road itself and by the disturbance associated with the adjacent field margins.

Immediately to the SE, two sarsen boulders remain in position on either side of the road, consistent with being further settings (53b and 54b) along the SW limb of the Avenue. The survey data to the W of these, whilst not showing evidence for any other stone positions, does unexpectedly include two linear low resistance anomalies some 17m. apart, running parallel with the road but well into the field and W of the Avenue (Plate 62B). Whilst parallelism with the road arouses the suspicion that these anomalies may be of relatively recent origin, perhaps agricultural, there is nonetheless a possibility that they might instead reflect a previously unidentified ditched avenue alignment.

These linear anomalies are weakly but clearly distinguishable from the background; if ditches, they are each about 2m. wide, extending S, but traceable NE for about 90 and 120m. respectively, before apparently petering out. They lie at an angle of some 70 degrees to the very broad anomalies which distinguish the ridge and furrow (Plate 62B) which here run at right-angles to the contour (see also Stukeley 1743, tab. xxi). Their potential significance in the context of Keiller's pre-excavation comments on the Avenue, quoted above, remains to be determined.

Further survey work, preferably in conjunction with simple test trenching, would establish whether or not these anomalies represent an important prehistoric feature. If this were indeed the case, then attention would have to be drawn to the obvious parallel provided by the Stonehenge Avenue, first recorded by Stukeley at much the same time as he was mapping the Kennet Avenue. Comparison with the Stonehenge Avenue is especially significant in view of the possibility that this too may have been associated with stone rows (Bartlett and David 1982). In support of this latter notion we may refer to a statement by Stukeley which, as far as we know, has previously escaped comment:

> It may be reckond bold to assert an Avenue at Stonehenge when there is not one stone left. but I did not invent it. having been able to measure the very intervals of almost every Stone. from the manifest hollows left in their stations & probably they were taken away when Christianity first prevaild here. (Stukeley 1722–4b, 129; Appendix II)

From the point of view of locating former stone positions, the extended survey (Plate 62B) is disappointing, although a former field boundary shows up clearly on the W side of the road and a similar feature exists to the E of it (Plate 62B). Unlike the initial survey (Plates 59 and

62A), where most of pairs 38–44 were located with some confidence, only in occasional instances further to the S can stone positions be conjectured. The variation in resistivity response was slighter and more dispersed than in the previous survey, perhaps owing to differing moisture regimes at the time when each survey was executed. In fact, as in our search for the Beckhampton Avenue (see section o, below), there is little objective reason for identifying any one anomaly as against another as a possible stone position; only by extending a regular pattern derived from Aubrey and Stukeley is it possible to suggest that, of the range of high resistance anomalies present, four may be identified for instance with stones 46, 47, 48 and 49. If, however, we were to disregard any preconceived patterning, other anomalies, off the supposed alignment, become no less significant than those just mentioned. Although these latter anomalies present no convincing alternative pattern, they prompt a warning: the course of the Avenue may well have contained irregularities, unrecorded by any of the antiquarians. More recently still it has been possible to extend the exploration of the Avenue alignment farther to the SE and also to the E of the road where the West Kennet Cove might conceivably have been located (Plate 62B and C). Linear features, similar to those already discussed above, were detected on the E side of the road, somewhat lessening the likelihood of the prehistoric ditched alignment proposed above. The evidence for a stone avenue over the ground covered by the whole of this latest extension S of the survey (Plate 62C) is unconvincing (although one may pick out the occasional specific anomaly and suppose that it might represent a stone placement). Either the avenue never did exist here, or it has been totally obliterated for reasons unknown, or it deviates from the expected alignment as plotted by Crawford (Crawford MS.), or our techniques have been unsuccessful in detecting its true course. Clearly, therefore, there is a strong case for extending coverage laterally before drawing any final conclusions.

n. The Sanctuary

Farther S along the Kennet Avenue, beyond our present geophysical survey areas, we have already reviewed the nature of the evidence for the angle/turn of the Avenue towards the Sanctuary in the region of West Kennet village. Continuing up Overton Hill, the kink at the point where the standing stones join the Sanctuary, shown both in Aubrey's plan B (Plate 8) and in his detailed record of the 'brow of the hill' (Plate 27), can still not be confirmed or denied archaeologically (Smith 1965, 208): however, it may well have existed, possibly as a counterpart to the 'anomaly at the approach to Avebury' (Cunnington 1932, 321).

On plan B Aubrey shows the Sanctuary as two concentric circles, the inner one comprising 14 dots, as compared with the 15 stones shown on his detailed plan, and the outer one 29 dots, as against 22 stones (shown as well as stated) on the plan. This record presents us with further information on the extent to which Aubrey was recording the actual occurrence of stones, for he says, 'The Stones are fower and five foot high . . . in number: most of them (now) are fallen downe' (Aubrey's elision) (Aubrey 24, 43; Fowles and Legg 1980, 50; paraphrased in Cunnington 1932, 300; and Burl 1979, 196): this strongly suggests that the site was still largely intact. Yet, though Cunnington's 1930 excavations confirmed that the inner circle contained 16 stones – very close to Aubrey's total of 15 (Stukeley recorded 18) – the outer circle had 42. Here Stukeley recorded 40 (Piggott 1985, pl. 16), which constitutes an impressively close near miss and apparently reveals gross error on Aubrey's part, unless we postulate that on this occasion Aubrey was only recording those stones which were still standing.

Despite Aubrey's (partial) unreliability regarding the number of stones, however, his record of their disposition as circular is correct – and in sharp contrast with Stukeley's later illegitimate transformation of their settings into ovals (Piggott 1935, 31; Piggott 1985, 107; and see Chapter II, vi).

Another piece of evidence regarding Aubrey's reliability is provided by his vertical side-note concerning the Sanctuary (the 'Monument as in plate III. fig.1'), beginning 'I doe well remember, there is a Circular Trench about this Monument or Temple ...' (or, as he wrote in the Camden (1695) version, the temple was 'encompass'd with a circular trench'). This has already been discussed (Chapter I, iv) in connection with the comment by Moray that Aubrey quoted in connection with it. Here we must note that Stukeley's view that Aubrey 'erred in saying there was a circular ditch on *Overton-hill*' (Stukeley 1743, 32), has been substantiated by modern investigators, who concur with his view that the Sanctuary never had such a trench (Cunnington 1932, 311–12).

o. The W Entrance – and Avenue?

We must now turn our attention to the henge's W entrance and the possibility that a stone avenue led to/from it. It is here, in discussion of the vexed question of the existence of a Beckhampton Avenue, that the preconceptions of the investigators of Avebury generally receive their only mention – in connection with Stukeley's theory that the avenues depicted a snake, which, it is often asserted, caused him to claim that an avenue of standing stones led from Beckhampton to the W entrance of the Avebury henge (Burl 1979, figs 84, 85). In fact, as we saw in Chapter II, v–vi, such views have hitherto invariably been based on an oversimplification of the situation. For one thing, it is clear that from 1719 until 1723, Stukeley had not recognized more than the one S entrance opening onto the Kennet Avenue (Long 1876, 6 n.1). Then, when he initially postulated a second avenue and entrance, this was part of his conception of the antiquity as a geometrical artefact, the W avenue having a temple at its end matching the Sanctuary, and it was only when he failed to locate this that he postulated instead that it represented a snake's tail. Be that as it may, the 'snake' idea which ultimately materialized has become well known in its published form (Stukeley 1743, 34–7), and many commentators have gone so far as to claim that the reason that Aubrey failed to record such a Beckhampton Avenue was that its existence was a figment of Stukeley's imagination (e.g. Cunnington 1932, 300–1; see also Lukis 1881–3a, 154–6 for different emphases in the discussion).

An alternative view, however, is that 'the Beckhampton standing stones represent the remains of an independent stone circle with an avenue of which Stukeley saw the remains, running from it towards the Kennet' (Keiller and Piggott 1936, 417), in what was – mistakenly, as we have seen – deemed to be his 'sound' period, before he imposed a fanciful theoretical structure on his findings. This was based at least partly on the detailed evidence that Stukeley recorded (1743, 34–6 and see also Gough Maps 231 *passim*; see also Smith 1885, 146–7; King 1879). Since the 1930s the existence of a Beckhampton Avenue has been said to have gained some support from excavations in the area (e.g. Cunnington 1914a) as well as by some chance observations of buried stones (Vatcher 1969; Vatcher and Vatcher 1980, 41–2). Thus Burl's statements can be taken as fairly typical of most modern judgements – that 'in the 17th century many of [the Beckhampton Avenue] stones still stood right alongside the cove' (Burl 1979, 138), for instance, or that there is 'no substantial question that this [Beckhampton] avenue did exist even though Stukeley himself saw only the tumbled ruins of it' (Burl 1979, 191).

Here, therefore, we have a clear example of discrepancy between two witnesses' evidence – as has long been recognized. The question remains as to why Aubrey should either have missed seeing those stones or chosen not to record them, especially as so many of them were said by Stukeley to have been close to the W entrance of Avebury itself (e.g. Eng.Misc.b.65, 33 which records that 'several stones in [a close-by] pasture were demolished 1702' where plan E simply indicates '1702' opposite two 'stones fallen' apparently lying on the verge of the road). Further doubt about the accuracy of Stukeley's recording of the stones in the supposed Beckhampton Avenue could possibly be raised by the absence of any mention or depiction of stones in connection with the 1695 plan of Avebury Manor and its gardens (Plate 49) (section c above) – in an area which must at least be very close to where Stukeley records three fallen stones (one '1714') and two having been taken away (one '1710') (Plate 35).

We hoped that evidence confirming the existence of the Beckhampton Avenue might be obtained by a geophysical survey undertaken in January 1989 (Plate 45). Perhaps the most obvious location for such a search is the open ground around the Longstones, or Adam and Eve, two standing monoliths (one re-erected) some 1.3km. SW of Avebury. These were shown by Stukeley as forming part of a series of settings along the N limb of his Avenue. It is unclear whether or not the W stone was a component of the Avenue, since it was also claimed to form part of a tripartite 'cove' (Plate 60).

Apart from Adam and Eve, Stukeley saw no Avenue stones still standing, although he indicated many fallen ones, mostly at the NE edge of Longstones field and beyond, towards Avebury, while near the Longstones he recorded both a number of half-buried stones and others of whose destruction he was told by local informants (Plate 60). To the SW the course of the supposed Avenue becomes even less clear, passing somewhere between the Longstones long barrow and the Beckhampton roundabout. Contrary to earlier supposition (Vatcher 1969; Vatcher and Vatcher 1980) there is insufficient evidence to show that the sarsen found buried near the roundabout (at about SU 0875 6899) is on the Avenue alignment, which more probably lay to the N, skirting the S side of the long barrow (clearly shown in Stukeley's view dated May 26, 1724, reproduced in Burl 1979, fig. 25).

Although some of Stukeley's sketch plans and drawings provide a useful guide to the general direction that he supposed the Beckhampton Avenue to have taken, his record of its course is nonetheless piecemeal and in important respects both vague and contradictory. West of Avebury village street itself, the Avenue is 'fixed' only at the Longstones, on an alignment which is roughly NE–SW, but otherwise 'floats' over a considerable arc depending on which sketch one follows. The farther any survey moves from the Longstones, therefore, the greater the coverage required to be sure of containing the full span of possible alignments. A further complication in identifying the Avenue is the possible (indeed, probable) presence of naturally occurring sarsens which could of course have been burnt or buried in the same fashion as other monoliths. The only means of discriminating between natural and artificial stone positions, therefore, would be the identification of recurring geophysical anomalies conforming to the regularity of an avenue. Since it may be assumed that it is most unlikely for there to be a detectable geophysical response at every stone setting, a very large area would have to be covered in order to identify any such pattern.

Both magnetometer and resistivity surveys were attempted, although the latter was given preference, for the reasons described elsewhere (section a above). The magnetometer survey, which covered an area of 90m. × 90m. around the Longstones (grid squares 4–6, A–C), was unproductive. The magnetic response was distinguished only by a very general spread of reactions to iron litter, of the kind encountered in any field. That no concentrations of anomalies were found suggests either that the effects of any burning have now been dispersed by the plough or that such burning did not take place within the area surveyed.

The resistivity survey covered a much wider area which close examination of Stukeley's sketches suggested should have accommodated well over 300m. of his Avenue. Some 32,400 readings were taken, spaced at 1.0m. intervals, in one of the largest archaeological resistivity surveys yet undertaken.

Most apparent on the grey-tone plot (Plate 63A) are extensive and repetitive linear anomalies relating to previous cultivation patterns, most probably medieval ridge and furrow. This overlay of alternating bands of high and low resistance lends a criss-cross texture to the plot which very probably obscures subtler detail. Very much broader changes in background moisture levels further obscure large areas of detail where values are,

196

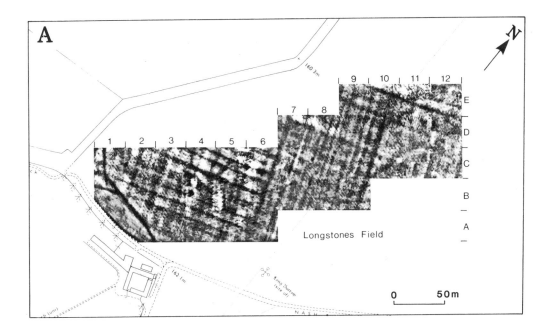

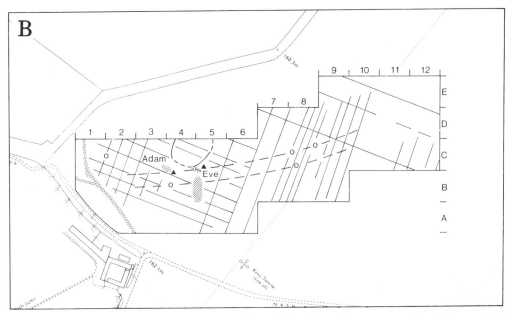

Plate 63 Resistivity survey in Longstones Field, Beckhampton: (A) grey-tone plot of data, and (B) interpretation. Key: ▲ standing stones (Adam and Eve); ○ possible stone positions; —— linear features; – – approximate course of Stukeley's avenue; stipple = other resistivity anomalies (see text).

respectively, too high or too low. The plot in Plate 63A minimizes these variations as much as possible.

Apart from the cultivation marks, the forked linear low resistance anomaly at the SW end of the survey (running through squares 2A, 1B and 1C) may be dismissed as of relatively recent origin. This feature, varying in breadth from some 3 to 5m., can be interpreted as a former trackway, superseded by the present track which skirts the modern field edge to which the earlier feature is roughly parallel. The ridge and furrow appear to respect this earlier alignment, and it was perhaps this, rather than the existing track, which features on Stukeley's sketches of the neighbourhood, on the southern side of which he shows two fallen stones (e.g. Plate 60). There are unfortunately no anomalies to confirm the suggestion that such stones once existed at this point.

Tackling the remainder of the survey plot in search of possible stone positions is daunting. There appear to be no appropriate high resistance anomalies. On the other hand, although some negative anomalies appear which might be candidates, these are spaced intermittently and do not conclusively define the linear pattern that might be expected.

There can be no simple explanation why stone settings should thus respond as negative anomalies in the Longstones field, whereas in the Kennet Avenue they appear as positive anomalies. Almost certainly, several variables – deriving both from the survey technique and from *in situ* conditions – interact to determine the response of any particular feature. A significant contributory factor may have been the soil conditions at Beckhampton, which perhaps inhibit the loss of moisture from stone burial or burning pits. That the negative resistivity response does indeed genuinely reflect the former existence of stones is indicated by just such an anomaly 12m. SSE of Adam. This is in a position closely corresponding to that of a stone ('C') sketched by Stukeley (Plate 60) on the S limb of his Avenue and described by him as 'destroyd by Richard Fowler among others' (Gough Maps 231, 42). The two missing stones of the Cove met the same fate and the site of their destruction appears to be indicated by a concentration of low readings to the W of their one remaining partner. A similar area of low readings S and W of Eve cannot be so explained, however, in that there is no documentary evidence that stones ever existed here: this may therefore be a local exaggerated response to a cultivation furrow with which it coincides. A further area of probably spurious values, but of high resistance, is located SE of Eve along the W margin of grid square 5B. This area of approximately 25m. × 12m. remains an enigma pending future investigation.

A search to either side (NE and SW) of the Longstones unfortunately does not reveal a succession of anomalies at appropriate intervals comparable to that exemplified by the survey of the Kennet Avenue (Plate 59). To the NE there are no likely anomalies for a distance of 90m. from Eve. From about this point, however, in grid square 8C, there are three weak negative anomalies disposed at the corners of a suitably oriented right-angled triangle. If an avenue indeed exists, then these anomalies, albeit very faint, might be taken to be suggestive of two stone positions on the N side of the alignment and a single one on the opposite side.

At present it must remain uncertain whether these anomalies distinguish the structure postulated by Stukeley from any other real or imagined features. Other anomalies, even less clearly contrasted with the background, could be drawn into the discussion, but they are too feeble to support any conclusions at this stage. To the SW of the Longstones, the picture is no more encouraging. Only one anomaly, on the margin of grid squares 1C and 2C, has the appearance of a stone position, but it is well to the N of the expected alignment; its nature could be determined by probing.

These findings plainly neither disprove not support Stukeley's firm assertion of the presence of an Avenue. More survey work is needed, both to re-examine certain areas already covered and, also, ideally, to extend coverage to other areas along the route. A wider probe-spacing, for instance, could 'see' rather deeper below the surface and would reduce the masking effect of the ridge and furrow. Survey at a time of year other than winter, with a more favourable soil moisture balance, would also help. Other areas requiring such investigation would include the ground S of the Longstones long barrow and on the NE side of Longstones field, where Stukeley noted thirteen fallen stones (Eng.Misc.b.65, 54). On the outskirts of Avebury some possible pits were noted in a trench near the bridge over the Winterbourne (Vatcher photos, Alexander Keiller Museum, Avebury) and this is another area where a search for an alignment might be profitable.

Thus, whilst not excluding the possibility, geophysical results at present provide no support for the existence of a Beckhampton stone avenue; one may wonder, therefore, along with the sceptical Lukis (1881–3a, 155), whether the Longstones do not, rather, represent the remains of 'a monument entirely distinct from Avebury' and whether other identifiable stones claimed by Stukeley, and consequently by others, to form part of an avenue were not in fact naturally occurring sarsens. It is worth recalling that it was partly because of his initial presumption of a symmetrical structure at Avebury that Stukeley was prone to expect a W avenue to balance an E one, while, though in the summer of 1724 he might have reconsidered his whole evidence afresh, the most he proved able to do was to translate the W part of his 'beautiful bell-like figure' (Stukeley 1722–4b, 175) into the tail of a snake (Stukeley 1743, tab. xxv; see also Chapter II,v–vi).

At this point it is instructive to remember that it is more usual for geophysical methods to be used in the location and definition of features such as pits, ditches, hearths, kilns and wall foundations than of individual stone settings (Clark 1975). Though we have here concentrated on a search for stones, the location of ditches, pits, and post-holes, and accumulations of organic or 'occupation-type' deposits would be of particular relevance to a better understanding of Avebury. With the exception of post-holes (elusive largely because they tend to be small, often with fillings poorly contrasted to the subsoil), such features are often readily detectable against a chalk background, and magnetometry in particular has been shown to be effective in such circumstances (Bartlett and David 1984).

These results and considerations constitute a timely reminder that – according to modern archaeological views – the nature of the Avebury monuments, and their associated cultural contexts and landscapes, will never be properly understood by examination of their upstanding stones alone. For instance, in the case of the Beckhampton Avenue, the resistivity survey (Plate 63) seems to have picked up evidence to the N of the Longstones for a ditched feature distinguished by the alignment of its component negative anomalies at an angle to the ubiquitous ridge and furrow. In attempting to see a recognizable pattern here, one is again at the mercy of all but invisible discrepancies camouflaged by irrelevant background activity. However, if the eye is not just being deceived by coincidental juxtaposition, one could interpret the above ditched feature as the partial outline of a circle defined by fragmentary curvilinear negative anomalies. Whether a circle or some other arrangement of ditches, this feature bears no comprehensible direct relationship to the standing stones.

The henge monument

p. The henge

Interest in Avebury – in the 20th century as much as in the 17th – has been focused on stones and earthworks. What is more, existing knowledge of the site has always to some extent taken into account the information available from the records of Aubrey and Stukeley. On the other hand, despite many generalizations in the existing literature as to the accuracy of the early records, there has been no detailed feature-by-feature published analysis such as is now attempted here. The nearest approach to this is an unpublished study carried out by

O. G. S. Crawford (Crawford MS.), which is significant for our purposes in various ways. It displays an impressive summary of knowledge about the site in 1927, just before modern excavations began, and, in doing so, provides an alternative view of stone equivalences to some of those presented in Smith 1965. It is largely because of the existence of Crawford's unpublished analysis of Stukeley's record of the Kennet Avenue – which is acknowledged as a major source by Smith (1965) – and the relationship of this to archaeological investigations, that we have felt able to refrain from detailed analysis of this avenue. Though Crawford's study was apparently based on only limited access to Stukeley's unpublished works, combined with considerable disdain for Aubrey's record, it has acted as a valuable independent check on some of the assertions in our book. It was encouraging to learn that Crawford's analysis had led him to many of the same conclusions about the reliability of the Stukeley record as we ourselves had arrived at; albeit in Crawford's case, Stukeley's internal contradictions as revealed by two of his unpublished records of the Kennet Avenue – held by Keiller at the time of Crawford's work – were explained as 'being probably due to additional information or more careful scrutiny' (Crawford MS., 13). Whenever pertinent, we refer to Crawford's unpublished assessments of details of Stukeley's record of other areas of the Avebury site.

Our own methods of correlating the evidence about the Avebury henge were rather different from those adopted by Crawford. In the first place we have managed to gain access to many more documents of the 17th and 18th centuries than he did. Secondly, and more important, we chose to start our comparative analysis by giving equal weight to all our sources – unlike Crawford, who unashamedly assigned much more weight to Stukeley's plan E than to any other record.

As a first step, therefore, we went to considerable lengths to make each available plan visually equivalent. Thus, where a particular map has a scale given, for example on Aubrey's plan A, 'This was projected at the half inch scale' (ie half inch = 1 chain; but see Welfare 1989), this scale has been used and the drawing optically enlarged or reduced to the common scale and drawn (Transparency 1). Where no scale has been given (or in the case of Stukeley's plan E, where the given scale is patently wrong) the drawings have been optically enlarged or reduced to a version of H. St George Gray's 1912 plan (Gray 1935, pl. 29) at the common scale (Transparency 2). However, since many of the early plans misrepresent the actual shape of the antiquity, this procedure can only provide an approximate comparison. In the case of the S circle, two versions of Aubrey's plan A depiction have been produced: one (Transparency 4) at his given scale and one (Transparency 5) enlarged to approximately Gray's 1912 actual size. All Stukeley's draft frontispieces (Transparencies 6–16) have been drawn to fit the common scale, as also have reconstructions of his 'tour' (Transparency 19) and his field measurements (Transparency 20) – thereby enabling the reader to overlay and adjust them to make his or her own comparisons.

Transparency 1 shows how in Aubrey's plan A the bank or ditch merely repeat each other's irregularities; the distortions caused by his surveying errors, discussed in Chapter III, A.15, are made quite clear when this plan is compared with Smith's (1965, based on Gray 1935) (Transparency 17). There is no sign of the 'fracture' made in the W bank in this Aubrey plan (see above); if Aubrey did get to hear of the ditch being filled and the bank destroyed before his death in June 1697, he did not amend his plan accordingly (and see Chapter III and section e above).

In Transparency 18 the henge in plan B is drawn to the same size as plan A (Transparency 1). Although, as we have argued, plan B was primarily intended to show the relationship between henge, Avenue, and Sanctuary, it is remarkable how much of the character of plan A it manages to reproduce: indeed, as we shall see, in some respects it is more accurate than plan A. Whether plan B dates from before or after the September 1663 survey is unclear, though on balance it seems likely to post-date it. Like plan A, it differs from Aubrey's earlier plan C in that it avoids giving the impression of a completely regular circle (Chapter III, B.10). On the other hand, this small sketch considerably smoothes out the irregularities of plan A; no roads are shown, and the bank is not differentiated from the ditch. In general, this would lead one to expect that where plans A and B differ – as in the SE quadrant – the more detailed plan should be preferred, though this must not be taken for granted (see section u below).

As for Stukeley, his reasons for ignoring the actual irregularity of the earthwork and his depiction of it as a perfect circle have already been discussed. Here we may note that his plan E (Plate 14) shows details of the levelling of the bank in some three areas in the NW and SW quadrants. The phases of these works might, in principle at least, provide clues to the relative chronology of the draft frontispieces; apparently successive depictions do seem in this case to confirm that Stukeley did update his records as changes occurred (Chapter III, E.7).

q. The stones

In turning our attention to detailed recording of stones, it is imperative that each feature is examined in detail, and the accuracy of each recorder objectively assessed, taking all relevant factors into account. Such an approach is in strong contrast to some 19th-century and early 20th-century accounts of Avebury, which have been inclined to impressionistic, general comments: thus King (1879, 378–80) not only thought that Aubrey had 'dotted down the stones [in his plans] in the most "higgledy piggledy" manner and with the most utter disregard of their relative distances', but was even 'led to quesiton whether Aubrey did make frequent visits to Avebury, and still more strongly to question his accuracy of observation when he did make his visits'. Similarly, Long (1858b, 67) remarked that 'The slovenliness of Aubrey's plans can hardly be too much regretted; for had he laid down with care the stones which remained in his day, their original number and arrangement could scarcely now have been open to doubt'. Lukis (1881–3a, 154ff.), on the other hand, dismissed Stukeley's overall recording of the Avebury monuments as a giving 'way to his imagination, he has added an appendage [the Beckhampton Avenue] to the monument which cannot have had any existence'.

Despite such strongly critical comments about the reliability of the particulars of the then-available early documents, all the authors concerned were still at pains to stress that some features were indeed accurate and that, without them, our understanding of the remains would be significantly impoverished. As Lukis himself put it, 'The monument has . . . been so sadly despoiled of its stones that unless we have recourse to the plans of Aubrey [and] Stukeley . . . the form in which the stones were placed is not easy to determine' (Lukis 1881–3a, 151). Even Crawford and Keiller, though generally critical of the value of Aubrey's observations regarding specific stones, admit to their occasional importance in having expanded the existing record (Crawford MS.; Keiller corresp.).

One of the main problems of a detailed comparative analysis of the evidence of the Avebury records concerning the stone arrangements is deciding what is the most appropriate reference point: circles of stones, pasture–stone relationships, or quadrants of the site? In what follows we have tried to assess the relative reliability of all these features. However, there is one immediate general problem relating to all the plans, namely that our ability correctly to interpret what is shown on them requires us to understand the conventions used by each mapper (see also Chapter II, ii).

Thus, in the case of Aubrey, we had no idea before we began this exercise whether his variable use of oblongs, oblongs and dots, and circles/squares in plan A was haphazard or an intentional device used to indicate different stone qualities and features. We would therefore have to try to test – by intensive comparisons of all available records – whether Aubrey's use of these conventions could be equated with any actual features which he might have observed in 1663.

As we have seen in Chapter III, E.6–7, a particular set of problems surrounds Stukeley's records. In an attempt to establish some base-lines for their assessment, we resolved to investigate his recording of those stones (both fallen and standing) which had been still visible to Gray and others prior to 1936 (Smith 1965, fig. 67). As far as is known no stones had been replaced or re-erected in the main Avebury monument (in contrast to the Kennet Avenue and Beckhampton 'Cove') prior to this date (Stuart Piggott, pers. comm.). In undertaking this study we are also able to use Stukeley's written 'tour' (Appendix II), and his unpublished map of measurements (Plate 15).

When we compare the standing stones still visible in the 1930s (Smith 1965, fig. 67) with Stukeley's drafts, plan E and his other records, we are rewarded with a remarkable degree of consistency. All nine pre-excavation standing stones at Avebury recorded in the outer circle (Smith 1965, nos 1, 8, 32, 33, 44, 46, 50, 68 and 98) are present on all the plans which distinguish standing from other stones, as well as in the measured plan and in Stukeley's 'tour' of the site. (Even draft plans T and U – of which only half the pages remain – respectively show the four and five standing stones that would be expected.) Likewise, all Stukeley's records which distinguish standing stones show the expected two stones in the S circle (Smith 1965 nos 101 and 103). (These standing stones are shown with Smith's 1965 numbers on Transparencies 6–16 and on the Quadrant comparisons, all of which are located in the folder.)

It is these standing stones which have enabled us to undertake the detailed matching of the various Stukeley drafts – thereby revealing some of the problems that confronted Stukeley and which now re-emerge for those attempting analysis of his records. Thus, for example, in comparing draft plan Q (Transparency 9) with draft plan X (Transparency 16) we find that when standing stones 44, 46, 50 and 68 are matched, they agree over the number of stone positions equivalent to Smith's 73–38 (but not with their details) (Transparency 17); a similar agreement is found with stone positions 77–98–1 when standing stone 98 is matched, as also 8 to about stone 24 when standing stone 8 is matched. The details of stones 29–33 are the same in both plans when standing stones 32 and 33 are matched, although they are displaced in draft plan X due to the presence of an extra standing stone and a gap within this section. However, there are also more noticeable discrepancies. Counting from standing stone 44 the two draft plans show the same details until position 37, but on draft plan X this stone is followed by a vacancy and two fallen stones, whereas Q has only one fallen stone before standing stones 33 and 32. Beginning as from standing stone 68, draft plan Q shows five vacancies followed by one fallen stone in positions 75–80, whereas draft plan X shows a fallen stone, two vacancies, another fallen stone, one standing and another vacancy (or, alternatively, starting from standing stone 98, where draft plan Q shows the above-mentioned stones and positions, draft plan X shows three fallen stones, two vacancies and then one fallen); and where Q has a vacancy, a hollow and three vacancies between stones 1 and 8, draft plan X shows a gap, a hollow, a huge gap, a hollow and then a fallen stone.

We find, therefore, that – despite Stukeley's accuracy in recording the existence of actual standing stones (a consistency almost equally matched for the ten *fallen* stones which were still visible in the 1930s) – his various records differ significantly in the number of stones and stone positions indicated, as well as in the placement of them in relation to known standing stones. Looking at the overall recording of the area between standing stones 32/33 and 8 on draft plans Q and X, we find that the variations are due to only two discrepancies: X has a fallen stone at position 27 where Q has a gap followed by a vacancy (when counting from stones 32/33), while X has a standing stone in position 14 whereas Q shows one fallen (counting from stone 8). Probably such variation in the spacing and number of stone positions between given points represents the practical result, in the field, of Stukeley's

202

preconceptions regarding the overall numbers of stones which would make up his various circles, the background to which has been fully discussed in Chapter II.

This kind of variability makes it exceedingly difficult to assess the significance of the fact that draft plan Q shows Smith's 1965 stone 35 (when counting from stones 32/33) as a standing stone. It is convenient, in such a case, to presume a simple error. It is not so easy to decide on a satisfactory interpretation when *several* drafts agree that a particular stone, represented as standing in other sources, was in fact a fallen stone or the place of a stone taken away. It is tempting to assume that the sources are here recording the chronological sequence of a stone first seen by Stukeley intact, which then fell and/or was then destroyed by villagers: but if so, at least one instance (Smith 1965 stone 78) appears to show categorically that Stukeley's published plan E should not be considered the authoritative version of his knowledge of the site (and see Chapter III, E.). As we will see shortly, a straightforward chronological sequence of events does not explain the variation in the record. Nevertheless, Stukeley *was* concerned in his various versions with giving an accurate account of the number and location of stones which he could observe at first hand. This holds good however much he may have 'had' to 'add' stones to ensure the expected numbers, and however difficult this may make it to match the archaeological evidence with other parts of Stukeley's record of the site. Whatever his deficiencies in the actual locating of individual stone positions, the Baconian tradition which enthused Stukeley like his predecessors (see Chapter II, i) was clearly in evidence in these attempts to preserve an accurate record of what was visible at Avebury for posterity.

Let us now, therefore, turn to an intensive comparison of the Avebury stones, feature by feature, as they were recorded by the 17th- and 18th-century antiquaries and as we are now aware of them on the basis of archaeological evidence. This will enable us to make comparisons within the records of Aubrey, Charleton and Stukeley and to evaluate the respective quality and accuracy of their recording.

The outer circle(s)

r. North-west quadrant

The easiest stones to start with for comparative purposes are those of the NW quadrant in the outer circle. Here Aubrey shows only seven stones in plan A (Transparency 1), and his plane-table survey results are not too badly distorted at this point. This quadrant was also chosen to be examined first because Keiller (1939) had attempted a similar exercise (possibly based on Crawford's unpublished comparison of plan E with the archaeological record), although not, of course, for the same reasons.

What seems clear is that, subsequent to his initial record of only three stones in this NW quadrant (plan C), Aubrey later (plan A) increased his identifications to seven stones, all of which Stukeley's plan E also records as standing (Transparency 2). However, Aubrey omits three others which plan E records as being in the same intact, upright state. Of the seven on plan A, only four remained standing in Keiller's (1936) time, two more being found by him in 1939 in burning holes (apparently, therefore, having been destroyed after Stukeley's time), while the last stone was in an area inaccessible for excavation.

Stukeley's plan E also records the positions of the stumps of three other stones, two of which Keiller also saw, protruding from under a medieval field boundary, the other no longer visible but found by excavation in 1937. These three stones (Smith's 1965 40–42) exemplify some of the problems of matching the archaeological and antiquarian records. Stukeley describes these stones on plan E as 'broke off to the stumps' (similarly annotated on draft plans R, V, W and X, described as 'broke' on version S, and bracketed together on

A Prospect of Abury Aug. 1722.

Plate 64 Stukeley's 'A Prospect of Abury, Aug. 1722' (Bodleian Library MS. Gough Maps 231, 218).See Key to Stones in folder.

version O). This is extended in his 'tour' (Appendix II) as: 'broke off at the root like the pedistal of a pillar'. However, his unpublished drawing of this area of the site (Plate 64) shows vacancies in positions 40 and 41, a small stone at 42, and apparently standing stones in Smith 1965 positions 43–46. However, although Keiller's record (Smith 1965) shows stones 40 and 41 as fallen and 42 and 43 as missing, Smith claimed that stone 40 was, in fact, 'the only undamaged one' (Smith 1965, pl. XXIXa). It is possible to imagine that stone 40 was undamaged but prostrate in Stukeley's time and that he simply confused its appearance with the broken stumps of 41 and 42 on plan E and other drafts. Perhaps, when drawing this particular view of the site, he could not see it (or stump 41) because it was hidden in the bank. Keiller, it appears, saw stone 40 when it was partially buried, without discovering that it was complete; he appears to have been in error with regard to the vacancies at stone positions 43 (where Stukeley shows a standing stone) and 42 (where a stone which 'lacks its upper part' undoubtedly exists (Isobel Smith, pers. comm.)). None of these three 'broke off to the stumps' stones seem to have been remarked by Aubrey.

Plan B shows one more stone overall than plan A in this quadrant (Transparency 18). However, when matched by quadrant with plan A, the three W stones are an almost perfect fit for placement and spacing (see Quadrant comparisons, in folder); the four N stones still appear in the same area near the N causeway (without the apparently inaccurate clumping of three of them shown in plan A), while an additional stone is shown, possibly in the region of Smith's 1965 37–39 (all of which were burnt). How far such apparent accuracy might have arisen by chance must remain an open question but, at first sight, plan B is strikingly accurate, in this NW quadrant at least, closely conforming – with only one possible exception – to positions of stones which can be readily accepted as having been standing in Aubrey's time.

As we continued with our detailed comparisons and matching of stones, so we learnt more about the recording methods and conventions of the antiquarians concerned, and about their limitations. Thus, Keiller (1939, 231) reports that one of the standing stones recorded by both Aubrey (in plans A and B) and Stukeley (in plan E) was inclined obliquely due to slippage during its original erection, but neither Aubrey nor Stukeley appears to attempt to represent this characteristic of the stone (although Stukeley, on other occasions in plan E, does show individual stone shapes and angles).

If the stone nearest to the N causeway in Aubrey's plans A and B was indeed Smith's 1965 stone 46 then we know that it was unusual, as compared to the other stones of the Outer Circle, in having a visible height of 14.7ft (full length 18.5ft) (Smith 1965, 196). This exceptional height is fairly clearly conveyed in plan E (and versions V, W and X – although not in S and U which also use a representative mode for showing standing stones), but it did not tempt Aubrey to depart from his apparent policy in plans A and B of not indicating stone sizes (with the exception of the Cove).

What can we conclude about Aubrey's records of the NW quadrant? If we were to treat his plans A and C as equally reliable records, we would have to conclude that Aubrey originally saw only one of three closely placed stones near the N causeway. We would also have to accept that he originally saw two specific stones in the S part of the quadrant, stones which had been destroyed by the time of his later visit, or which he simply failed to record on his plan A. Given the degree of concordance revealed for this quadrant of the site in all other plans (see Quadrant comparison, in folder), it seems much likelier that Aubrey's plan C was intended to be indicative rather than representational, a conclusion already reached from our analysis of the depiction of buildings and boundaries (see section d above). Furthermore, because of the nature of plan C with its concentric circles, it is not possible – apart from most exceptional cases such as the Cove stones (see section y below) – to match its record of specific stones with those on other plans or with those attested archaeologically. Plan C will therefore normally be omitted from the detailed comparisons which follow.

When we examine the whole Stukeley record of the NW quadrant in detail we observe that certain features differ between his draft frontispieces and his 'tour' on the one hand and, on the other, his published Frontispiece with accompanying text (plan E), despite there being no evidence that he returned to Avebury after his final (1724) fieldwork there (Chapter I, viii). Thus, for example, five of his versions (Q, R, V, W, X) resemble plan E in showing ten standing stones of the Outer Circle – albeit with varying degrees of spacing between the stones – while draft plan N shows only eight, draft plan O nine and versions S and U eleven. Draft plans N and O are similar in showing only three of the four standing stones at the N edge of pasture III, the 'tour' confirming that there were four (Appendix II).

Still in the NW quadrant, but farther to the SW, even more important discrepancies begin. For instance, where plan E shows three standing stones, followed by a stone taken away and then two fallen stones before one comes to what the 'tour' describes as 'pails going across the ditch', the latter records the three standing stones but then only one 'broke & tumbled a little out its place too much westward' and one 'broke off by the root' (Appendix II). Even if one assumes that the palings had been moved between the two recording sessions involved, it is not possible to match the remaining stone details, the draft frontispieces again revealing different numbers of stones, and differing states of preservation. The problems are epitomized by the written comment (Eng.Misc.b.65, 18), that the number of stones in the NW quadrant of the outer circle is '22 in all', whereas published plan E shows 21. All this presumably shows the difficulty that Stukeley had in determining stone details, and the frequency with which he changed his mind.

We come now to one of the most controversial of all Stukeley's claimed stone positions at Avebury, the stone which he shows on plan E in pasture III, somewhere to the E of Smith's 1965 stone 33 (Transparencies 2 and 17). Stukeley (Appendix II; Gough Maps 231, 31v) takes this stone as evidence for the second of his proposed 'two great Circles with their inner concentrics' (and see discussion of the 'ring-stone', section w, below). Not surprisingly, therefore, this pasture III stone has been a focus of archaeological interest but, since no trace of it has been found by excavation, the existence of a second outer circle is nowadays usually dismissed (Smith 1965, 190 and fig. 68, I).

As we saw in Chapter II, vi, Stukeley was clearly aware of the weakness of an argument for the existence of a whole circle of standing stones simply on the basis of one survival. Yet Stukeley appears to have maintained his view of the significance of this stone throughout his fieldwork at Avebury, several of his plans describing the positions in this postulated circle of stones as 'places of a stone taken away'. By the time of his published text, however, Stukeley appears to have given up at least some of his previous insistence on double circles (see Chapter II, vi) and *Abury* is totally silent about this 'Inner Circle', and the supposed number of its stones is omitted from his total listing (Stukeley 1743, 37).[4] Again, it is clear that the published Frontispiece (plan E) – with the stone in pasture III shown as fallen – was drawn up with a different, earlier, concept in mind, reflecting Stukeley's views at the time of his fieldwork.

Can we gain any further insight on Stukeley's change of mind about an 'Inner Circle' from his draft plans, and his plan giving measurements? The single fallen stone in pasture III is clearly shown not only on plan E but also on versions S, U, V, W and X. No such stone appears in versions N, O, P, Q or R, nor is a stone mentioned in this location in Stukeley's measured plan (Plate 15, and Transparency 20). It would be tempting to suggest that these two groups of plans date respectively from before and after this stone had been found. However, first we must note that although version R has no pasture III stone, it has a stone position (perhaps a hollow) on the circumference of the 'Inner circle' in the hedge dividing pastures IX and X. More surprisingly, version S has not only the pasture III stone but several others on the same 'Inner circle' circumference: a fallen stone across the E verge of the S road (just outside the hedge of pasture X), another fallen in the hedge of pasture I, and two other possible fallen stones, one projecting from pasture IV into the N road, and one within the N roadside hedge of pasture V. Here what we appear to have is, not a developmental sequence based on actual discoveries, but the results of preconception on 'evidence' in the field. Perhaps uniquely we may be witnessing Stukeley's opinion about the very existence of stones waxing and waning as his interpretations were modified, until, by 1743, the double 'Outer circle' had disappeared altogether.

Modern investigations have, if anything, complicated the picture even more, reflecting the disarray in our archaeological knowledge of Avebury. Keiller calculated the position of the pasture III stone from Stukeley's published Frontispiece prior to excavating for it, but it appears that, when he did so, he did not correct for the inaccurate scale given on the published engraving.[5] When this error is corrected, the stone's distance from the outer circle turns out to be 77ft, not 96ft, and it is therefore about 7ft W of the trench which was actually excavated (Smith 1965, fig. 60)! However, even this may not be the full story, since plan E's position of the stone is not borne out by other evidence. Stukeley's unpublished 'tour' (Appendix II) records that this 'stone of the lesser circle lyes in pasture VIII [i.e. Pasture III of plan E] over ag[ains]t that which is tumbled awry over ag[ains]t the parsonage barn end', which conforms quite well with the position of this stone as shown on plan E and on versions V, W and X. However, its location on version U is at least one stone position farther to the N than on the published Frontispiece, while on version S it is both farther N and farther E.

Although it would therefore appear that archaeological investigation has failed to come to grips adequately with the Stukeley record, it is important to note that no stone was claimed by Aubrey in any part of this particular area in either plans A or B.

s. South-west quadrant

The SW quadrant provides confirmation that Aubrey was not concerned with distinguishing the angles at which standing stones leaned, and that he probably included both standing and fallen stones in his plans without differentiating between them. Keiller – whose comment that 'Besides stones 9, 13, 18, five more stones [presumably Smith's 1965 nos. 4–6, 9, 10] were found buried, all at considerable depth' is in any case obscure – had to conclude that '9 stones, but whether standing or fallen is not indicated, appear on Aubrey's plan [A], the identity of some of which cannot however be fixed with certainty' (Keiller 1939, 230). Keiller's remark anticipates some of the observations made above about the overall problems involved in correlating the details of stones on the different plans and Stukeley's draft frontispieces; thus while plan B shows only eight stones in this area, plan A shows nine (and plan C has only five).

The stone closest to the S causeway in plans A and B should possibly be equated with Smith's 1965 stone 4, but this, according to Smith (1965, 190), had been buried (in medieval times?). If we are to assume that Aubrey was recording what he could see, and if burial of stones really ceased after medieval times (see section h above), this stone must be better matched with Smith's stone 3; which was burnt (presumably, therefore, after Aubrey's recordings).

We must assume that the next stone to the N would be Smith's 1965 standing stone 8; in Keiller's time it was standing, but leaning obliquely – a characteristic not recorded by Aubrey. We have already seen that all Stukeley's draft plans as well as plan E indicate a (standing) stone in this area of the SW quadrant (Smith's 1965 positions 2–8): however, draft plans Q and R show it in stone position 7, S and V in stone position 9 (as also may plan E and draft plans W and X which all indicate a gap hereabouts), and draft plans N, O, P and T placing it in the tenth stone position. Stukeley's 'tour' (Appendix II) confirms that he experienced considerable difficulties in determining the nature of these particular stones, at that time apparently not remarking four of the stone positions shown in his plans. Only his measurement plan (Plate 15 and Transparency 20) actually shows a stone – either standing or fallen – in the eighth position (and cf. Plate 44).

North from this point (i.e. the second stone in the SW quadrant in Aubrey's plan A) the situation becomes very unclear. But Aubrey's next three stone depictions in plan A are so close together (unlike plan B where they are quite evenly spread) that it is difficult to imagine that they would not cover the locations of at least Smith's stones 9–11. If so, they include not only the Barber Stone and stone 10, both of them buried (apparently with no pre-excavation holes visible in the 1930s), and only found during excavations in 1938, but also a stone (Smith's 11) which is very probably one of those shown by Stukeley to be fallen, presumably later destroyed by firing, and found again during the 1938 excavations. It therefore seems archaeologically impossible that Aubrey could have seen all the stones that he depicted here. Either his plan A was impressionistic or he was not differentiating between actual stones, hollows where stones might once have stood, and locations suggested by local informants.

The next two stones in plan A, to the N, can apparently be equated with Smith's 1965 stones 14 and 15, the former apparently still standing as late as 1812 (Keiller 1939), the latter a burnt stone. However, the last two stones in this quadrant of plan A were presumably two of Smith's 19–21, all of which are reported as having been buried and subsequently burnt (Smith 1965, 190). As we have seen earlier in this chapter, most commentators have simply assumed that burials occurred only in medieval times, in which case Aubrey could not have seen these stones. To accept Aubrey's general reliability in recording stones in this area would require us to believe either that he was recording oral history about the burial of stones (although without specially remarking the fact), or that Stukeley (1743, 15) did not mean (or was not correct in claiming) that stone burial ceased once the locals had discovered how to break up the stones by fire and water. Two of these stones (19 and 20) are shown by Stukeley in plan E (and in all the draft plans except N and S – which show nothing on this point) as forming part of a group of four cavities of stones 'taken away AD 1720', while position 21 is shown on plan E and versions W and X in a different style from normal, apparently to indicate that it 'lyes there partly above ground' (Appendix II). However, this apparent consistency is belied by Stukeley's 'tour' (Appendix II) which makes no mention of a date but specifies that the physical evidence for these stone positions were 'cavitys ... visible full of nettles'. Stukeley's measurements plan (Plate 15), in contrast to all other records which show four cavities, apparently marks an extra stone or vacancy before reaching a garden. Within this garden, plan E shows a charming, but unexplained, detail, which also appears on versions R, S, U, V, W, X (and possibly Q). It is explained in his 'tour' (Appendix II): 'we goe thro' a little garden carryd into the ditch where [the stones] are buryd in the mold'.

The other stone which is said to have been buried and subsequently burnt (Smith 1965, 196, stone 24) is shown by Stukeley in plan E and one of its drafts as a fallen stone. Stukeley's 'tour' (Appendix II) fortunately allows us further to examine the implications of such descriptions of stones as being buried but subsequently disinterred and burnt. He makes it clear that Smith's 1965 stones 7, 11, 12, and 13 were 'fallen and buryed flat in the ground', presumably signifying that some parts of the stones remained visible to both Aubrey and Stukeley (the latter not differentiating partially buried stones from fallen ones on plan E), and presumably also to those who later dug them out and burnt them. Confirmation of this conclusion exists for Smith's 1965 stones 7 and 12 which were found by Keiller to have been partially buried.

From the analysis of this quadrant, then, it is not possible to say categorically whether Aubrey's plan A or B can have matched the existing reality of the Avebury monument when he surveyed it in 1663, but it is clear from his omission of Smith's 1965 stones 13 and 24 (both 'buried' stones shown by Stukeley as fallen) that his record is unlikely to have been comprehensive.

t. North-east quadrant

One of the most interesting features of Aubrey's depictions of the NE quadrant of the site in all three of his plans concerns the two stones nearest to the N and E causeways. The former must presumably be Smith's 1965 47 or 48 – either way it must be the stone 'of a most enormous bulk' to which Stukeley refers (1743, 22). As usual in plan A, Aubrey does not appear to distinguish size in any way, but the second stone away from the N causeway in plan B is a bigger than usual – almost double – dot. This is a further example of a surprising accuracy of some of the features in the latter plan compared to plan A.

The stone nearest to the E causeway, which appears in virtually the same place in plans A and B, is presumably Smith's 1965 stone 73, which Stukeley's plan E indicates as lying within a hedge; Stukeley also shows two fallen stones lying across the verges of the road to Marlborough which are not indicated by Aubrey at all. Even were one able to judge only from his published plan E, it would appear that it may have been Stukeley who was inaccurate here. Unless stone 73 was still standing in Aubrey's time but fallen in Stukeley's, Aubrey would presumably have looked over or through the hedge in which the stone was lying, to see into the road. He is presumably also likely to have walked along the road to carry out his surveying. In addition, it seems unlikely that two stones fallen not far from the middle of the road would have been left there for long to hinder travellers. Confirmation of our suspicions is provided by Stukeley's 'tour' of the site (Appendix II) (also incidentally again revealing the shortcomings of his decision to rely on the Frontispiece as the main method of communication and recording). This makes it clear that the two stones shown in plan E as fallen and *in situ*, were assumed stones only, for he writes that they were 'no doubt thrown into the ditch when they filld it up to make this road' (Appendix II). In strange contrast, draft plan T shows these two stones in the road as actually standing – which can only suggest that, in this draft plan at least, Stukeley's intention was to restore the site, in some details, to its assumed original state.

We have to conclude that Stukeley's plan E rendition at the N entrance is itself problematic. Thus he says of stones 48 and 49 that their places were 'great hollows', fragments 'of the stones ... tumbled into the ditch to make the north entrance', whereas they can in fact be seen (once one knows what to look for) on plan E, both clearly indicated as present but fallen (see also Plates 43 and 64, Gough Maps 231, 218 and 326). All this abundantly confirms that Stukeley's views on Abury from the north (Plate 43) were based on the assumption that this entrance, like the eastern, was a modern one (and see section j above). Thus Stukeley's presumption that there were only two ancient causewayed entrances led to his not only surmising but actually depicting stones which may never have existed.

We now come to a further possible source of confusion within Stukeley's own records, in the form of an example of what appears to be a field boundary change between the time of compilation of Stukeley's written 'tour' (Appendix II) and draft plan S on the one hand, and plan E on the other – unless it is a simple case of inaccuracy or engraver's error. Accepting the two standing stones shown in plan E and version S in this quadrant as Smith's 1965 stones 50 and 68, plan E shows a hedge boundary between hollows 53 and 54, while the tour speaks of – and draft plan S indicates – a group of three 'vacancys in a little grip under the hedg ... [before, moving E–W] we come to the VI pasture' (i.e. pasture V of plan E): in addition, whereas both plans are agreed in all details regarding positions 68–59, 57, 56 and 50–52, the position of hollow 58 on plan E is left as a gap on draft plan S (and is said to have been a vacancy in the 'tour' (Transparency 19)).

Attempts to correlate stone recordings on the basis of pasture and other divisions shown in Aubrey'a plan A and Stukeley's plan E (Transparencies 1 and 2) may therefore be liable to error. The possible inaccuracy of plan E – or the changing nature of boundaries over time – is apparently confirmed by plan E's representation of stone 72's position as 'the place of a stone taken away' from within pasture VI, whereas the 'tour' (Appendix II) appears to place stone 72 under a hedge, with trees growing on it.

Unfortunately, the field bank running W–E along the inner perimeter of the outer circle in this area (Plates 52 and 67, and see section d above) – no doubt a continuation of the field boundary in the NW quadrant in which Stukeley and Keiller had remarked stones – has masked any resistivity responses for stones in Smith's 1965 positions 47–58.

Finally we must note that Smith (1965) appears to show one less stone in this area of the quadrant than does plan E. This is due to the fact that her tentative reconstruction of the circles (1965, fig. 70), in opting for a regularly spaced circle of stones (see Chapter V), takes no account of 17th- and 18th-century evidence for variable spacing.

u. South-east quadrant

In the SE quadrant, the situation we have found characteristic when comparing Aubrey's plan A and Stukeley is, in part, reversed. Of the nine stones which Aubrey shows in this quadrant in plan A, he records seven in an area where Stukeley has only three standing. Aubrey's 7 stones must, therefore, somehow correspond to Stukeley's plan E total of three standing stones in this area of the quadrant, four 'place[s] of a Stone taken away', two 'Cavit[ies] visible where a Stone stood', and one 'stone fallen'. These ten Stukeley stones and stone positions should probably equate with Smith's 1965 stones 1 and 90–98, but we must remember that all are in an area where there has been no excavation, and Smith's regular, circular arrangement for these stone positions is simply a suggestion.

Given the apparent accuracy of Aubrey's plan B at various other observed points, and despite the fact that it appears to be much more grossly distorted than plan A in this quadrant, we cannot afford to ignore the fact that it shows the same number of stones in this quadrant as does plan A, although in B they are much more evenly distributed, so as possibly to conform to something like every second stone in Smith's 1965 distribution 98–75/74.

On the basis of this evidence, it is difficult to reconstruct the events which could have resulted in such different recordings. Comparison of Transparencies 1, 2 and 18 clearly highlights the problems for interpretation: without further information, Aubrey's plans A and B and Stukeley's plan E appear mutually contradictory.

Aubrey's plan A (Transparency 1) seems so specific in its indication that there were no stones in the outer circle within Stukeley's 'Pasture VIII' and most of Stukeley's 'Pasture VII' (Transparency 2), that it is difficult to conceive that the apparent correspondence between this plan A distribution and the plan E record of stones 'Demolished by Tom Robinson' should be fortuitous. But this apparent congruence of record creates several problems. If Aubrey's plan A was accurate in this area of the SE quadrant, Stukeley's reiterated information about these particular stones being removed in 1700 must have been erroneous – clearly they would have had to have been removed by 1663. However, Aubrey's plan B (Transparency 18) adds a further complication since it appears to depict stones which could reasonably be taken to equate with Smith's 1965 positions around stones 79–89. This can only be explained as being due to it being schematic, perhaps attempting to reconstruct the original state of the antiquity, conceivably on the basis of local oral history about Smith's stones 79–89.

In assessing Stukeley's record, we again have the 'tour' and draft plans to turn to, and these again cast doubt on the reliability of Stukeley's published plan E. The text (Appendix II; Transparency 19) makes no mention of the first stone shown as a 'vacancy' in the hedge between plan E's pastures VIII and VII, but it does agree with plan E that there was a lying stone thereabouts (Smith's 1965 stone position 88 on plan E: i.e. Smith's position 89 in the textual version when counting from standing stone 98; and Smith's stone 89 position on E (or 90 in the 'tour' version) when counting from standing stone 68 (since the 'tour' has one additional stone position between Smith's standing stones 98 and 68)). It is from about here that Aubrey's plan A starts its long stretch without stones while plan B continues with a regular stone distribution. Fascinatingly, Stukeley's unpublished text appears to show up a double change of mind when compared with plan E: '9 [del.] < 10 > of them all contiguous on the south eastern side, were destroyd by one man < Tho. Robinson > in the year 1700 their places perfectly leveld', while plan E (and versions Q, R, V, W and X) revert to nine (dots) 'Demolished by Tom Robinson AD 1700'. Further scrutiny of the variant plans casts doubt on the reliability of any particular figure for this series of vacancies: draft plan N shows twelve vacancies (without giving a date), S shows nine vacancies but writes in the number ten, draft plans O, P and T show eight vacancies (and are the only ones not providing Robinson's name), while the actual measurements recorded by Stukeley (Plate 15 and Transparency 20) appear to deal with only seven vacancies.

Such variations could have occurred on the basis of observation alone, but it would seem more than likely – in the context of the evidence in Chapter II – that Stukeley was simultaneously influenced by a need to ensure the right number of stones in the 'Outer circle' to conform to his idealized concept of such prehistoric monuments. Hence his exact numbers must be treated with caution. In addition, the possibility remains that Stukeley's oral history was wrong, and that destruction of these stones – whatever their number – might equally well, in fact, have taken place prior to 1663.

We next come to a highly controversial stone. Moving further NE towards the E road, plans E and version X show an apparently leaning standing stone, followed by a fallen one – presumably corresponding to Smith's 1965 78, and 77 or 79. Draft plan R (which has three more stone positions in this area than does Smith 1965) shows stone 78 (counting from standing stone 98) as a (hatched) rectangle but it appears to have been crossed out and is accompanied by the word 'leaning'; this is followed (in Smith's position 77) by another hatched rectangle, this time with 'leaning' crossed out and 'f' (fallen) substituted. Draft plan S (with the same number of stones in this area as Smith 1965) has a crossed-out hatched rectangle – acompanied by the word 'vacancy' – which is in Smith's 1965 stone position 80, with a hatched rectangle captioned 'leaning' in Smith's position 79. Draft plan W (also with the same number of stones in this area as Smith 1965) shows a fallen stone in position 78; draft plan V (with one more stone than Smith) also has a fallen stone at position 78 (counting from standing stone 68); draft plan Q (with three more stones than Smith) has a fallen stone in this same position 78 (but counting from standing stone 98). In draft plans O and possibly P (with one less stone in this area than Smith) a fallen stone is also shown in position 79, counting from standing stone 68, while draft plans V (with one more stone in the area than Smith) and Q again (with three more stones than Smith), have a fallen stone shown in position 77 when counting from standing stone 98.

It is obviously tempting to assume a chronological sequence in these records, from standing, to leaning, to fallen stone (Smith's 78, as still visible in 1936), were it not for the fact that in Stukeley's 'tour' (Appendix II) stone 78 (counting from stone 98) appears as supposedly the tenth stone destroyed by Robinson (this text, as we have seen, only belatedly deciding on ten stones rather than nine). Whether or not part of all this confusion came about because a stone in Smith's position 78 was, indeed, a leaning stone which subsequently fell, is a matter of conjecture. What does seem clear is that Stukeley's variable record of this part of the SE outer circle derived, in part at least, from the confusion about the Robinson stones.

Happily we are, at this point, able to include archaeological evidence about stones supposedly demolished by Robinson: the probings and limited excavation made by Lukis and Smith in July and August 1881. They found eight stones in the area immediately S of Smith's position 78 or 79. However, they were obviously unable to provide information of the date of destruction. It seems incontrovertible, therefore, that if plans A and E were correct in showing no stones, plan B (unless after all, very early) was an idealized version indicating what Aubrey assumed to have been the original state of the monument, and that, in any case, Stukeley's local information was incorrect about date, destruction and name. Stukeley was, therefore, in a position allowing him maximum flexibility (or creating maximum uncertainty) in the number of stone positions which he could claim to exist to complete his desired number of 100 stones for his Outer Circle (see Chapter II, iv).

We must now return to the S part of this SE quadrant in an attempt to clarify another apparent confusion on the published plan E. Our problems start with Aubrey's two most S stones, shown in plan A as clearly within one pasture (Smith's stones 1 and 98) – as opposed to the three (Smith's stones 1, 98, 97) shown within Stukeley's plan E pasture X (and several other draft plans), the stones on either side apparently standing within hedge boundaries. The first clue to a possible inaccuracy in plan E comes from tab. xii of Stukeley's *Abury*, where stones 1 and 98 are clearly shown within the same pasture – and not, in any way, part of hedges – with stone 97 clearly in the next pasture to the E. This latter displacement is confirmed in Stukeley's 1723 'A Prospect of Abury from the South Side of the Vallum' (Plate 44), in which stone 97 appears to be placed as far from any division between pastures IX and X as stone 98 is from stone 1. Tabs. xvi and xvii of *Abury* (cf. Plates 22 and 23) both also demonstrate that plan E is in error, as does version R, while this distribution is confirmed in the 'tour' (Appendix II), 'the two first stand in the first pasture, in the 2[n]d, the other', as well as by the pre-excavation record (Plate 53). Interestingly, a similar conclusion about the inaccuracy of this pasture division on plan E was arrived at independently by Crawford in his unpublished manuscript (Crawford MS.). So far, therefore, Aubrey's plan A (and probably B) and at least the bulk of *unpublished* Stukeley are in full agreement.

According to plan E (Transparency 2) pasture IX has a vacancy, followed by a visible cavity, followed by two more vacancies, while the unpublished 'tour' (Appendix II and Transparency 19) has two hollows, followed by a vacancy followed in turn by another vacancy near to railings. Despite the difference in details here, the number of stone placements is the same – and it is also identical with the three hollows and the vacancy that existed prior to excavation in the 1930s (Plate 52). If we are to accept the evidence presented in plan A, it seems that Aubrey's first four recorded stones going N in this pasture must all have been destroyed prior to Stukeley's record: although perhaps unlikely, this is clearly not impossible.

Pasture VIII, according to plan E, has a fallen stone, followed by a vacancy and then a hollow, with another vacancy in the dividing hedge to pasture VII. The unpublished 'tour' (Appendix II) reports that the first stone in its pasture III (pasture VIII of plan E) 'was standing when I was first here but now three vacancys perfectly leveld'. This tallies with Aubrey's plan A (and possibly B) – though plan A omits the pasture boundary between IX and VIII – since the former clearly shows the standing stone which only fell after Stukeley's first visit to Avebury. The Stukeley evidence, however, appears, once again, to be both complex and possibly self-contradictory. Using the interpretation of Stukeley's symbols set out earlier, we can say that four draft plans (S, V, W and X) show the first stone as fallen, as does plan E; two (Q and T) shows it standing, as may others (N, O and P); while version R indicates a stone which has been subsequently deleted (thus providing a perfect fit to the written description, quoted above). We may, therefore, here have evidence that Stukeley was, at different times, recording different stages in the preservation of the monument.

Encouragingly, all plans, as well as the 'tour' (Appendix II), agree that the second position was a 'vacancy'. However, here the unanimity ends: plan E's third hollow position is confirmed by draft plans W and X (and possibly V), but contradicted by the vacancy shown on draft plans O, P, Q, R and T (and possibly draft plan N, if the depiction there of a fallen stone has been corrected by a 'v'? (for vacancy)). (Draft plan S remains ambiguous with regard to this third position, showing either a vacancy or a hollow.) At least two points are clearly confirmed by this – first, plan E does not fit Stukeley's written 'tour' of the stones (Appendix II); second, Stukeley's record of the stones is particularly variable for this part of the site.

Geophysical examination of this area of the SE quadrant (Plate 66) has revealed clearly distinguishable buried stones or burning pits in the area of Smith's stone positions 88–92 and 97. One of these (perhaps Smith's 1965 stone position 91, which was a visible depression in 1936), appears to have been located by probing by Smith and Lukis in 1882 (Lukis 1881–3a, 153); it also presented a significant resistivity response in our survey. The area around Smith's proposed stone position 92 did not show up in 1936 but was also positively probed by Lukis and it also gave a significant resistivity response.

As we have seen, Smith's idealized reconstruction (1965, fig. 70) was based on the presumption that the stones were regularly spaced as well as being placed a regular distance away from the ditch. It is not possible, because of the nature and resolution of the 17th- and 18th-century plans, to calculate such distances and spacings to the required accuracy to allow comparisons to be made. It therefore becomes tempting simply to assume a correlation between the two farthest N of the outer stones in this quadrant, and the spacing between them on both Aubrey's plans A and B, with the only two visible (fallen) stones recorded by Keiller (1939, fig. facing p. 224). However, to do so would demand a much greater distance between these stones (Smith's 1965 nos. 77 and 78) than apparently existed. It would obviously be more convenient if they could be matched with the Stukeley's one standing (Smith's 77) and one fallen stone (Smith's 88) which Stukeley records in this area, but to do so would imply that stone 88 had been plotted by Stukeley much too far to the S while, in any case, he has shown it as being located near a 'hedge'.

In conclusion, therefore, the evidence of this quadrant confirms not only that Stukeley's published record was anything but infallible, but also suggests that the physical condition of the stones of the Avebury monument could indeed have changed drastically over certain very short periods of time.

At least parts of Aubrey's plan A – and perhaps surprisingly of plan B also – could be as accurate as anything of Stukeley's record. As before, we are left with doubts about the status of plan B, which sometimes appears to represent the monument at a different stage in its destruction from plan A, though it remains impossible to be sure that such occasional 'accuracies' on plan B – especially when, as in this quadrant, apparently incompatible with plan A – were not merely coincidental.

Inner circles

w. Southern circle(s)

Charleton's plan D and Aubrey's plans A and B all indicate one inner S circle, while Stukeley shows *two* concentric ones, focused on a circular stone 21 ft high and 8 ft 9 ins in diameter (the Obelisk) which was apparently already recumbent when he did his recording work.

Smith's 'tentative reconstruction of the Avebury Circles' (1965, fig. 70) also shows a clear S circle of 29 stones (nos. 101–129), and, within it, the Obelisk, pits, stones i–xii in a rectangular arrangement, with an isolated stone D in the S (Transparency 21). Basing herself on the results of the 1939 excavations (Chapman 1939, 11), Smith dismisses the possibility that stone D originally formed part of a second internal S circle as claimed by Stukeley (Smith 1965, 198–9) (Transparency 22).

At first sight, the differences in detail between the S 'circles' in Aubrey's plans A (Transparency 4), B (Transparency 23), and Charleton's D are more striking than any common features, particularly when compared with Smith's (1965) ideal S inner circle (Transparency 21). However, closer investigation shows such a view to be oversimplified. Thus, it is true that both Charleton, and Aubrey in plan A, record the 'circle' as consisting of 13 stones: but in plan A these make up only one 'segment' of a 'circle', whereas Aubrey's plan B, which shows only one less stone, is, like Charleton's, the representation of a *complete* circle. Smith's hypothetical 29 stones apparently coincide with Stukeley's claimed 30 stones (Transparency 22) for the S *outer* ring, while Aubrey's plan A and Charleton's record are close to Stukeley's complete proposed S *inner* ring of 12 stones.

The potential significance of this information in terms of interpretation is strikingly demonstrated by Crawford's discussion of – and subsequent inference from – Aubrey's plan A record in his unpublished Avebury MS.: having concluded to his own satisfaction that Aubrey intended 15, rather than 12, stones in the S circle, he continued:

> Three others which he shows *may* have belonged to this circle: two of them, in the NE quadrant near the barn, almost certainly did belong to it. If so, the number shown by Aubrey (14) would agree exactly with that given by Stukeley, but some of them certainly did not.

If Burl's 1979, Table I, measurements are used, Aubrey's plans A and B are at first sight strikingly similar in their inaccurate depiction of the S circle, showing it as much too small in diameter (205 ft in plan A) to fit either Stukeley's outer circle (Burl, 416 ft; corrected to c.330 ft (see Chapter III, E.8)) or Smith's reconstruction of it (340 ft). On the other hand, it would be wrong simply to assume that these were renderings of Stukeley's inner circle (173 ft; corrected to c.138 ft); rather, we must attempt to compensate for the distortions resulting from the plan A plane-table survey (see Chapter III, A.15) – as we have done in Transparency 5 – and see what conclusion can be drawn from this. This survey may also have been the basis of the plan B depiction, at least so far as its irregular shape is concerned, even though we have discovered that several stone positions in plan B are unlikely to have derived directly, or exclusively, from plan A.

To compare Aubrey's plan A in detail with the archaeological evidence, it is necessary to convert it to the size of Smith's (1965) plan (Transparency 5). It may then be oriented in various ways. One achieves a good fit both because its SE external features and Smith's pits 122 and 124–7, and between Aubrey's most S stone (outside the 'circle') and Stukeley's 'ring-stone' (confirmed by excavation in 1939: Smith 1965, 202–3) (Transparency 21). There is also a close fit with the W arc of the 'outer circle', including all but two of the standing stones and stone holes known from that area (101–109/110), but including also one stone which has not been excavated. If Aubrey is indeed accurate in this part of plan A, it is important to note that he has also recorded the position of two stones, either of which could be candidates for stone D. However, plan A does not show these two stones forming part of a second internal S circle and thus gives no support to Stukeley's claim for stone D. On the other hand, in this rendition of the S circle in plan A at the same size as Smith's (1965), most of the other stones here recorded by Aubrey do not seem to have been recorded by others; the excavated stones i–xii seem to have been totally unremarked by Aubrey, except possibly for stone xi or x, the former apparently being visible as a hollow before the 1936 excavation.

In addition, when one examines Aubrey's plan A at this size, the most immediately notable of its internal features is also its most obvious discrepancy with Charleton's plan D – the absence of (or lack of any special emphasis on) the Obelisk. This could be explained simply in terms of the failure of plan A to distinguish the relative sizes of different stones (see above), just as there is nothing in this plan to distinguish the 'ring-stone' morphologically from any others. But on this orientation of the plan no stone equivalent to the Obelisk appears to be shown in the correct position.

These problems force us to consider an alternative, namely that the S circle in plan A was in fact depicted at a correct scale. At Aubrey's own scale (Transparency 4) it is almost possible to locate the 'Obelisk' and also stone D (cf. Transparencies 21 and 4); on the other hand, the result sets all the other stones in the plan grossly askew, most particularly those which form the E arc of the circle (the only possible exception to this is stone position 129).

Comparison of Stukeley (Transparency 22) with plan A at Aubrey's own scale (Transparency 4) fails to produce any support for Stukeley's inner ring, with only Smith's 1965 stone D falling into place (although on the wrong side of the hedge). Aubrey's plan B (Transparency 23) provides no assistance in the interpretation of plan A in this segment, as it simply picks up the roughly circular shape of this single S arrangement of stones and refrains from including anything at all within it. If any reliance was placed on it in this instance, it would indicate either that Aubrey had noticed neither the Obelisk nor stone D, or that he thought them part of the circle. But plan B does seem to confirm that neither the three N stones, nor the four in the E–W road, of plan A were seen by Aubrey as forming part of the SE quadrant's stone arrangements: the latter four are, indeed, actually part of the N inner circle.

Prior to excavations in 1936, only stones 101 and 103 were still standing (Smith 1965, fig. 67): this is confirmed by all Stukeley's records which distinguish standing from other stones. With two exceptions, they all also indicate both 'stone D' and the 'ring stone'. One exception is draft plan N which, while indicating three further standing stones (Smith's 1965 125, 126 and 129), shows very little detail of the S circle, most noticeably omitting the Obelisk. The other exception is draft plan T which shows both the ring stone and the Obelisk (in pencil) but not 'stone D': like draft plan N, it gives little detail of the S circle, but it indicates four further standing stones (Smith's 1965, 102, 105, 106 and 107). All of the other draft plans which distinguish standing from other stones depict at least one of these further standing stones (draft plan Q – 102; draft plans R, S, V, W, X and plan E – 125 and 126).

We are confronted, therefore, with a strange record whereby draft plan N is in agreement with most of the others as to which stones were standing, but is unique in also including stone 129, while version Q is exceptional in showing only three standing, one of which is stone 102. Curiously, Stukeley's measured drawing (Plate 15 and Transparency 20) – which does not differentiate standing from fallen stones – records eight, in adition to 'Stone D' and the 'ring stone', including stones 102, 105 and 106 (all three shown as standing in draft plan T, and still visible as fallen stones in 1936), but not 129. Fallen stones 104, 105 and 106 may be included on draft plans O, P and N and are certainly shown on all other draft plans, except plan Q (and version T, unless one can assume displacement of stones whereby the three shown as standing on this draft plan should be equated with positions 104, 105 and 106 rather than with 105, 106 and 107). Despite the written 'tour' being imperfectly preserved with regard to the S circle, it appears to confirm the presence of several of the above stones (Transparency 19).

Can some of the apparent disparity again be ascribed to inadequacies in Stukeley's record? One way to approach this problem is through the evidence of pasture boundaries, particularly in this quadrant, where the change in the alignment of fence and trees around the Obelisk in plan E was not corroborated by the pre-excavation 1936 record of this area of the site. In fact, the layout of the pastures, and the numbers of stones in each, constitute one of the chief differences between Aubrey and Stukeley in this area, the former showing eight stones of the S circle clearly within pasture X, while the latter shows eight and a stone position in the hedge. As with the stones of the outer ring in this pasture – and as independently confirmed in Crawford's unpublished study (Crawford MS.) – Stukeley's published plan E seems again to be in error. The unpublished 'tour' makes it clear that Smith's 1965 stone 101 has been wrongly placed in this pasture by Stukeley's engraving; in fact it stood in pasture IX (Appendix II). The placement of Smith's 1965 107, 106, 105 and 102 (all fallen), and 103 (standing) are all happily confirmed both by the unpublished text and by analysis of various of Stukeley's detailed drawings (e.g. Stukeley 1743, tabs. xvi, xvii) (Plates 22 and 23). Even the location corresponding to Smith's position 104 (a pre-excavation hollow) can be seen in Stukeley's tab. xvi to have been empty. Given that Aubrey's plan A and unpublished Stukeley records agree in the number of stones in pasture X, and that their locations can be well matched at Aubrey's unaltered scale (Transparency 4), the interpretation of plan A in terms of this unaltered scale could well become the preferred one (despite the remaining problems already referred to).

The relocation of the boundary on plan E so that Smith's stone 101 is clearly situated in pasture IX necessitates moving either the boundary or the position of standing stone 126 – still within pasture IX – towards the boundary between pastures IX–VIII, with standing stone 125 more or less on the boundary with pasture VIII. All these adjustments are clearly justified both by Stukeley's 'tour' and by various of his drawings.

Stukeley's *Abury* departs from its normal practice of largely refraining from written description when it comes to the N arc of the circle, echoing the unpublished text concerning all the stones supposedly incorporated in, or destroyed by, houses or a barn (i.e. Smith's 1965 110–119). Both texts contradict the accompanying general statement that 'but [the unpublished text says, 'about'] fourteen [stones] are still left, whereof about half standing' (Stukeley 1743, 24): in fact, both describe only four recumbent stones. Curiously, *Abury* combines its version with the observation that many of these stones had been destroyed twelve years earlier by a farmer called John Fowler who confirmed that he had himself burnt five of them: the 'tour' restricts a similar remark about them – 'several have been destroyed 12 and 13 ys ago <John Fowler avowed he burnt 5 of them>' – to the supposed (twelve) stones making up Stukeley's inner S circle (Appendix II).

As is well known, Stukeley's claim for an inner circle actually depended on only one (confirmed) stone, shown clearly by him in plan E in the NW corner of pasture IX (Transparency 2): This also appears as a small stone firmly within pasture IX on all except one (N) of his draft frontispieces, in several of his drawings (e.g. Plates 22, 23, 44) and in his 'tour' (Transparency 19), which explicitly remarks on this circle: 'Whereof at present only one standing'. Smith (1965, 198–9), however, advances arguments to suggest that Stukeley must not only have confused various oral accounts but also have wrongly located the stone. Although we have seen many examples of Stukeley's inconsistencies and inaccuracies, Smith's interpretation has several points against it, not least that, as Stukeley repeatedly indicated, the stone he depicted was not in that part of pasture IX, on the border with pasture X, where Smith wanted to locate it as stone 'D' (cf. Transparencies 21 and 22). Furthermore, Stukeley's unpublished statement (Appendix II) that his pictured stone was 7½ celtic rods from the Obelisk fits closely with its planned distance of c.21 metres from the latter stone, also shown in his measurement plan (Plates 15 and Transparency 20), in contrast to Smith's location for stone D of c.39 metres. It would seem much likelier that Stukeley never saw or recorded Smith's stone D, which before excavation was apparently only represented by a hollow.

The unnamed stone (which Stukeley thought had formed part of an inner, S circle) in fact fits perfectly with the locations of ix, x or xi (Smith 1965) (Transparencies 21, 22), one of which, as we have noted in our discussion of Aubrey's plan, was a pre-excavation hollow. As described and reconstructed by Smith (1965, 199), the history of the burial, destruction and/or burning of these and the other small stones (i–viii) in the area – the position of at least one of which appears to have been visible as a pre-excavation hollow – is complex and somewhat difficult to follow. It seems far from improbable that one of these stones remained standing in Stukeley's time and was depicted by him on his engravings (Plates 22, 23) in its correct location (as was also assumed by Crawford (MS., 13)). It is also conceivable that Stukeley might have taken some of the pre-excavation hollows (Transparency 3) to form part of his claimed S inner circle, although the positions do not match exactly (Transparencies 21 and 22).

This raises the possibility, therefore, that Aubrey's plan A – at Aubrey's own scale (see above, and Transparency 4) – may also have been recording Stukeley's unnamed stone, Smith's 1965 stone D, or the pre-excavation hollows, in addition to any other of the group of small stones i–xi which might still have been standing at that time (although it may be worth noting that the pre-excavation hollows to the N of the Obelisk (Transparency 3) seem to be in an area which Aubrey leaves devoid of stones).

In attempting to weigh up the nature and quality of Stukeley's evidence for one, or even two inner S circles, it is impossible to forget the evidence presented in Chapter II for Stukeley's preconceived expectations of finding double circles of stones. These expectations clearly were in part based on the evidence of stones that we know did exist. As we have seen, almost all Stukeley's plans record those standing and fallen stones of both 'circles' which we know were still visible in 1936. However, it is almost impossible to ignore the inconsistency of his further 'evidence' for the outer of the suggested circles, as presented in plan E and the draft frontispieces – ranging from four standing and ten fallen (plan E, versions W and X), to four standing and eight fallen (version V), four standing and seven fallen (version S), four standing and five fallen (with four more standing or fallen) (version R), three standing and ten fallen (version Q), five standing and four definitely and three probably fallen (version N), or six standing (version T).

Many of the above considerations, as well as those involving the measurements of angles discussed in Chapter III, E.6–7, seem to come together when we move to the last of the stones in this area of the site – the so-called 'ring-stone'. Now that we have ascertained that archaeologists were wrong to have identified Smith's 1965 stone D with a stone recorded by Stukeley, we might conjecture that something similar may have occurred with regard to Stukeley's 'ring stone' – a name which, incidentally, it appears that he only inserted in ink onto draft frontispiece X (Plate 42) at the very last moment. Is it possible that Smith might be incorrect in accepting as Stukeley's 'ring-stone' a '"stump" found [in the 1939 excavation] between its stone-hole and burning-pit', placed in 'a rather deep hole', 'set at a high(er) level in order to display more prominently some features it possessed' (Smith 1965, 202–3)? Stukeley's own location of this 'odd stone standing, not of great bulk' (Stukeley 1743, 25) is, on the face of it, far removed from the archaeologically identified position. However, the apparent error in location is only so with regard to the location of the 'ring-stone' *vis-à-vis* the S circle which, as we have seen (cf. Transparencies 2 and 17) has been incorrectly located both on plan E and on all the other draft plans except O and T (these appear somewhat more accurate, especially in their placing of the circle in relation to the roads). Whether or not such erroneous locations make sense in terms of Stukeley's considerations in the summer of 1723 about the asymmetrical placing of his two inner temples (Chapter II, v) is unclear. However, when the 'ring-stones' in Transparencies 2 and 17 are matched, the bank/ditch and causeways fit almost perfectly. It seems probable, therefore, that the partial stone found in the excavations *is* Stukeley's belatedly named 'ring-stone': before excavation, it was apparent as a depression which Crawford (MS.) records as being 25 ft west of an extended line from the Cove to the Obelisk.

It would have been tempting to think that this stone might have been a relatively late discovery by Stukeley, since it is almost certainly absent from his 'tour' (Appendix II): however, it is clearly marked (albeit unnamed) standing as within pasture IX on all the draft frontispieces; most significantly, it is locatable in Stukeley's measurement plan (Plate 15 and Transparency 20).

Of the 'ring-stone', Stukeley wrote in *Abury*: 'Exactly in the southern end of the line that connects the two centers of these temples, *viz.* in that pasture mark'd IX in our ground-plot, is an odd stone standing, not of great bulk. It has a hole wrought in it, and probably was design'd to fasten the victim, in order for slaying it. This I call the *ring-stone*' (Stukeley 1743, 25) (Plates 22 and 23). Nowhere in either his unpublished or published work does Stukeley appear to have explicitly claimed this stone as a *second* survivor of his putative 'lesser Outside circle' (see section r above), though this identification is implicit in its location on the arc of the inner outer circle. But on draft plan X – on which the name 'Ring-stone' is added in ink (perhaps in handwriting of c.1730) – is added an ink line, linking this stone to the Cove (see section y below) via the Obelisk, a line which is not reproduced on published plan E. For whatever reasons, it seems as if Stukeley's early discovery of this stone had not made much impact on him; later, however, and apparently subsequent to both his initial and his revised opinions about the design of Avebury (Chapter II, v, vi), this particular stone became of immense significance – apparently in the context of his incorporation of sacrifice into his overall view of activities on the site. How else to explain Stukeley's published statement about this stone, considering that he had written earlier of the 'Inner circle' stone (Stukeley 1722–4b, 129), 'I dont wonder so much at the 99 which are gone as at the poor one remaining ... which certainly has the honour to preserve the memory of the rest ... Some perhaps may say it was a stone necessary in their sacrifices, it might be a god or twenty such meagre suppositions, which are not worth answering as mere trifles, altogether abhorrent of the Noble Majesty of this Work'. Without doubt we are here witness to a fresh reinterpretation by a man who had already been forced to re-think his whole approach to his chosen subject (see Chapter II, v, vi).

This also explains a disjunction between published Frontispiece (plan E) and the published text concerning Stukeley's outer 'Inner circle'. Though marked, as we have seen earlier, on all draft frontispieces except T – albeit, on version P, most curiously positioned with the 'ring-stone' where the S circle would have been expected to be – and although championed as an originally complete circle of stones that formed an integral part of a narrative (Chapter II,vi) – it receives no recognition in the text of *Abury*. The only possible reference in *Abury* to a double outer circle might conceivably be Stukeley's use of the word 'colonnade' (Stukeley 1743, 25), as Crawford has perceptively pointed out (Crawford MS.). Yet, though frustratingly imperfect, it is clear from Stukeley's earlier text (Appendix II) that he then thought in terms of a 'circular Colonnade', clearly referring in his 'tour' to an 'inner circle of 100 lesser Stones' whose width – *as demonstrated by the ring stone* – he notes as 60 celtic feet,

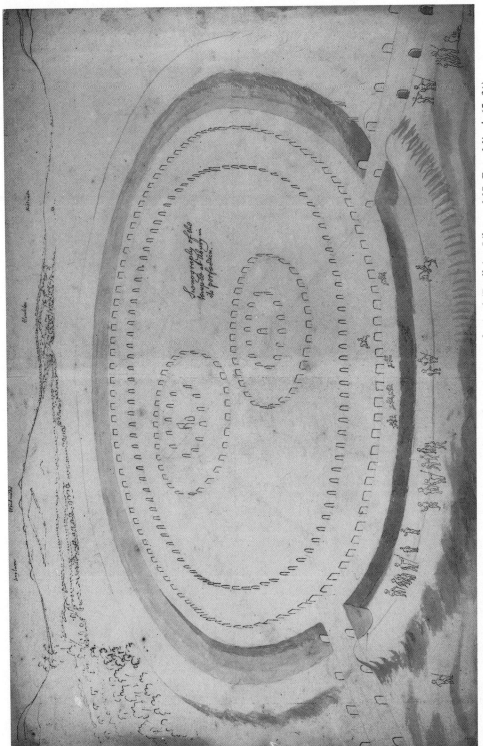

Plate 65 Stukeley's drawing of 'Scenography of the temple at Abury in its perfection' (Bodleian Library MS. Eng. Misc.b.65, 31).

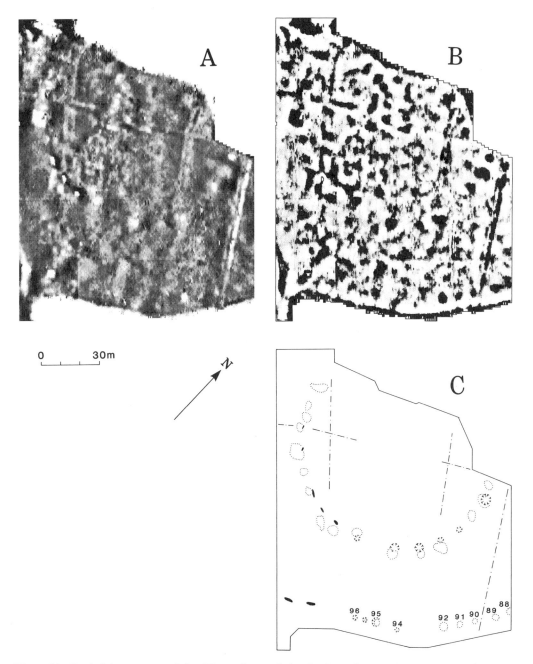

Plate 66 Resistivity survey of the SE quadrant of the Avebury henge: (A) grey-tone plot; (B) negative plot of (A); (C) interpretation: Key: —·— old field (pasture) boundaries; ▲ standing stones; ✿ extant depressions; ◌ selected resistivity anomalies.

and which he thus takes to be a continuation of the similarly dimensioned Kennet Avenue (cf. Plate 65).

Finally, we must return briefly to the question of Aubrey and the 'ring-stone'. The partial fit between its archaeological location and one of the stones shown on plan B, when other features of the monument in this rendition are matched, could, presumably, be coincidental. But this seems less likely to be the case for Aubrey's plan A (Transparency 5), when its size is adjusted to that of Smith's and both sides of the arc of the circle are matched (Transparency 21), whereby the 'ring-stone' is in the correct place.

In connection with these analyses and the problems involved in reconciling them, a resistivity survey (Plate 66) was carried out over some two-thirds of the S circle, containing the arc of Smith's 1965 stone settings 101–109 and c.121–129 (Transparency 21). High resistivity values, although irregularly placed, might be referable to stones 121, 122, 123, 125, 126, 127 and 129. Other anomalies can be seen close to stone settings 101–108, and are presumably indicative of related pits and/or excavations. Although resistivity anomalies are present throughout the survey data, it is not possible to discriminate with any confidence between those reflecting possible prehistoric features and those which are natural or spurious. This SE quadrant is more 'noisy' or disturbed by superficial interference than is the case in the NE quadrant (see section x below). The area excavated by Keiller and found to be largely devoid of features now demonstrates a range of resistivity anomalies similar to most of the remainder of the survey plot (Plate 66). No Obelisk setting is discernible, and pits and post-holes seem to be entirely elusive. In particular, there is thus no confirmation of Stukeley's assertion that five stones of the S inner circle were destroyed by burning by John Fowler (Appendix II).

The whole of this area of the site therefore continues to be an enigma, conceivably all the more so if a very recent discovery of a possible prehistoric stone setting (Hawkes, Heaton and Trott 1989) were to be confirmed. Located in the N area of the S circle, such a stone position could even re-open questions regarding the exact relationship between the circle and the Obelisk.

x. Northern circle(s)

Smith's (1965, fig. 70) 'tentative reconstruction of the Avebury Circles' (Transparency 24) clearly shows a N circle of 27 stones (nos. 201–227) surrounding the three Cove stones (I–III), with three more, scattered, stones to the N and E of the Cove (E, F, G). In an addendum, Smith reports the finding of a burning pit SSE of the Cove (Transparency 24: 1964): she takes this as confirmation of Stukeley's second concentric and internal circle, relying for its circumference on this new stone position and stones F and perhaps G (Smith 1965, 223). On this reading, only stone E, probably 'three small individual stones buried in a communal pit' (Smith 1965, 202), is off the perimeter of any circle.

As noted in Chapter III, A.14, it is not obvious from plan A alone (Transparency 26) that the four stones in the E–W road were supposed to form part of a N circle around the Cove. However, now that we have concluded on the basis of plan B that they undoubtedly must have done, Aubrey's plan A (Transparency 26) – taken in conjunction with plan B (which has 17–18 stones) (Transparency 25; see discussion, above) – could be interpreted as showing one circle of 16 stones around the Cove. This is a configuration that has already received support from our analysis of the S circle (Transparency 23). Neither Aubrey's plan C, nor Charleton's, shows any circle, while plan E shows two, supposedly with thirty and twelve stones respectively (Stukeley 1743, 37) (Transparency 27).

It is worth noting parenthetically that Aubrey apparently did not intend any archaeological discrimination, in his plan A, between oblong-with-dots stones and others, since the only reason why he should have sought to distinguish these particular four stones would seem to have been to emphasize that, unlike others, they lay in the road.

Comparison of the depiction of those particular stones and their locations in plan A and plan E simultaneously casts light on the reliability of both (or, in the latter case, of Stukeley's local informants). Stukeley shows four stone positions in the road here, the westernmost being immediately within the S end of the N road: this is presumably the stone 'at the corner of the lane', mentioned earlier in this chapter as having been 'us'd as a stall to lay fish on'. Aubrey, on the other hand, nowhere depicts or mentions such a corner stone, and in any case a direct equation between his four and Stukeley's can be made only at the cost of debiting Aubrey with a formidable eastward displacement of his westernmost stone. The next stone E of Stukeley's four in the road is said by him to have been taken away in 1711. While in its proximity to the junction with the N road it appears not to correspond to any of Aubrey's four, the combined evidence of plans A and B (together with Stukeley's first sketch plan of Avebury dated May 1719 – Plate 11) persuades us to view it as the westernmost of Aubrey's. The first of Stukeley's stones, which he reports as a 'stone fallen', is on the very edge of the road – immediately following one said by him to have been removed in 1694 – this is also the first of these stones to be described in Stukeley's unpublished 'tour', where it is said to have been 'lying at the Inn gate most obvious to Strangers: tho' many a slash has been given it & great peices knocked off yet tis of a vast bulk' (Appendix II). This is presumably Aubrey's easternmost stone in the road. Given that Stukeley was clearly reliant on oral history for locating three of the four, Aubrey's positioning of these stones should in principle take precedence.

Aubrey's plan B (Transparency 25), enlarged to the same size as his plan A, matches the regular disposition of the N circle postulated by Smith (1965) (Transparency 24; see also Chapter V): it is even possible to make a good match with the only two standing stones in the circle (201, 206), though only by assuming that the Cove stones are displaced and by ignoring the details of other stones, whether burnt, fallen or assumed. Any such circular regularity is, however, belied by plan A (Transparency 26) when it is drawn to the same scale as Smith's idealized picture of Avebury (1965, fig. 70) (Transparency 24). If the Cove stones are taken as the matching points, five stone positions can be equated with other evidence: 219 (for which Stukeley gives a date for stone taken away), 222 (a Stukeley standing stone confirmed by resistivity), 223 and 209 (Stukeley fallen stones) and 207 (an extant stone, shown prostrate by Stukeley) – but only with pasture divisions and roads significantly out of place. If one ignores the position of the Cove stones and takes stones 201, 222, and 106, the N road and the pasture boundaries as the matching points, the position of most of the arc of the proposed circle is relatively good – but the S stones are far too far to the S, and the W ones depart at a tangent. Perhaps, therefore, the stone arrangements were not a regular circle at all.

This would certainly help to make sense of the fact that some observers completely missed this feature. The most obvious discrepancy between Charleton's plan D and Aubrey's plan A is Charleton's failure to note a N circle surrounding the Cove: it is possible to argue that Charleton, in this area of the site, was the less observant of the two, and that having picked up its most prominent feature – the Cove – he simply overlooked other stones there. But this does suggest that a distinctive circle of stones, let alone two as claimed by Stukeley, was not immediately obvious on the basis of a simple visit to the site. That this was so seems also to be confirmed by the evidence reviewed above of Aubrey's plan A, although it is apparently contradicted by his more or less circular depiction in plan B.

When we turn to Stukeley's record of stones which were still visible in 1936 (201 and 206 standing, and 207 and 210 fallen), all his plans except draft plan N conform to the record, as does his measured plan (Plate 15 and Transparency 20) (though versions O, P and R fail to indicate whether stones are standing or fallen), except that on version Q stone position 207 is indicated by a dot instead of the normal faintly or partially filled rectangle (while draft plan U fails to indicate stone 210 because it is incomplete). The exception is version N which fails to show any stone E (or F), indicates 210 as a vacancy and appears to record stone 207 as standing, but of a peculiar, small shape. The written 'tour' confirms the other versions.

It is interesting to note that, whereas we might have assumed from the pre-excavation record of 1936 alone (Gray 1935, 109; Crawford MS.), that Smith's 1965 stone E would have been one of the stones that were visible to Stukeley, in fact Stukeley's 'tour' tells of his having 'observd one Star-light night that the stone standing in the lesser circle of the temple before the Cove looking over that standing by the hedg side the most northerly ... of the outer circle points directly to the northpole star' (Appendix II): this suggests that it might rather have been Smith's 1965 stone F (together with stone 201) that he saw (cf. Plates 43 and 71).

It must be said, however, that Stukeley's record – both published and unpublished – is at its most confusing in this NE quadrant. Even allowing for the four stones in the road, already discussed, the stone positions indicated on plan E number 29, instead of the 30 claimed in Stukeley's published text. Fortunately, the draft frontispieces confirm that the missing stone position – equivalent to Smith's 1965 no. 205 – is likely to be located behind a tree on plan E. Even so, there is further discrepancy in the various versions of the record, especially in the N area to the E of the N road (and see below) where – according to Smith's 1965 assumed spacing of stones – there would appear to be at least three stone positions too many. It is important to realize that we are here concerned with only four actual stones supposedly fallen, several of the other presumed positions being covered by Stukeley's statement in his 'tour': 'Many taken up 1717' (a date also marked on plan E). There is, however, no mention in the 'tour' of the dot-position on plan E apparently showing a stone lying on a verge within the N road.

In view of all this uncertainty, and in order to try to assess the quality of the oral information given to Stukeley, we decided to look in detail at Stukeley's records for the area around Smith's 1965 stones 201, 227–212. This area was also of particular interest in the light of an unpublished claim that a 'sarsen burning pit' had been found 'in Red Lion Yard July 1973' (Vatcher MS.). Ostensibly, this is to be equated with Smith's 1965 stone 213, but this would put it much too far SE, so her stone position 217 seems likelier, in a position close to Stukeley's 1714 date on plan E. In Stukeley's 'tour' (Appendix II) he says that a stone adjacent to a hollow created in 1715 had been 'demolisht since last year', and that many other stones in this area had been destroyed in 1717. When this information is compared with plan E, the '1715' hollow appears to become '1717', 'last year' appears to be 1715, and the 'hollow, vacancy and two hollows' of the written record have all been transferred into 'cavities', supposedly with stones taken away in 1719. As we have seen, plan E also records a further stone removed in 1714.

None of the dates referred to are many years prior to Stukeley's first fieldwork (Chapter I, viii); they are found (in various combinations) on all except two or three of the draft frontispieces – only draft frontispiece R standing out markedly, with a date of 1723 being added (in later handwriting) to the fallen stone which in other plans is marked 1715. It is tempting to match this inserted date of 1723 to the remark, 'demolished since last year', which would again suggest that plan E did not present the results of the most up-to-date recording of the site.

Even in the E arc of this N 'circle', and despite several Stukeley drawings to confirm some parts of the record – e.g. Plate 71 showing the 'bulky' nature of Smith's 1965 stone 204 – there is conflicting information within Stukeley's own record. Thus the position of the apparently tall and thin fallen stone 207 – S of standing stone 206 – is described in the 'tour' as being within the hedge dividing garden from pasture, but it is not so indicated in plan E.

If anything, the records make us even more uncertain when we move to Stukeley's claimed inner N circle – which is, of course, unsupported by anything shown on plans A–D. In his manuscript 'tour' (Appendix II), Stukeley claims 'of the inner circle only three stones left', a statistic matched by draft plans Q (2 standing and 1 fallen) and S (1 standing and 2 fallen) as well as versions O and P (which do not distinguish standing from fallen stones). But it is contradicted by published plan E, and draft plans W and X, which firmly indicate one

A

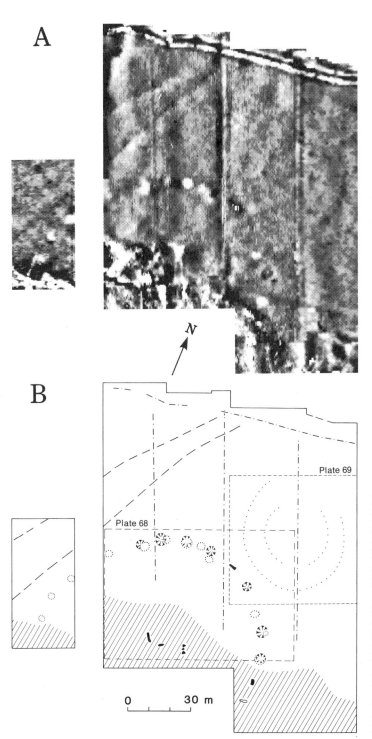

B

N

Plate 69

Plate 68

0   30 m

Plate 67 Resistivity survey of the NE quadrant, and part of the NW quadrant, of the Avebury henge: (A) grey-tone plot, and (B) interpretation. Key: –·–·– old field (pasture) boundaries; ◣ standing stones; ✿ extant depressions; ○ resistivity anomalies on the arc of the N Inner Circle; ...... tentative concentric circles; — — — other linear resistivity anomalies. Shaded area = zone of resistivity disturbance caused by later activity.

standing stone and five fallen ones, as well as one 'place of a stone taken away' in 1717. Draft plan R, however, shows only two stones (whether fallen or standing), while version V shows one standing and five fallen. Unfortunately, the Stukeley 'tour' is incomplete at this point (Appendix II): but it does appear to indicate that one of the three stones lying along the E side of the N road in plans E, and versions W and X was, in fact, taken away (and should, therefore, have been shown by another dot).

Given the conflicting nature of what was then known, it is perhaps not surprising that both excavation and probing were carried out in the 19th century with the explicit intention of testing Stukeley's reliability (e.g. Lukis 1881–3a, 151). However, they still left the question of the former existence of any twelve-stone inner circle in considerable doubt.

In an attempt to resolve some of these problems we carried out a resistivity survey covering some two-thirds of the NE quadrant of the henge, including the surroundings of the Cove, and extending across the NE arc of the N circle (approximately covering the course of Smith's 1965 stones 222–227 and 201–207). A 0.5m. probe spacing was used and readings were taken at 1.0m. intervals along traverses spaced at 0.5m. across the survey grid.[5] A plot of the resulting data, enhanced to clarify potential archaeological features as much as possible, is shown in Plate 67A.

In discussing the geophysical response around the Cove (as in many other parts of Avebury), it is first of all important to recognize the serious limitations imposed by the extensive disturbance to the ground caused by medieval and later building activity in the area. The response to such disturbance is very clear in the set of data illustrated in Plate 67A. Here, all the ground around and to the S of the Cove has clearly been much interfered with, obscuring any subtle response to extant archaeological features. This zone of disturbance extends E along the rear of buildings and gardens aligned on Green Street. In order to reduce the effect of this disturbance in the Cove area and within the N circle, we have also utilized the (previously unpublished) results of a survey undertaken in September 1975 using a 1.0m. probe spacing, the effect of which has been to 'look' somewhat deeper, reducing the 'noise' of more superficial anomalies. These results (Plate 68A) are of considerable interest.

To the N of the Cove there is a group of three concentrations of high values suggestive of buried stones or the sites of their destruction. The largest of these anomalies – a roughly circular area about 3–4m. across – is centred approximately 6m. NNE of Cove stone II. If it is not of relatively recent origin, this anomaly might be explained as a response to the site of destruction of stone III (Plate 68 and Transparency 24).

Apparently unrelated to it, and centred a further 5m. to the N, is a rather smaller anomaly more in keeping with the position of A. C. Smith's stone 18 (1867, pl. V) – stone G (Transparency 24) – which can be matched with the stone whose destruction is dated 1717 on Stukeley's plan E (this is almost certainly the stone drawn in his tabs. xiii and xiv (Plate 71, 72)).[6] Two further anomalies lie on a N–S alignment some 5m. to the E of the latter and may be a response to one or more stones or pits for which there has, until now, been no documentation (Transparency 24). However, when one studies Plate 72 in detail, a fallen stone is clearly shown located between stones F and G. Not recorded at all on plan E, such a stone must surely be equated with one or both of the latter resistivity anomalies (Plate 68).

Some significance may reasonably be attached to the resistivity anomalies described above because they occur to the N of the Cove, away from known building disturbance. That they are unlikely to be spurious is also suggested by the location of similar anomalies at stone positions E and F (Transparency 24), visible on the same plot. The survey confirms previous suggestions that stone E – which still breaks the surface of the turf – is the southernmost of three stones currently all together in one pit. Stone F, shown as standing by Stukeley in plan E and almost certainly also in his Plates 71 and 72 (cf. Crawford MSS.), was measured by Crocker as standing 83 feet from the easterly corner of the nearest Cove stone (I) (Colt Hoare 1812–21, pl 13). This stone F was eventually detonated with gunpowder in c.1825. Crawford

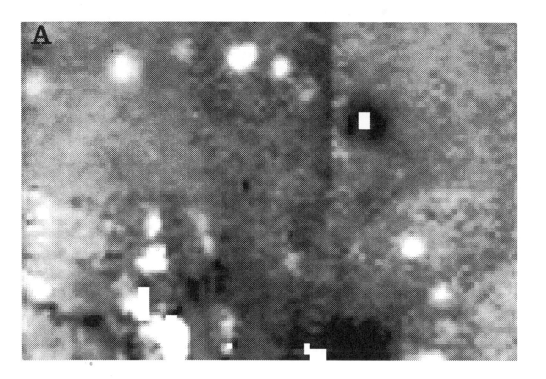

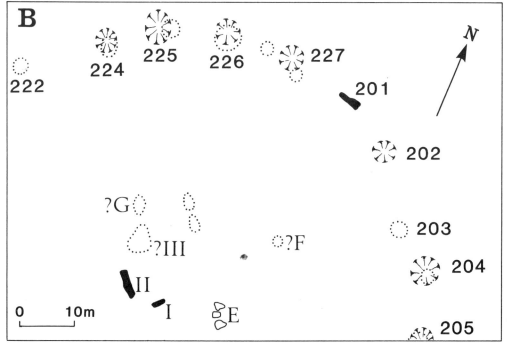

Plate 68   Resistivity survey (Sept 1975) of N Inner Circle: (A) grey-tone plot, and (B) interpretation. Key: ▰ standing stones; ✳ extant depressions; ◌ resistivity anomalies.

(MS., 4 and 4v) devotes considerable space to an attempt to discover its location, as well as the precise data of its destruction. A high resistance anomaly at the location given by Crocker is clearly identifiable on the plot. The most S of Stukeley's stones – as Crawford almost certainly also thought (Crawford MS., 6) – is the one which 'lyes in the Corner between the two barns' (Plate 72; Appendix II), whose position is marked in Transparency 24 as S. This was outside the resistivity survey area.

The arc of a concentric circle, centred slightly to the N of stone I and drawn through the anomaly marking the former position of stone F, intercepts no other anomaly which cannot be explained as of modern origin (for instance stemming from the garage which formerly stood between the Cove and the Swindon Road). The anomaly attributed to stone G falls off the line, at a position inside the circuit, possibly due to the burial or burning pit of the stone being different from its original position when standing. All in all, there appears to be little geophysical support for features disposed in a recognizable pattern; from the combined material presented here, it must be admitted that the evidence for an inner stone circular setting within the N circle remains at best highly equivocal.

The arc of the N 'circle' itself, however, *is* visible, with small variations, in both the 1975 and 1989 sets of resistivity data (Plates 67A and 68A). Overall, it is outlined by several isolated concentrations of high values which could be coincident with pits or buried stones. The results are of considerable interest in their own right, since some definitions are better than others and such variations are a challenge to explanation. In the first place, it is necessary to remember that two of the fallen stones shown by Stukeley (and cf. Plate 43 and 71) (Smith's 1965 stones 202 and 204) were visible as shallow depressions. Whereas there was no anomaly over setting 202, the resistivity response from stone position 204 is most unusual, having been detected as positive in 1975 and negative in 1989. This phenomenon presumably demonstrates the acknowledged variability inherent in resistivity surveys carried out under different soil moisture conditions, which are seasonally as well as locally changeable (Clark 1975, 301). In this case the feature responsible – presumably the particularly 'bulky' stone shown in Plate 71 – may be rather deeper than the others and may also, for some unexplained reason, have different water-retentive properties.

The resistivity results show a considerable number of other variations. Whereas the depressions of positions 224, 225, 226 and 205 were all confirmed, that at 227 produced two resistivity anomalies (Transparency 24). Although no depression was visible at position 203 – where Stukeley indicated a vacancy (Transparency 27) – there was a clear anomaly in the resistivity response, possibly, therefore, indicating a buried stone. The case of Smith's 1965 position 223 is particularly interesting; recorded by Stukeley, quite exceptionally, as a 'fragment' (and one of only two stones to be shown as an unfilled-in rectangle on plan E – see Chapter III E.5.ii(a)), it has not been detected by resistivity. According to Crawford, it had left no visible hollow (Crawford MS.). Given our earlier discussions about how to interpret the records of the 17th and 18th centuries (Chapter III, E.5.ii), it could be concluded either that the stone had neither been buried nor burnt and that its stone hole had been too shallow to be detected either visibly or through geophysical methods, or that there never had been a stone in Smith's 223 posited position at all, and that Stukeley had been in error in marking one. If this were the case, it would throw doubt on the existence of a complete N circle in this area of the site.

Very significantly, three stone positions, which continued the circuit of the N circle, were found in an extension of the resistivity survey to the W of the N road (Plate 67). The implications of these three anomalies (corresponding very approximately with Smith's 1965 stone positions 219, 220 and 221) are immense, since they fall significantly outside the projected perimeter of Smith's 1965 circle and are in an area where Stukeley's record is internally inconsistent (Transparencies 24 and 27). Each of them falls successively farther off the circuit, stone position 219 lying as much as 8m. to the W. This displacement is greater than is likely to be explained by the offsetting of burning or burial pits and must therefore suggest that the N 'circle' was not necessarily geometrically exact and may have had a centre significantly W of that usually proposed. It is therefore at least possible that Aubrey's plan A version of this area (Transparency 26) may yet turn out to be the most accurate of all – conceptually, if not in detail! On the other hand, if we retain the presumption of circular configurations, this rearranged 'circle' would have had its centre significantly N of the position currently presumed.

As has been seen, much of the interpretation of the resistivity data depends on pattern recognition and, like the observers of the 17th and 18th centuries, we are in this almost certainly concentrating on patterns which we somehow expect to be present (see Chapter V). It is perhaps significant, then, that there is no geophysical evidence for the third (N) circle once suggested by Keiller (1939) and recently claimed anew by Burl (1979, 163–4, fig. 7) (see Chapter V).

Although most of the area surveyed outside the N circle appears devoid of significant detail there is nevertheless a temptation to see circles in the results (Plate 67A). There is one faint image, barely emerging above ordinary levels, to which it may be worth drawing attention as possibly more than wishful pattern recognition (Plate 69). To the NE of stone 201 (Plate 67), straddling a former field boundary ditch, may be one and, possibly, two previously unrecognized concentric circles, some 30m. and 50m. in diameter respectively, comprising very weak and intermittent negative anomalies. So faint and partial are these, indeed, that it must be admitted that the suggestion that they represent genuine features can only be extremely tentative at this stage. Even if not imaginary, the anomalies responsible are unlikely to relate to stone settings: they might instead be caused by post-holes. No relevant magnetic anomalies were detectable here and no features of any kind are marked in this area on any of the plans of Aubrey, Charleton, or Stukeley.

γ. The Cove

Aubrey's plan C and Charleton's D coincide in large measure in their views of the Cove. The top left-hand inset in plan C (Plate 29) appears to leave little doubt that Aubrey wished to depict the presence of four stones in the Cove, the fourth stone lying flat on the ground: the depiction of the Cove within the plan itself (Plate 30) is compatible with such an interpretation (see Chapter III, C. 14). There is absolutely no ambiguity about a fourth stone in Charleton's plan D (Plate 5). As we have seen, his notes clearly state: 'G – the three high stones, standing in the North-east quadrant of the greater Circle, in a Triangle. ... I – a Triangular stone, of vast magnitude, lying flat on the ground; but (probably) at first imposed on the heads of the other three, in manner of an Architrave'. Although Aubrey's plan B may be too schematic to be relied on in this context, it too appears to show a disposition of four grouped and one rather solitary stone (Plate 8 and Transparency 25): if not random, this might possibly represent stone E (Smith 1965, 202) or even stone F which, as we have just seen, was probably the only standing stone in Stukeley's inner N circle. In showing the Cove as composed of four stones, all three plans differ significantly from Aubrey's plan A (Plate 7) and, at first sight, also from Stukeley.

Burl (1979, 43), ignoring any differences between the 'sketch' and the 'plant' in plan A (see Chapter III, A.12(c)), uses this plan and its detail to draw attention to Aubrey's 'very good' and accurate work. His readers are asked to note 'the sketch and plan of the undamaged Cove inside the North Circle', and he speaks (1979, 44) of the 'irreplaceable sketch of the three stones called the Cove inside the North Circle'. According to Burl, Aubrey saw the three Cove stones still standing, the furthest N of them falling down and being broken up 'not long afterwards' (Burl 1979, 44). This is an event which Stukeley recorded as taking place in 1713 (Stukeley 1743, 24), adding in an unpublished note that the stone had had a (s)piked end

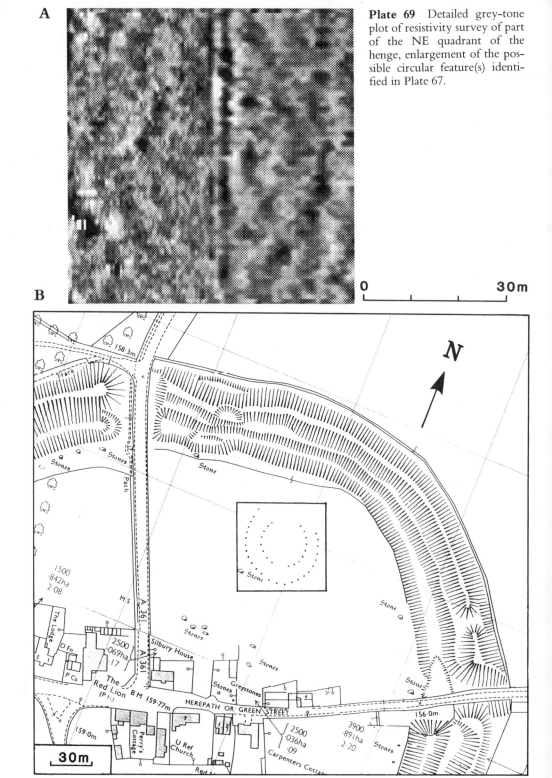

A

B

Plate 69 Detailed grey-tone plot of resistivity survey of part of the NE quadrant of the henge, enlargement of the possible circular feature(s) identified in Plate 67.

0   30m

and had been supported all round with little stones (Gough Maps 231, 9). The number of three Cove stones is also consistent with Stukeley's published total number of stones considered by him to constitute the Avebury monuments (Stukeley 1743, 37). It is also consistent with plan E – while all except one of those of his draft frontispieces which include such detail show two standing Cove stones and the date of 1713: the addition of the position of the third Cove stone on one of his published engravings was a retrospective addition (Stukeley 1743, tab. xiv, and cf. Note 72).

However, and remarkably, the written description that Stukeley published to accompany his representation of this three-stone Cove itself suggests that he thought that there had once been a fourth stone in the Cove area, for he says (Stukeley 1743, 24; Long 1858a, 325), 'the altar properly lay upon the ground before this superb nich [of three stones]. That, no doubt, was carry'd off long ago, as not being fix'd in the earth'. As we saw in Chapter III, E. 7, Stukeley's draft plan P (dated 1721) does appear to show a circular Cove of four stones, two apparently as extant, and the other two presumably as stone positions (Transparency 8 and Plate 34).

Independently of plans C and D, which were apparently wholly unknown, particular attention was paid in the 19th century to this claim for the existence of a Cove 'altar'. Browne stated (1823, 34–5; Long 1858b, 17) that 'Before the central one of the three [stones], facing, like the altar trilithon of Stonehenge, the north-east, was placed the stone on which the sacrifices were burnt. This I ascertained myself by digging, the place being still apparent where it lay, but now filled up with rubbish. The stone before which it was placed is evidently marked by the action of the fire of the sacrifices.' Burl (1988, 9) has recently interpreted this report as showing that Browne 'unknowingly ... had chanced upon the results of eighteenth century burning rather than prehistoric ritual', adding that Hunter had been told by a labourer that 'the earth had been examined to the depth of a yard or more, at the foot of the cove stones, to see if there were any evidence of sacrifices having been performed there, but nothing peculiar was observed' (Hunter 1829, 6). In 1865, when Smith and Cunnington undertook excavations in search of burials in order to test claims then current that Avebury was a vast burial-ground (Smith 1867, 209–16), they also searched for 'the remains of an "Altar stone" which might once have stood in the centre of the three stones of the "Cove" and since have been destroyed'. These excavations uncovered some stone flakes which 'at first I was inclined to attribute to the remains of an altar ..., but this theory is not supported by any tangible facts' (Smith 1867, 211). What Smith meant by this is explained by handwritten notes accompanying the 'Examinations at Avebury Sept 29th 1865' in the Wiltshire Archaeological and Natural History Society library in Devizes where the final subclause of the quotation above is deleted and replaced with the words, 'There was no hollow in which such stone [sic] could have been placed'.

As a result of Browne's excavations, Lukis (1881–3a, 153) wrote, 'I reject Stukeley's ideas as regards the altar ...'. This rejection is echoed by Burl (1988) in his recent attempt to establish 'as unquestioned coves' 'two basic forms', both with three standing stones, deriving from earlier rectangular burial chambers. Yet the chief conclusion to be drawn is that the cumulative effect of disturbance by excavation has been to close this off as a viable avenue of enquiry. In addition to the excavations referred to, there were possibly others by a farmhand in 1829 (Hunter 1829, 6) and by Thomas Leslie in 1894 (Gray 1935, 103), thus highlighting one of the basic problems in the philosophy of archaeological enquiry – whether, and when, to excavate. In addition, the fact that buildings lay right up against the Cove stones at least until 1935 (Plate 72; Gray 1935, pls 29, 33), and that a garage until recently occupied the ground between the Cove and the Swindon road, means that no light can be shed on the original structure of the Cove from resistivity data (Plates 67, 68), except that the concentration of high values nearest to stone II is likely to equate with the pit for stone III.

Unfortunately the relevant part of the 'tour' of the site in Stukeley's 'Celtic Temples' is

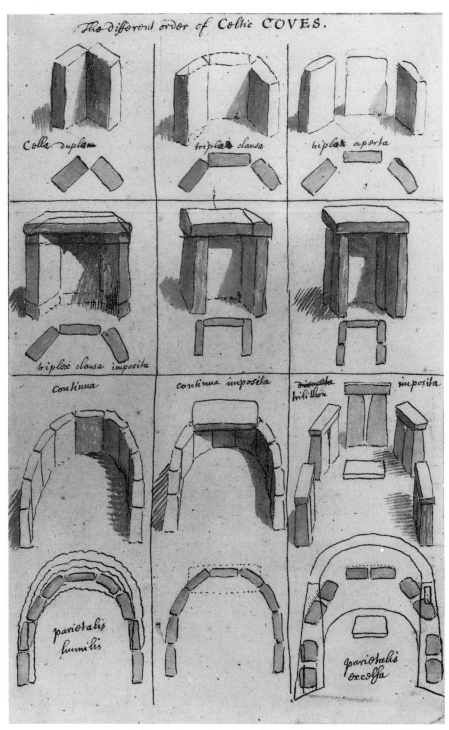

The different order of Celtic COVES.

colla duplex   *triplex clausa*   *triplex aperta*

triplex clausa imposita

continua   *continua imposita*   *disrupta trilithon*   *imposita*

parietalis humilis   *parietalis excelsa*

Plate 70 Stukeley's comparative chart of Cove types (Bodleian Library MS. Top.Gen.b.53, 8v).

missing and there is hence no detailed topographic description of the Cove, though there are speculations about its overall significance as the 'great gate of the gods ...' (Chapter II, iv). Moreover, elsewhere in 'Celtic Temples' Stukeley attempted a functional typology both of 'cove'-like structures (Plate 70) – very like, though not noted by, Burl 1988 – and of 'Celtic Temples' generally (Stukeley 1722–4b, 21ff; Top.Gen.b.53, 9, 11). It is evident that Stukeley was well aware that stone monuments of presumably similar character could take a variety of forms; for example, he recognized that circles of stones, could occur in varying concentricity, from double to 'quincuple'. Perhaps more important in the present context, Stukeley shows an awareness that what appeared to a contemporary observer as a three-stone arrangement might originally have comprised more stones. In words strikingly reminiscent both of Charleton's comments on his plan D (see also Chapter II, iii) and of Aubrey's remarks about his plans A–B (as also his box-like cove 'plant' on plan A), Stukeley writes of 'The Cove' (as a general category of monument):

> most often this is composd only of 3 large stones sett in a semilunar figure, as twice, if not oftner at Abury [here he presumably refers to the Cove currently under discussion, the so-called Beckhampton Cove, and the 'Devil's Coyts' Cove reported by Aubrey and accepted by Stukeley within the Kennet Avenue]. Sometimes tis perfectly square resembling a box made of 3 stones sett on three sides of a square, with another great flat stone covering the whole & then it becomes properly a Niche. (Stukeley 1722–4b, 23)

This is not an isolated statement: of Kits Coty Stukeley writes, 'three Stones stood ... as some at Abury on the top of which lay another, & probably before them lay one on the Ground as an altar stone', while, when he compares this site to the main Avebury Cove, it is almost as if Charleton were writing: 'The Covering stone now lyes with its western end in the ground' (Stukeley 1722–4b, 39, 41).

In his expectation that there might have been a fourth Cove stone Stukeley was not alone among the 18th- and 17th-century investigators, each of whom was working within interpretative frameworks which would have led them to expect the presence of a fourth stone – albeit not always for the same reasons. An expectation of an altar-stone of some kind was also part of 19th-century accepted wisdom and these concerns echo a concern with altar-stones in Stukeley's unpublished writings where he wrote that these were: 'sometime set in the middle of the circle or coves, or they make part of a Cove, sometime sett at a distance from the Circle' (Stukeley 1722–4b, 25). As for the notion of a capping-stone, Fergusson (1872, 62) advanced the same interpretation – 'a cove consisting of three upright stones supporting a capstone – a dolmen, in fact'. Even in the 1920s Crawford may have been doing no more than reiterating commonplace expectations when he wrote:

> There seems no reason to suppose that the fourth or eastern side of the cove was ever blocked by a stone. There is no evidence of such, & analogy with the chambers of Long Barrows suggests that it would have been open. Whether we are justified by the same resemblance in postulating a capstone resting on the three uprights is a question that cannot *now* be answered. Such a capstone would have [had] to be nearly 30 feet square. (Crawford MS., 6)

It is therefore more than merely incidentally interesting that there is no actual physical evidence of the existence of an original Cove capstone.[8]

Whatever its purpose, what *does* seem to be the case is that the weight of the evidence is in favour of there having originally been a 'Cove' with at least four, if not five, stones. The history of digging and survey reported above certainly does not disprove the existence of an original (altar- or cap-) stone lying on the ground as late as the 17th century.

To adopt a cap-stone or altar-stone thesis about the Cove area would, of course, seriously damage the main evidence behind a number of current views, notably a recent argument

(Burl 1988, 6, 10–11) that coves were 'put up in regions of dense populations and were, themselves, important ritual centres' providing space for 'a great number of onlookers ... which the open nature of coves afforded'; this leads Burl on to suggest an association of some sort between coves and funerary miming. On the other hand a three-stone Cove interpretation would entail rejecting, or at least reinterpreting, the oral evidence recorded by Stukeley, both in his text and on his draft plan P, together with the written and illustrated evidence of Charleton, and the illustrated evidence of Aubrey's plans C and perhaps B, in favour of the representation of the Cove (and its detail) in Aubrey's plan A – which clearly indicates only three stones.

It is possible to speculate that the Aubrey of plan C, Charleton and Stukeley were all so conditioned to expect an altar- or cap-stone (or possibly both) at Avebury that the original existence of such a stone was, literally, beyond any doubt. But it seems strange to dismiss three relatively independent authorities on the basis of a single one, which, though hitherto accepted as almost wholly authoritative, we have come increasingly to doubt in many of its details in the course of this book. Instead, we need to explain why plan A shows the Cove with no stone on the ground in the centre of it. It is possible that this was a conscious revision, the rationale of which may be suggested by Aubrey's comments on Stonehenge in 1666, when he had become convinced that Jones had been wrong in claiming that there was an altar there, noting, perhaps significantly: 'Perhaps they used no Altar; for I find the middle of *these* monuments voyed' (Aubrey 24, 58; Fowles and Legg 1980, 75; our italics). This could allude to Avebury. Alternatively, we may have recourse to the suggestion made in Chapter III, A.12(c), as to when the drawing of the Cove was actually inserted on plan A, which introduces the possibility that the omission of the fourth stone was a simple error. If, as was postulated there, the detail of the Cove might have been recopied – perhaps at the point when Aubrey produced his fresh copy of 1688–9 – from an illustration in his 1660s text, the elapsing of over twenty years might have meant that he simply failed to include the recumbent stone (though this would entail the presumption that Aubrey did not perceive this stone as significant enough to be worth remembering). This, too, is not a particularly satisfactory hypothesis; but the balance of testimony clearly necessitates 'explaining away' plan A as a source in this instance. We leave the reader with the balance of probabilities, so that he or she may judge the evidence for him or herself. In any case, the nature of the Avebury Cove remains one of the most intriguing of unanswered questions in British prehistory.

z. Summary

The Quadrant comparison in the folder encapsulates the information presented above about the outer circle from Aubrey's plans A and B, Stukeley's plan E and archaeological evidence.

Some of the evidence seems reasonably clear: thus, there is no reason to doubt that both Aubrey and Stukeley were recording Smith's 1965 standing stone 68 which is still visible today. The same is true for Smith's 1965 stone 73 (apparently fallen by Stukeley's time but – since we have discovered that Aubrey does not distinguish between standing and fallen stones – possibly still standing in Aubrey's). Plan A may well have recorded two further visible (standing or fallen) stones (Smith's 1965 positions 63 and 64) in this NE quadrant, while by Stukeley's time both may have been removed – leaving visible hollows. Alternatively – and we cannot be certain because of the distortions which all the plans incorporate – Aubrey's two stones may have been depictions of those slightly farther to the N, which Stukeley also recorded (as fallen). Both Aubrey's plans – as well as Stukeley's plan E – can be assumed to have recorded Smith's 1965 stones 77 and 78, the latter apparently still standing in Stukeley's time.

Much of the same sort of confidence surrounds the recording by both Aubrey and

Stukeley of the first three stones E of the S causeway (despite the confusion of boundaries in Stukeley's record), with all the adjoining stones to the E which were probably seen by Aubrey, having been removed by Stukeley's time – some leaving visible hollows in the ground, others not. The clear evidence that the records provide real evidence of stones and stone positions, make it seem highly likely that both Aubrey and Stukeley were recording Smith's 1965 standing stone 50 (albeit somewhat displaced in Aubrey's records), suggesting that at least one of Smith's 1965 stones 47–49 – for which there is currently no direct archaeological or resistivity evidence – was still visible in the 17th and 18th centuries.

The record of the W half of the Outer Circle is also convincing, with at least the first four stones W of the N causeway having been observed by both Aubrey and Stukeley, two of them being subsequently burnt. Thereafter – moving S – it is particularly difficult to match Aubrey's plan A record to either Stukeley's plan E or to archaeological evidence. However, the appearance of two closely spaced stones on both Aubrey's plans in Smith's 1965 positions 32 and 33 can be matched with the two standing stones on Stukeley's plan E – two stones which are still visible today. Such reliability in the 17th- and 18th-century records makes it seem likely that the currently fallen stone 14 as well as standing stone 8 were both represented on plans A, B and E – the former probably still standing in Stukeley's time.

It is much more difficult to make any sense of the various records of the S inner circle (which is why we have not attempted a comparative drawing): thus, plan B has only 12 of the 28 stone positions shown on plan E, and, while plan A is – for whatever reason(s) – so distorted in this region that close matching is impossible. However, by analogy with the evidence derived from analysis of the outer circle, Aubrey and Stukeley are both likely to have recorded Smith's 1965 stones 101–103 and 105–106: if so, Stukeley saw the same two standing as in the 1930s and, in addition to the three fallen by the 1930s, stone 107 seems also to have been visible in the 18th century. Positions 104 and 108 – both confirmed archaeologically – were only remarked as hollows in Stukeley's time. In other segments of the southern circle the likely reliability of Stukeley's plan E record cannot really be assessed: several fallen stones are in places which have not been investigated archaeologically: some vacancies are in localities where there is archaeological evidence for a stone hollow or burning pit, while still others are in areas where there is no archaeological support for there ever having been a stone.

It is possible to make an inexact match between plan A's stone depictions and stone positions 101–109: stone 104 (Stukeley's hollow) being out of circular alignment and stones 107–109 much closer to each other and to stone 106 than expected from either the archaeological evidence or from Smith's 1965 reconstruction of the S circle. If such an alignment for plan A is accepted, it could be argued that Stukeley's other two stones (in Smith's 1965 positions 125 and 126) could be present in Aubrey's cluster of six stones shown to the S of the presumed Obelisk depiction.

The situation regarding the N circle is, if anything, even harder to assess. On the basis of the above presumptions of accuracy of recording by Aubrey and Stukeley we may start by assuming that both of them must have recorded stones 201 and 206 as standing, and 207 and 210 as standing or fallen. Stukeley shows only three standing stones, two of which could match Smith's 1965 positions for stones 201 and 206 – whereas his third standing stone is in Smith's 1965 posited position 223 for which there is no archaeological evidence of any kind. With 201 and 206 matched, one can indeed also match fallen stone positions 207 and 210 in Stukeley's record, suggesting, perhaps, that 208 and 209 (for which there is no archaeological evidence) were also fallen stones in Stukeley's time. However, if Stukeley's stones 201 and 206 are matched with Aubrey's plan A (with the Cove stones roughly in the correct area) on Aubrey's plan A we are left with no Aubreyan record for the existence of any stones in positions 207–210.

Two overall impressions remain. The first is that, perhaps not surprisingly, apparent

233

A View of the Remains of the Temple of the Moon at Abury. Aug. 1722.

Plate 71 Stukeley's view of the 'Temple of the Moon. August 1722' on which tab. xiii was based.

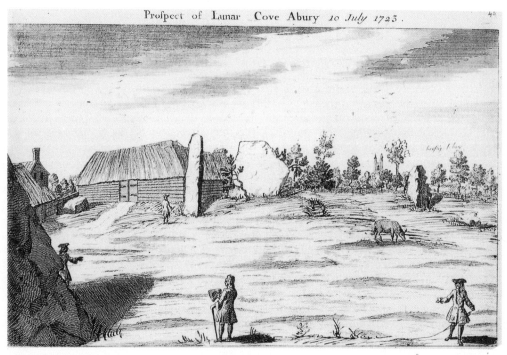

Prospect of Lunar Cove Abury 10 July 1723.

Plate 72 Stukeley's view of the 'Lunar Cove. 10 July 1723' on which tab. xiv was based.

inaccuracies in the record of these early plans derived either from particularly inaccessible areas of the site (e.g. around the W causeway, on either side of the W–E road, etc) or from information presumably derived from oral testimony (e.g. the area of Smith's 1965 stones 79–89). The second is that consequent reliability or inaccuracy may additionally vary between area or quadrant for several other reasons: the nature of hollows in the ground may have been variable, the visibility of stones breaking the ground would have varied at different times, and slight mounds of earth would have been open to differential interpretations.

Notes

1. The geophysical survey plots chosen to illustrate the text are a selection from many attempts at drawing optimal information from the available data. Comments on the survey results are therefore drawn from experience of many survey plots for which the space available here only allows the reproduction of the most representative. These plots have all been numerically treated to some extent. For instance, all the resistivity data has been interpolated using bilinear interpolation to increase the density of data points. The resulting plots have had rogue values removed using a local thresholding method. With the exception of the 'raw' plot (Plate 58 A), all the other resistivity data has been 'smoothed' using a directionally sensitive convolution mask. All resistivity plots have also been contrast-enhanced by subtracting a local mean from each reading typically calculated from an 11×11 window centred on each sampling point.

2. Keiller's and Piggott's report (1936, 426) that some stones had fallen prior to the early Iron Age and that Iron Age inhabitants had ignored the stones, making use of the stone holes as rubbish pits, was apparently based on misinterpretation of the pottery concerned, which is now said to be medieval (Smith 1965, 243).

3. These form part of a series of bearings written on a loose sheet inserted in Stukeley's 'Stonehenge' MS., mostly between different sites in the Avebury region. Not all are now identifiable but the bearings of those which are can be checked using a modern map. Most appear to be reasonably accurate. True north appears to have been used except at Windmill Hill where an error has occurred and all the bearings are offset. The bearings to the East Kennet long barrow are the least accurate but, surprisingly in view of the distance and lack of intervisibility, a bearing to the Mount at Marlborough taken from the Sanctuary is very good.

One set of 8 bearings is taken from the supposed West Kennet Avenue Cove but unfortunately few of the bearings can be used because of problems of identification, obvious errors and imprecise targets (e.g. 'Abury').

Using the two bearings which can be confidently identified and one which is less certain and assuming that the site lies on the line of the Avenue, the location of the Cove can be found by resection. Using this method the site would lie just to the north of the point where the Avenue is crossed by the modern road to Avebury from West Kennet Farm.

4. A list of the number of stones at Avebury appears on a manuscript sheet endorsed 'A Prospect of STONEHEN[GE]'. Preserved in a folder of loose Stukeley manuscripts at Freemasons' Hall (1130 Stu), it differs significantly from the list published in *Abury* in that it itemizes 100 stones for Abury's Inner Circle – an entry which has been subsequently crossed out. The total number of stones itemized amounts to 749, a total which is also crossed out and 750 subsituted. *Abury*'s total of 650 comprises, in addition, the ring-stone – and omits the Inner Circle 100 stones. Unfortunately, there is no possibility of exactly dating this manuscript page, though it is in a fairly early hand.

5. The easternmost 30m. of the grid was surveyed with the transverse spacing widened to 1m.

6. Here we differ from Crawford's conclusion about Stukeley's tabs. xiii and xiv (Plates 71, 72), which he claimed show an extra stone in the N part of the outer circle (Crawford MS., 6). In preference to accepting such an extra unidentified stone in the outer circle – which would, in addition, be a rare example of Stukeley presenting a distorted angle in his tabs. – we consider this Stukeley record as more likely to show the location of stone G accurately, despite the statement on plan E that it had been demolished in 1717.

7. Inspection of the tops of the two remaining Cove stones by Michael Allen (Trust for Wessex Archaeology) at our request (on 31 December 1988) revealed two very shallow, parallel concave grooves, c.10cm. wide, on the furthest NW stone which might, presumably, have been made by the laying of a stone on top of it, but could have been natural. On the southernmost stone, however, a distinct triangular natural ridge appeared totally unmarked and it would seem impossible for a large stone to have been anchored across the top of this stone without that ridge showing some effects of such an 'imposition'. Mr Allen concludes, therefore, contrary to Charleton's claim, that no fourth stone had 'probably' formed an 'architrave', a feature which would have suggested that the Cove was analogous (had it had a capstone) to a large Megalithic dolmen or quoit, as found in Wales and the west of England.

V Plans, perceptions and preconceptions: from the 1660s to the 1990s

The reader may feel somewhat bewildered by the sheer detail of the previous chapter, and it seems appropriate at this point to draw some more general conclusions. First, we will briefly recapitulate what we have learnt about each of the 17th- and 18th-century plans by collating the information that they provide with other data about the site. More important, we will draw together scattered hints contained in the previous chapter to make some broader points about the significance of the plans, the impact that they have had on the existing interpretation of Avebury, and the fresh lines of enquiry that our analysis of them has suggested.

Taking the early plans in turn, we may begin with Charleton's plan D, which in some respects is the least problematic. In contrast to painstaking surveys like Aubrey's plan A and Stukeley's plan E, the conventionalized nature of plan D clearly reflects an intention to give only a general idea of the site and its component parts, making no attempt to give an accurately measured depiction of the features which it shows, or their location. But its clear statements about the features of the site – particularly in its captions – are of critical importance. We have discussed these at length in connection with the Obelisk and the Cove, where Charleton's evidence is unequivocal; but the clarity of his statements about these is matched by what he says about 'the great stones at the four Entrances'. Though hard to correlate with certain other evidence itemized in the previous chapter, it must remain a real possibility that these putative portal stones were a former feature of the site. The one major feature which Charleton entirely missed was the northern circle surrounding the Cove, but here we may benefit from the evidence discussed in Chapter IV, x, which suggests that this was difficult to discern.

Moving to Aubrey's plan C, this second hitherto unknown document is at once one of the most intriguing and one of the most frustrating of our records. Perhaps the most important feature of it from an archaeological point of view is the detailed drawing of the Cove in its left-hand margin, which bears out Charleton's record in clearly showing a fourth stone; in addition, the marginal depiction of Avebury parish church is quite accurate, closely resembling the depictions of the church by Stukeley in the early 18th century which were considered so accurate in the 19th that they served as the basis for the restoration of the building (King 1879, 380–1). In both these respects, this plan is to be preferred to Aubrey's later plan A. In addition, this plan echoes Charleton's in showing a pair of stones outside three of the four entrances, and its independent verification of Charleton's testimony on this point provides further strong evidence that such portals may indeed have existed.

In other respects, however, our investigations in the previous chapter have suggested that virtually all the details in this plan, though ostensibly realistic, are not to be relied upon. Thus we have the false location of the river between the henge and the church; the profuse depiction of buildings along both the E–W and the N–S streets within the antiquity; the complex pattern of what are apparently field boundaries interspersing the stones; the arrangement of the stones themselves into four concentric circles, around a crossroads itself misleadingly perfect; even the apparent verisimilitude of the depiction of the profiles of the stones themselves. In each of these cases, careful correlation of plan C with other records suggests that the details are impressionistic rather than true to life. In other words, though at first sight the asymmetrical placing of the buildings and stones appears to attempt accurately to record such features' exact position on the site, we must conclude that all that is given is an *impression* of irregularity, the actual disposition of features being arbitrary. The same appears to be true of the shapes of the stones – apart from those of the Cove – for our attempts to correlate these with evidence from other sources have proved fruitless. Yet, though disappointing as a record of the site, it may be argued that plan C is an artefact characteristic of Aubrey's antiquarian method as a whole: in the way in which it was closely focused on detail, but more impressionistic in the manner in which the detail was collocated, it is perhaps not fanciful to see it as a pictorial equivalent of Aubrey's celebrated preface to his *Wiltshire Antiquities* (cf. Hunter 1975, 174ff.).

Plan A evidently reflects a conscious revision on Aubrey's part, and in various respects it has a verisimilitude which his previous effort lacked, establishing the basic pattern of Avebury as we now recognize it. The plan's positive merits are obvious: the plane-table survey of the ditch and rampart; the delineation of the actual disposition of the cross-roads, contrasting with the exact cross shown on plan C; the revision of the arrangement of the stones to reflect discrete internal features as against simple concentricity; and the attempt to mark the positions of stones and to indicate where gaps existed. Yet this plan too has major shortcomings, which careful examination in the previous chapter has shown to be greater than has often previously been presumed. Some of the anomalies can be attributed to limitations in Aubrey's survey practice, some to complications caused by his intentions in formulating the plan as we have it, and we will deal with these in turn.

It seems as if there were clear limits to the amount of accurate surveying that Aubrey did, both in extent and in time: his measurements seem to have been confined to defining the inner edge either of the ditch or the bank, and the overall dimensions of the earthwork were drawn in regular proportions around that. This may reflect the likelihood that the survey had already taken him three or four days, making him reluctant to devote even more time to the project. In addition, the overall dimensions for the site that Aubrey gives are underestimates of 10–16%; his rendition of the southern circle is approximately a third too small; the bend in the eastern half of the E–W street is certainly inaccurate; and the spatial relationships between the different components of the antiquity are distorted. It seems likely that, although the arrangement of the roads is relatively accurately shown, the pasture boundaries and stones were 'eyed in' within the quadrants thus imprecisely delimited. Probably the stones were added to the composition last of all and, though their number and general disposition carries some conviction, it lacks any secure precision.

More serious are the implications of the hypothesis (Chapter III, A. 6(a), 12(c)), that certain features of Plan A as we have it may be retrospective additions. There is a strong possibility that both the church and the detail of the Cove were added to the plan after it was originally drawn up, the church probably early, but the Cove (judging by its detailing) later, perhaps in the late 1680s – though there is an unfortunate element of circularity about this argument, which has been invoked partly to explain discrepancies between this and other records in connection with these features. Initially, the plan may have been deliberately defined by the circumvallation which Aubrey had surveyed, and this could also explain why the portal stones were omitted (the captions to the roads may also be later additions). Indeed, paradoxically, the initial pursuit of exactitude in plan A may be the reason why some features which appear on its predecessor either fail to appear here, or appear in a cruder and derivative form, something that applies particularly to the depiction of the Cove. In addition, plan A makes no attempt to distinguish the different sizes of stones, which explains why it fails to echo Charleton's clear observation of a particularly large stone standing within the southern circle: this is a further limitation to its value as a source. It is ironic that one of our findings in this study is that this plan is a more problematic document than has generally been realized.

Plan B is a rather different artefact. As a general view of the Avebury to Overton complex, intended to illustrate the mutual relationship between the main henge and 'the Walke, and the lesser Temple appendant to it', its primary intention was different from that of plan A – and, for that matter, from that of the more detailed plan of the Sanctuary which appeared elsewhere in Aubrey's *Monumenta Britannica* (Plate 27). In a plan of this kind, one would not necessarily expect as much attention to detail as in plan A, and this may also explain why items like the stones at the entrances were omitted. Yet, considering its more schematic quality, plan B is often surprisingly accurate in its mapping of stone emplacements, at times even comparing favourably in this respect with plan A. The evidence of revision that survives, seen, for example, in the careful cutting out of sections of the plan, also increases our respect for its value as a source. More important, the very fact that this plan is somewhat schematized means that it makes some points clear which are not obvious from the more detailed plan A. For instance, plan B shows that Aubrey did perceive as part of the northern inner circle the four outlying stones which plan A depicts lying along the E–W street – something which plan A leaves far from clear.

Lastly, we come to Stukeley, whose record – though, like Aubrey's plan A, hitherto taken for granted – proves to be at once much more extensive, more complicated, and more ambiguous than has generally been supposed. For one thing, our investigations have revealed that the Frontispiece published in his *Abury* (1743) is not as definitive as its position at the head of that volume, and the remarks about it in its text, imply. In fact it has to be read alongside an extensive series of overlapping records drawn up between 1721 and 1724, including many drafts of the frontispiece itself, together with the detailed written description of the antiquity which – with a perhaps surprising faith in visual testimony – Stukeley omitted from his published book, and which is edited here as Appendix II. Taken together with illustrations, notes and associated material, this record by Stukeley comprises one of the fullest examples of archaeological recording in Britain before modern times, outweighing all the previous descriptions of the site in density of detail. But, though it might have been hoped that there would be a cumulative increase in accuracy within these records, this does not seem to be the case: rather, Stukeley appears to have worked on various drafts in parallel, so that none of them is entirely devoid of evidential value, their overlapping testimony instead creating a picture of considerable complexity.

Undoubtedly Stukeley was conscientious according to his lights, but his record raises problems not dissimilar from those which arise with Aubrey and plan A. Some are due to simple error; some to experimentation in his method of notation and his use of symbols to distinguish whether stones were standing, existed in a recumbent state, or had been removed. He was also inconsistent in what he recorded concerning earlier destruction, both in terms of the numbers of stones affected, and of what fate befell specific stones. There are problems as to what he was aiming to describe – whether the original state of the site, or its state when he first saw it in 1719, or its state in some later year. Lastly, Stukeley was particularly transparent in the way in which his record was influenced by his preconceptions (Chapter II, vi). It is symptomatic that, in giving his evidence concerning formerly existing stone positions, he juxtaposed 'the report of the Inhabitants of their own memory & *the Symmetry of the work*' (Stukeley 1722–46, 121; our italics). In sum, therefore, our research has added to the richness of the record, but has at the same time made it more complicated, and the difficulties in Stukeley's evidence need to be taken much more fully into account than hitherto in assessing both the stone placements within the main henge and features such as the Avenue(s).

All this may have made some readers wonder why, in view of the clear inaccuracy of various features of the different plans, we did not categorically dismiss one or more of them as worthless at the outset. The answer – which some may find frustrating – is that this is not possible. As should by now be clear, none of the plans is without some degree of evidential value, however schematic other aspects of it may be. This is perhaps most clearly illustrated by the new plan C, for, though Aubrey's plan A clearly supersedes this as a record of the topography of the site, it is inferior to the earlier document in its depiction of the Cove and the church. With Stukeley's extensive records, too, there is no simple progression from the less to the more accurate, while, though Charleton's plan is stylized in some respects, it has clear evidential value through the clarity of the statements in its captions.

It is also worth re-emphasizing the value of *any* evidence about the state of the site prior to the destruction of stones that occurred in the late 17th to 18th centuries, since it crucially supplements an archaeological record that will never be complete. Even at the lowest estimate, the plans provide important information which would not otherwise be available. In part, this may be illustrated by specific features which would not even have been suspected without these early records. Thus the location and subsequent excavation of the Sanctuary was due entirely to Aubrey's and Stukeley's testimony, while, within the henge, the records dealt with here are the chief source of evidence concerning the Obelisk and elements of the Cove structure. None of the above features could have been deduced from the ground surface alone, or simply by projection from existing remnants of patterns; and the same is also true of many of the individual characteristics of stones, now lost, recorded by Stukeley and others. At the very least, any attempt to understand the prehistory of the Avebury complex must be indebted to the 17th- and 18th-century antiquarians for all this.

It is perhaps also proper to add the features which have come to light as a result of the fresh investigation inspired by the plans and divulged in the present study, such as the ancient road at the E entrance. Finally, a number of more speculative questions are opened, or re-opened, by the data contained in the early plans. These include the real possibility that portal stones stood at and/or within the entrances to the henge; the nature of the putative Beckhampton Avenue and/or Cove; and the possible existence of a Cove in the Kennet Avenue. In addition, Aubrey's suggestion of 'habitations' near West Kennet Farm, and his postulate that the avenue turned a sharp right-angle at that point, now bears reconsideration in the light of recent discoveries at West Kennet Farm (Whittle and Smith 1989). Indeed, had Aubrey been taken more seriously by later commentators, attention might long ago profitably have been directed to this location, thus forestalling the regrettable encroachment by the road and buildings to either side of it, which has so irrevocably disturbed this pivotal area.

Such matters outweigh the 'negative' factors of discrepancy between different records, and even simple inaccuracy, which have hitherto fuelled the condescending attitude that archaeologists have often adopted when trying to match Stukeley's and Aubrey's efforts with those of more 'objective' recorders. As we have seen, a number of the inconsistencies between different records, and even some of their 'inaccuracies', make sense in terms of the differing intentions underlying their composition. We have also dealt sympathetically with the preconceptions with which the antiquaries approached the site, and illustrated how these affected their assessment of features like the Cove or the general disposition of the antiquity, without being exclusive of empirical observation.

Hence the black-and-white attitude towards these early recorders shown by some 19th-century commentators (Chapter IV, q) does not seem in order here. Indeed, it is disturbing to find a similar line being taken by Caroline Malone in her recent study, in which she appears to dismiss all the 17th-century sources as more or less worthless, writing: 'Thanks to the work of Gray and Keiller this century, we do not need to take the early sketches of Aubrey and Charlton [sic] too seriously' (Malone 1989, 22).[1] In fact, it is hard to avoid the suspicion that she adopts this negative approach largely as an excuse for not going into the matter in the detail that it deserves. It is revealing that she contradicts herself in an adjacent passage by saying: 'much valuable information would have been lost for good without the interest taken in Avebury by two men, one in the 17th and one in the 18th century', in other words, Aubrey and Stukeley (Malone 1989, 21). Moreover, although she invokes the work of Keiller in dismissing these earlier records, Keiller's own interest in the early documents concerning the site is shown by the care with which he collected and preserved them (cf. Piggott 1950, 193–6).

What is equally important is to recognize how, for better or worse, all subsequent interpretation of the site – up to the present day – has been affected by these early records. Indeed, none of the archaeologists involved with Avebury in the 20th century has ever been able to free him- or herself from preconceptions derived from these earlier sources, and from ideas inherited from the interpretative structure of the antiquarians whose work has been outlined here. We may therefore now turn to assess the influence that these records and interpretations have had on subsequent perceptions of Avebury; and to consider how such perceptions have evolved and, in their turn, directed approaches to·the excavation and archaeological interpretation of the monument up to the present day.

The then-known antiquarian records were first openly exploited by the 19th-century successors to Aubrey and Stukeley – men such as the clerical antiquaries Bryan King, A. C. Smith and W. C. Lukis. Their discussions of the relative accuracy of the plans have already been referred to, while in 1865 Smith and King collaborated with William Cunnington III in excavating at Avebury with 'the desire to thoroughly ascertain the sites of certain of the great sarsen stones which had been removed in former days, and whose position was as yet more or less defined by depressions in the ground where they once stood' (Smith 1867, 210). Here, we have the beginning of a long-lived tradition of excavation designed almost exclusively, though not always explicitly, to test the records of the early antiquaries. This was not only continued in subsequent excavations by Smith (and Lukis) but, many years later, by Keiller and Piggott.

The nature of some of these 19th-century excavations has been briefly reviewed in Chapter IV. Despite their unsatisfactory nature – described in the case of one investigation of the bank as 'slight and random tappings in its mighty sides' (Smith 1867, 213–14) – Smith did succeed in finding the presumed site of destruction of the Obelisk. On the other hand, on extending his trench, he was unable to find evidence for Stukeley's inner southern circle. In addition, two partially buried stones were found in the SW quadrant and, on returning to dig and probe at Avebury in 1881, Smith and Lukis managed to locate 18 stones of the Outer Circle, several of which had been recorded by Stukeley as 'demolished'. In the same vein of setting-the-record-straight they were able to criticize not only Stukeley but also Crocker – who surveyed the site for Colt Hoare in 1812 – for failing to observe additional destruction pits.

If the influence of the antiquarian tradition on Victorian archaeologists like these was only to be expected, it is perhaps more surprising to find that it continued to be important even at the time when it is usually considered that systematic and scientific archaeology really began at Avebury. This was in 1908, when a campaign of five seasons of excavation (1908–9, 1911, 1914 and 1922) was inaugurated at the behest of the British Association for the Advancement of Science. The work on Avebury was to be the culmination of a more general enquiry into 'The Age of Stone Circles' on which the appointed archaeologist, Harold St George Gray, had been engaged since 1901. It was symptomatic of the confidence in prehistoric studies, which owed much to pioneering excavations elsewhere in Wessex, that it was considered possible to date stone circles solely on the principles of stratigraphy and artefactual association. Gray evidently felt able to interpret the Association's directive with considerable latitude, since he proceeded upon the most formidable digging campaign yet witnessed at Avebury.

Previous work at Avebury and at other circles had already shown them to be prehistoric (Gray 1935, 103–5) and Gray's cuttings into the bank and ditch were aimed at producing stratigraphic evidence for a relative chronology. Despite the fact that dating and relative chronology were the priority for research and investigatory design, however, Gray acknowledged the helpfulness of the earlier plans, including Aubrey's (Gray 1935, 99). Although his own excavations did not concern themselves with the pattern of the monument, both his survey of 1912 and passing remarks in his reports show that he was, in fact, influenced by Stukeley's record. Despite seeing no trace of it, Gray 'ventured to dot in a circle on the plan' (Gray 1935, 109 n. 1) within the northern inner circle. Again, within the southern circle he observed four apparent stone-holes happily disposed concentrically about the central depression thought to mark the position of the former Obelisk. This inner ring was also dotted in. Support was found for these conjectures in the supposed congruence of another depression, to the S, with Stukeley's 'ring-stone'. It remains remarkable that such ready acceptance of features attested to only by the antiquarian record was coupled with Gray's scrupulous examination of the topography of the site – exemplified by his refusal even to accept the 25-inch OS map as a reliable basis for his survey, and his insistence that every detail be measured anew, the resulting plan remaining as yet unsurpassed (though see below).

During the twelve years between the completion of Gray's excavations and the publication of his final report, considerable advances were made in identifying the relative chronological sequence expressed in prehistoric pottery assemblages. In particular, finds of sherds from the Avebury excavations were examined alongside the sequence then recently available from Windmill Hill (excavated 1925–9) and other Wiltshire sites. Stuart Piggott – to become the acknowledged expert on Stukeley – was then pioneering such pottery studies, and he was able to conclude that the Avebury material could 'be assigned to the overlap period in North Wiltshire between the end of the Neolithic ... and the dawn of the Bronze Age' (Piggott in Gray 1935, 136). Gray's principal objective of establishing Avebury's date therefore appeared to have been satisfactorily achieved.

Independent of but overlapping with Gray's fieldwork were the researches of Crawford during the years 1920–7, when he compiled notes and parts of the text for a projected book on Avebury. This very largely consisted of a dogged and painstaking correlation of the extant remains and of information derived from 19th-century excavations with Stukeley's published plan and engravings, and also, in the case of the Kennet Avenue, with two unpublished plans then in the possession of Keiller (Crawford MS.). This assessment helped, it is claimed, in the location of stone positions during the excavations of 1957–60 (Smith 1965, 185). What is striking is how seriously Crawford took Stukeley's evidence, despite the shortcomings in it that the 19th-century excavations had revealed. Indeed, the admiration of Crawford and others associated with him for Stukeley was often unconcealed: 'any modern archaeologist who has had occasion to test the accuracy of Stukeley's field-work ... will have proved the complete reliance that can be placed upon it' (Piggott 1935, 28).

Crawford's work exemplifies the manner in which Stukeley's materials have been used and interpreted by archaeologists virtually ever since. The main tendency has been to deploy the evidence of the antiquarians to 'discover' features which were not currently visible, both within the Avebury henge and outside it. Thus Crawford attempted to locate the Beckhampton Avenue on the basis of Stukeley's plans and views; failing in this, he tried photographing the Longstones field from the air, but was unable to identify any suggestive cropmarks (Crawford and Keiller 1928, 210–13, and pls xxxvii and xxxviii). A few years later a similar attempt was made to locate the site of the Sanctuary from the air: this also was unsuccessful, but the Sanctuary *was* eventually located using evidence deduced from Stukeley's various drawings and engravings of relevant features (Cunnington 1932). On another occasion Crawford made use of alignments derived from the engravings in *Abury*, together with the evidence of Stukeley's plan E, to identify the depression within the henge which he then equated with Stukeley's 'ring-stone' (Crawford MS.).

Comparable use of the antiquarian record to supplement archaeological evidence concerning particular sites has continued more recently (e.g. Barker 1985; Lambrick 1988; Whittle 1989). For example, at the site of the Millbarrow long barrow near Winterbourne Monkton, where the archaeological evidence on its own was clearly inadequate, Whittle (1989, 7) concluded that 'the excavation has confirmed the general indication given by Aubrey and Stukeley that a large barrow with stone structures existed at Millbarrow'. In fact he is here making use of the antiquarian record to interpret – and therefore to presume – details of the facade and other features which could not be directly substantiated by excavation (Whittle 1989, 5).

Such deductions take for granted that the antiquarian record was substantially accurate, yet even in Crawford's time certain key discrepancies made it clear that it was not, and again his response to this is revealing. One important question is how he dealt with discrepancies between the evidence of Aubrey and Stukeley. On the whole, Stukeley's record was preferred to Aubrey's, presumably because of the apparently greater detail that it provided, and Crawford's MS. reveals him as highly equivocal in his evaluation of Aubrey. In one place, he attempted to show that Aubrey's records supported Stukeley's interpretation. When further enquiry showed that they did not, he deleted those parts of his manuscript approving Aubrey, substituting for the suggestion that 15 stones recorded by Aubrey could have formed part of the outer southern circle the following passage: 'others which he shows may have belonged to this circle, but some of them certainly did not' (Crawford MS., 13). The overall impression is that where Crawford thought that information deriving from Aubrey or Stukeley confirmed the archaeological evidence, it was quoted with approval; where there was perceived conflict between Aubrey and Stukeley, it was usually but not always the latter who was given credence; where the 19th-century archaeology was perceived to be in conflict with Stukeley it was often the nature of the archaeological investigation that was criticized. Crawford was especially scathing towards the publications of A. C. Smith, whose stone locations were impugned as often erroneous and whose plan 'is about as bad as it could be' (Crawford MS., 13).

As for the discrepancies between Stukeley's various records, Crawford was to some extent aware of these (Crawford MS.). But it has to be said that it is doubtful if the early 20th-century archaeological fraternity would have continued to accord such trust to the work of Stukeley had they been fully aware of all his 'inconsistencies' through studying his unpublished notes and draft frontispieces, the bulk of which had been bequeathed to the Bodleian by Richard Gough. That they did continue to take his work very seriously is certain. Would the debate regarding the possible existence of the Beckhampton Avenue have raged – and continue so to do today – if it had been generally known how radically Stukeley's views changed concerning the nature and exact location of its termination, as has been revealed here (Chapter II, v)? In fact – and as acknowledged, for example, by Piggott (1985, 95) – Stukeley saw no standing stones between the so-called Beckhampton Cove and the supposed termination of the continuation of his avenue: he also recorded only three stones standing in the entire length of the avenue between the Longstones and

Avebury, in an area probably scattered with naturally occurring sarsens. Were his fragmentary alignments of fallen stones merely fortuitous? Or invented? Or was his recording indeed a remarkable feat of intuitive fieldwork and observation.

Insofar as archaeologists did take cognizance of the problems of Stukeley's own evidence, their main reaction was to have recourse to the thesis, the inadequacy of which has been exposed here (Chapters I and II), that a division could be made between the sound and the unsound in his work. As Crawford put it: 'He may have been fanciful and absurd in his conjectures, but he was diligent and generally accurate in his record of facts ... Let us once for all [sic] pay a tribute of esteem and gratitude to Stukeley's memory' (Crawford and Keiller 1928, 211). This was then developed by Piggott, first in his article of 1935 – in which Stukeley's distortion of the shape of the Sanctuary was invoked in this connection – and then more fully in his biography (Piggott 1950; 1985), in which a sharp dichotomy was claimed between a period of accurate recording on the one hand, and, on the other, the fantastical meanderings exemplified in his published *Abury*. This presumed chasm has had profound effects on archaeological interpretation: for example, it has become 'the orthodoxy of modern use of Stukeley to discount any records based on 'his theory that the monuments had been laid out in the form of a serpent', as opposed to the 'objective observation' during Stukeley's early years of fieldwork at Avebury (Smith 1965, 217). We must repeat that such a basis for assessing the reliability, or otherwise, of Stukeley's data is not valid. Yet we would argue that such an unwarranted discrimination in the treatment of his observations has crept unquestioned into the archaeological portrait of Avebury. One particular consequence has been the 20th-century conclusion (Smith 1965, 217 n. 2) that some of Aubrey's observations (about a West Kennet Cove) should be discounted on the basis of Stukeley's records from his 'sound' period.

We may now turn to the excavations at Avebury from 1934 to 1939, largely the work of Alexander Keiller, which transformed 'the outstanding archaeological disgrace of Britain' – as he called it – into the partially restored and somewhat sanitized monument we know today. It is undoubtedly significant that there was a direct personal link between Crawford and Keiller – the former launching Keiller 'into the turgid waters of British archaeology' in the 1920s and continuing to provide appropriate sympathy and support thereafter (Piggott in Smith 1965, xx). Thus Crawford's plotting of the Kennet Avenue was probably partly responsible for stimulating Keiller's and Piggott's own work there. Another link between Keiller and earlier work at Avebury was provided by St George Gray who – ironically as it would turn out – was engaged for the excavation of Windmill Hill in 1925 as a sop to those who felt that Keiller lacked experience (Malone 1989, 64). This partnership was an unhappy one, perhaps because Keiller's 'fantastic perfectionism' was obsessive quite beyond practical necessity (Piggott in Smith 1965, xxii).

Keiller – 'erratic and at times infuriating' (Crawford in Piggott 1983, 32) – nevertheless remained consistent in seeing 'our task [as] primarily that of those in the field, viz to record facts for the arm-chair theorists of this and future generations' (Keiller corresp. to Gray, 1925). He thus echoed A. C. Smith – and, beyond him, Colt Hoare – in his aspiration to eschew 'theory' in favour of 'tangible facts' (Smith 1867, 211; Colt Hoare 1812–21). In 1934 Keiller and Stuart Piggott, who had taken private employment with him a year before, began to excavate and to restore the northern part of the Kennet Avenue, continuing this work in 1935 and 1937. The excavations within the henge took place under Keiller's sole direction in 1937–9, but were then interrupted by the outbreak of war. In the NW and SW quadrants his main efforts were directed towards the clearance and restoration of the 'Great Circle'. His final season, in the SE quadrant, was devoted mainly to investigating and restoring what remained of the southern inner circle and examining the southern entrance causeway. As is well known, almost none of this work was published during Keiller's lifetime: this considerable feat was to be achieved ten years after his death in the now classic account by Isobel Smith (Smith 1965).

Keiller claimed that his exclusive aim was the judicious and exact restoration of Avebury, together with the retrieval of fundamental facts about its cultural and chronological setting: 'The primary purpose of these excavations [on the Kennet Avenue] was to establish the exact course followed by the avenue, and furthermore, if possible, to arrive at a definite date and culture for the construction of the monument' (Keiller and Piggott 1936, 418). From what he said in other contexts Keiller considered himself to be dispassionate in his assessments, and clearly viewed his reconstruction work at Avebury as inherently factually based. Thus he wrote that:

> It has been brought to my notice that in some quarters it has been suggested that I have re-erected certain fallen stones in this section of the West Kennet Avenue, not upon any scientific principles but in order to conform with some involved but unspecified theories of my own as regards the original significance or purpose of these monuments. I desire to take this and, indeed, every, opportunity of categorically denying any such suggestion. I should consider that I had grossly betrayed the trust which has been placed in me by those who have consented to my taking charge of these operations had I for an instant failed to apply my invariable principle that, while theory may well be the natural corollary of excavation in the field, the sole immediate purpose of the latter must be the establishment of demonstrable fact. ('Note for preface to report of erection of stones, by Alex Keiller', Keiller corresp.)

This outburst may have been related to his supposed identification of Avenue stone position 30b, for which no stone-hole was in fact located. Despite a total absence of evidence, Keiller had felt it acceptable to estimate this stone's probable position, which he identified with a distinctive plinth.

This latter episode appears to be not atypical of Keiller's presumption that the nature of the real Avebury could be established by a judicious use of past records and contemporary archaeological investigation, and that once the nature of the evidence had become clear to his satisfaction it should be presented in appropriate form for everyone to enjoy. He appears not to have suffered from doubts about the possibility that he might misinterpret evidence, whether derived from the antiquarian record or from his own direct enquiries (Malone 1986, 9). It also seems unlikely that Keiller would have recognized the value of questioning, for example, the appropriateness of his policy of marking stone-holes with 'concrete blocks ... deliberately made as unlike the megaliths as possible in case they should be confused with them' (Chapman 1939, 14), even when this resulted in having a plinth in 'pyramidal' shape to mark the assumed spot of Stukeley's 'Obelisk'. Given the detail of the shape and dimensions of the latter stone as recorded by Stukeley, which Keiller's own excavations partly confirmed, it is interesting that Keiller chose to represent the centre of the southern 'circle' by a symbol at once so out of place within the context of British megalithic stone arrangements, yet – ironically – so reminiscent of Stukeley's conviction of a direct linkage between Avebury and ancient Egypt.

Had the war and ill-health not intervened, Keiller would no doubt have proceeded with his intended reinstatement of the entire Avebury monument, adopting whatever signs and symbols he considered appropriate. But it is symptomatic of the limitations of this enterprise – to which we will return later in this chapter – that Piggott has said of his joint work with Keiller: 'As the Avebury excavations continued, and became to my mind more like megalithic landscape gardening than research archaeology, I became increasingly bored and in need of some more congenial intellectual activity' (Piggott 1983, 32).

How far was Keiller influenced by the antiquarian record? We have already seen the degree to which Crawford was influenced by Stukeley's work, and this would establish a *prima facie* case for Keiller's inheriting similar concerns. Keiller's interest in such sources was evident early on, when he acquired many of Stukeley's original manuscripts at the sale of family papers in 1924. Indeed, at this point he was clearly enthralled by stone circles and he indulged in a speculation worthy of Stukeley when he wrote, after the first season at Windmill Hill: 'might it not be that Windmill Hill was originally a monstrous stone circle; that the stones were removed, presumably to Avebury, and that thereupon the area within the ditch surrounding the outer circle of standing stones was utilized as a habitation site, and one or two other ditches added. This would account for the stone holes and also for our finds of pottery, bones etc etc which all point to a dwelling site of considerable magnitude' (Keiller corresp. to Gray, 1925). Thereafter, as Piggott acknowledges, it was Keiller who first made him aware of the importance of Stukeley's work and who encouraged him to make a close study of Stukeley's unpublished manuscripts: this led Piggott to his major contributions both on Stukeley himself and on the history of antiquarianism more generally (Piggott 1935, 23 n. 2; cf. Piggott 1937, 1950, 1976, 1985, 1989).

On the other hand, Keiller – who probably commented in 1924 on Crawford's analysis of Stukeley – was not an uncritical devotee of Stukeley, let alone of Aubrey (Chapter IV, q). He was sometimes willing to accept the usefulness of the antiquarian record, but equally capable of pointing out when he thought it inadequate. It is revealing to find that he produced a comparative diagram entitled 'Avebury – the Earlier Plans' showing the stone positions within the outline of the henge as compiled by Aubrey, Stukeley, Colt Hoare and A. C. Smith, although he never published it. Moreover, his excavations were conceived at least in part as a direct 'check' on Stukeley. In 1937 a special trench was dug to find evidence for a single stone shown by Stukeley as lying on his inner 'Outer circle' in the NW quadrant. Keiller believed that his results 'proved conclusively that no stone had ever stood here or in the immediate vicinity' (Keiller 1939, 225) – though in fact, as we have argued (Chapter IV, r), he had singularly failed to do so. (It is ironic that it was in a separate cleaning-up operation that season that Keiller stumbled upon the northern causeway – totally unsuspected on the basis of Stukeley's record.) Even in 1960, an excavation was specially undertaken to check whether or not another of Stukeley's stones had really existed (Smith's 1965 stone H; Piggott 1964).

Such examples of attempts to locate stones recorded by Stukeley highlight the way in which views of the monument derived from antiquarian records have continued to play a significant role in archaeological enquiry at Avebury. But it is not only in the continued search for proof or negation of particular stone arrangements recorded by Aubrey or Stukeley that we find such influence: it is also to be seen in what archaeologists have attempted, and continue to attempt, to recognize as significant features in the archaeological record.

For instance, it is striking how the concept of the circle has maintained its traditional grip on interpretation. As we saw in Chapter IV, the evidence for at least three of the stone circles claimed by Stukeley is suspect. What is more, our resistivity results suggest that, if there *was* a northern 'circle' within the Avebury henge at all, it may well not have been exactly in any of the locations proposed by Aubrey or Stukeley and accepted by subsequent archaeologists, and neither was it necessarily of the regular circular shape which has been assumed to have been the intention of the builders of other putative circles at the site. In the light of these results it is remarkable how the slender evidence for such circles has, until now, withstood the test of time. For it would be wrong to give the impression that these problems belonged only to the 17th and 18th centuries and have now vanished: in fact, such symbols as the circle continue to exercise immense power, and the same is true of the cross (see Chapter VI). In the case of prehistoric Avebury circular concepts have recurred ever since the time of Aubrey, Charleton and Stukeley. Thus, with the henge itself, circular presumptions are enshrined in that most powerful of modern archaeological symbols, the 'tentative' reconstruction, exemplified in diagrammatic form by Smith (1965, fig. 70); similarly, in the 19th century, Lukis even suggested that Longstone Cove was the 'remains of a large circle – a monument entirely distinct from Avebury' (Lukis 1881–3a, 155). Even in 1960, when Piggott briefly returned to Avebury looking for a new feature which was not evidenced in the antiquarian record at all, it was a circle that he looked for. In 1937, he had suggested to Keiller that three apparent stone-holes in the NE quadrant of the henge had formed a third stone circle (Stuart Piggott pers. comm.). This third circle – for which the evidence was very partial (Keiller 1939, 226–7; Chapman 1939) – would have existed prior to the 'Great Circle' and the bank and ditch, and would therefore have provided the first good evidence from Avebury for any sort of structural phasing such as had been demonstrated for Stonehenge. In the event Piggott demonstrated that no such circle had existed (Piggott 1964, 29; and see Smith 1965, 191). Yet this third circle now again lives on in the National Trust-sponsored work of Burl (1979, 164, fig. 7).

It is not only the presumption of circularity which has survived from the 17th to the 20th centuries but also the presumption of regularity. We may recall that Stukeley assumed regularity in the numbers of stones and the intervals between them because of his expectations about the sophistication of Avebury's builders; we have also seen how these affected his recording of what was actually to be discerned in the field, and how such preconceptions may have led him to decide in different locations whether or not there were traces of hollows representing once-present stones (Chapters II, vi and IV). The pattern of a regularly spaced circular setting is one which we are attuned to perceive and accept, and it has continued to be at the centre of interpretations of megalithic (and other) prehistoric monuments. Like Stukeley, Smith assumed (rather than deduced) regular stone intervals at Avebury, and it was on this basis that she arrived at her reconstruction (Smith 1965). As a consequence, and perpetuating one of Stukeley's shortcomings, stones for which there is no physical evidence have been irrevocably allocated position numbers; in addition, and in contrast to Stukeley, simple hollows in the ground are assumed to be burning-pits and, whether excavated or not, have also been given numbers. We therefore have before us in the 1990s a no less idealized picture of Avebury than Stukeley's, shaped in the 1720s.

The presumption of regularity has also affected the interpretation of linear features in the Avebury complex, and not least the Kennet and Beckhampton avenues. Excavations at West Kennet between 1957 and 1960 by W. E. V. Young, previously Keiller's foreman, were undertaken in the expectation of finding several of the Avenue stone positions underlying the present road. In part, such expectations were founded on the work of Aubrey and Stukeley, and the transcription of the latter's record onto the OS map by Crawford (see above, and Smith 1965, 187). But, in addition, it is important to realize that Young had a clear expectation of a regular 'avenue' at West Kennet, and this affected the way in which he and others came to interpret features excavated there. As we have seen (Chapter IV, m) resistivity survey has so far not been able to confirm the expected course of the Kennet Avenue. This raises the real, if unlikely, possibility that the chalk-cut features found by Young could be of various ages and be susceptible to other explanations. For example, were it not for our preconceived ideas about the Avenue's likely route, we would undoubtedly be placing more weight on the evidence that sarsen boulders are, or were, abundant in these valley bottoms (Smith 1965, pl. xxxviiia). In the valley bottom north of West Kennet, for instance, Stukeley noted their presence in certain of his plans of the area (e.g. Eng.Misc.b.65, 43), and even today, despite generations of clearance, scores of sarsens are still ploughed into. Such stones could presumably have received the same destructive treatment as any deliberately placed prehistoric monoliths, leaving comparable burning pits and other traces.

There seems to be a continuing fascination in attempting to fit the occasional find of sarsens, pits and other features into Aubrey's or Stukeley's presumed circular or linear patterns (e.g. Smith 1965, 223; Hawkes, Heaton, and Trott 1989). Thus, even recent Royal Commission/Ordnance Survey records maintain that 'Stukeley's theory was supported by the finding in 1968 ... of (i) the possible robbing pit of a stone in the High Street ... and, (ii) a buried stone beside the A4 road' and that 'a large buried sarsen and a possible stone robbing hole were encountered in October 1965 in a GPO trench. Identified by Mrs Vatcher as almost certainly part of the Beckhampton stone row recorded by Stukeley' (RCHM, SU06 NE62; Vatcher 1969; Vatcher and Vatcher 1980).

Even our own interpretation of resistivity data illustrates comparable presumptions, for pattern recognition in this context raises problems very similar to those which confronted our archaeological forebears. Once we have recorded the data from geophysical survey it is still largely a matter of inference as to what recorded features are taken to be of archaeological significance. It remains a matter of discretion and experience as to when 'noise' on our plots is taken as significant or when it is adjudged subsidiary to particular anomalies. Thus, in the surveys, as in our Avebury studies generally, it is clear that our interpretation within the data has in places been selective of the more 'probable' of a range of potential choices. In at least one case we have made conscious use of the antiquarian record to argue against the likelihood that an otherwise significant resistivity anomaly is evidence of a buried stone or burning pit (Chapter IV, o). In other cases we do not wish to deny that our 'recognition' of repetitive anomalies on certain axes has been encouraged (nor, indeed, that we have been inhibited from searching for other possible 'patterns') by knowing that the area which we were investigating included the extension of a line of visible stones or of stones recorded by Aubrey and Stukeley. But we must admit that it is quite possible that other people, lacking our presumptions, might discern a different set of possibly significant patterns in our resistivity plots. Such a realization, however, in no way implies that the patterns that we have claimed to recognize are not in fact present.

At this point we may generalize more broadly still about the way in which interpretation has been affected, as in the 17th and 18th centuries, by preconceptions, sometimes the same ones. We may note the commonsensical deduction that the fact that the ditch was inside rather than outside the bank suggested that it was non-defensive and that it formed a kind of amphitheatre from which spectators might have viewed ceremonies carried out in the inner 'sacred area . . . without being allowed to get closer' (Aubrey 24, 31; Fowles and Legg 1980, 34; Coupland 1988; Gray 1935, 161). This latter suggestion, based on implicit analogy with classical and more recent public arenas, is to be found in Stukeley (1743, 15), in Gray (1935, 161), and in the present owners of Avebury, the National Trust, who even go so far as to say that 'Henges [in general] seem to have been temples in which the ditch defined the sacred ritual area while the banks could have seated large congregations' (Muir and Welfare 1983, 90).

A more questionable example of the impact of presumptions is provided by 20th-century deductions about the burial of stones at Avebury (Chapter IV, h). Young categorically dismissed the idea that the stones were buried to get them out of the way of the plough as 'to my mind utterly unreasonable': he argued that shallowly buried stones were more of an obstacle than stones above surface which could easily be seen and ploughed round, 'with the loss only of the small space of ground they occupied'. It was this presumption that the stones were not buried on grounds of simple economic rationality that spawned the idea that they might have been treated thus for 'ritual' (i.e. irrational) reasons. However, it is interesting to turn to Stukeley in this connection, for, in his eyes, his contemporaries *did* act irrationally. He thought that local inhabitants sought to get rid of the stones 'chiefly out of covetousness of the little *area* of ground, each stood on', despite the fact that the 'expense of digging the grave, was more than 30 years purchase of the spot they possess'd, when standing' (Stukeley 1743, 15). In other words, Young was presuming that it was obvious what people in the past would see as economic good sense, yet in fact it was not. Without caution and self-awareness it is all too easy to make presumptions based on our concepts of such matters as economic rationality, and on this basis then to slip unthinkingly into the catch-all category of the 'ritual'.

Unsubstantiated presumptions about the 'ritual' realm also appear in 20th-century views about the significance of the shape of stones in different parts of the antiquity. In the 18th century, Stukeley believed that stones were selected for their regular 'rhomboid' shape, while he also thought that 'they took care to set the smoothest & most sightly side of the stones innermost where most in view . . . so they placd the best stones of the outer circle towards both entrances, of the avenues. all along observing the best effect that could be producd from such materials & with much judgment' (Stukeley 1722–4b, 122). Stukeley claimed that in this respect Avebury resembled Stonehenge. Nowadays this interpretation is not usually mentioned in connection with Avebury, where the original claim of Keiller and Piggott (1936, 420) that certain stones had been artificially shaped (and carved on) has been generally rejected. In its place, attention has been drawn to the opposition of tall and thin stones with squat and wide ones – apparently intentional, though expressed in different ways, both in the Avenue and within the henge circles: this has been supposed to reflect an assumed general fertility cult (Smith 1965, 251) though details of the practice of this are rarely specified (see, however, Dames 1977).

Perhaps the most tenacious of traditions of this kind is the assumption of a profound relationship between human burial and the site of Avebury, a theme which has preoccupied many commentators throughout the period covered by this book. We have already seen how Charleton claimed that 'a Monument of some Danish King' was to be found at the heart of the henge, a suggestion which he may have owed to his mentor Olaus Worm. A comparable presumption is seen in Charles II's command to Aubrey to excavate within the site 'to try if I could find any humane bones', a suggestion which may also owe something to an established royal and aristocratic tradition of barrow digging, going back at least to the Anglo-Norman period (Marsden 1974).

The presumed link between megaliths and burials may have been strengthened by discoveries made by such early barrow diggers, for they would almost certainly have encountered large stones in or near some of the mounds that they explored. Moreover, this link was explicitly canvassed by Stukeley, who was aware of the juxtaposition of standing stones with burials at sites like Millbarrow (Stukeley 1722-4a, 113): it was this that lay behind the theory that he adopted in 1723, that Avebury itself represented a two-dimensional mausoleum focused on Silbury Hill, which he believed to be the burial site of Avebury's founder (Chapter II, v). Perhaps more surprising is the fact that such presumed associations live on. Thus, in an unrevised speculation, Richard Atkinson suggests that Silbury contains the body of a Bronze Age potentate, architect of Stonehenge: 'a figure as shadowy and insubstantial as King Brutus of the medieval British History. Yet who but he should sleep, like Arthur or Barbarossa, in the quiet darkness of a sarsen vault beneath the mountainous pile ...' (Atkinson 1979, 167).

In terms of excavated evidence the link between stone circles and burials was apparently confirmed in 1678 when workmen '(digging not far off the ro[a]d)' at the Sanctuary reported that they 'throw upp many bones here, but know not of what creatures' (Aubrey 24, 14; Fowles and Legg 1980, 52). These were identified as human by Robert Toope, a local physician, who reported to Aubrey in a letter of 1685 how he made 'a noble medicine' from them on this and other occasions (though others were worried by the element of sacrilege involved, and a local informant later told Stukeley that 'Took [sic] never thrived after it[:] his daughter went a begging' (Gough Maps 231, 48v)). Indeed, Toope assured Aubrey that the bones lay 'soe close one by another that scul toucheth scul', the whole site being thought to be 'full of dead bones' (Aubrey 24, 14v; Fowles and Legg 1980, 53). No clearer indication that a stone circle was used as a cemetery could be needed, although the dating of the bones was, and is still, in doubt. Within the Avebury henge itself, the search for comparable remains inspired the first excavations there, those initiated by the Wiltshire Archaeological and Natural History Society in 1865. These were stimulated by perhaps the most idiosyncratic of 19th-century commentators on Avebury, the indigo merchant turned architectural historian, James Fergusson (Watkin 1980, 82–5). Fergusson came to the study of Avebury from an extensive acquaintance with the architecture of the East, and it was not least on this basis that he claimed of Avebury 'that it was, like almost all the circular buildings throughout the world, dedicated to the memory of the dead, and not to the worship of any living God' (Fergusson 1860, 210). Fergusson's views on Avebury were more fully elaborated in his *Rude Stone Monuments in All Countries: Their Age and Uses* of 1872, which has been described as 'the first general survey of megalithic architecture' (Daniel 1981, 96). In relation to Avebury, Fergusson's main purpose seems to have been to throw contempt on the 'Ophite heresy', as he described Stukeley's 'Dracontia'. Although we have seen that many people have had their suspicions of Stukeley's work (see Chapter IV and above), Fergusson's opprobrium reached almost paranoid levels:

> Stukeley, however, cut the vessel adrift from the moorings of comon sense, and she has since been a derelict tossed about by the winds and waves of every passing fancy, till recently, when an attempt has been made to tow the wreck into the misty haven of prehistoric antiquity. If she ever reaches that nebulous region, she may as well be broken up in despair, as she can be of no further use for human purposes. (Fergusson 1872, 15–16)

However, Fergusson's own theory for Avebury appears to us no less dubious, based on a strained reading of the evidence, in ignorance of dating clues which now seem crucial:

> I feel no doubt that it will come eventually to be acknowledged that those who fell in Arthur's twelfth and greatest battle were buried in the ring at Avebury, and that those who survived raised these stones and the mound at Silbury in the vain hope that they would convey to their latest posterity the memory of their prowess. (Fergusson 1872, 89)

In support of this date and of the funerary purpose of the monument, he adduced various more or less convincing evidence, including the fact that all extant traditions associated this and comparable monuments with the post-Roman era, and the reference to 'burying places' at the end of the 'stone row' (see Chapter I, i) (Fergusson 1860, 209; 1872, 73–4). But – just as his claim that Silbury post-dated the Roman road was quickly challenged by Sir John Lubbock (Lubbock 1865, 54–5) – so Fergusson's assertions concerning a funerary function for Avebury were undermined by the 1865 excavations of A. C. Smith, William Cunnington III and Bryan King. By the end of these, they could exult in dismissing Fergusson's theory: they had found no human bones (Smith 1885, 139).

The perennial theme of Avebury and human burials did not, however, disappear, for the 20th-century excavations brought to light human inhumations in the ditches surrounding the henge and at the base of four Avenue stones. Not only was the inhumation of a so-called adult female dwarf found in the filling of one of the ditch terminals;[2] in addition, some twenty other human bones were recovered in ditch deposits (Gray 1935, 148). Gray himself appears to have drawn no special inference from these human remains, but subsequent writers have (e.g. Smith 1965, 251), and Burl has even risked a calculation that perhaps three hundred such bones could still lie within the henge ditch (Burl 1979, 68).

What is perhaps more surprising is that Crawford, who epitomizes several of the themes we have reviewed above, continued to associate the circular stone arrangements at Avebury with a funerary tradition: 'The purpose was probably sepulchral. We may imagine that the Cove originally contained an interment – its arrangement when perfect recalls the burial-chambers of Brittany and Cornwall; and a similar cove probably occupied the now empty place of the obelisk, at the centre of the southern circle' (Crawford and Keiller 1928, 213). However we regard this speculation, it reflects the continuing belief that central physical features at Avebury, and particularly the Cove, formed the focal points of rituals, whether these were assumed to be burials or sacrifices. While the 19th-century excavation by Smith and others was focused on the Cove with a view to assessing whether or not there were burials there, in Chapter IV, y, we saw other approaches to its function, culminating in Burl's (1988) suggestions regarding funerary miming.

Clearly, therefore, the idea that funerary activities were centrally involved in what went on at Avebury is still fashionable. Whereas Crawford's view may no longer seem appropriate, some present-day suggestions have much in common with antiquarian concerns and assumptions, being inherently based on the view that such a mighty structure cannot simply have been of secular intent. Among the factors favouring such views is the discovery at the West Kennet Long Barrow of jumbled disarticulated bones, presumably the result of funerary rites involving successive burial and other activities (Piggott 1962, 21–4, 65–8). Following Aubrey's assumption that the Avenue was a processional way from West Kennet to Avebury, and in the light of the discoveries of bones at the Sanctuary and at Avebury itself, it is easy to see why some would still wish to view the entire Avebury complex as a kind of funerary landscape.

We may end with a sobering reflection about the nature of the record itself, and the way in which this has been affected by pre-existent assumptions. For it is important to recognize, not only that conceptions of what constitutes a proper degree of 'accuracy' in recording are continually changing, but also that, as our preconceptions become modified, so do our very assessments of what may or may not be significant features in the archaeological record (and therefore worthy of such precise record). In Chapter II, ii, we discussed how the antiquarians who initially undertook field observation had no accepted guidelines either as to what should be recorded in the field, or as to the means by which to do so. Since then, a tradition of such recording has developed, with the cumulative result that plans produced in successive generations which were considered satisfactorily accurate by their makers – Crocker, A. C. Smith, Lukis and so on – have subsequently been superseded. Even Gray's plan, considered adequate until 1989, has now beeen adjudged insufficient: for present purposes, greater topographical detail, as well as the up-dating of the current village holdings, is required. So, in 1990, Aubrey's initial intentions in plan C have again become relevant: a new survey, taking in the entire World Heritage area, is to be undertaken by the Royal Commission for Ancient and Historical Monuments with a view to establishing the most precise record yet achieved. Yet however valuable a new survey is, we can guarantee that at some future date it will itself be deemed inadequate.

On the other hand, although such a cumulative growth of accuracy is undoubted, it is not uncomplicated; for, at every point in this process, decisions have had to be made as to just what should be recorded with the appropriate degree of exactness. When Aubrey decided to use a black dot to indicate presumed stone positions as well as visible – lying or standing – stones for his plan A, he clearly did not consider the distinction between these three important enough to be differentiated visually on his plan. Again, Stukeley experimented extensively in his draft frontispieces with different conventions and lettering in an attempt to convey as much information as possible through the use of symbols – stones standing, recently fallen, fallen, taken away, hollow, stone fragment, etc. He also pondered about the advantages of such symbolic representation over verbal description. By deciding to publish plan E and drastically to reduce his proposed written text, he removed all details regarding the depth and nature of the hollows and 'cavities' in which he thought that stones had once stood. He took this decision on the implicit assumption that such detail was not – and presumably would not in the future be – of concern. Yet his belief that his visual record would be adequate without the written commentary with which he initially furnished it has been shown by our investigations in this book to be unfounded.

This is not, however, a problem unique to the 18th century, for a similar state of affairs is to be found in the 20th, in connection with the record of Keiller's excavations at Avebury as reconstructed by Smith (1965). Since we are aware of the problems involved in the dating of the burial of stones at Avebury, it is clear that the depth and nature of surviving hollows in the ground may assist in establishing the history of a stone's disappearance. Whereas Keiller's recording of excavated stone hollows, pits, and destruction sites was very precise, no published attempt has so far been made to characterize unexcavated hollows except – in some cases perhaps mistakenly – as 'burning pits' (e.g. Smith 1965, fig. 70). Since 1965 we have been presented with the concept of a 'typical stone-hole' (Smith 1965, 203), although such holes could in fact be the result of several very different activities. Detailed topographic survey, as envisaged by RCHM (see above), can be expected to clarify the nature of hollows and other surface features in the area, and to shed new light on such questions.

Somewhat similarly, changing perceptions of what may or may not be relevant in the archaeological record have led to problems in interpreting the significance of ancillary finds recorded by archaeologists and others throughout the centuries. As we have seen in Chapter IV, h, the question of how to date the burial of stones at Avebury is insoluble insofar as there is an absence of detailed information, not only about which burial pits had medieval material within them, but also about the precise nature of any 'association' between such material and the buried stones. We have very little detail from Stukeley about the nature of the 'association' between his reported Roman skeleton and the stone found with it (Stukeley 1722–4b, 132; Appendix II) but it is disappointing to find comparable inadequacies in the 20th-century record. Clearly, as knowledge grows, and the possibilities for interpretation become greater, so the need for a clear definition of an 'archaeological association' becomes more acute. The Avebury story leaves no doubt that Stukeley's and, for example, Smith's understanding of when – quite apart from why – stones had been buried in the past was very different. Their consequent assumptions undoubtedly coloured the ways in which they chose to present the 'facts' of the Avebury record.

It is also the case that the ambitions of those associated with Avebury have been conditioned by inherited presumptions as to what were appropriate parameters of investigation. To identify a stone or a possible stone placement within a regular pattern has all too often been taken as some kind of end in itself. It is otherwise difficult to understand how, in the 1990s, when archaeological research is clearly focused on the attempt to place sites within their wider cultural and economic environments, a megalithic site such as Avebury remains virtually unexamined from any point of view except that of its monumental earthworks and stone placements. It is almost as if the ability to match the jigsaw pieces to the antiquarian-derived outline model has obviated the need to seek for archaeological evidence of habitation, activity areas, or other non-monumental features.

As we see, therefore, our perceptions are as inescapably interrelated to our preconceptions today as was the case with the early antiquaries. This is not to say that we are enslaved by such preconceived ideas, but that we need to be aware of them, and that we should attempt to test and re-examine them. One way of doing this, as illustrated in this book, is by looking at the remains of an antiquity like Avebury through the alien eyes of our 17th- and 18th-century forebears.

Notes

1. She continues: '[We] should see them as part of the academic discussion of the seventeenth century that has developed into the archaeological science of this century' (Malone 1989, 22). It seems worth pointing out for the benefit of potential readers of her book that Malone's summary of the antiquarian discovery of Avebury (Malone 1989, 21–2) contains almost as many misunderstandings or errors as it does sentences. It was not after reading 'written descriptions' of the site by Aubrey that Charles II asked to be shown it; Charleton's name is misspelt Charlton throughout; Aubrey's and Charleton's papers were not 'on the geometrical significance' of Avebury, and neither were 'all the arrangements of stones' 'set in exact geometrical alignment'; Charleton did not show four avenues of stones, and neither did Aubrey show 'only the outer circle and a single, centrally placed inner circle'. It is also far from clear what is meant by her claim that 'It would seem that these drawings were the result of philosophical argument, rather than observation on the ground'. This list could be continued, but it is perhaps worth adding a final comment about p. 82, where she says that Aubrey recorded the Sanctuary in 1648, which must be a garbled reference to his discovery of Avebury in 1649 (see Chapter I, ii): the exact date at which Aubrey made his observations of the Sanctuary is not known, but it was almost certainly later than his original discovery of Avebury. In addition, she is wrong to state on the same page that it was Aubrey who recorded that local people called it the Sanctuary: in fact it was Stukeley.

2. Don Brothwell (pers. comm.) has informed us that the use of the term 'dwarf' was incorrect, the size of bones from the individual in question being within the normal range of adult stature. He estimates that the individual would have been perhaps 5 feet tall.

VI *The future*

The past two years have been critical ones for Avebury. This book stems from one event during this period, the discovery in August 1988 of two hitherto unremarked plans of the site dating back to 1663, which has stimulated the complete re-evaluation of 17th- and 18th-century records of Avebury offered here. But this has been juxtaposed with a series of developments which have raised in acute form questions relating to the preservation and interpretation of the monument and the relationship between the two. Because of this, we feel it imperative to place the significance of our work firmly within the context of the future of Avebury and its surrounding monuments. Here the nature of the present interdisciplinary study of Avebury may be instructive in itself, for it is exceptional in combining historical, archival, geophysical and archaeological skills, including the application of subsurface detection to landscapes in a specific research project. As a result, it has revealed some of the difficulties engendered by current structural and organizational divisions between aspects of archaeological endeavour: universities, laboratory-based archaeological science, archives and the 'heritage industry' – in its own hierarchy of manifestations from supra-national (UNESCO) via National Trust and English Heritage, to local enterprise.

One inescapable fact is that these monuments are major tourist attractions; in addition, several of them, including the Sanctuary and part of the Kennet Avenue, are Guardianship Sites, 'monuments of such outstanding archaeological quality that they ... constitute relatively rare cases where English Heritage have taken over the management of sites in order to present them to the visitor' (English Heritage n.d.). They are also part of the 'World Heritage': as we saw in the Introduction, 'the joint site of Stonehenge, Avebury and their associated sites' forms one of the eleven World Heritage Sites in the United Kingdom. It is described as being one of the 'most important and characteristic prehistoric monuments in Britain. [It] represent[s] the Henge monument *par excellence*, as the largest, most evolved and best preserved prehistoric temple of a type unique to Britain. Together with the associated sites and monuments [it] provide[s] a landscape without parallel in Britain or elsewhere and provide[s] an unrivalled demonstration of human achievement in prehistoric times.' (English Heritage n.d.). Currently, both English Heritage and the National Trust are deeply involved in plans which will have a major effect on Avebury's future.

While this book has been in progress, Avebury and its surroundings have been discussed in several significant contexts. First, there was an official inquiry into the possible merits and demerits of constructing a hotel/hostel and information centre to replace the current Ridgeway Cafe situated opposite the Sanctuary site. In April 1989, the proposed redevelopment was rejected by the Secretary of State for the Environment, and in 1990 the National Trust acquired the Ridgeway Cafe site (for £250,000). The Trust had already 'owned some 920 acres [including the stone circle and the restored part of the Kennet Avenue] since 1942, when the bequest to the nation by Alexander Keiller was assigned to it in perpetuity' (*British Archaeological News* 1989, 81). In October 1989, by 'using a bank loan of £750,000' (*British Archaeological News* 1989, 81), the National Trust also acquired a further 480 acres of the land comprising the bulk of the area between the Ridgeway and the Sanctuary and Avebury itself, thus making it a real possibility to implement Keiller's original concept of continuity with prehistory by means of present-day walks and control of the archaeological landscape.

However, while these acquisitions were under way, 'unauthorized works' in the grounds of Avebury Manor (a Grade I listed building) were being carried out to develop 22 acres into a 'Tudor theme park'. The avowed intention of the 16th-century Manor's new owner, after alterations rumoured to cost between £1 and £2 million, is to create a 'unique Elizabethan experience', with wax effigies of past owners of the manor, licensed restaurant, rose and herb centre, gift shop, tuck shop, car park, tea rooms, 'armour for children', 'jousting tournaments', torture chamber and falconry. The Manor and its grounds were opened for the 1989 Easter weekend although many of the proposed alterations had been stopped on legal grounds before their completion; this ruling is currently (May 1990) subject to appeal. Despite some lack of 'facilities', visits are encouraged by enthusiast groups, some of them large: the Sealed Knot Society are planning to take many of their 6000 members to the Manor in August 1990 to stage an English Civil War mock battle in its grounds.

As we write, Avebury is under a third distinct threat from tourist development, with the proposal by Marlborough Homes Ltd. for 'a multi-purpose complex, including [a 90-bedroom] luxury hotel' at 'West Kennett Farm' (a Grade 2 listed building). The proposed development is clearly within the cultural ambiance of the Kennet Avenue, and would partially overlie a newly discovered, and previously quite unsuspected, 'palisaded enclosure', dated to around or a little before 2000 BC, as well as several other features (Whittle 1988, 180; Whittle 1989, 8; Whittle and Smith 1989; Smith and Trott 1989). The discovery of this major new site, with its use of large wooden posts, 'in an area [which] may well have much more to offer' (Whittle 1989, 8) demonstrates most emphatically how much there still is to be learnt about the cultural environment of Avebury, and how easy it is to prejudice the future. The development, if allowed to proceed, would include not only renovation of existing farm buildings, but the construction of new ones and the laying out of car parks, swimming pool, gardens and a playground over an area of 3.2 hectares.

In 1989 English Heritage scheduled part of this newly discovered site, but only the NE part of the enclosing ditch, leaving the area within the prehistoric structure unprotected. The Secretary of State for the Environment has rejected any suggestion of postponing this proposed development at West Kennet Farm until a national plan of management for Avebury exists; however, a public enquiry into this specific proposal was held in August 1989, the outcome of which is still awaited.

In a recent debate in the House of Lords (February 13, 1989) Lord Kennet stressed that, in his view, any one of the three proposed changes would so alter the character of Avebury that it could lead to the site(s) being struck off the World Heritage List. Nevertheless, the Government has rejected proposals for a Planning Enquiry Commission, a form of enquiry reserved for developments considered to be of national importance.

At this point, it is worth recalling the major part that Avebury has itself played in raising the consciousness of the public concerning the importance of ancient monuments. This was not the least of Stukeley's aims in recording it: 'The particularity of this description is designd to preserve the memory of this most illustrious Work of the highest Antiquity ... which may rescue some part from impending ruin when the Country finds an advantage in preserving its poor reliques.' (Stukeley 1722–4b, 173). Stukeley was prophetic of developments which were to follow over a century later, when Avebury was to play a vital role in the formative stage of the introduction of such measures to protect archaeological monuments as currently exist in Britain. The key figure here was Sir John Lubbock, whose comments on Avebury and the unstable relationship between the village and the antiquity have already been cited (Introduction). Lubbock added to his account the following revealing footnote:

It is impossible to mention Abury, without regretting that so magnificent a national monument should have been destroyed, for a paltry profit of a few pounds. As population increases, and land grows more valuable, these ancient monuments become more and more liable to mutilation or destruction. We cannot afford them the protection of our museums, nor, perhaps, would it be desirable to do so, but it is well worthy of consideration whether Government would not act wisely in selecting some competent archaeologist, who might be appointed Conservator of the National Antiquities; whose duty it would be to preserve, as far as possible, from wanton injury, the graves of our ancestors, and other interesting memorials of the past; to make careful drawings of all those which have not yet been figured, and to report, from time to time, as to their condition. At a very trifling expense the Danish Government have bought for the nation a large number of tumuli, and have thus preserved many national monuments which would otherwise have been destroyed. (Lubbock 1865, 55n.)

This was written in 1865, and the ethos that underlay the introduction of preservationist legislation in this country is clearly in evidence – the awareness of an imminent threat, the concept of 'national monument', the sense of antiquities as the guarantors of historical identity, and the invocation of other European countries where measures were taken earlier than in England (Hunter 1981; Ucko 1990). Six years later, in 1871, Lubbock took the most practical step possible to protect Avebury, when he was warned that further destruction of the circle was imminent, by buying the land in question himself: he thus avoided 'the irreparable injury' of Avebury, including the 'threatened profanation of the great circle' itself 'by the building of villas within the area and the destruction of the stones – which caused a thrill of horror within the breast of every Archaeologist' (Smith 1872). Later, in 1900, Lubbock was to take the title of Baron Avebury: the experience at Avebury undoubtedly contributed to his conviction of the need for legislative protection for national antiquities, which bore fruit in the Ancient Monuments Bill which first appeared in the House of Commons in 1873 and finally reached the Statute Book in 1882 (Hutchison 1914, i, 126–7, 131, 150, 167–8; Keith 1924, 93–4).

Today, with an apparently formidable structure of legislation in position to protect relics of the past, which is yet palpably threatened by increasing pressures, we need again to take stock. The situation is particularly crucial where sites as important as Avebury are concerned. The significance of the monument itself is surely the first

257

point to be taken into account. For preservation is not an absolute: the more important the site is adjudged to be, the more carefully it needs to be protected, and developments which might be deemed acceptable elsewhere may be found unacceptable here. What need to be decided, therefore, are the criteria by which what *is* acceptable should be fairly and disinterestedly adjudicated.

One option is presented by the view that Kennet District Council has adopted in its draft Avebury Local Plan, itself due for public debate in the summer of 1990 (1989, 18, 40). This states that the objective should be 'to restrict additional tourist oriented development to that which is related to the greater appreciation and enjoyment of the neolithic monuments, ancient landscapes and prehistoric character of the area'. As a result, 'Proposals for development related to tourism will not be permitted unless . . . it can be demonstrated that such development will not adversely affect [the] monuments and their settings'. The rationale for such views was given by those who spoke recently at the National Trust Appeal (see below): 'In the Avebury landscape lie embedded the very roots of our prehistoric past: it is truly unique and of incomparable value' (Cunliffe), and 'At Avebury a sense of quiet power is drawn partly from the neolithic remains but also from the setting of the circles. If more of the unspoilt land around Avebury is developed then the site will lose its integrity' (Thackray) (both quoted in *British Archaeological News* 1989, 81). One implication of such views – however unpalatable – is presumably that those physically living at any given moment in Avebury must not necessarily be allowed to determine future policy.

On the other hand, we are more conscious than we once were of the conflict of interest that such well-intended and ostensibly objective assessments entail. 'Heritage' and its politics have now been widely discussed (Cleere 1989; Ucko 1989a), and we need to be aware of the extent to which the concept of a 'World Heritage' – to which Avebury has belonged since 1984 – carries with it a concept of the past in which all people of the world are deemed to have an interest (Ucko 1989b), which in turn may be in conflict with locally perceived concerns. In such circumstances there is a risk that archaeology may be seen as reactionary, a force against change – such an image risking the future of the very monuments which it seeks to protect.

This is illustrated clearly enough at Avebury, where the opinions of the heritage commentators are in direct conflict with the views of many of those who actually live there. As BBC-TV's recent (16 May 1989) 'Enterprise Culture' recorded, major tourist development at Avebury is supported by many who see the opposition to 'moving Avebury into the 1990s and the 21st century' as coming only from archaeologists and 'snooty blow-ins who've hardly been in the village more than a couple of years [as distinct from] the real old villagers [who] are all very much in favour'. Nor is this the first time that the views of the residents of Avebury have been asked to take second place to those of a different circle of opinion – as 1937 letters from Avebury residents to the newspapers, and *The Times*' article about their problems at that time (quoted in Coupland 1988), make clear. Manifestly, a *modus vivendi* between the different interests has to be found.

It should also be remembered that, contrary to the way in which the term appears to be being used in some of the speeches quoted above, the essence of any landscape is that it is a human artefact; at any particular moment it is the result of a complex set of interactions with the human population. There can be no doubt that the landscape around Avebury was not exclusively created by the neolithic inhabitants who built the monuments in the first place. If the argument is to prevail that the Avebury landscape is to be preserved as it currently exists, such a decision deserves to be seen in its true context – which involves the clearing of forests, agricultural activities of post-neolithic times, decimation of the grey wethers, the 18th-century planting of ornamental trees, and a whole range of other changes over a very long period indeed.

A case in point is Avebury Manor itself. We may feel that the building repairs and refurbishment of 1955, which were carried out to prepare the Manor for its first round of public visiting in 1956, were trivial compared with what has recently been done to that site (Knowles 1956, 369; Barrington 1975, 434–5). But what about the earlier history of the surroundings to this house 'built by William Dunch c.1560' (Knowles 1956, 359)? Contrary to the claim (Knowles 1956, 366) that 'the seventeenth century at Avebury Manor seems to have been a time [with] no evidence of alteration to the house or its grounds', we have seen how Farmer Skeate was instructed in 1695 to carry out all manner of planting and replanting of different kinds of trees, whose roots could well have affected the future well-being of the building, quite apart from the damage which they may have done to possible stone settings in the neighbourhood (Chapter IV, c and e).

Yet, though we need to be sensitive to this ongoing process of cultural change, we may still feel that it is now appropriate to control it. This is particularly the case in the late 20th century. In an overpopulated country, with an almost unlimited demand for tourist facilities and with unprecedented power to alter our inherited environment, we cannot afford to trust the results of *laissez faire*. Here we may return to the recent works at Avebury Manor. We can leave on one side the proprietor's disregard for planning procedures, which, though stemming from an understandable frustration with bureaucracy, could as easily have resulted in the demolition of the house as its 'beautification', and which draws attention to the inadequacy of the practical measures available to enforce the statutory controls that exist. The point for judgement is whether ancillary uses like these are to be encouraged on a site which is of such importance for its prehistoric remains. Moreover, whatever the damage to possible stone positions done in the late 17th century, there can be little doubt that the recent works at the Manor will have done irreparable damage to crucial subsurface evidence of both 17th-century and earlier features.

However well disposed we may feel towards those living on the site either now or in the past, we would surely not have allowed a free hand to the 'vile humor of the occupyers of these lands' in Stukeley's time, who 'seem now to pride themselves in this mischievous practise' of destroying the stones (Stukeley 1722–4b, 80): such attrition inspired Stukeley to reflect on the irony of an ancient monument left by its priestly builders 'in its own constitution eternal till at length in these wicked ages desecrated by a mean set of villagers' (Stukeley 1722–4b, 246). Today, we should surely err on the side of preservation at such a site. Moreover, it is right that the equivalent of this in current archaeological orthodoxy should be the shift away from destructive exploration and excavation towards the educative presentation of prehistoric monuments. This echoes Keiller's attitude in the 1930s (1939, 223) – possibly itself an echo of the view taken by John Aubrey in 1663 (see Chapter I, iv).

On the other hand there is no reason for archaeologists to be complacent, for there are lessons to be learnt by them too. If it is admitted that the preservation and interpretation of archaeological remains is to take priority at Avebury, we need to decide *what* it is that we are preserving and interpreting. As Keiller would undoubtedly have agreed, the onus on the heritage industry is to check the facts and to show them in the light of alternative interpretative parameters (see Keiller 1939, 223). Yet the present study's careful re-examination of the extant evidence in the light of the data from the 17th- and 18th-century plans has illustrated the inadequte nature of our knowledge of many key aspects of Avebury and its surroundings, including the impact that developments since the neolithic period have had on the henge and associated monuments.

One lacuna which this study has made clear is the fact that 20th-century reluctance to excavate has not gone hand in hand with the facilitation of archaeological geophysical investigation which, in Britain, is more or less limited to surveys of threatened sites. The results which geophysical prospecting has begun to reveal have been set out in Chapter IV, and, to give one example, it would surely have been academically irresponsible to have taken a decision about the future conservation, let alone display, of the northern quadrants of the Avebury henge without having had access to this resistivity data. Thus, amongst other observations in this area, two linear resistivity anomalies run diagonally across the north-western corner of the plot (Plate 67) as if to converge at the lip of the ditch of the henge. Apart from the lack of any obvious recent explanation, the possibility of their prehistoric origin is strengthened by the presence of the southernmost of the two alignments to the west of the north road. Could these therefore represent previously unknown features pre-dating the main north–south route through the henge, and what sort of Avebury management plan would it be that ignored such information? Indeed, what sort of management regime will it be if it opts to remain in ignorance of other features no doubt characterizing other unexamined quadrants within the henge (Plate 73)?

This may suggest a frustrating provisionality, when in practice firm action is constantly having to be taken in the light of what is currently known. But it may be that wise decisions as to display will include proper recognition of this provisionality – which only emphasizes the irreplaceability of each site and artefact. Archaeological knowledge is, and always will be, a matter of interpretation. For example, it is not long since Avebury was supposed by archaeologists to have had only two ancient entrances. As we have seen (Chapter V), it was only in 1937 that the northern entrance was found during excavation, to the complete surprise of those responsible (Keiller and Piggott 1936, 417; Smith 1965, fig. 67).

Equally important is the question of the relationship of the monument with its total, and archaeologically rich, surroundings. Without more than a superficial knowledge of their context, and thus of the prehistoric culture(s) which constructed the henge and its related stone arrangements, we necessarily have a rather warped view of the monuments themselves. Given the inevitable limitations of archaeological investigation, it may remain strictly impossible ever to fully appreciate the position of Avebury within the landscape. However, it is vital to remember that such limitations are not fixed: new techniques and new approaches constantly arise and with them the hope of learning more. Until we know much more about where (and how) the users of Avebury *lived*, how can we ever begin to make sense of the 'monumental'?

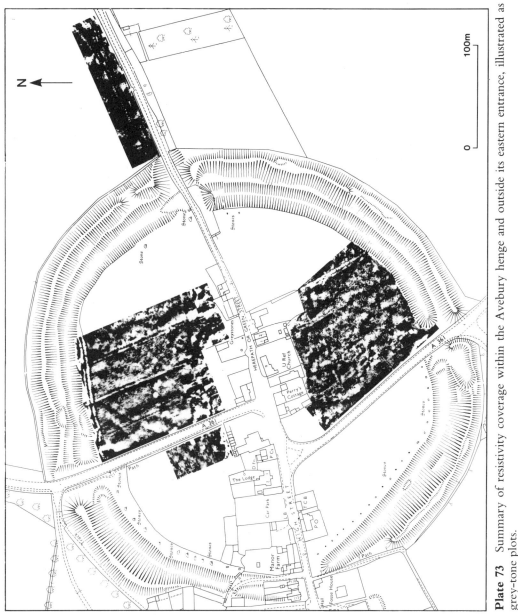

Plate 73 Summary of resistivity coverage within the Avebury henge and outside its eastern entrance, illustrated as grey-tone plots.

Such questions pose immense challenges of decision-making for archaeologists, necessitating not only the ordering of research priorities, but also the raising of finance to enable them to be carried out. It is not only further non-destructive geophysical and other surveys which are needed (Holgate 1987; Smith 1984), but also (costly) archaeological and palaeo-environmental investigations throughout the landscape, especially amongst, and beneath, the sediments of the valleys. This may provide the fuller cultural context needed to comprehend (and therefore to be able properly to display) the funerary or the monumental.

Indeed, it may be that Avebury's importance is such that a whole swathe of surrounding countryside needs protection, and a step in this direction has been taken by the National Trust. Since the Trust acquired a large part of the area, it has launched (October 1989) a public appeal for £250,000 towards its total costs of £750,000 to keep all the land in its care in inalienable ownership. Its 'long-term intention is to mark the mile and a half long route of the Avenue to the Sanctuary for visitors and to put much of the arable back into grass so that visitors can walk from the Stone Circles to the Sanctuary along the "ceremonial route"'. Without further geophysical investigation of the kind reported in Chapter IV we might be about to deceive the public, for instance by imposing our continuing presumption that what existed some four thousand or more years ago was a 'route' *between* the uprights of 'avenues' of standing stones. The findings summarized there could be taken to imply that the wear was as much on either side of the parallel rows as within them, and it is conceivable that future survey and excavation will reveal whether people are likely to have walked between the Kennet Avenue stones rather than, say, on either side of them. It may be that the notion of walking 'within' an avenue is as much a preconception derived from the classical world as any of the ideas which influenced the record of our 17th- and 18th-century predecessors – perhaps reflecting the presumptions of a regimented society, whereas in actuality the 'avenue' might have been reserved for spirits while mere mortals trod a humbler route.

This is, of course, highly speculative, but it is indicative of the need constantly to reconsider preconceptions, the message which has been at the heart of this book. For the evidence we have presented demonstrates all too clearly how powerful some symbols have been, and continue to be, in attempts to understand the evidence of past societies. As was indicated in Chapter V, a range of preoccupations such as circularity and symmetry have affected scholarly interpretation of the site. At a more popular level these have been supplemented by other, equally deep-rooted symbols, such as the cross. Like the circle, these can be expected to be loaded with symbolic meaning not only for the tourist, but also for the home-viewer. One public reaction to the discovery of plans C and D in 1988 was epitomized by the suggestion in *The Independent* (31 October 1988) that they showed the possibility 'that avenues led off from the rings to the four cardinal points, forming a massive cross-shaped design with the circle at its centre', a hypothesis ingeniously developed by ITN National News to suggest that 'most excitingly, there is evidence that Avebury was in the centre of a massive cross which probably linked it to other sites in the area, such as Beckhampton and Stonehenge'. Amazingly, even the National Trust's own current and newly revised map-brochure on Avebury announces that 'There were avenues of stones to at least [sic] four of the entrances of the circle'.

Whatever we may think about such theories, it is clear that they raise questions about how Avebury related to its environs to which we need full and systematic answers. Despite Aubrey, Charleton and Stukeley, and everything which has happened since, we remain in a state of considerable confusion about the early Avebury region. Without a concerted re-analysis of the archaeological and written evidence, completing that begun here, we will not have a serious basis on which to decide what it is that should be presented to the wider public, both outside the henge and, equally importantly, within it. One stone avenue or two, or more, and running exactly *where*? One extending as far as West Kennet farm, but by what route? How many coves, of how many stones? Double or single circles in the north or south of the henge? Until we decide *what* should be presented, we certainly cannot determine *how* it should be done.

Hence, the provisionality of our interpretative views does itself have implications for preservation in the Avebury area. We surely owe it to the memory of the 17th- and 18th-century pioneers to do all in our power to preserve and present the heritage in a way that cannot, as sometimes in the past, be criticized as having been based solely on preconceptions and concerns of living 'antiquarians' – or, for that matter, only on the immediate interests of living 'villagers'. Preservation needs to be arranged so that it is open-ended rather than restrictive, while also being as sympathetic to the legitimate desires of local residents as possible. This in turn demands that archaeology should recognize its own limitations of method and interpretation, in order not to restrict but to enhance its legitimate authority. It is also essential that archaeologists should come to terms with the social, economic and political nature of their enquiries. Whether they welcome it or not, they cannot remain distinct from the heritage industry – and all that that implies – not the least being the realization that they are not alone in claiming rights over the remains of the past.

What we have to do is not only to determine the archaeology of the Avebury area without destruction of the evidence, but also to decide how to present it to visitors of all ages from a wide variety of backgrounds (from Britain, Europe, the world). The challenge of Avebury in the 1990s and beyond demands a whole set of re-alliances between archae-ologists, English Heritage, the National Trust, and the public, to avoid any possible repetition of the sorry saga of the Sanctuary. That site, originally described by Aubrey and

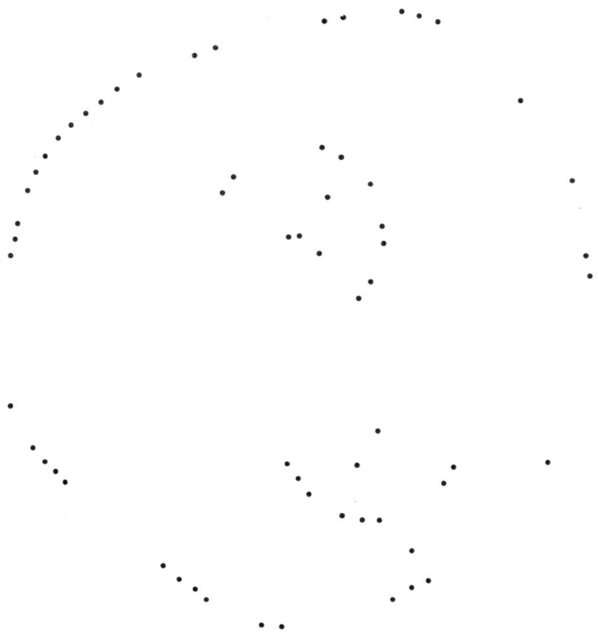

Plate 74 Reconstruction from Stukeley's Measured Plan (Plate 15 and Transparency 20) of the stones in the positions that Stukeley probably saw them.

Moray in the 17th century, rediscovered in the 20th century solely on the basis of Stukeley's 18th-century records, and consequently excavated in the 1930s, is still, in 1990, referred to by Stukeley's apparently romantic but perhaps genuinely local name (Stukeley 1743, 31). Yet 'The Sanctuary' remains a total failure of public presentation, its component parts represented only by nondescript markers. 1990 also leaves Avebury itself 'looking more like a tank trap than our most remarkable prehistoric site' (Ponting 1969, x), if not 'somewhat resemb[ling] a military cemetery in France' (Avebury residents in 1937, quoted in Coupland 1988).

Sanctus [handwritten marginal note]

Some difficult decisions are long overdue, involving matters of preconception and taste, and questions about the range and nature of archaeological information that should be freely available to the public. Should display concentrate exclusively on what we now, for the first time, know was the evidence of the stones which Stukeley *actually saw* (Plate 74), and should limited excavation be undertaken designed to test particularly crucial features and areas of the monuments? Should reconstructions be undertaken like that recently announced for the neolithic henge with megaliths at Stanton Harcourt (Oxon) (Wainwright 1989, 27) – and, if so, should it be done for the Avebury henge (or parts of it), the Avenue(s) and the Sanctuary? As emerges all too clearly from this book, such a course would almost certainly demand further limited excavations. Should the display and presentation of the Avebury region continue to be almost exclusively focused on the prehistoric period, or should Roman and medieval (and later?) activities there be granted some importance? Is it really appropriate for lessons in dowsing to be freely offered at the World Heritage site of Avebury in order to trace the shapes of long vanished Stukeley-described stones – with no cautionary advice to the contrary?

Most significant of all, however, is the bald fact that – despite an English Heritage Working Party composed of members of all interested parties, an Avebury Environs Forum and new interest from the Royal Commission on Historical Monuments – Avebury still remains without any national plan for its future management and care. Is this an appropriate state of affairs for what Stukeley, with some justice, described as 'the noblest monument, which is probably on the face of the globe; which has stood so many ages, and was made to stand as many more' (Stukeley 1743, 37)?

Appendix I
A few observations in the country to Bathe [1663]

by Sir Robert Moray

Royal Society Classified Papers, vii(1) 10

These notes by Sir Robert Moray are written in his own hand. For their association with the royal visit to Bath in 1663, see above, Chapter I, iv, where attention is drawn to the significance of various details in Moray's record. After beginning with information on antiquities in the Marlborough region, Moray includes observations made at Bath and in excursions from there, and others made while the royal party was on its way back to London via Cornbury Park and Oxford. When back in London, he brought up some of the matters referred to in these notes at the meeting of the Royal Society on 7 October 1663.[1] At the top of the first page the manuscript is endorsed 'Sir R: Moray' in a contemporary hand, almost certainly Oldenburg's. In addition, it is marked 'read Oct. 19: 64' in an 18th-century hand: cf. Birch 1756–7, i.476, which records how on that date 'Sir Robert Moray gave an account of what he had observed in his late excursion into the country'. However, since this echoes Oldenburg's endorsement of a different manuscript, Classified Papers, vi.17: 'Observations of Sir Robert Moray, Sir P. Neile and Dr Wren, made by them in their late excursion into the Country, brought in by Sir R. Moray Nov. 9 1664', it may refer to that rather than this (cf. Birch 1756–7, i.483). The manuscript carries the original foliation (89), (90), (91), (92), thus confirming, as does the list of the series in Classified Papers xxiv.78, that it was originally kept in the same sequence as plans C and D, which were fols. (60) – (63). Deletions and insertions have been noted in the footnotes. The ink/nib changes after the first seven words on fol. 24.

In the lord Seamors Garden at Marleborough there is a round Mount which may be reasonably supposed to have been an Auncient Tumulus such as there are divers in that Country being in figure lyke a frust[um] of a Cone whose Diameter at the base is guessed to be about 160 foot, at the top 70 & its hight 200. the way up to it is a spiral of 4 entire turns & about a quarter making a very insensible ascent of some 700 yards in all, the walk being some 6 foot broad handsomely gravelld a fine quickset hedge on the outside with fruit trees of severall kindes set in it & at[2] orderly & convenient distance on all sides of bankes of the sloping hill in spirall foot-paths, therof being green everywhere. about the end of the third turn there is a pretty arbor or resting place of hewn stone covered & at the top a pretty green compassed with the quickset hedge & fruit trees as the rest of the spirall walk, and in the Middle a very fair & handsom Octagonall arbor or room so[me] 24 foot wide with a pair of staires of one side, rising some 15 or 16 foot to a platform leaded, with a fair Cistern in the middle of some 18 foot over,[3] & 4 foot high, into which there is water forced up by a water mill & force pump in lead pipes of some 3/4 inch bore and between 3 & 400 yards long the Mill set upon a brook, & the water rising as the Gardner or overseer of work affirmes 140 foot. every stroke of the pump being hard[sic] at the Cock by which the water is let into the Cistern as clearly as if it were not 20 yards off./fol. 22v/

Selberry Hill is an Artificiall Mount or Tumulus standing in a Meadow higher & broader than the L[ord] Seamors mount but narrower somewhat yet flat at the top all over green, and of a steep ascent. It affordeth store of a sort of snail[4] with a flat shell slender & having 3 or 4 entire turns. There are in the subiacent meadow near the foot of the mount, (which of one side touches a bank of rising ground some 20 or 24 foot from the bottom) vestiges of a Ditch out of which it seemes the earth may have been taken to raise the mount appearing some 90 or 100 foot broad (at a guess) but not above 5 or 6 deeper than the rest of [the] meadow at any place, filled up as it seemes in process of time by the growing earth, seeing there is no appearance so much earth as the Tumulus contains could be taken out the ditch that appears. where usually in winter there stands some water which may conduce to the growing up of the earth.

Between Marleborrow & Selberry passing over a rising ground some 200 yards wide[?] of the highway on the left hand there are to be seen some 50 or 60 stones[5] part of a greater number many of which are entire, some broken & others carried away from their places which are still conspicuous. they are soe in 2 Circles or figures intended for Circles as it seemes. one within the other, the biggest about some 18 or 20 yards in Diameter, the other 9 or 10. And on the west side where the Hill descends with an easy declivity there seemes to have been 2 rowes of great stones lyke the other set as trees are in a walk some 8 or 9 yards wide & the stones placed one against another & distant from one another some 7 or 8 yards. thus [?] hath there /fol. 23/ been a great many placed in walk somewhat winding at the lower end tending towards a Village. diverse of the stones are entire, others broken and others it seemes have been carried away for use yet leaving sufficient Vestiges to discern where they stood. Some 16 or 18 have been placed upon the hill, & that being cut off by a hedge where its declivity ends some stones appear in the pasture within the hedge & some in the hedge that runs along the highway opposite to the others.

Not farre from the 2 Circles towards[6] the southeast there is a small Tumulus of about some 10 or 12 foot high & some 15 or 16 at the bottom, the Ditch out of which the earth that raised it seems to have been taken is grown almost level with the rest of the ground about it. The 2 Circles were taken notice of & described by Mr Aubry & one by S[ir] P[aul] Neile. & the Tumulus & Growing up of the Ditch by Mr Aubry.

At Aveberry is the noblest monument that I ever saw of the kinde, already observed & spoken of at[7] a meeting of the Society sc. by Mr Aubry & Dr Charleton wherof I shall forbear to make any description, knowing that Mr Aubry intends to take the exact measures of every particular there to be noted & to bring a perfect account thereof to the Society./fol. 23v/

The hot springs at Bathe are treated of by learned men: but the cause of their heat may furnish yet some work for philosophers after all hath been suggested hitherto. I could not learn that anybody had ever digg'd deep in the rysing grounds between Bathe & the top of Lansdown in order to the finding of those Mineralls which apparently are there lodged: & were possibly worth the paines, aswell in regard of the Emolument might thereby accrue to the owners of the Ground, as of the light it might afford towards the discovery of the cause of the heat of the Springs. that[8] seem to proceed from the Hill already named, which cannot be elevated less than 300 yards above the place where the springs break out. the Ascent being pretty steep for above a Mile together and there being on the Highest part of the Hill a Noble plain, exceeding levell between 2 & 3 miles long & of unequall breadth, some places[9] half a mile, some more, some less.

Upon the high way from Bathe to the Top of Lansdown within some 3 or 4 yards of the brim of the level ground on the top, there is a litle well to be seen whereof one side is a stone some 2 foot long lying about 8, or 9 Inches above the ground, which dammeth up the water in an oblong figure some 2 foot in length & one in breadth. this Well His /fol. 24/ Maiesty observed to be a running spring: which is no small rarity upon a high hill, so near the Highest place of it.

The Guides of the Baths[10] at Bathe have a way of Guilding silver coines in a Tryce; they first scour the peece and then sometimes dipping it amongst stale piss taken up at the pissing places of the streets with the dirt & mudd mixt with it, sometimes letting dropps of that durty stuff fall upon it & spreading the same upon it with the finger, and then suddainly washing it in water taken out of the Bath, (as if the Secret lay in that) till the piece have acquired the right Colour, then they dry it & lap it up in clean white paper. the colour will be black if it be too often dipt or toucht, otherwise it will look perfectly lyke gold but vades if long exposed to[11] the Air, or being often handled.

At Draycot Mr Longs house there is to be had in great quantity a black light stony stuff lyke a Minerall the taste of it is very strong & rellishes both of Vitriol & alom and it smells lyke brimston. or makes the finger smell so that touch it.

266

Mr Fr[ancis] Godolphin[12] hath a ground near his house where there is a kinde of stone of a soft fine greet not unlyke chalke wherein are frequently found in the heart of large stones that have no crack nor rent in them small round stones that look lyke Iron, which being broken are of the Colour of brass within having streakes or beames shooting from the Center to the Circumference every way. Whereof he gave me 2 & promised 20 more./fol. 24v/

About a mile below Bristol there is a Copious spring flowing out of a vast rock that[13] looks as if it had been cleft of purpose to let the river run through it the passage being no broader than the bed of the river, the rock rysing steep on both sides. this spring is about 25 foot below the high-water Mark, & almost as warm as milk newly drawn from the Cow & affording no discernable taste and just[?] opposite to it on the other side of the river there is such another spring of cold water. Women there take up the warm water for straungers, find amongst the rockes thereabouts the Bristol Diamonds.[14]

In Corneberry Park the Dear have hornes the first year nothing near so fair as elsewhere, the second worse by much: but the third there is none above a finger long & commonly crooked some[15] one way some another. This is said to have happened since the park was stored with rabbets, though the dear be as fair & fat as in other places and as is reported before there were rabbets in the park, the dear there had as fair heads as any other.

Doctor Wallis relation of a new improvement of Tame pigeons is a pretty story[.] not unlyke that His Maiesty relates of a young blackbird that was bred & fed by a Thrush scarce a Moneth older than itself.

The lord Hawley presented the King with a kinde of sallet called Laver, scrapt off the rockes that are overflowed by the sea in Sommersetshire, not unlyke Cavear in Taste.[16] It is said to grow /fol. 25/ again the next day after it is scrapt off.[17]

Notes

1. See Birch 1756–7, i.310 (Godolphin's and Long's minerals), 311 (Wallis' pigeons). Cf. ibid., 313–14. For biographical information on Moray, see Stevenson 1984, Stevenson 1988, ch. 7.

2. replacing '&', deleted. Later in the sentence, 'in' replaces 'with', deleted. Earlier, 'walk … broad' is inserted above the line.

3. replacing 'diam', deleted. Later in the sentence, 'falls a' is deleted after 'which', and '4 & 500' before '3 & 400'.

4. before snail, 'shell' has been deleted. 'Standing … Meadow' and 'to raise … appearing' are inserted above the line. At the end of the paragraph, 'of onely' has been deleted after 'where'.

5. After 'stones', '(or pieces of stones)' deleted; within this, 'pieces' replaces 'the Vestiges', deleted; 'part of a greater number' is an insertion, perhaps to replace the deleted phrase. Later in the paragraph, 'the' is deleted before 'one within the other'; 'in Diameter' replaces 'distant', deleted; 'the other' is accidentally repeated; 'not' is deleted after 'declivity ends'; and 'ends' is altered from 'is'.

6. 'to the' is deleted before 'towards'; 'of the Tumu' is deleted after 'of the Ditch'.

7. 'at' is changed from 'in'; later in the sentence, 'sc' is written over 'b' after 'Society'; and the second 'Aubry' replaces 'Aveb', deleted.

8. 'that' replaces 'which', deleted.

9. replacing 'times', deleted; later in the sentence, 'times' has been deleted after 'some' before both 'more' and 'less'.

10. At the end of this word, 'e' has been deleted and replaced by 's'. Later in the sentence, 'coines' replaces 'money' (both above the line), and 'peece' replaces 'it first', deleted. After 'sometimes', 'touch' has been deleted, as has 'till' before 'and then'.

11. 'if long exposed to' inserted, replacing 'in', deleted. In the next sentence, 'foun …' has been deleted before 'had'.

12. Presumably Francis Godolphin of Coulston, Wilts. Later in the sentence, 'greet' = 'grit' (O.E.D.).

13. 'seemes' deleted after 'that'. In the next sentence, 'about' replaces 'above', deleted, before '25 foot'; the first letter of 'newly' has been altered from something else ('freshly'?); the first letter of 'Cow' has been altered to a capital; while '& affording … taste' is inserted above the line. Presumably Moray is here describing Clifton Gorge.

14. I.e. the name given to brilliant crystals of colourless quartz found in St Vincent's Rock, Bristol.

15. 'times' deleted after 'some' here and again three words later; 'there' is inserted in the last sentence of the paragraph.

16. On 'Lavor, a seaherb, found in the Severn-Sea', see Hunter 1989, 111. Francis Hawley, Baron Hawley of Duncannon, was captain of a troop in the Royal Regiment of Horse.

17. The remainder of fol. 25r is blank, as is fol. 25v except for the title which the piece has here been given, which is in Moray's hand.

Appendix II
A reconstruction of Stukeley's original description of the Avebury henge

from 'Celtic Temples', Bodleian MS Eng.Misc.c.323
(Stukeley 1722–4b)

In his published *Abury* (1743, 22) Stukeley explains that he has refrained from giving a detailed written description of the site, relying instead on his 'great frontispiece plate' (see Chapters I, viii, III,E). In fact, however, a much fuller treatment than the cursory one given in his published text does survive: part of Stukeley's 'Celtic Temples' MS., this appears to be his original extended description of the Avebury henge. Its existence has been recognized by Piggott (1985, 89), who praises its style as 'clear and almost colloquial, and invariably fresh, lively and enthusiastic'. However, he then quotes only one full sentence (that beginning 'I shall take the reader a fine tour along with me'), citing none of the rich but intricate detail either of the 'tour' itself, or of passages associated with it. On the other hand, it has to be said that Stukeley's text is not straightforward, owing to extensive alterations and deletions to which this Appendix will try to do justice.

Apparently in 1722, Stukeley began a description of Avebury in the form of a continuous text written on the rectos of the MS. (i.e. the odd-numbered pages); during the same year he may have made the first notes and additions on the facing versos (the even-numbered pages), following the procedure we have described in Chapter I,viii. In 1723 this text was extended with a series of annotations, sometimes keyed and interlinked, inserted mostly on the facing versos, but occasionally towards the foot of rectos. After this, at an unknown date or dates, large sections were lightly deleted (see 'Editorial conventions', below). Further, on the same or different occasion(s), whole pages were cut out (their stubs remain visible), with the result that the original continuous text, while much supplemented on the versos, now has several long gaps in it. Similarly, occasional sets of annotations on versos survive in the absence of the facing text to which, whether keyed or unkeyed, they were related. The resulting MS. text is therefore both incomplete and potentially highly confusing.

In spite of this, there are luckily few stone settings within the henge of which a description does not survive. One of the now absent items, unfortunately, was obviously a description of the Cove, but what else is missing is unclear. It is worth noting here that the volume as a whole is nominally of [x] + 268 pages, those from 3 to 259 being numbered by Stukeley, but of these some 27 leaves have been cut out. No fewer than 17 of the leaves that have been removed belonged to the section in which Avebury was described, following the heading 'Abury' on p. 101: these are pp. 103–108, 111–114, 125–128, 133–136, 141–156. The present transcript draws on most of the remaining pages of this section – especially pp. 101, 109, 115, 117–124, 129–132, and 137–139.

In order to present the extant descriptive material in full while respecting the way in which the MS. was originally composed – i.e. in two or more phases – it has seemed to us best to intersperse quotation from Stukeley with commentary, rather than to attempt to give a unitary text. Conventions used are given below.

It should be noted that on p. 122 Stukeley refers to an accompanying 'Groundplot': from what he says about the notations used on it, this does not appear to be among the eleven surviving draft frontispieces discussed in Chapter III,E. Because of this, we have prepared a visual reconstruction of the state of the site as encapsulated in the account that follows, and this appears as Transparency 19.

Editorial conventions

Editorial notes inserted into Stukeley's running text are enclosed within brackets and italicized [*thus*]. Empty brackets [ ] show spaces left by Stukeley.

The MS. page number of each passage quoted is shown in bold at its beginning within brackets, e.g. **[115]**, and at internal page-breaks within double slashes, e.g. **//115//**. Where several discrete additions or notes appear on a single page, we assign a consecutive Roman number to each, e.g. **[120[i]– 120[ix]]**.

Editorial headings are also bracketed in bold, e.g. **[Pastures I–IV]**. Stukeley's own occasional centred headings are shown unbracketed in bold, i.e. here **Name**, **Circus**, **Solar Temple**. Words following full-stops have been capitalized in accordance with modern usage, while punctuation has also been modernized, for the convenience of the reader, except where ambiguity appears to allow alternative readings.

Unusual spellings are retained, with occasional expansion to avoid uncertainty. Non-standard abbreviations are expanded. We have ignored vertical lines which appear in the margin of various rectos – pp. 119, 121, 131, 137, and 139 – some of them continuous, some not. Neither the date nor the significance of these is clear.

Deletions. Stukeley's extensive deletions in 'Celtic Temples' are done usually by a single horizontal pen-stroke through each line which leaves both the text and any earlier specific deletions quite legible. In this fashion, within the 'Abury' section with which we are concerned, Stukeley has cancelled almost all of the recto text, and occasional parts of the verso notes and additions. Since we aim to base our transcript on the earliest text, we do not show the blanket deletions; instead, we note **D** (deleted) or **U** (undeleted) following the page number of each passage quoted. Specific contemporary deletions, followed by *del.*, are enclosed within brackets.

Additions. Stukeley's own insertions and revisions are transcribed in place, within pointed brackets < >, if they appear to be virtually contemporary with the original text. If they appear to be significantly later, they are footnoted.

It must be remembered that in 1722–3 Stukeley was still using his anti-clockwise series of pasture numbers (I–X): he did not go over to the familiar clockwise series (also I–X) until the making of plan E and its preceding engraved variants (see Chapter III,E.7). We have reproduced the anti-clockwise numbers here, as Stukeley gives them, with no specific comment.

'Celtic Temples' opens with general material, including the section 'Of the Manner of Celtic Temples', already referred to (Chapter IV,y), and Stukeley's topographical survey of such temples throughout the British Isles and beyond. From this, he went on to draw wider conclusions about their origins, including criticism of the theories of earlier writers, particularly Inigo Jones, and ending with an assertion of the Druids' archetypal religious context (cf. Chapter II,iv). At this point, the centred heading 'ABVRY' is preceded by the following introductory words:

> **[101 U]** We shall next pursue the chief Topic of this discourse The Temples of the Antient Celts in the particular description of Abury & Stoneheng which are the most perfect & magnificent Works of this kind we have among us. Their parts & uses include all the rest. First of Abury.

There is then a (deleted) section on the preference of the Celtic priests for island strongholds – 'as more private & secure. Here they pursud their studys to more exalted heigths & more noble productions' – concluding with 18 lines of verse on the subject. The next three leaves (103–108) are cut out, and the recto text resumes on 109. Here, uniquely in this volume, Stukeley has inserted a leaf: headed 'Druids p[ro]phets', its pagination duplicates that of the following leaf, 109–110. The text on 109 proper resumes in the middle of a section on historiography, overlapping with that in the published *Abury* (1743, 15). Here, however, Stukeley is more forthright about Holland's lack of perception, and he deploys the mention of Munster directly to back up his criticism. Stukeley then professes:

> **[109 D]** I have therefore contributed what my mean abilitys could produce towards doing justice to so noble a Theme; the revival of the glory of our ancestors, Men gigantic in thought, if not in bulk.

The celebratory passage on Avebury which follows includes an encouragement to 'the Ingenious' to visit and study such places, 'by which means they may preserve many valuable Antiquitys & curiositys in our Island, without the hazard & expence of Foreign Voyages'. This is cut off in mid-paragraph by the removal of two more leaves (111–114).

When the text resumes, Stukeley is discussing the source of the henge stones, in the first of two descriptive paragraphs. Some elements of these are to be found condensed in *Abury* (e.g. the references to Lord Pembroke, and to 'moor stones', 1743, 17), but in the present context they are worth reproducing *in extenso*:

> **[115 D]** no doubt but that they were taken from the surface of the ground, from among them we call the grey weathers, & we may see many cavitys & holes there, whence probably they came. These stones, we said, are Massy rocks lying upon the ground in vast numbers all over the Downs about this Country, especially in vallys & declivitys[;] which together with their color gave occasion to the name: for at a distance they resemble a flock of sheep. This kind of appearance of vast rocks lying dispersed above the turf, is pretty com[m]on in *Derby* <shire>, in most downs about *Plymouth* this is what they call moor stone. My Lord *Penbroke* causd several of them to be dug under, & found 'em lying loos[e], without any connexion to a rock or quarry, & certainly this opportunity encouragd the Inhabitants hereabouts to raise these mighty works therewith, for they might pitch upon stones, to what size they pleasd, requiring little work of hewing to a Scantling, & none of raising them from the bed of a quarry. It seems to me a greater difficulty to solve this appearance & assign the reason of their lying there, than to transport 'em to their seats at present. I observd some lye flat, others on an edg & their plains <no way> correspondent, for a considerable group together.[1]
>
> The bulk of the stones at *Abury* is really amazing. They seem at present very rude, yet we have room for suspicion that they were originally pretty shapely, tho' I beleive not squard so nicely as even those of Stoneheng. At a *medium* tis easy to determin them about 16 foot broad, as many high above ground, & four or five foot thick. My Lord *Penbroke* has computed the quantity of one of them to be about 50 tuns & that little less than 200 yoke of Oxen is sufficient to draw it. They are pitchd upright & very little below the surface of the ground. A bed of lesser Stones [are, *del.*] <is> placd at bottom, as a firm foundation for their support. Moreover the soil is hard chalk which favors their stability. By what method they were raisd in early times is hard to conceive, since it would exercise the skill of a Modern Architect with his best machines, to perform the same work & the great number of them still enhances the miracle.

The next paragraph (deleted) on p. 115, continuing on p. 117, begins with Stukeley remarking how 'in the works of Antiquity, a simple majesty & magnificence, a greatness & marvaillous affect [is] producd, what <ever> is the design or materials'. In a vein alluded to in Chapter II,iv, he goes on to give an account of the genesis of architecture 'immediately after the [F]lood', emphasizing that 'the first ages of the world were intent upon grandeur only', remarking that 'the pillars of *Seth* are thought to have been Obelisks', and noting also that '*Semiramis* hewd an obelisk 150 foot long'. The ancients 'thought it not enough to make a temple where the order & all the parts should be exact & beautiful but it must be large too', whereas 'now adays':

> **[117 D]** A certain minuteness of thought possesses us, as in the whole, so in the parts & ornaments of an edifice. What is the reason, but that our Gentry do not study Architecture. They goe to see the magnificent works of *Rome* & know nothing of the Principles by which they were made ...

He also criticized modern architects for ignorantly throwing together the components of classical architecture, 'just as if a composer for the press should throw a parcel of letters upon a table, expecting to make a fine book' **[117–119 D]**. Keyed to the end of this passage is a further (undeleted) note on

p. 118, about the nature of beauty as consisting in harmonious proportions.

At the top of p. 119 is the cross-heading, 'Name'. Under this are the last few lines of the section just quoted, which are immediately followed by the start of Stukeley's original description of Avebury, a continuous text occupying the successive rectos 119, 121, 123. What followed is unclear, since pp. 125–128 have been cut out, but the original text stops short of the bottom of p. 123, and this particular section may originally have ended there. At that point a reference appears to a continuation passage on p. 130, which seems to be one of his 1723 additions and is reproduced in place below, in our series of transcriptions from the versos.

It will be noticed that the long transcript we are about to give contains, on p. 121, the internal date 1722. At the foot of that page is an important but unkeyed note, quite possibly belonging to that year:

[121 D] A stone of the lesser circle lyes in pasture VIII over ag[ains]t that which is tumbled awry over ag[ains]t the parsonage barn end.

[119 D]   **Name**
The [Town, *del.*] < village > of Abury [with an ill omen, *del.*] < which has the hon[o]r to stand in one of the most remarkable works in the w[or]ld > is placd in the middle & built with the Ruins of the Temple we are about to describe, containing about 30 houses. Tis a fine scituation, for this spot is a plain or rather a gently rising knoll, in the midst of a large concavity 5 or 6 mile in diameter, for you descend to it from < on > all sides, from hills which overlook it two or three miles distant, so that tis a sort of large Theater, admirably well chose for the magnificent purpose, had not the soil been rather too good, & too near the River Kennet; for all three heads thereof rise within a mile of it or little more. Indeed tis not impossible but that this very thing may have been one regard, that determind the choice of our Ancestors here, the manifest blessings of the element of Water claiming as good a pretence to divinity as any other. The present name of *Abury* seems to hint at this, which is no more < than > the Water-farm, then it should properly be written AEa, thus *Abury* on the River *Wey* above *Guildford* in Surrey, *Abunger* a town at its head. Not far off < here > is *Auburn* at the head of a brook running into the *Kennet* below *Marlborough*. It alters not the case tho' sometime it be wrote *Albury*, for so is the said town upon the *Wey* called sometime *Albury* [*in margin* Aubury] & *Auburn* is sometime called *Alburn*, as the chase hard by; & with both these names are they written in the Maps. Mr *Baxter* conjectures well that the River *Kennet*, or *Kunnet* as still calld by the Country people, took its name from the Roman Town *Cunetio*, now *Marlborow*, as was the manner of later times, & that the most antient name of this River was *Morlais*, from the sound of its Waters, for tis quick & its descent considerable enough. One of its Springs rises a little west of *Abury* & goes Southwards, till it meets with another coming from *Bekampton*, they unite just by *Silbury* hill. Both at present afford but little water except in wet seasons, but running half round *Silbury* hill they meet with the *Swallow head*, & properly the Fountain head of the River *Kennet* which is a little more than a bowshoot off. This Spring is very famous among the Country people: one would think they still retain some of the antient veneration for the place, they talk of it with so much awe & pleasure. This Spring affords a good deal of Water & descending between East & West *Kennet*, passes by *Overton* & so to *Marlborough*. The Temple in which stands this Town of Abury is comprehended in a circular ditch of < above > eleven hundred feet in diameter withinside. This is very deep, like the Foss that encompasses an old castle, fourscore foot broad at top, the great quantity of earth which is //

121 D//   **Circus**
is thrown out of it, forms on the outside a mighty *vallum* or rampart of earth, the compass whereof on the outside Mr *Roger Gale* & I measurd 4300 & odd feet. This bank of earth so placd forms a fine terrace, like the uppermost walk in the Antient Amphitheaters, & presents a perfect view of every thing within. The included *Area*, I observe, has a very gentle descent both eastward & westward. Without the Ditch westward stands the Church, the best of any hereabouts, with a pretty square steeple: the Parish comprehends both West *Kennet* & *Beckampton*. This rampart is a good security to the Town against winds & hinders a sight of it near. Which prompted the People to build in it first & the ground is pretty good, tho' in the main chalk or marl as everywhere this way.

271

[Main circle]

[121 D] Thirty foot within the verge of the ditch is sett [<in> *del.*] a Circle of Stones at equal intervals, upon an edge, with their planes parallel to the side of the Ditch, or at right angles with a *radius* of the circle.[2] This Range in the whole, consists of the compleat number of one hundred stones. Each 16 foot broad, as many high & full four foot thick. This circle is 1040 foot in diameter. The intervals between the stones are equal to the bredth & heigth of the stones, so on the outside between this circle & the ditch is an esplanade, or walk quite round, 30 foot broad. The quick sett hedges now upon the ground sometime take the row of the stones & sometime the verge of the ditch. The distance between the center of each Stone is nearly *35 of our feet*. Out of this noble circuit of these mighty Stones theres still left Anno 1722 40 in number whereof 17 standing, the rest thrown down or reclining. [9, *del.*] <10> of them all contiguous on the south eastern side, were destroyd by one man <Tho. Robinson> in the year 1700.[3] Several more 1718, & again 1720, immediately after the first time I saw the place, <& more 1720> so that there were in the beginning of this Century above half the whole number remaining. Most of the cavitys whence the rest were taken are now visible. One now lyes buryd underground in the garden on the left hand as you goe to the church,[4] & in some places trees are planted in their stead. Upon the method I have marked them in the Groundplot of Abury is this: the Stones that are shadowd, note such as are standing, the single outline those that are left but fallen, the shadow without an outline thos which are gone but where the cavity of them is still visible, the point shows the places of such as are carryd away & the turf leveld thereupon: which the report of the Inhabitants of their own memory & the Symmetry of the work sufficiently demonstrate. Very likely some others are buryed but the tumor not apparent, because they might disperse the superfluous mold to render the pastures level, for the benefit of the grass & convenience of mowing. Some of these Stones measurd above 17 foot broad, for as they were not squard, some exceed a little & //

123 D//   **[Solar *del.*] Temple**

& some fall short a little of the common measure, the Symmetry of the whole being only regarded of the Architects. So some of the stones thrown down I measurd 20 foot long, <[122 D] that at the North entrance 22 foot long>, therefore such no doubt were lett farther into the ground to preserve the regularity. This great circle then resembles a Colonnade of the Pycnostyle kind, if we would speak in the manner of the Greecian Architecture, where the intercolumniation & bases of the pillars are equal: which can be only proper in Structures of the largest size, because the voyd between would otherwise be too small, in proportion of human body.

We are supposed now to be within the limits of the sacred ground.[5] What next is presented to our consideration, are the two great circles environed by the last standing in the middle of the *Area*. If we take the whole for a temple, these must be esteemd two *Sacella* or chappels, consecrated to particular Deitys, as in the manner of our Cathedrals, but if they be properly Temples, which is my opinion, then the *Area* comprehended between them & the outer circle, must be thought a kind of Church yard. <[122 D] but not for the abominable use we put 'em to at present of burying the dead but grandeur, beauty & use in the holy ceremonys.> The centers of these two temples are upon a diameter of the whole passing nearly from Northwest to Southeast, the line that crosses it at right angles regards the northeast. Thes[e] two centers are 372 foot asunder, for at the distance of 186 foot from the center of the whole on each side, are they fixt upon the first mentiond diameter. Each of these circles is above 320 foot in diameter,[6] [each, *del.*] <and> consisting of the just number of 30 Stones of the same dimensions with the former, [&, *del.*] set at the same intervals. That which is southward of the other has [*above line:* χ [*chi*] *unkeyed*] about 14 Stones still left, whereof about half standing, some lying along in the pastures, two lett into the ground under a barn, others under the houses. One lys above ground under the corner of a house, over against the Inn (now the sign of the Catharin Wheel), one buryd under the earth in a little garden. The hollows of some more are visible; in the places of some are trees sett; I beleive all those in the pastures were standing within the memory of Man. Each of these Temples are formd of two concentric circles, for within this we are describing, upon half the diameter of the outermost is another vizt *about 160 foot*. Whereof at present only one standing but several have been destroyd 12 & 13 year agoe.[7] In number there seems to have been twelve. In the very Center there's now a Stone higher originally than the rest & of a circular form at base, of a vast bulk & conical. This I call the [Solar, *del.*] <Southern> Temple. V[ide] p. 130.[8]

272

As already noted, the content of the pages following 123 is unknown, since they have been cut out. At 129 and 131 a continuous text returns, and here Stukeley is commenting first on his postulated 'inner circle of 100 lesser stones', then on destruction at the site generally:

[129 D] such as have intimately considerd these things, which at first sight may appear too bold to those that are strangers to these antient works. It may be reckond bold to assert an Avenue at Stonehenge when there is not one Stone left. but I did not invent it. having been able to measure the very intervals of almost every Stone. from the manifest hollows left in their stations & probably they were taken away when Christianity first prevaild here. Millions of People have traversd the ground over many times without ever discerning it, & Many have with great assurence denyd the possibility of it to me, when upon the next view & being warned of the thing they have been fully convincd of it. Now no one will expect that there should be the tracks of those stones at Abury, supposing they are less than the rest & run directly athwart the middle of their pastures &c. & when it would be easy to fill up their holes & level the ground. It seems to me that at the time of first building the town here these stones were all taken away, being as easily broke as the other they must have fetchd off the Downs, especially we may well suspect the Church is [entirely, del.] <mostly> raisd from them, for tis the very same stone,[9] the Lord of the Mannors house & outhouses in all likelyhood partook of the plunder, perhaps the parsonage house & large barns. Truly supposing the thing for a real fact, which I am thro'ly convincd of my self: I dont wonder so much at the 99 which are gone as at the poor one remaining[9] upon which such as love these speculations will greatly felicitate themselves, which certainly has the honor to preserve the memory of the rest & of which according to my notion there can no tolerable account be given but upon our <this> supposition. Some perhaps may say it was a stone necessary in their sacrifices, it might be a god or twenty such meagre suppositions, which are not worth answering as mere trifles, altogether abhorrent of the Noble Majesty of this Work. But if we have but the least tincture of the spirit of the Founders, if we think like them, we must allow this was a fine walk, like the porticos of the antients, a circular Colonnade at a *medium* 3000 foot in circumference to which I know nothing equal but the Portico's of Solomons Temple: they indeed were coverd & it was their purpose to shelter the people from rain, but this was a delicacy, we well believe wholly disregarded by our hardy Ancestors. But what relates to state & grandeur & the magnificent or ornamental Parts of sacred structures was well presented to us by Ours, & in my private opinion its effect must be more admirable, than that of a strait portico or common gallery. In that you see the whole at one end & there is no variety for the eye all the way, you see all the com-//131 D//pany at once as in the Mall, but in walking round so mighty a Curve as this, which takes in no less than [ ] acres of ground, every step gives you entirely a new view. You meet the company <unseen before> at a reasonable distance & in every sort. The effect must be admirable. As for the use of it I shall speak of it by & by. But the coincidence of the stone <being exact 60 celtic feet distant from the out[er]> upon one of the denary points of the diameter of <the circle> made me immediately suspect its purport when I first laid down this groundplot <for tis the same bredth as the avenue>.[10] This portico is [70, *altered to*] 60 foot wide which with the 30 comprehended between the outermost circle & the edg of the ditch makes up 100, a 10th part on each end of the whole diameter.

Thus from the Ruins of this bulky Carcass, as the Antiquarians from the fragments & *rudera* of Old Rome, must we fish out a model of its pristine state, & in this Critical time when the Compass of an ordinary life saw it well nigh in its original perfection. The *aera* of its desolation exceeds not 30 years, except what we spoke of the inner circle of 100 lesser Stones. *Walter Stretch*, Father of one of the chief inhabitants, first found out the way of breaking the Great Stones by Fire about that time. The first he exercisd the base art upon, was one of the outer circle of the [Lunar, *del.*] Temple standing in the highway over against our Inn, about 1694. Whilst it was upright in the road it surprizd the Passingers among the rest, but falling down I suppose incommoded them by its enormous bulk, this put him being the Innkeeper upon practising upon it, & probably some Traveller might help him to the unlucky hint, some subtle *Iconaclast* whose name ought not to be recorded, unless as that of *Herostratus* for infamy. Since then *Tho. Robinson* has been a terrible Mallet, tho' he ownd to us two of them cost £8 breaking, & upon our remonstrances has promisd to spare all those that are standing in his ground. The destruction of the rest that stood in the road was much resented by S[i]r *Robert Holford* who had an estate in the Town. One Stone thereof containing the quantity 20 load built the dining room end of the house at the Inn. Since then

Farmer *Green* pulld down many of the < lesser circle of the > [Solar, *del.*] Temple to build his house & walls at *Beckampton*. In short all the Town & houses hereabouts are built of these sacred Materials, & the genealogy of every one may be tracd from the [Sun and Moon, *del.*], tho' like the *Arcadians* they are not *Prosel 'enites*[?]. For a while we will leave the holy confines & retire without the ditch & huge rampart which bounds it & gives us an agreeable walk like the walls of an old Town where we may take an airy prospect of all the adjacent Country, of *Silbury* hill a mile off, a *tumulus* of an astonishing bulk, of the rich cornfields extended upon all the lawns & levels, of the naked eminences //

Here the text breaks off again, pages 133–136 being removed, but at 137 it returns, dealing with the ditch and rampart, and the lie of the land within the henge:

[137 D] The ditch & Rampart which include the Temple of *Abury* are together 160 foot broad, the half of which is allotted to each; they form a circle tho' not a Mathematical one but accurate enough for the rudeness of thos[e] times. This is not the only place where the rampart is sett on the outside, but it was the Celtic practise < commonly > in holy places. The reason can certainly be for no other purpose than to demonstrate it to be so sacred[a] Place, the reason why tis so excessively large here, is only that it may bear a proportion to the work which every where was well observd by these people. That it was not a Camp would be absurd to endeavor to defend, in words as < in > reality, and only necessary to convince some of the weakest of the Country people who fancy so, & that the Stones are for security, that the soldiers might lye behind them & shoot their Arrows thro'. Tho' the vastness of the labor in making such a trench, which at a *medium* in length amounts to above 3600 feet, might show their regard in seperating profane from sacred ground, yet they would nevertheless by the manner of it, inculcate a supposition that it needed no other defence, than its own prerogative, which forbids any violation or inroad even in the minds of the most barbarous heathens. Further it is plain by this means they provided more for the perpetuity of the Work: had it been a Really fortifyd place like the Temple of *Apollo* at *Delphos* or the like, which were Castles withal, & many more of Antiquity, it would one time or other < have > brought on the havoc of war, for thither upon a hard necessity the people would have retird as to a defensible place. & there can be no better argument than this to prove it a Temple, but I think I may spare my self the trouble of [prov, *del.*] enlarging upon that Topic. Besides if they had thrown this great body of earth within side, the whole monument had long since been defacd; at least those stones nearest would have been thrown down & coverd over there with. But without question they have by the present disposition well provided against the inconvenience of rains, which immediately drain off into the ditch, & keep the *area* dry & hard. For had it been otherwise, they would have found two great disadvantages, that the water pent up within the banks, must have sometime overflowed the place & rendered it unfit to serve their purpose in Religious assemblys: & that the softning the ground might have endangerd in time the fall of the Stones, especially when much trampling of Cattle at those time. & after all it cannot be denyd by those that see the place, it makes the whole look more august & solemn.

I observe too that the plain of the ground has naturally a ridg or rising going from Northwest to Southeast exactly, with the Diametrical line upon which the two Centers of the two Temples stand, & that both ways from thence the water falls < by an easy descent >, the middle of the temples being upon this highest ground, which is an admirable contrivance.//

On the following recto Stukeley again writes in a speculative and reflective vein. Whereas all the passages quoted so far were deleted, this page is undeleted:

[139 U] As a contemplation of a work of this magnitude cannot but be highly entertaining to the curious, & present to us a dilated notion of the founders; so from its order & propriety of parts, we may observe somewhat to persuade us, that not strength alone was employd in this mighty collection of stones. I flatter my self that we may be able to discover the very measure of the people that erected it, & that it was designd by an Artist of a very just as well as capacious thought, who was sensible of the beauty of proportions, without which bulk alone fails of a considerable part of the pleasure & surprize. Nor is it to be thought that the conducting so operose a labor as this, is inconsiderable, where little less than an Army for a long while must be imployd, & where provisions & previous regulations, order & discipline are to be regarded, or the work must certainly at last be left more rude & unsightly than time has renderd it. Where so many hands must cooperate in each single stone, a *Genius* that presides & directs is as necessary as the force that executes: & of which we may gather some notion from the Schemes of the famous *Fontana* when he raisd an Obelisk in *Rome* with great pomp & solemnity. While dubious passions filld the breasts of the whole City present, with apprehension of the event. This will appear still more weighty when we have finishd the whole description of the vast appendages belonging to it, & upon considering too that its not to be suspected, that little more than plain human strength was applyd in such early times, or the help only of the most simple mechanic powers, such as the leaver, rollers & tho' they had ropes in all likelyhood, yet scarce is it to be thought they were masters of pullys & other like auxiliary Engines. The majority too of these materials must be fetchd from 6 or 7 miles distance & over great inequality of ground. Tis plain from sight of the groundplot that the Scheme which the architect prepard, as the rule & model of this stately composure, was adjusted with great skill & judgment, both with regard to use & to produce a proper effect. The number of the stones tho' so very considerable yet are no more than necessary, nor can we chuse to add any without deforming its simplicity. In all points tis well adapted to its purpose. As all sacred places ought to be, tis entirely different from buildings of private use. It strongly affects the beholder & inspires him with a Religious Awe, forcible as the Spirit that engagd 'em in its erection. People must needs think well of that principle [that, *del.*] which produces a work seeming so much above human strength, & rather the effect of the Powers they there adore: which takes in so wide a Scope, as even in its present tatterd condition to exhibit the appearence of a ruind city, yet with a characteristic so entirely different from the desolation of other structures, for here we cant see one stone upon another.//

Here, as already noted, the recto text is interrupted by a whole series of excised pages.

In 1723, when Stukeley returned to the site, he began to rewrite the original account which we have been presenting so far, evidently intending to recast the whole in a new form. Some of his additions were piecemeal second thoughts. Others, however, comprise a new departure, in that he now seems to have decided to include much more detailed information about specific stone settings than had seemed to him appropriate in 1722. The result is a rather unsatisfactory juxtaposition of original and newer material. Since many of the passages on stone settings are longer in their own right than the original passages to which they are keyed, we shall consistently quote these *in extenso* here. On the other hand, in the case of passages which simply comprise second thoughts on the original text, we have used our discretion, in an attempt to minimize confusion to the reader, sometimes presenting them here and sometimes consigning them to footnotes to the places in the 1722 text to which they refer.

To confuse matters still more, these 1723 additions are interspersed with others which, on grounds of handwriting and sometimes also of placement on the page, we are inclined to date to 1722, while there are also a handful of evidently late brief additions. Here, we shall transcribe only material directly germane to the description of the site, simply drawing attention to the existence of other notes.

Thus the notes on p. 102 comprise classical quotations only; those on p. 110 are additions to a lost page of text, including an interesting note about climbing on to an architrave at Stonehenge, and the better sense of the bulk of the stones thereby acquired. The notes on p. 116 comprise either classical quotations (at least some of them in a perceptibly later hand) or brief notes supplementing passages that we have not transcribed. On p. 118 Stukeley has made eight varied additions to the general section on Avebury on p. 119, of which the first is the long note on beauty (see above). Five subsequent notes (one of them in a later hand) deal with names connected with water and rivers, and there are the following two unkeyed reflections on further virtues of the site:

[118[iii] D] One reason why they pitcht upon this place was the solid chalk affording a firm basis for their work & throwing off showers quick. I took notice by the parsonage barn the great bank thrown out of the ditch is pure chalk & the roads hereabout are very hard chalk < tho > so public & worn & never mended are not very deep.

[118[vi] D] Tis particularly sheltered from the east by Whitehill < hakpen > & the continuation of its ridg parallel to Kennet Avenue as far as Overton hill, the most general descent of this ground meets the tepid Zephyrs, there is a visible declension of the ground, on the north side of the town immediately from the outside of the vallum. very considerable on the east & indeed quite round the Town, the lowest part within is between the two avenues the [sla,[?] *del.*] southwest part of the outer circle, so its opposite is the highest. the diameter that answers to Silbury hill or midway between the two avenues.

The tours of the henge

At p. 120, however – on which the additions dealing at length with stone settings begin – Stukeley provides what is in effect an alternative beginning to the entire description of the site (this is the sentence quoted by Piggott 1985, 89):

> **[120[i] U]** I shall take the reader a fine tour along with me quite round the verge of the temple, but how much more agreeable upon the Spot tho' accompanyd with the trouble of climbing over the hedges.

These words seem to have been added by way of preface to the next passage, the beginning of the 'tour' of the outer circle. Topographically it is the first of a series of passages keyed to places in the original text and/or to each other. The order in which these were added is not entirely clear, especially since in some cases their position on the pages is dictated by the position on the facing recto of the passage to which they are keyed. We have therefore presumed that, as his sequence of keys tends to indicate, Stukeley intended them to appear as a pasture by pasture tour of the outer circle (as similarly, later, of the northern and southern 'temples'). This sometimes involves intercalating keyed passages from p. 122 into those from p. 120.

The opening phrase reveals the date of this series:

> **[120[ii] U]** In order to record their p[resen]t state A[nn]o 1723. We will begin from the road going to the right hand by the ditch side that we may have our left towards the center after the manner of the conversion of the Britons. The three first stones from the road are standing & present us with a most stately copy of what the whole was when compleat: this view I have delineated Tab.[   ]. The two first stand in the first pasture, in the 2[n]d the other. The[re] follows two hollows & a vacancy near which is set a young ash tree but nearer the ditch than it ought. Next is a vacancy by the rails side. In pasture III the 1st stone was standing when I was first here but now three vacancys perfectly leveld one [*or?*, ore (=over)] entering pasture IIII. the 2[n]d lys on the ground & level with its sup[er]ficies.

The next section, topographically speaking, is keyed to the passage in Stukeley's earlier text, on the facing recto 121, dealing with Tom Robinson's destruction of stones in the NE quadrant. For clarity's sake, we prefix this passage in italics:

> *[121] Out of this noble circuit of these mighty Stones theres still left Anno 1722 40 in number whereof 17 standing, the rest thrown down or reclining. [9, del.] <10> of them all contiguous on the south eastern side, were destroyd by one man < Tho. Robinson > in the year 1700.* **[120[vii] U]** & their places perfectly leveld. Next follows one reclining, then one on the ground, then a vacancy the hedg side of a little garden where another was placd. Two more in the middle of the east[er]n road are no doubt thrown into the ditch when they filld it up to make this road. Next one of excessive bulk lying resting it self on a side which I suppose fell upon wearing away of the road. Another lyes under the hedg & trees grow upon it. Entring the V pasture after 3 vacancys You come to a stone standing: after 3 vacancys more a very large hollow where the outline of the Stone that lay upon it is very visible & one would be apt to imagine it had pressd so deep a bed in the hard chalk by its incumbent weight.

A symbol (circle atop cross) then leads to a passage, farther down the page, which continues on to p. 122:

[120[ix] U] After another hollow a stone lys among bushes as if ashamd to see the desolation of the place. Next two flat in the ground & here the hedg on the right hand by the ditch side which hitherto stood upon the edg of the ditch retires inward & accompanys the circle of Stones leaving a pretty walk or terras behind it. & hereabouts too is the highest peice of ground in the whole circumference being the north point thereof. Next follows two vacancy[s], then two stones lye upon the ground in situ between the hedg & the ditch. Next follows three vacancys in a little grip under the hedg, & we come to the VI pasture, wher[e] under the hedg is a vacancy, a hollow, then a stone standing, then [a, *altered to*] g[rea]t hollow < s of two > [the next, *del.*] stones < which > (at least fragments [of it], *del.*] are tumbled into the ditch to make the north entrance. Then we come to that which lys in the road split in its fall. Its bulk is astonishing. This minute [lyes, *del.*] < are > three or 4 wooden wedges driven into **//122[vi] U//**[11] into a great crack in order to rend it in pieces which Lord Winchelsea & I saw with much regret. Entring the terras at the end of the VII pasture we have the agreeable sight of 4 stones standing together. Against the end of the VIII pasture the next is broke off at the root like the pedistal of a pillar: the like of the next. & the next to that. Then you come to 3 standing. The next is broke & tumbled a little out its place too much westward, the next is broke off by the root when you come to the pails going across the ditch to the end of the great Parsonag barn. All this way from the north road the top of the vallum on the other side of the ditch was leveld by S[i]r Rich[ar]d Holford whos name ought ever to be mentiond with honor & his memory dear to Antiquarians for his great care in preserving these glorious remains & worthily imitated by his descendant the present possessor Mr [   ] Holford Esqr. S[i]r Rich[ar]d usd to take great delight in walking upon that agreeable terras & planted a little parterr of trees upon the end of it. From hence to the W entrance the vallum is thrown intirely into the ditch for the outhouses standing along it. & the ditch is planted with trees. Passing over the pales we view 2 standing < in pasture VIII >, one vacancy & one hollow. The next is standing in the yard, then 2 vacancys over ag[ains]t the barn. Next you come to a little tenement & a garden in the ditch, which comprehends one vacancy more[:] then another great stone lyes in the garden under a great beech tree standing at the corner of the house by the great road side leading to the Church. Then, crossing this road at the beginning of Beckampton or longstone avenue, one that stood in the middle of it is quite gone. The next lys under the pails on the other side of the way, then we goe thro' a little garden carryd into the ditch where they are buryd in the mold.

After 'mold', Stukeley has written the parenthetical cross-reference '(next page backwards ⊕)'. Stukeley's cross within circle here keys back to the word 'buryd', in the middle of a clause in his original text (p. 121); the end of this clause is keyed on (by an X) to another addition on p. 120. Again we prefix the earlier sentence, in italics:

[121] One now lyes buryd underground in the garden on the left hand as you goe to the church, **[120(viii) U]** another lyes there partly above ground. In the pasture < IX > next it 4 cavitys are visible full of nettles, in the next one is leaning, one standing, 4 fallen & buryed flat in the ground. Now you come to Kennet avenue, one Stone stone [*sic*] full in the middle of the road & avenue the three next

The paragraph breaks off thus in mid-page, although there is a line or more of space to continue had Stukeley wished. However, it may at first have ended more conventionally, since the words 'the three next' – presumably referring to the three stones in Pasture I with which the tour began – could perhaps have been added a little later. Alternatively, Stukeley may have left this sentence incomplete because he intended to supersede it by a further passage higher up the same page, which is keyed, by an X within a circle, to the end of the sentence ' . . . buryed flat in the ground':

[120[iii] U] In pasture X there are two vacancys quite obliterated, one hollow very conspicuous by the hedg close by the lane & entrance of Kennet Avenue, which brings us to the place where we began & compleats our circuit & the number of 100 stones.

The two remaining items on p. 120 are an unkeyed note about the N entrance:

[120[v] U] Reuben Horsal when a boy remembers that stone standing on this right hand of the North entrance. which fell down at noon time of day a loaded cart going by which probably shook

.it being almost undermind by wearing away of the road which is hard chalk, it split into two by the fall as it now appears & of prodigious bulk.

and then the sentence:

[120[vi] U] I reckon all in the groundplot that ever I saw from my first observation.

On p. 122, apart from the section already quoted, there is also a further passage not yet dealt with. This constitutes a composite whole although divided by an existing note, transcribed above because it seems to be an early addition to the text on p. 123. The first part of this originally contained phrases concerning Celtic measures, now fully deleted by scribbling. While some of these may eventually prove decipherable, they are ignored in our transcript:

[122[ii] D] I took care to be very accurate in finding out the founders intent in this outer circle, & discoverd that the stones are two parts broad as many high, the intervals are 3 [*altered from 2 and/or 4*] <each a celtic foot>. so that a celtic rod at 3 & ½ goes from center to center of the stones of this circle quite round. The 1000 celtic foot is the diamet[er] of the middle line of the out[er] circle & of the out[er] circle of the two temples. There seems to be some little difference according to the bulk of the stones but in the main the same proportion goes round & preserves the same effect as **[122[iv] D]** if they were hewn & mathematically exact, & particularly as in general they took care to set the smoothest & most sightly side of the stones innermost where most in view as at Stonehenge, so they placd the best stones of the outer circle towards both entrances, of the avenues, all along observing the best effect that could be producd from such materials & with much judgment. Some of the stones are above 16 celtic foot broad therefore the intervals between them are somewhat more.

On p. 124 are nine short miscellaneous notes, all probably relating to material formerly on the cut-out recto 125, although only two of them are keyed. These are:

[124(iv) D] X About 8 a clock at night one winters evening.
[124(vi) U] + I saw a rough piece of such a black marble lye before the blacksmiths door without the dich towards the church.

Apart from four deleted classical quotations, not transcribed here, the other notes are:

124[ii] D] Mr Bray of Monkton informs me that his Mother told him she saw K[ing] Charles II in his progress this way ride into the yard to see this prodigious cove.
[124[vii] U] containing about 22 acres of ground.
[124(viii) D] The lunar cove <Kebla> opens precisely 10d[egrees]. eastward of the N.E. just as that of Stonehenge.

It will be seen that two of the above refer to the Cove, thus hinting that it was probably the subject of original text opposite, now removed. This appears confirmed by the two longer paragraphs on p. 124, since these constitute a tour of the northern circle(s):

[The Northern Circle(s)]

[124[iii] U] Let us begin <our [lunar, *del.*] [   ]> at that Stone lying at the Inn gate most obvious to Strangers: tho' many a slash has been given it & great peices knockd off yet tis of a vast bulk. Going forwards Eastward the next stone lys in the Garden behind the next little house in the street. Another stood in the middle of our Landlords garden, the next in part lys in the hedg between the garden & pasture V, entring which a stone stands wellnigh perfect & most straitly embracd by some elm trees which almost hide it & with which probably its fate is united. The next place is perfectly vacant & the ground leveld ore. The next stone very bulky spreads its carcass on the ground, some trees growing around it. The next vacant, then one fallen & one handsom stone standing by the hedg side. Pursuing our track into Pasture VI we find a hollow, next a vacancy, then two hollows.

Of the next a fragment is left; the next is standing by the lane side, then it gos across the lane into pasture VII where many were taken up in 1717. Two year before was one destroyd where now is a hollow, the next to it has been demolisht since last year to build a wall by the garden side.

[124[v] U] Of the inner circle onely three stones left one gone since I saw it in the hedg by the road side, one lyes in the Corner between the two barns & one stands in pasture VI fronting the Cove, this pasture has the honor to possess that Stately work the [Lunar, *del.*] Cove. I observd one Star-light night that the stone standing in the lesser circle of the [lunar, *del.*] temple before the Cove looking over that standing by the hedg side the most northerly in pasture V of the outer circle points directly to the northpole star.

Pages 125–128 being cut out, the next verso is 130, at the head of which are two paragraphs keyed on from the discussion of 'the southern Temple' on p. 123, and constituting Stukeley's tour of it:

[The Southern Circle(s)]

[130[i] U] We shall follow the former method in describing the [Solar, *del.*] < South > circle as before & begin in Pasture I, entering from the Town Street where on the left hand is a garden wall built the [*sic*] Stone that stood in its place, next to which are two hollow holes, the seats of as many Stones of the outer circle of this temple. Three stones next are fallen but lye upon the ground not much diminishd; by the side of each is growing an ashtree, whence probably the Stones were thrown down. The next is standing, of a handsome figure, another lys along by the hedg side. Entering pasture II the first stone is standing, the lodgment of the next is visible & a young ash tree planted in its room, the next has a little rising above the level of the ground, the next has a great cavity left & a young elm tree planted therein, the next to that is standing. In pasture III the first is standing, the 2[n]d has a hollow, the next a p[er]fect vacuity, the next to that a very deep hole & great bredth, the next stood by the pails of the garden.

[130[ii] U] In that garden were two, & two in the barn adjoyning one whereof remains in the floor[:] the next destroyd since last year to build the next house, one or two more lye or did lye in the floor of that house. The next lyes now by the Street side under the corner of an house directly over ag[ains]t the Inn. The next that was in the garden was destroyd to build the meeting house, the next is left in a barn or stable floor. The next stood in a garden but now demolishd, the last is at present buryed in the same garden which compleats our number of 30.

Following this are notes 130[iii], quoted in n.8 below, and the deleted **[130[iv]]**: 'The inner circles is the diameter of 1000 celtic feet'. The interpretative passage 130[v], again deleted, is quoted almost entire in Chapter II,iv: it begins 'In the middle of thes[e] two circles is the cove of 3 stones which magnificent & awful structure is no other than the great gate of the gods . . . '. Finally, 130[vi] is a still later, but deleted, interpretative addition, beginning 'the central obelus was a kibla – to worship towards, a patriarchal custom'.

Of seven miscellaneous notes and quotations on p. 132, two at least suggest that the missing recto 133 may have dealt with the avenues. The first of these is quoted in Chapter IV,h, and the second, in part, in Chapter II,iv.

[132[iii] U] Several Ro[man] coyns found with the bones of a man under one of the stones of the avenue over ag[ains]t the white hart alehouse close by the Ro[man] road, but illegible: one I had given me. Probably some Roman was buryd under it & the stone thrown down over him for a monument & these coyns of little value laid with him to show his country.

[132[vii] D] The brook running thro' & crossing the tail of the serpent indicated the moisture necessary for heat to work upon in order to further generation or the warm steam or fiery humidity the author of it. So the whole temple is placd near a spring head to indicate that water is the sustenance of all life.

After this, with pp. 133–136 and 141–156 cut out, Stukeley has removed so much that it is not feasible to attempt to give a complete text. Some of the major surviving pages deal with features outside our present scope, such as Silbury Hill (p. 158, obviously added to the missing 159) and barrows in the Avebury vicinity (pp. 163ff.). There is also Stukeley's hypothesis about the overall structure of the monument, dated 17 July 1723 (p. 175), and a page dealing with the termination of the Beckhampton Avenue, where Stukeley writes:

[157 D] Why it should end here I cannot give a reason unless here was a temple dedicated to the Manes or Infernal Deitys, which upon frequent reflection I have persuaded myself is fact, & that these stones are the remains thereof beside what has been consumd in building all the houses hereabouts.

Other passages deal with Stukeley's interpretation of the site more generally, as surveyed in Chapter II, but, although some of these are of interest in their own right, and might merit publication, in view of their incompleteness and the extent to which they overlap with Stukeley's fieldnotes in Gough Maps 231, we have not attempted to include them here. It seems appropriate to end with Stukeley's memorable peroration:

[173 U] The particularity of this description is designd to preserve the memory of this most illustrious Work of the highest Antiquity, & writing it upon the spot made me catch at every appearance that I thought tended that way & had a regard in the eye of the Founders. If it be not too dry for the entertainment of the present age it may assist in their contemplation of what reality remains & I hope will tempt them strictly to survey it, which may rescue some part from impending ruin when the Country finds an advantage in preserving its poor reliques. But future times may hence be able to ascertain its purport, when this sort of learning will be more cultivated. Such sort of accounts being modern & untouchd, I think I have done my part in recording its history as pregnant materials for them to work upon, & when others of like nature shall be brought in competition therewith, & many monuments of a kind compar'd together mutually explain each other. But as they that carry a candle light themselves first I shall not be unwillingly [sic] to answer the readers expectations in delivering my present sentiments upon the matter, & leave them to be canvassd by the curious & Ingenious admirers of Antiquity as a debt due to the memory of the antient Britons, who contrivd as far as men could a work of perpetuity, to astonish & delight. To pronounce this a Temple I think there is all the reason in the world without one negative suspicion, & that it was their compilement the thing its self shows loudly: the whole Scope & manner, all its parts & what accompanys it, what has been found in the barrows around, conspire with the fullest evidence, & conviction.

Notes

1. After 'for' and 'together' in this clause appear raised keys (X and + respectively), presumably relating to notes on the cut-out verso 114 formerly opposite.

2. Opposite this passage is a quotation used in similar context in *Abury* (1743, 22):

3. After 'in the year 1700' is a key – dot within circle – leading to 120[vii, ix], then 122[vi], then 121. In the margin opposite 'these mighty Stones' is written '20 C'; lower on the page, opposite 'measurd above' is '10 cub'.

    [120[iv] U] pro molli viola, pro purpureo narcisso
           carduus & spinis surgat paliurus acutis.
           Virg.

4. After 'One now lyes buryd', a key – cross within circle – leads to/from end of 122[vi]; after 'goe to the church' an X-key leads to 120[viii]. We transcribe these passages in their appropriate places.

5. After 'the sacred ground' is a key (a lozenge) leading to note (iii) at foot of page (see n.6 below): 'with us enter ... '.

6. After originally writing 'above 320 foot', Stukeley altered this to '330', but he later added 'stet' above the line, and indicated by underlining that he wished the original to be reinstated. In the margin between 'and' and 'consisting' has been added '200 C | 190'.

7. After '12 & 13 year agoe' the key asterisk leads to a deleted note (122[v]) on the facing verso: 'John Fowler avowd burnt 5 of them.' Below this is the quotation (cf. Stukeley 1743, 22):

        – nec ipso
    monte minor procumbit. Virg.

Just above this, opposite 'about 160 foot', '144' appears in the L margin, while opposite this in the R margin appears '100C | 80'.

8. After the continuous text on 123, Stukeley made the following four discrete additions:

[123[i] U] Of the inner circle of the [Solar, *del.*] <Southern> temple but one is now standing 7½ celtic rods distant from the central obelus: this is in Pasture II. On the other side the pails nearer the houses were many left, which met their fate A[nn]o 1710.

[123[ii] D] The [dot within circle, here = Sun symbol] central obelisc is 21 f long, 8 [or] 9 thick.

[123[iii] U]
[lozenge note,   with us enter with lucky omen
Keyed in text]   – neque[?] ad tua limina phoebe
            Ipse manu multo suspensum
                   Numino ducas.

[123[iv] D] The stones round Abury are 15 f. br. 13 high. The int[er]vals as 2 to 3 22½, the bredth of the avenue double that 45. The distance of the stones of the avenue sideways 72½[sic], the same ratio.

In the bottom margin appear two undeleted sums, the significance of which is unclear.

9.   After 'same stone' is a raised asterisk, and after 'poor one remaining' a raised X; these presumably keyed to notes formerly on the facing verso, 128, now cut out.

10.   After the phrase < for tis the same bredth as the avenue >, a lozenge in the margin keys to a note on the facing verso:

[130[iii] U] : to which it is only a continuation, which is the strongest argument in the world that it was in reality as I have supposd it, for otherwise there is no reason to be assignd Why these measure [sic] should both ways so exactly measure 100 celtic f. the thickness of each stone inclusive.

In the margin opposite the earlier part of this sentence are the words 'stet 4thly'. This evidently implies that he wanted to reinstate the words 'upon one of the ... diameter', in place of his insertion.

11.   The first (part-)sentence of this passage on p. 122 is deleted, by Stukeley's customary single horizontal line.

Works referred to
(Books and individual MSS)

Almost all the bracketed citations in the text refer to entries in this list of references. The exceptions to this are as follows: all references in the form Eng.Misc., Gough Maps, or Top. Gen. are to manuscripts in the Bodleian Library, Oxford. All references to items by Alexander Keiller which do not feature in the list of references are to manuscripts in the Alexander Keiller Museum, Avebury: since these are not classified it is impossible to give precise references. Lastly, 'WANHS Stukeley MS' refers to the Stukeley commonplace book in the Library of the Wiltshire Archaeological and Natural History Society at Devizes.

Allen, M. J., and Carruthers, W. J. 1989. Environmental Assessment of the Alluvial Deposits (Trench H). In Smith and Trott, 1989, Appendix 2.

Annable, F. K. 1959. Excavation and Fieldwork in Wiltshire: 1958, *Wiltshire Archaeological and Natural History Magazine*, **57**, 227–39.

Anon. 1862. Fac-similes of Aubrey's Plans of Abury, *Wiltshire Archaeological Magazine*, **7**, 224–7.

Atkinson, R. J. C. 1979 (revised 1956 edition). *Stonehenge* (London).

Aubrey 1. John Aubrey, *The Naturall Historie of Wiltshire*, part 1, Bodleian Library MS Aubrey 1.

Aubrey 4. John Aubrey, *A Perambulation of Surrey*, Bodleian Library MS Aubrey 4.

Aubrey 12. Letters to Aubrey, A–N, Bodleian Library MS Aubrey 12.

Aubrey 24. John Aubrey, *Monumenta Britannica or a Miscellanie of British Antiquities*, vol. 1, Bodleian Library MS Top. Gen.c.24.

Aubrey 25. John Aubrey, *Monumenta Britannica or a Miscellanie of British Antiquities*, vol. 2, Bodleian Library MS Top.Gen.c.25.

Aubrey, John. 1847. *The Natural History of Wiltshire*, ed. John Britton (London).

Aubrey, John. 1898. *Brief Lives, Chiefly of Contemporaries*, ed. Andrew Clark, 2 vols. (Oxford).

Aubrey, John. 1972. *Three Prose Works*, ed. John Buchanan Brown (Fontwell).

Bakker, J. A. 1979. Lucas de Heere's Stonehenge, *Antiquity*, **53**, 107–11.

Barker, C. T. 1985. The Long Mounds of the Avebury Region, *Wiltshire Archaeological and National History Magazine*, **79**, 7–38.

Barrington, E. J. W. 1975. Francis Gerald William Knowles, 1915–1974, *Biographical Memoirs of Fellows of the Royal Society*, **21**, 431–46.

Bartlett, A., and David, A. 1982. Geophysical Survey of the Stonehenge Avenue. In M. Pitts, On the Road to Stonehenge: report on investigations beside the A344 in 1968, 1979 and 1980. *Proceedings of the Prehistoric Society*, **48**, 90–3.

Bartholinus, Thomas. 1663–7. *Epistolarum Medicinalium Centuriae Quatuor*, 4 vols. (Hafniae).

Bartlett, A., and David., A. 1984. Geophysical Prospecting. In P. D. Catherall et al., eds., *The Southern Feeder, the Archaeology of a Gas Pipeline* (London), 197–205.

Bennett, J. A. 1982. *The Mathematical Science of Christopher Wren* (Cambridge).

Birch, Thomas. 1756–7. *The History of the Royal Society of London*, 4 vols. (London).

Birch, W.de G. 1887. *Cartularium Saxonicum: a Collection of Charters relating to Anglo-Saxon History*, vol. 2 (London)

Borrichius, Olaus. 1983. *Olai Borrichii Itinerarium 1660–1665, The Journal of the Danish Polyhistor Ole Borch*, ed. H. D. Schepelern, 4 vols. (Copenhagen).

Borthwick, A. M. 1985. *Avebury 1985: Report of Archaeological Evaluation Work by the T.W.A. on Behalf of Wiltshire County Council ... Car Park at Avebury* (Trowbridge).

Borthwick A.[M.] 1989. *West Kennet Avebury – a Landscape Study*. Unpublished report to English Heritage.

Boyle, Robert. 1744. *Works*, ed. Thomas Birch, 5 vols. (London).

REFERENCES

British Archaeological News. 1989. The Future of Avebury, *British Archaeological News*, **4**, 81.

Britton, John. 1845. *Memoir of John Aubrey* (London).

Browne, H. 1823. *An Illustration of Stonehenge and Abury* (8th ed., 1867) (Salisbury).

Burke, Sir Bernard. 1883. *A Genealogical History of the Dormant, Abeyant, Forfeited, and Extinct Peerages of the British Empire*, new ed. (London).

Burl, Aubrey. 1979. *Prehistoric Avebury* (New Haven, London).

Burl, Aubrey. 1988. Coves: Structural Enigmas of the Neolithic, *Wiltshire Archaeological and Natural History Magazine*, **82**, 1–18.

Camden, William. 1600. *Britannia* (London).

Camden, William. 1607. *Britannia* (London).

Camden, William. 1610. *Britain*, trans. Philemon Holland (London).

Camden, William. 1695. *Britannia*, ed. Edmund Gibson (London)..

Chapman, D. Emerson. 1939. *Is This Your First Visit to Avebury?* (Basingstoke).

Charleton, Walter. 1663. *Chorea Gigantum, or, The Most Famour Antiquity of Great-Britain, Vulgarly Called Stone-heng, Standing on Salisbury Plain, Restored to the Danes* (London).

Childrey, Joshua. 1661. *Britannia Baconica: Or, The Natural Rarities of England, Scotland, & Wales* (London).

Chippindale, Christopher. 1983. *Stonehenge Complete* (London).

Clark, A. J. 1975. Archaeological Prospecting: a Progress Report, *Journal of Archaeological Science*, **2**, 297–314.

Cleere, H. 1989. *Archaeological Heritage Management in the Modern World* (London).

Colt Hoare, Sir Richard 1812–21. *The Ancient History of Wiltshire*, 2 vols. (London).

Colvin, H. M., 1968. John Aubrey's 'Chronologia Architectonica'. In Sir John Summerson, ed., *Concerning Architecture* (London), 1–12.

Coupland, Lawrence. 1988. *The Avebury Monuments: A Study Pack for Teachers* (English Heritage) (London).

Crawford, O. G. S. MS. [Alexander Keiller Museum, Avebury; held within envelopes numbered 78510456].

Crawford, O. G. S., and Keiller, A. 1928. *Wessex from the Air* (Oxford).

Crook, J. Mordaunt. 1968. John Britton and the Genesis of the Gothic Revival. In Sir John Summerson, ed., *Concerning Architecture* (London), 98–119.

Cunnington, M. E. 1914a. The Re-erection of Two Fallen Stones and Discovery of an Interment with Drinking Cup, at Avebury, *Wiltshire Archaeological Magazine*, **38**, 1–11.

Cunnington, M. E. 1914b. A Burial Stone in the Kennett Avenue, *Wiltshire Archaeological Magazine*, **38**, 12–14.

Cunnington, M. E. 1932. The 'Sanctuary' on Overton Hill, near Avebury, *Wiltshire Archaeological Magazine*, **45**, 300–35.

Curl, J. S. 1982. *The Egyptian Revival* (London).

Dames, Michael. 1977. *The Avebury Cycle* (London).

Daniel, Glyn. 1981. *A Short History of Archaeology* (London).

David, A. 1984. Avebury Car Park, *Ancient Monuments Laboratory Report Series No. 4449*.

Defoe, Daniel. 1724–7. *A Tour thro' the whole Island of Great Britain*, 3 vols. (London).

Defoe, Daniel. 1748. *A Tour thro' the whole Island of Great Britain*, 4th edn., 4 vols. (London).

Desgodetz, Antoine. 1682. *Les Edifices Antiques de Rome Dessinés et Mesurés Tres Exactement* (Paris).

Devine, M., ed. 1977. *The Cartulary of Cirencester Abbey, Gloucestershire*, vol. 3 (Oxford).

Dolley, R. H. M. 1968. The Irish Mints of Edward I in the Light of the Coin-hoards from Ireland and Great Britain, *Proceedings of the Royal Irish Academy*, **66** sect. C, 235–52.

English Heritage. n.d. *Avebury World Heritage Site: Management Plan*.

Evans, Joan. 1956. *A History of the Society of Antiquaries* (Oxford).

Evans, J. E., Limbrey, S., Mate, T, and Mount, R. J. 1988. *Environmental Change and Land-Use History in a Wiltshire River Valley in the Last 14000 Years*. In J. C. Barrett and I. A. Kinnes, eds., *The Archaeology of Context in the Neolithic and Bronze Age: Recent Trends* (University of Sheffield), 97–103.

Evans, J. G., Pitts, M. W. and Williams, D. 1985. An Excavation at Avebury, Wiltshire, 1982, *Proceedings of the Prehistoric Society*, **51**, 305–10.

Evans, R. J. W. 1979. *The Making of the Hapsburg Monarchy, 1550–1700* (Oxford).

Evelyn, John. 1955. *The Diary of John Evelyn*, ed. E. S. de Beer, 6 vols. (Oxford).

Fauvel, J. et. al., eds. 1988. *Let Newton Be!* (Oxford).

[Fergusson, James]. 1860. Stonehenge, *Quarterly Review*, **108**, 200–25.

Fergusson, James. 1872. *Rude Stone Monuments in All Countries; their Age and Uses* (London).

Fleitman, Sabina. 1986. *Walter Charleton (1620–1707, 'Virtuoso': Leben und Werk* (Berne).

Fowles, John, and Legg, Rodney, eds. 1980, 1982. *John Aubrey's Monumenta Britannica*, parts 1–2, 3 (Sherborne).

Fox, H. B. Earle, and Fox, Shirley. 1909–13. Numismatic History of the Reigns of Edward I, II and III, *British Numismatic Journal*, **6–10**, 197–212, 91–142, 137–48, 181–206, 95–124.

Frank, R. G. 1980. *Harvey and the Oxford Physiologists. A Study of Scientific Ideas and Social Interaction* (Berkeley and Los Angeles).

Gelbart, N. R. 1971. The Intellectual Development of Walter Charleton, *Ambix*, **18**, 149–68.

Godwin, Joscelyn. 1979. *Athanasius Kircher: A Renaissance Man and the Quest for Lost Knowledge* (London).

Gray, H. St.G. 1935. The Avebury Excavations, 1908–22, *Archaeologia*, **84**, 99–162.

Harding, A. F., and Lee, G. E. 1987. *Henge Monuments and Related Sites of Great Britain* (B.A.R. British Series 175) (Oxford).

Harington, Sir John. 1591. *Orlando Furioso in English Heroical Verse* (London).

Harrington, P. 1986. Excavations at Avebury 1982. *Wiltshire Archaeological and Natural History Magazine*, **80**, 217–221.

Hawkes, J., Heaton, M., and Trott, M. 1989. *Avebury Chapel, Wilts*. Trust for Wessex Archaeology, Project Code 32922 Summary Report (Salisbury).

Hearne, Thomas. 1915. *Remarks and Collections*, vol. 10, ed. H. E. Salter, Oxford Historical Society, vol. 67 (Oxford).

Heawood, E. 1950. *Watermarks, Mainly of the Seventeenth and Eighteenth Centuries* (Hilversum).

Henry, John, 1988. Walter Charleton. In J.-P. Schobinger, ed., *Grundriss der Geschichte der Philosophie begrundet von Friedrich Ueberweg: Die Philosophie des 17. Jahrhundert 3: England* (Basel), 376–82.

Henry, John. 1990. Magic and Science in the 16th and 17th centuries. In R. C. Olby, G. N. Cantor, J. R. R. Christie and M. J. S. Hodge, eds., *Companion to the History of Modern Science* (London), 583–96.

Holgate, R. 1987. Neolithic Settlement Patterns at Avebury, Wiltshire, *Antiquity*, **61**, 259–63.

Hooke, Robert. 1665. *Micrographia* (London).

Hoppen, K. T. 1976. The Nature of the Early Royal Society, *British Journal for the History of Science*, **9**, 1–24, 243–73.

Hoskin, Michael. 1985. Stukeley's Cosmology and the Newtonian Origins of Olber's Paradox, *Journal for the History of Astronomy*, **16**, 77–112.

Hoskins, W. G. 1953. The Rebuilding of Rural England, 1570–1640, *Past and Present*, **4**, 44–59 (reprinted in *Provincial England* (London, 1963), 131–48).

Hunter, J. 1829. Present State of Abury, Wilts., *The Gentleman's Magazine*, **99** pt. 2, 3–7.

Hunter, M[ichael] C. W. 1971. The Royal Society and the Origins of British Archaeology, *Antiquity*, **45**, 113–21, 187–92.

Hunter, Michael. 1975. *John Aubrey and the Realm of Learning* (London).

Hunter, Michael. 1980. Laying the Foundations, *Times Literary Supplement*, 28 November 1980, 1362.

Hunter, Michael. 1981. The Preconditions of Preservation: A Historical Perspective. In D. Lowenthal and M. Binney, eds., *Our Past Before Us: Why Do We Save It?* (London), 22–32.

Hunter, Michael. 1982. *The Royal Society and its Fellows, 1660–1700: the Morphology of an Early Scientific Institution* (Chalfont St Giles).

Hunter, Michael. 1989. *Establishing the New Science: the Experience of the Early Royal Society* (Woodbridge).

Hunter, Michael. 1990. Pioneer Prehistorians, *Times Literary Supplement*, 9 February 1990, 153.

Hutchinson, H. G. 1914. Life of Sir John Lubbeck, Lord Avebury, 2 vols. (London).

Iversen, Eric. 1961. *The Myth of Egypt and its Hieroglyphs* (Copenhagen).

Jackson, J. E. 1860. Lost Vol. of Aubrey MS. *Wiltshire Archaeological Magazine*, **7**, 76–80.
Jackson, J. E., ed. 1862. *Wiltshire. The Topographical Collections of John Aubrey* (Devizes).
Jones, Inigo. 1655. *The Most Notable Antiquity of Great Britain, vulgarly called Stone-Heng on Salisbury Plain, Restored* [ed. John Webb] (London).
Jope, E. M. n.d. *Avebury: Saxon and Medieval* [unpublished MS].

Kargon, R. H. 1966. *Atomism in England from Hariot to Newton* (Oxford).
Keiller, Alexander. 1934–5. *West Kennet Avenue: General Notes 1934–5*. MS, Alexander Keiller Museum, Avebury.
Keiller, Alexander. 29 June 1938 (Correspondence). In Coupland 1988.
Keiller, Alexander. 1939. *Avebury: Summary of Excavations, 1937 and 1938*. Morven Institute of Archaeological Research (Avebury), *Antiquity*, **13**, 223–33.
Keiller, Alexander, and Piggott, Stuart. 1936. The West Kennet Avenue: Excavations, 1934–5, *Antiquity*, **10**, 417–27.
Keith, A. 1924. Anthropology. In U. G. Duff, ed., *The Life-Work of Lord Avebury (Sir John Lubbock) 1834–1913* (London), 67–104.
Kempson, E. G. H. 1955. The Anglo-Saxon Name for the Avebury Circle, *Wiltshire Archaeological and Natural History Magazine*, **56**, 60–1.
Kendrick, T. D. 1950. *British Antiquity* (London).
Kennet District Council. 1989. *Avebury Local Plan. Draft Plan*.
Kerridge, E. 1954. The Sheepfold in Wiltshire and the Floating of the Water Meadows, *Economic History Review*, **2nd series 6**.
Keysler, J. G. 1720. *Antiquitates Selectae Septentrionales et Celticae* (Hanover).
King, B. 1879. Avebury. The Beckhampton Avenue, *Wiltshire Archaeological Magazine*, **18**, 377–83.
Knowles, Francis. 1956. Avebury Manor, *Wiltshire Archaeological and Natural History Magazine*, **56**, 359–70.

Lambrick, G. 1988. *The Rollright Stones: Megaliths, monuments, and settlement in the prehistoric landscape* (London).
Lees, D. 1984. The Sanctuary: A Neolithic Calendar? *Bulletin of the Institute of Mathematics and its Applications*, **20**, 109–14.
Leland, John. 1907–10. *Itinerary*, ed. Lucy Toulmin Smith, 5 vols. (London).
Levine, J. M. 1977. *Dr. Woodward's Shield. History, Science and Satire in Augustan England* (Berkeley and Los Angeles).
Levy, F. J. 1967. *Tudor Historical Thought* (San Marino).
Long, W. 1858a. Abury, *Wiltshire Archaeological Magazine*, **4**, 309–63.
Long, W. 1858b. *Abury Illustrated* (Devizes).
Long, W. 1862. *Abury Illustrated. With Additions* (Devizes).
Long, W. 1876. *Stonehenge and its Barrows* (Devizes).
Long, W. 1878. Åbury Notes, *Wiltshire Archaeological Magazine*, **17**, 327–35.
Lubbock, Sir John. 1865. *Pre-Historic Times, as Illustrated by Ancient Remains, and the Manners and Customs of Modern Savages* (London and Edinburgh).
Lukis, C. 1795. *The Old Serpentine Temple of the Druids at Avebury in North Wiltshire. A Poem.* (Devizes).
Lukis, W. C. 1881–3a. Report on the Prehistoric Monuments of Stonehenge and Avebury, *Proceedings of the Society of Antiquaries of London*, 2nd series **9**, 141–57.
Lukis, W. C. 1881–3b. Report on the Prehistoric Monuments of Wilts., Somerset and South Wales, *Proceedings of the Society of Antiquaries of London*, 2nd series **9**, 344–55.

Machin, R. 1977. The Great Rebuilding: a Reassessment, *Past and Present*, **77**, 33–56.
Malone, Caroline. 1986. *Alexander Keiller's Avebury: Fifty Years Ago* (Southampton).
Malone, Caroline. 1989. *The English Heritage Book of Avebury* (London).

Marsden, Barry M. 1974. *The Early Barrow-Diggers* (Princes Risborough).

Mayhew, N. J. 1983. *Sterling Imitations of Edwardian Types* (Royal Numismatic Society, Special Publication No. 14) (London).

Meyrick, O. 1955. "The Broadstones", *Wiltshire Archaeological and Natural History Magazine*, **56**, 192–3.

Meyrick, O. 1959. An Early Eighteenth-century Visitor to Avebury, *Wiltshire Archaeological Magazine*, **57**, 225–6.

Moir, Esther. 1964. *The Discovery of Britain. The English Tourists, 1540–1840* (London).

Montfaucon, B. de. 1721. *Antiquity Explained, and Represented in Sculptures*, trans. David Humphreys, vol. 2, pt. 2 (London).

Morgan, Victor. 1982. The Cartographic Image of 'the Country' in Early Modern England, *Transactions of the Royal Historical Society*, 5th series **29**, 129–54.

Morris, William. 1984. *Collected Letters*, ed. N. Kelvin, vol. 1 (1848–80) (Princeton).

Mowl, Tim, and Earnshaw, Brian. 1988. *John Wood: Architect of Obsession* (Bath).

Muir, R. and Welfare, H. 1983. *The National Trust Guide to Prehistoric and Roman Britain* (London).

Musson, C. R. 1971. A Study of Possible Building Forms at Durrington Walls, Woodhenge and the Sanctuary. In G. J. Wainwright and I. H. Longworth, *Durrington Walls: Excavations 1966–68* (London), 363–77.

Oldenburg, Henry. 1966. *Correspondence*, ed. A. R. and M. B. Hall, vol. 2 (Madison).

Ovid, 1931. *Fasti*, trans. Sir J. G. Frazer (London).

Owen, A. L. 1962. *The Famous Druids* (Oxford).

Palmer, R. 1976. Interrupted Ditch Enclosures in Britain: the Use of Aerial Photography for Comparative Studies, *Proceedings of the Prehistoric Society*, **42**, 161–86.

Passmore, A. D. 1926. Avebury – a New Stone in the Kennet Avenue, *Wiltshire Archaeological and Natural History Magazine*, **43**, 341–3.

Pepys, Samuel. 1972–83. *The Diary of Samuel Pepys*, ed. Robert Latham and William Matthews, 13 vols. (London).

Piggott, Stuart. 1935. Stukeley, Avebury and the Druids, *Antiquity*, **9**, 22–32.

Piggott, Stuart. 1937. Prehistory and the Romantic Movement, *Antiquity*, **11**, 31–8.

Piggott, Stuart. 1940. Timber Circles: a Re-examination, *Archaeological Journal*, **96**, 193–222.

Piggott, Stuart. 1946. The Destruction of 'The Sanctuary' on Overton Hill, *Wiltshire Archaeological Magazine*, **51**, 470–1.

Piggott, Stuart. 1948. Destroyed Megaliths in North Wiltshire. *Wiltshire Archaeological Magazine*, **52**, 390–2.

Piggott, Stuart. 1950. *William Stukeley: an Eighteenth-century Antiquary* (Oxford).

Piggott, Stuart. 1962. *The West Kennet Long Barrow: Excavations 1955–56* (London).

Piggott, Stuart. 1964. Excavations at Avebury 1960, *Wiltshire Archaeological Magazine*, **59**, 28–9.

Piggott, Stuart. 1965. Archaeological Draughtmanship: Principles and Practice. Part I: Principles and Retrospect. *Antiquity*, **39**, 165–79.

Piggott, Stuart. 1968. *The Druids* (London).

Piggott, Stuart. 1976. *Ruins in a Landscape* (Edinburgh).

Piggott, Stuart, 1983. Archaeological Retrospect 5, *Antiquity*, **57**, 28–37.

Piggott, Stuart. 1985. *William Stukeley: an Eighteenth-century Antiquary*, revised ed. (London).

Piggott, Stuart. 1986. William Stukeley: New Facts and an Old Forgery, *Antiquity*, **60**, 115–22.

Piggott, Stuart. 1989. *Ancient Britons and the Antiquarian Imagination* (London).

Pitts, Michael. 1986. *Footprints through Avebury*, 2nd ed. (Avebury)

Pitts, Michael and Whittle, Alisdair. forthcoming. Radiocarbon Dating of the Henge at Avebury.

Ponting, K. G. 1969. Introduction to the 1969 Printing. In John Britton, ed., *The Natural History of Wiltshire; by John Aubrey, F.R.S.*, reprinted (Newton Abbot).

Powell, Anthony. 1963. *John Aubrey and his Friends*, revised ed. (London).

Rattansi, P. M. 1964. Paracelsus and the Puritan Revolution, *Ambix*, **11**, 24–32.

Rawlinson, Richard. 1718. Introduction. In John Aubrey, *The Natural History and Antiquities of the County of Surrey*, vol. 1 (London), i–xl viii.

Renfrew, Colin. 1973. Monuments, Mobilization and Social Organization in Neolithic Wessex. In C. Renfrew, ed., *The Explanation of Culture Change: models in prehistory* (London), 539–558.

Ronan, Colin, and Hartley, Harold. 1960. Sir Paul Neile, F.R.S. (1613–86), *Notes and Records of the Royal Society of London*, **15**, 159–65 (reprinted in H. Hartley, ed., *The Royal Society: its Origins and Founders* (London, 1960), 159–65).

Rossi, Paolo. 1984. *The Dark Abyss of Time. The History of the Earth and the History of Nations from Hooke to Vico*, Eng. trans. (Chicago).

Rowse, A. L. 1950. *The England of Elizabeth* (London).

Seaton, Ethel. 1935. *Literary Relations of England and Scandinavia in the Seventeenth Century* (Oxford).

Sharp, Lindsay. 1973. Walter Charleton's Early Life, 1620–59, and Relationship to Natural Philosophy in mid-Seventeenth-century England, *Annals of Science*, **30**, 311–40.

Simpson, A. D. C. 1984. Newton's Telescope and the Cataloguing of the Royal Society's Repository, *Notes and Records of the Royal Society*, **38**, 187–214.

Smith, A. C. 1867. Excavations at Avebury, *Wiltshire Archaeological Magazine*, **10**, 209–16.

Smith, A. C. 1872. General Meeting of Society 1871. Report for 1871, *Wiltshire Archaeological Magazine*, **13**, 221–2.

Smith, A. C. 1885. *Guide to the British and Roman Antiquities of the North Wiltshire Down in a Hundred Square Miles around Abury*, 2nd ed. (Devizes).

Smith, I. F. 1964. Avebury: the Northern Inner Circle, *Wiltshire Archaeological and Natural History Magazine*, **59**, 181.

[Smith, I. F.] 1965. *Windmill Hill and Avebury. Excavations by Alexander Keiller, 1925–39* (Oxford).

Smith, Roland J. C., and Trott, Martin. 1989. *West Kennet Farm, West Kennet, Marlborough, Wiltshire. Archaeological Evaluation 1989*. Trust for Wessex Archaeology, Project Code 32731 (Salisbury).

Smith, R. W. 1984. The Ecology of Neolithic Farming Systems as Exemplified in the Avebury Region of Wiltshire. *Proceedings of the Prehistoric Society*, **50**, 99–120.

Stevenson, David. 1984. Masonry, Symbolism and Ethics in the Life of Sir Robert Moray, F.R.S., *Proceedings of the Society of Antiquaries of Scotland*, **114**, 405–31.

Stevenson, David. 1988. *The Origins of Freemasonry. Scotland's Century, 1590–1710* (Cambridge).

Stewart, Ian. 1984. Bishop Bek and the Durham Coins of Edward I and II, *British Numismatic Journal*, **54**, 81–5.

Stukeley, William. 1722–4a. *Celtic Religion*. Cardiff Central Library MS 4.26.

Stukeley, William. 1722–4b. *The History of the Temples of the Antient Celts*. Bodleian Library MS Eng.Misc.c.323.

Stukeley, William. 1722–4c. *Stonehenge*. Cardiff Central Library MS 4.253.

Stukeley, William. 1724a. *Itinerarium Curiosum, Centuria 1* (London).

Stukeley, William. 1724b. *The Hieroglyphics of the Egyptians*. Freemasons' Hall, London, MS 1130 Stu (3).

Stukeley, William. 1740. *Stonehenge: a Temple Restor'd to the British Druids* (London).

Stukeley, William. 1743. *Abury: a Temple of the British Druids* (London).

Stukeley, William. 1776. *Itinerarium Curiosum, Centuria 2* (London).

Stukeley, William. 1882. *The Family Memoirs*, vol. 1, ed. W. C. Lukis (Surtees Society, vol. lxxiii, for 1880).

Stukeley, William. 1883. *The Family Memoirs*, vol. 2, ed. W. C. Lukis (Surtees Society, vol. lxxvi, for 1883).

Stukeley, William. 1887. *The Family Memoirs*, vol. 3, ed. W. C. Lukis (Surtees Society, vol. lxxx, for 1885).

Sullivan, R. E. 1982. *John Toland and the Deist Controversy: a Study in Adaptations* (Cambridge, Mass.).

Thom, Alexander. 1967. *Megalithic Sites in Britain* (Oxford).

Toland, John. 1726. A Specimen of the Critical History of the Celtic Religion and Learning. In *A Collection of Several Pieces by Mr John Toland*, 2 vols. (London), i. 1–228.

Turner, Anthony. 1973. Mathematical Instruments and the Education of Gentlemen, *Annals of Science*, **30**, 51–88.

Twining, Thomas. 1723. *Avebury in Wiltshire, the Remains of a Roman Work* (London).

Ucko, P. J. 1989a. Foreword. In Stone P. and MacKenzie, R., eds., *The Excluded Past: Archaeology in Education* (London), ix–xxiv.

Ucko, P. J. 1989b. Foreword. In H. Cleere, ed., *Archaeological Heritage Management in the Modern World* (London), ix–xiv.

Ucko, P. J. 1990. *Whose Culture is it Anyway?* Unpublished Frazer Lecture, University of Glasgow.

Vatcher, F. de M. MS, Alexander Keiller Museum, Avebury.

Vatcher, F. de M. 1969. Avebury: Beckhampton Avenue, *Wessex Archaeological Magazine*, **64**, 127.

Vatcher, F. de M., and Vatcher, L. 1980. *The Avebury Monuments* (London).

V.C.H. 1983. Avebury. In *The Victoria History of the Counties of England. A History of Wiltshire*, vol. 12, ed. D. A. Crowley (Oxford), 86–105.

Wainwright, G. J. 1989. *Archaeology Review 1988/9* (London).

Watkin, David. 1980. *The Rise of Architectural History* (London).

Webster, Charles. 1967. The College of Physicians: 'Solomon's House' in Commonwealth England, *Bulletin of the History of Medicine*, **41**, 393–412.

Welfare, Humphrey. 1989. John Aubrey – the First Archaeological Surveyor? In Mark Bowden, Donnie Mackay and Peter Topping, eds., *From Cornwall to Caithness: Some Aspects of British Field Archaeology; Papers Presented to Norman V. Quinnell* (B.A.R. British Series 209) (Oxford), 17–28.

Whittle, A. 1988. West Kennett: Palisaded Enclosure (SU111682): Late Neolithic and Romano-British, *Wilshire Archaeological and Natural History Magazine*, **82**, 180.

Whittle, A. 1989. *Excavations at Millbarrow, Winterbourne Monkton, 1989: Preliminary Report* [unpublished MS; 8 pp.].

Whittle, A., and Smith, R. 1989. West Kennet, *Current Archaeology*, **118**, 363–4.

Williams, James. 1969. *An Edition of the Correspondence of John Aubrey with Anthony a Wood and Edward Lhwyd, 1667–1696*. University of London Ph.D. thesis.

Wittkower, R. 1967. *Architectural Principles in the Age of Humanism*. 3rd ed. (London).

Wood, Anthony. 1813–20. *Athenae Oxenienses*, ed. Philip Bliss, 4 vols. (London).

Wood, John. 1747. *Choir Gaure, Vulgarly called Stonehenge, on Salisbury Plain, Described, Restored, and Explained* (Oxford).

Woolf, D. R. 1988. The 'Common Voice': History, Folklore and Oral Tradition in Early Modern England, *Past and Present*, **120**, 26–52.

Worm, Olaus. 1643. *Danicorum Monumentorum Libri Sex* (Hafniae).

Worm, Ole. 1968. *Breve Fra og til Ole Worm, III, 1644–54*, ed. H. D. Schepelern (Copenhagen).

Wren, Christopher, jr. 1750. *Parentalia: or, Memoirs of the Family of the Wrens* (London).

Young, W. E. V. 1938. *Diary with Archaeological Notes, June 14 to September 10*. MS, Devizes Museum.

Young, W. E. V. 1961. The West Kennet Avenue, *Wiltshire Archaeological and Natural History Magazine*, **58**, 30.

NOTE

The following publication appeared after the book went to press:

Pitts, M. 1990. What Future for Avebury, *Antiquity*, **64**, 259–74.

Malone, c. 1990. *Prehistoric Monuments of Avebury* (London).

Index